WITHDRAWN

A NATION OF ENEMIES
CHILE UNDER PINOCHET

A Nation of Enemies

Chile under Pinochet

Pamela Constable

AND

Arturo Valenzuela

W · W · NORTON & COMPANY

NEW YORK LONDON

The text of this book is composed in 11/13 Sabon,
with the display set in Sabon Bold.
Composition and Manufacturing by
the Maple-Vail Book Manufacturing Group.
Book design by Margaret M. Wagner.

First Edition.

Library of Congress Cataloging-in-Publication Data
Constable, Pamela.
A nation of enemies : Chile under Pinochet / by Pamela
Constable and Arturo Valenzuela.
p.   cm.
Includes index.
1. Chile—Politics and government—1973–   2. Pinochet Ugarte,
Augusto.   I. Valenzuela, Arturo, 1944–   . II. Title.
F3100.C64   1991
983.06′5—dc20   90–27236
ISBN 0–393–03011–3

W.W. Norton & Company, Inc., 500 Fifth Avenue, New York, N.Y. 10110
W.W. Norton & Company, Ltd., 10 Coptic Street, London WC1A 1PU

1 2 3 4 5 6 7 8 9 0

Contents

ACKNOWLEDGMENTS

FROM among the hundreds of Chileans, of all backgrounds and political views, who enriched this book by giving us of their time and personal insights, we would like to mention a few whose kindness, knowledge, or inspiration was especially valuable: Mario Agliati; Carmen Gloria Aguayo; Andrés Allamand; Pilar Armanet and Rafael Astaburoaga; Genaro Arriagada, for his indefatigability; Sergio Arellano Iturriaga; Sergio Bitar and Eugenia Hirmas; Edgardo Boeninger; Rosemarie Bornand, for her perseverance and love; Hugo and Nora Castillo; Ascanio Cavallo; Edgardo Cavíz; José Luis Cea; Germán Correa; Camilo Cortés, for his abiding faith; Flavio Cortés; Marco Antonio de la Parra; Gonzalo Falabella; Angel Flisfisch; Fernando Fuentealba of La Florida; Arturo Fontaine Talavera; Judge René García Villegas; Manuel Antonio Garretón; and Oscar Godoy.

Also, our loyal friends Renato and Edith Gómez; Hernán and Rina Gutiérrez, for Sunday tea and brainstorming; Jaime Guzmán; Patricio Hales; Eugenio Hieremans; Judge Germán Hermosilla; Ricardo Lagos; Cristián Larroulet; Miguel Angel Larrea; Bernardo and Anita Leighton, for their courage; Marta Leiva; Fernando Léniz; Yerko Ljubetic; Liliana Mahn; General Alejandro Medina Lois; Mario Muñoz in Conchalí; Heraldo Muñoz; Ricardo Núñez; Claudio Orrego, for a life of democratic commitment; Máximo Pacheco Hijo; José Piñera; Roberto Pulido; Ronald Ramm, for his creative indignation; Colonel Alfredo Rehren; Germán Riesco; the Reverend Flor Rodríguez and the members of her San Miguel church; Orlando Sáenz; Lucía Santa Cruz; Domingo Santamaría; General Horacio Toro; and Carmen Vivanco. We are also grateful to a number of individuals, especially in the justice system and the armed forces, who agreed to speak with us anonymously.

We are professionally indebted to the writings of a number of Chilean journalists and scholars, especially the staffs of *La Epoca* newspaper and *Hoy* magazine, and researchers at the Corporación de Investigaciones Económicas para Latinoamérica (CIEPLAN), the Centro de Estudios Públicos (CEP), and the Facultad Latinoamericana de Ciencias Sociales (FLACSO). We are deeply grateful to our colleagues and friends at FLASCO, where we spent many quiet hours of research; and to the lawyers of the Vicaría de la Solidaridad, who gave us access to many of their files. The Alicia Patterson Foundation provided generous support for this project, and the Fulbright Commission and the Heinz Foundation also gave us vital assistance.

Our thanks also to the friends who offered thoughtful comments on our manuscript, especially Jorge Olave, Iván Jacsik, Richard Newfarmer, and José Luis Cea. Special appreciation is due Josiane Bonnefoy, our diligent and good-humored research assistant; Hilary Hinzmann, our patient and insightful editor at Norton; Mark and Jenny, who tolerated a father's commitment to a far-flung cause: and Missy, our faithful friend through many cloistered months of writing. Finally, we would like to express our gratitude to and admiration for two distinguished non-Chileans, Professor Federico Gil and Ambassador Harry G. Barnes, Jr., and our deepest appreciation to our parents, Dorothy and Raimundo Valenzuela and Priscilla and Cheston Constable, who have given us a lifetime of love and encouragement in our work.

PREFACE

THIS book was born during the tumultuous Santiago spring of November 1984. It was a moment of exhilarating change in Chile. The military-ruled nation, divided by hatred and frozen by fear for a decade since the 1973 coup, was erupting in massive protests. General Augusto Pinochet, the sixty-nine-year-old president, had declared a state of siege, but each night young demonstrators swarmed into the streets, defying tear gas and water cannons, and raising their chant against the regime: "It's going to fall, it's going to fall!"

One evening, choking and trapped between phalanxes of protesters and police, we hailed a taxi. Its gray-haired driver steered us grimly out of harm's way. Then, in a voice both anguished and apologetic, he blurted, "What has happened to this country? I used to be so proud to live in a democracy. Now there is such malignancy, such power. The only ones brave enough to fight it are the youth. Today, I am ashamed to be a Chilean."

Something about this threadbare but dignified man, and the values to which he had quietly clung through a decade of dictatorship, struck us as a key to understanding the impact of political trauma and military rule on Chilean society.

For 150 years preceding the overthrow of President Salvador Allende, Chile had boasted a tradition of stable democratic rule and a culture of austere, enlightened civility. Now it had become a very different country—orderly and efficient, but suspicious and cowed. The values of the past, eroded through a period of bitter ideological warfare beginning in the 1960s and intensifying during Allende's socialist government, had been abandoned in a vortex of rage and panic. During a decade of military rule, these values had been trampled underfoot, yet they had survived in the hearts of many Chileans, and now they were struggling to resume their place in society.

That struggle was to take another five years, until a national referendum on military rule was held in October 1988, and Pinochet was forced to step down after presidential elections in 1989. During that time, we visited Chile repeatedly and interviewed hundreds of people—carpenters and colonels, priests and politicians, torture victims and technocrats. Some Chileans had prospered under dictatorship, finding reassurance in the order it brought to a chaotic, polarized society. Others shared tales of indignities endured, hopes crushed, families torn apart or forced to make painful choices to survive in a climate of comformity and intimidation.

Often we were struck by the vast psychological and cultural gap between these two Chiles—the winners and losers of the Pinochet years. The coup had frozen society at a point of great trauma and divisiveness, and all sectors—right and left, rich and poor, military and civilian—remained locked within separate microcosms, nursing their mutual fears and private dreams. Chile had become a nation of enemies. Not until the late 1980s did this hostility begin to thaw, as debate challenged propaganda and a spirit of reconciliation began to replace the climate of war.

We hoped this book could serve as a window into each sector of society, airing the multiple conflicting perceptions within and thus aiding in the process of healing. It was not an easy task; the years of unexorcised pain and anger had taken a terrible toll. Most searing were the testimonies of brutality and humiliation inflicted on thousands of leftists in the secret police dungeons: the sixteen-year-old girl who nearly went insane from electric shock; the elderly mayor who was forced to eat excrement. Even for those who escaped physical reprisal, the overthrow of Allende brought terror, guilt, and disillusionment. As one socialist friend told us sadly, "It was like the death of a son, the end of a world."

But our aim was not to polemicize the plight of a relatively small number of Chileans—perhaps tens of thousands—who suffered from direct political repression. It was to place such suffering in context, to understand how an aberrant value system had taken over the gamut of social relations, and to show how it affected daily life. To this end, the hundreds of accounts we heard of small tribulations and survival techniques were no less compelling, from the carpenter who was forced to pawn his wedding rings to the state bureaucrat who secretly visited his son in prison each weekend.

Determined opponents of military rule formed collective mechanisms to keep political and intellectual life alive: underground party networks, church support groups, small academic institutes. Some groups were crushed by the regime or rent by internal conflict, but others nurtured the flame of resistance and eventually coalesced around the values of tolerance and consensus that had once made Chilean democracy strong.

On the other side of the abyss, we found a very different Chile, a world where many people, convinced that communism had nearly destroyed their society and had to be crushed, retreated behind the bulwark of modern authoritarianism and became insulated from the suffering of their fellow citizens. There was the banker's wife who earnestly suggested that Chile wasn't ready for democracy yet, the penniless widow who wept with gratitude over supplies donated by the first lady, the judge who sought refuge in legal formalities when desperate families tried to save their sons from torture.

Well-to-do Chileans often reacted with suspicion when anyone sought to interview them, yet it was crucial to understand how members of an educated Western elite had discarded the civic values they had once mythologized. To hear their nightmares of mass uprising, their still-vivid rage at Allende's food-rationing system, was to sense how they could harbor such bitterness after so many years—and how 42 percent of the country could vote for an aging dictator in 1988.

Many supporters of military rule also saw it as a chance to create a modern, prosperous Chile, and they embraced a bold experiment in free-market economics imposed by the regime and its civilian aides. The state was dismantled, businesses were forced to become competitive, and a dynamic entrepreneurial class emerged. Eager young technocrats worked to eradicate poverty and inefficiency, isolated from the darker side of dictatorship. "Pinochet created compartments: the cavalry, the artillery, the economists," explained one former aide.

Chile's military establishment was the most difficult sector for us to penetrate, a hermetic and hierarchical world that was hostile to all outsiders. Nervous about being interviewed, some officers hinted at chafing under the rigid command structure or disapproving of abuses by the secret police. But most expressed an unswerving commitment to the principles of anticommunism, patriotism and duty, and pride in the achievements of the regime. We did not share their perceptions of Chilean reality, but we did gain insight into what had shaped their beliefs and, by extension, into the powerful but contradictory personality of Augusto Pinochet.

This book is neither a diatribe against Chile's dictatorship nor an apology for it; it is an attempt to explain how military rule dominated and shaped a society for nearly seventeen years, only to be rejected by the people. We admired the economic progress fostered by Pinochet's technocrats, but we found that much needless suffering was imposed in the process, and we lamented the replacement of an austere, public-spirited culture with a fast, aggressive consumer culture. We came to respect the dedication and discipline of the armed forces, but we saw how these qualities had been perverted by an excessive concentration of power in one man.

We found that many sins had been committed by the Marxist left during its brief time in power, when doctrinaire fervor and arrogance undermined the ideals of a generation inspired by the Cuban revolution. But we became convinced that the hate-driven repression following Allende's overthrow was far more damaging, debasing civilized rule and making a monster of the state. We regretted the bickering of Chile's politicians, but we admired their ability to survive and finally come together in a triumphant display of civic maturity: the peaceful electoral defeat of a dictator.

Ultimately, what inspired this project was the profound democratic conviction of so many Chileans we interviewed or came to know: the former cabinet minister who could not bring himself to hate the men who had nearly assassinated him; the shy architect who joined the anti-Pinochet electoral campaign out of sheer indignation; the church lawyer who pursued hopeless cases from court to court—and the elderly taxi driver who wept for the democracy he had once known. It is to them, and to thousands of others who never lost their faith in what it meant to be Chilean, that this book is dedicated.

Washington, D.C.
September 1990

A NATION OF ENEMIES
CHILE UNDER PINOCHET

CHAPTER ONE

THE WAR

General Arellano: "How many casualties?"
Commander Jaña: "My General, the garrison is without
  incident."
Arellano: "What are you talking about? How many casualties?"
Jaña, bewildered: "There are none. . . ."
Arellano, angrily: "Don't you realize we're at war?"

—*Talca, October 30, 1973*[1]

AT 11:52 A.M. on September 11, 1973, two Hawker Hunter
fighter jets streaked across the late-winter sky over downtown
Santiago, the sprawling capital halfway down Chile's 2,000-mile
Pacific coast. The jets dipped and fired a round of rockets into La
Moneda Palace. As they banked gently away in tandem and returned
for six more passes, windows shattered and curtains ignited in the
pristine, sand-colored colonial mansion, which had stood for 130
years as a symbol of Chilean democracy.

Inside the palace, President Salvador Allende had been pacing
the halls with a submachine gun, calming frightened friends on the
telephone, refusing military offers of safe-conduct out of the country, and coming to grips with the collapse of his elected Socialist
revolution. For months he had struggled to salvage the Popular
Unity government from economic and political ruin. Now Chile's
military commanders had risen against him, too, flouting a cen-
tury-old tradition of obedience to civilian authorities, and the end
seemed near.

A bespectacled medical doctor and impassioned leftist vision-
ary, Allende faced the mutiny with defiance and serene fatalism,

determined to defend his revolution but expecting to lose his life in the process. At midmorning, he telephoned a progovernment radio station and broadcast his final message to the nation. Asking to be remembered as "an honorable man who was loyal to the revolution," he urged followers to defend "but not sacrifice" themselves in resisting the coup.

"I am certain that the seed we planted in the worthy consciousness of thousands and thousands of Chileans cannot be definitively uprooted," Allende declared. "They have the strength; they can subjugate us, but they cannot halt social processes by either crime or force," he vowed. "History is ours, and the people make it." The words were a signal of reassurance and conviction amid chaos, the desperate last gesture of a proud leader facing his final moments.[2]

As Chile's president came to terms with his defeat, a man ensconced in an army communications complex was tasting his first moments of power. In late August, Allende had named General Augusto Pinochet Ugarte, a deferential career officer, army commander in hopes of averting a confrontation with the military. Reluctantly, the general had joined the coup at the last minute. But now he turned against the elected government with deadly fury.[3]

From his telephone command post in Peñalolen, a Santiago suburb in the Andean foothills, Pinochet barked out orders to hunt down dozens of officials and ranted against the leftist civilian leaders he had obeyed for three years, revealing a vengeful anticommunist streak that had been hidden to virtually all who knew him. "That whole pile of pigs there . . . all that filth that was going to ruin the country," he roared to an aide. "They must be seized and up, into the plane, without clothes, with whatever they have, out!"

As for Allende, Pinochet repeatedly demanded his "unconditional surrender," in military language salted with vulgar remarks about the president. According to one account, he even suggested putting Allende on a plane into exile and letting it crash. Finally, impatient with the president's refusal to abandon La Moneda, Pinochet issued an ultimatum. Within minutes, the Hawker Hunters were airborne.[4]

As flames spread through the palace, tanks and infantry troops advanced toward the building, exchanging gunfire with bodyguards in the windows and snipers on surrounding rooftops. Within ninety minutes, the resistance had petered out. Choking in the smoke and tear gas, two dozen figures emerged from a side door, poking a white cloth on a broomstick ahead of them. Allende was not among them. Nervous soldiers shoved the men down onto the sidewalk and stormed into the flaming palace behind General Javier Palacios.

A handful of Allende's guards still fought back, and a bullet grazed Palacios in the hand, sending his men into fits of fury. Lieutenant Armando Fernández Larios stanched the wound with his handkerchief, and later treasured the bloody cloth as a memento of his proudest hour as a soldier. Bursting into one ornate, ceremonial hall, the troops encountered Patricio Guijón, one of Allende's doctors, keeping vigil over a gray-haired figure slumped forward on a red velvet couch.

The president's head had been demolished by machine-gun fire, and his hands were covered with gunpowder. Leaning against him was a Soviet-made automatic rifle inscribed with a gift plaque: "To Salvador from your companion in arms. Fidel Castro." The military men contemplated the scene somberly. Moments later, the radio in Pinochet's command post crackled with a curt, triumphant message from Palacios: "Mission accomplished. Moneda taken. President found dead."[5]

The confusion surrounding Allende's death remained the subject of passionate debate for years. Admirers insisted he died fending off military attackers, while detractors claimed that he committed suicide rather than face defeat. Although the evidence suggests the president did take his own life, the event acquired an enduring mythical stature and an intense personal meaning for Chileans on both sides of a divided society.[6]

While the palace drama was unfolding, combat troops swept through working-class areas of the capital, seizing Popular Unity supporters, searching for weapons and fully expecting to encounter massive resistance. Since dawn Radio Magallanes, operated by the Communist party, had exhorted workers to assume their "combat posts" and "stop the fascist coup," asserting that the "masses are alert and disposed to make the greatest sacrifices" in defense of Allende's revolution.[7]

In a few factories and universities, where militants from the Movement of the Revolutionary Left (Movimiento de Izquierda Revolucionario, or MIR) and the Socialist party had hurriedly distributed weapons, handfuls of students and workers attempted to repel invading troops. At the Sumar textile plant, about forty union activists armed with rifles and machine guns held an army helicopter at bay, then fled into the leftist shantytown of La Legua, where a battle continued for several days.[8]

But the great majority of the "masses" offered no resistance at all. By midday, Radio Magallanes's urgent exhortations had been replaced with military broadcasts pledging to "liberate the fatherland from the Marxist yoke." Despite months of bravado, leftist leaders had no real defense plan and few weapons. Their followers had little stomach for a lopsided fight, and troops entering most factories encountered only confused, frightened men.

Years later, Pinochet himself acknowledged that armed resistance had been much weaker than expected, although his explanation was contemptuous. Having pushed the country toward confrontation for months, he wrote, Chile's revolutionaries "fled like rats when it came to pass."[9]

IF fighting was subdued in the capital, it was virtually non-existent elsewhere. By early morning, the navy had secured the principal port of Valparaíso with almost no bloodshed. Anti-Allende journalists reporting from the provinces stressed the "absolute calm of the population and the almost total inaction of the extremists."[10] Regimental commanders, ordered to prepare their troops for war against armed peasants, secured notorious leftist strongholds with startling ease.

To the north, army officials were particularly worried about Chuquicamata, the world's largest open-pit copper mine and a bastion of Popular Unity forces. They envisioned armed miners overrunning the nearby Calama regiment, allowing Cuban troop planes to land and launch a civil war.[11] Major Fernando Reveco advanced on the silent mining compound with heavily armed troops, kicked in the manager's door, and felt like a fool. "Everything was quiet, not one weapon. . . . I could have turned the handle instead," he recalled. Later, the major was awarded a combat medal for taking Chuquicamata.[12]

To the south, officials also expected to encounter trouble in the industrial city of Concepción, a MIR stronghold, and in the nearby coal-mining region dominated by Communist unions. General Washington Carrasco forbade troops to advance on the town of Lota for fear of a counterattack. Instead, he ordered the local police colonel to pacify the city and call for supporting air strikes if necessary. To the colonel's relief, most of the miners stayed home, and almost all labor and leftist leaders turned themselves in peacefully.[13]

In Concepción, the MIR was caught completely by surprise and its leaders fled underground, their revolutionary rhetoric suddenly hollow. In the ten provinces under his command, Carrasco noted, "Happily we have had only three dead and three wounded. Cooperation is widespread, even from persons who were partisans of the previous government. To them I am particularly grateful."[14]

Military intelligence had warned that numerous cooperatives and forestry centers in the south were equipped as guerrilla camps, but once again rumor proved more dire than fact. Colonel Alfredo Rehren, for example, was told that one farm contained a major arsenal. "Maybe it was hidden, maybe it didn't exist, but the truth is we found nothing," he acknowledged after retiring. Like his colleagues, Rehren remained convinced that civil war had become inevitable. But he also noted, "A lot of speculation about conflict was pure rhetoric on both sides."[15]

By late afternoon, the armed forces were in complete control and a twenty-four-hour curfew was declared. At nightfall, a four-man military junta swore itself into power—but pledged to respect the 1925 constitution and to restore the institutional structure and "character" of Chile.[16] Pinochet would act as president, joined by General Gustavo Leigh of the air force, Admiral José Toribio Merino of the navy, and General César Mendoza of the Carabineros, or national paramilitary police.

In a series of radio declarations, the junta described its "moral duty" to overthrow an "illegitimate" government, and vowed to protect workers' rights and preserve judicial independence. Over the next few days, the commanders reassured Chile's eleven million citizens they had no desire to seek revenge or absolute power. "This is not a coup d'état, but a military movement" aimed at "salvaging the country," stated Pinochet. There would be "no victors or vanquished," only Chileans united in a "brotherly task" of rebuilding the nation.[17]

Yet these conciliatory words contrasted sharply with the actions of Chile's armed forces. On September 12, the junta declared a state of siege, using constitutional provisions intended for "a state or time of war," which restricted civilian rights and expanded the purview of military courts.[18] One week later, with armed resistance reduced to a handful of rebel safe houses, the junta declared the entire country an emergency zone, giving military authorities power over virtually all civilian activities.

In a stream of edicts, the junta banned political parties and the major labor federation, closed down Congress, declared all news subject to censorship, and warned that anyone who maintained a

"belligerent attitude" would be "executed on the spot." Mass raids
continued day after day, until more than 45,000 people were held
for interrogation in army barracks, navy training camps, air force
hospitals, soccer stadiums, and even merchant ships anchored off
Valparaiso.[19]

"Our role was to restore tranquillity and give security to the
population. Obviously this meant doing disagreeable things,"
recalled General Alejandro Medina, who led the army's special
forces unit in house-to-house sweeps through working-class areas
of Santiago and who saved his beret with a sniper's bullet hole as
a memento of the coup. "No one likes to have his house raided,"
the trim, no-nonsense officer explained. "But if there are rats inside,
you accept that someone comes in to get them out."[20]

By December, at least fifteen hundred civilians were dead—shot
in confrontations, tortured to death, hunted down by vigilantes,
or executed by firing squads.[21] Thousands of detainees had been
shipped to military prison camps, more than seven thousand had
fled into exile after receiving safe-conduct passes, and the grounds
of the Venezuelan, Swedish, Argentine, Italian, and British embassies were jammed with asylum seekers. A revolutionary dream had
been crushed in a spasm of military fury, and a reign of professional state terror had begun.

THE coup shattered not only the brief socialist experiment of
Salvador Allende but also the myth that Chile's 150-year-old civilian constitutional government was invincible. The inhabitants of
this long, narrow strip of seacoast—stretching from arid, copper-
rich deserts in the north, through the lush farms and vineyards of
the central valleys, to pine forests and alpine lakes in the south—
had long believed that their society was more stable and enlightened
than those of the volatile continent that lay beyond the towering
Andes range.

While neighboring countries were regularly rocked by coups and
revolutions, Chile's presidents dutifully gave way to their elected
successors, and the army was kept in check. From 1830 to 1973,
Chile was under direct military control for only thirteen months:
once after the civil war of 1891 and twice during the years between
1924 and 1931. Elections were events of great civic pride for which
families donned their Sunday best. Respect for the constitution
was deeply ingrained, and the art of compromise was a highly
developed political skill.[22]

Through the nineteenth century, Chilean democracy was restricted to the landowning and urban elite, whose rival Conservative and Liberal parties shared fundamental beliefs about the proper economic order. But by the early 1900s this cozy arrangement was being challenged by working- and middle-class groups. In the textile mills of Santiago, the coal mines of the south, and the nitrate camps of the north, socialist and anarchist unions took root before the Russian revolution, spawning the development of the strongest Communist party in Latin America.

To thwart the rising power of the left, Chile's urban and rural elites reached a tacit agreement. Urban leftist movements were permitted to join the electoral system, and welfare laws were adopted. But in the countryside, landowners retained control over the peasants who labored on vast *fundos* (estates), bound to the *patrón* by tradition and ignorance and courted with wine and rodeos at election time. Thus, unlike the oligarchies of Argentina or Guatemala, Chile's ruling class avoided relying on military alliances to enforce its privilege.

By midcentury, however, Chilean society had developed strong political subcultures. Party affiliation defined one's identity and played a dominant role in one's choice of friends and spouses. Liberals vacationed at Liberal beaches; Radicals sent their children to Radical schools; Socialists rooted for Socialist soccer teams. Society was also narrow and ingrown, with intense competition for limited space at the top. Party politics dominated an unending stream of elections in labor unions, student leagues, and city councils, and shrill debates erupted regularly in Congress.

Yet Chile's strong, law-abiding traditions kept competition confined within certain rules and rituals, softening class hostility and ideological conflict. There was no argument, it was said, that could not be settled over a bottle of Chilean cabernet. "We were known as the English of Latin America, because nothing ever became so bitter it could not be discussed," explained Carlos Alberto Cruz, an architect and son of the conservative political aristocracy.[23]

The backbone of Chilean democracy was a large middle class, proud of its liberalism and subsidized by a generous state. The professional classes prized knowledge above wealth, and Chile's public education system produced six presidents and two Nobel Prize–winning poets, Pablo Neruda and Gabriela Mistral. Public service was a dignified vocation; ostentation and corruption were frowned upon. President Jorge Alessandri (1958–1964), an austere bachelor, endeared himself to constituents by strolling to work and waiting in line at the bank.

By the mid-twentieth century, this centrist middle class, represented by the progressive, anticlerical Radical party, commanded about one-third of the electorate, with leftists and conservatives each attracting about the same amount of support. Thus, no group could afford to become intransigent, and presidential candidates had to forge new coalitions every six years. The pragmatic Radicals, who held the presidency from 1939 to 1952, were always ready to negotiate with either side.

Under Radical tutelage, the state became the engine of economic growth. An ambitious development program subsidized and protected infant industries, ranging from steel to sugar beets. Public employment was greatly expanded, becoming an important source of political patronage. Yet by 1950 the system had run its course. Manufacturing was woefully inefficient, and agriculture had been neglected. For the next two decades, the economy grew at a painfully slow average rate of 3.9 percent a year.

Chile's per capita income remained one of the highest in Latin America—$1,064 in 1960—but it was sustained by deficit spending and bloated public payrolls, driving inflation upward.[24] Rural poverty remained widespread, and beyond the teeming factory belts that ringed Santiago, illegal shantytowns known as *callampas* (mushrooms) festered with tuberculosis, alcoholism, and raw sewage running through dirt alleys.

By the 1960s, the perception of economic exhaustion, combined with rapid working-class politicization, had begun to undermine Chile's culture of compromise. President Alessandri's orthodox economic policies had failed, and a new reformist party called the Christian Democrats—more utopian and intransigent than the Radicals—challenged them for control of the center. Meanwhile, a new generation of students and intellectuals, inspired by the 1959 Cuban revolution, pushed the political fulcrum further left.

To stave off the leftist ground swell, conservatives reluctantly backed the Christian Democrat Eduardo Frei for the presidency in 1964. Frei's campaign received strong endorsement from the Johnson administration in Washington, which viewed the Christian Democrats as a critical antidote to Cuban communism. The Central Intelligence Agency, working with U.S. multinational corporations, funneled a huge amount of aid to the Frei campaign. CIA support for Frei alone was double the amount per voter that the

Goldwater and Johnson campaigns together spent in the United States that same year.[25]

Advocating a "third way" between capitalism and Marxism based on progressive Catholic philosophy, Frei encouraged working-class activism, opened higher education to the poor, and launched ambitious social programs at the same time that he promoted greater industrial efficiency. But his boldest move, expropriating tracts of farmland to form peasant cooperatives, provoked a visceral upper-class resentment that has never diminished.

"Expropriation overturned the social scale and destroyed a way of life, like the American Civil War," asserted Carlos Alberto Cruz, whose class had always viewed society as unified by a natural hierarchy, in which everyone knew his place and everything could be negotiated between gentlemen. "The result was a loss of values and a political disaster whose permanent effects we still cannot measure."

Furious with Frei, the right abandoned the Christian Democrats in the 1970 race. This allowed Allende, a Socialist senator, to eke out a 36 percent plurality in a narrow three-way race and become the first freely elected Marxist head of state, committed to a platform of revolutionary change. With no absolute winner, the legislature had to choose between the two front-runners. The Christian Democrats agreed to back Allende, but only in exchange for his written pledge to respect the rules of democracy.

In Washington, the incoming Nixon administration was appalled at the rise of Allende. Henry Kissinger, Nixon's national security adviser, remarked impatiently, "I don't see why we need to stand idly by and watch a country go communist due to the irresponsibility of its own people."[26] The United States mounted a "two-track" operation to thwart Allende's election: while diplomats waged an overt political crusade, the CIA spent up to one million dollars on propaganda and other operations aimed at creating financial and political panic. When these efforts failed, Nixon ordered the agency to take more drastic measures, but its hasty efforts at fomenting a military coup backfired, and the new president was inaugurated on schedule.[27]

A complex, contradictory man, Allende had trained as a doctor in the 1930s but abandoned medicine for the more passionate vocation of politics. In between repeated terms as a legislator, he had run for president in 1952, 1958, and 1964. Myopic in appearance, he was a riveting orator and a dogged campaigner. Despite his commitment to the "democratic road" to socialism, he admired Fidel Castro and the romantic young rebels of the MIR. Yet his tastes were those of a bourgeois bon vivant; he drank imported Scotch, wore flamboyant capes, and often conducted political business until dawn.

Upon taking office, Allende exhorted the young and the poor to help him inaugurate a "second" path to socialism, transforming the political and economic order within a peaceful, democratic framework. Unfazed by his slim mandate and lack of majority support in the Congress, he launched ambitious plans to nationalize copper mines, take over factories and banks, accelerate land reform, and raise living standards. He was convinced that the sluggish, inefficient economy could be stimulated without leading to inflation.[28]

It was a euphoric time for students, professionals, factory workers, and peasant leaders caught up in Allende's Popular Unity movement, known as the U.P. With salaries rising and prices held down, the economy surged. There was great urgency in the air—a sense that capitalism was giving way to a new order of state-centered equality and justice. Student brigades taught janitors to read, housemaids were called "home advisers," and mill hands were organized to run "liberated" factories with the help of government intervenors.

"We gave our all to the U.P. We lived each moment intensely and worked terribly hard; we felt an immense responsibility. We were the generation that thought we had the world in our hands; we were building a new country," explained Estela Ortiz, a dedicated Communist who spent the Allende years as a party youth volunteer creating experimental kindergarten programs.[29]

Santiago became a magnet for intellectuals from Paris and Mexico, political refugees from Brazil, college students from California, and technocrats from Cuba, all eager to help forge a new society. Campuses rang with revolutionary rhetoric; Marx and Marcuse were on every tongue. Late-night cafés flowed with wine and Andean protest ballads by Victor Jara and Violeta Parra. One lyric, "The people, united, will never be defeated," became the rallying cry for a generation.

In the countryside, state technicians spread the gospel of land reform, urging peasants to shake off the bonds of servitude and invade estates whose owners resisted legal expropriation. "We were trying to promote dignity, to help peasants raise their heads," recalled Jorge Barudi, a wizened man with a white goatee, describing his years as an agricultural agent under Allende. "That was the most worthwhile thing I ever did," he said with a faraway look of pride and pain.[30]

But to prosperous farmers like Bernardo Olalde, the transformation of the old, paternalistic rural order brought only trauma and destruction. "The U.P. took away all my land, and they left me with nothing," he explained bitterly. "The workers destroyed the wheat crop and the eucalyptus stands, they took over the house and cut up my furniture for firewood, and they did it in a spirit of political vengeance and hatred."[31]

By the end of Allende's first year, the idealism of his followers was becoming tarnished by arrogance. The government's coalition frayed as rivalries formed; party militants vied for government posts and radical postures. The victory of the masses was at hand, and everyone wanted his share of glory. Economic planners, determined to produce a rapid rise in living conditions to bolster the U.P. in local and legislative races, ignored the pitfalls of heavy deficit spending and too-rapid wage increases. Within a year, the economy was spinning out of control.[32] When the Christian Democrats in Congress abandoned their tacit support for the new government, Allende's ministers resorted to extensive decree powers to implement their policies, many of questionable legality.

As ideological rhetoric intensified, Chile's tradition of political give-and-take was dismissed by the left as a bourgeois anachronism. Intoxicated by a dream of popular revolution, radical students from the MIR took up paramilitary training and attempted to infiltrate the armed forces, imagining that the troops would side with them to bring down capitalism forever. Despite Allende's paternalistic tolerance (his nephew Andrés Pascal was a MIR founder), the group accused him of betrayal and demanded a full-scale insurrection.

"People believed paradise was around the corner. There was an explosion of passion, a drunken binge of ideas, and a constant demand for political definitions. We all thought we were at the Sorbonne; we expected to find Ché Guevara in the next café," recalled Marco Antonio de la Parra, a writer and psychiatrist who was in college during the U.P. "But there was also a sense of violence, a feeling that it would all come crashing down. We suffered the calamitous impact of a utopian time."[33]

The widening reach of Allende's revolution horrified well-to-do Chileans, who saw their property being stolen and their privileges usurped. Fighting back, investors took their capital abroad, and truckers fomented strikes that created shortages of staple goods and fueled the black market. Right-wing "shock troops" like Patria y Libertad (Fatherland and Liberty) blew up electrical towers and vandalized factories to heighten the climate of tension and fear. For much of the right, democracy had also become an anachronism, a system of government incapable of protecting its fundamental interests.

Chile's experiment in revolution found another powerful adversary in the Nixon White House—especially with National Security Adviser Kissinger, who feared that a successful elected socialist regime in Chile would encourage the advance of the left in Western Europe. Having failed to prevent Allende from coming to power, the two men pressed to destabilize the Chilean economy. Aid was slashed from a peak of $260.4 million in 1967 to $3.8 million in 1973; American companies were urged to curb trade and cut off supply shipments.[34] There was little protest from Congress and strong cooperation from U.S. multinationals, infuriated by the loss of their investments and fearful that Allende's actions could encourage similar measures in other countries.

Without the public's knowledge, the U.S. government also spent at least $8 million on covert operations against Allende between 1970 and 1973, an enormous sum given the collapse of the Chilean currency on the black market. The CIA financed opposition by labor and business groups and political parties, as well as a massive propaganda effort by the powerful newspaper *El Mercurio*.[35] Day after day, alarmist headlines warned of food shortages and secret leftist guerrilla camps, reinforcing people's most primitive fears.

Government mismanagement exacerbated economic deterioration. The left's romanticization of the working class was accompanied by a contempt for profit and a belief that idealism could substitute for expertise. Prices were fixed at unrealistically low levels, bankrupting businesses and sending inflation to record levels of over 300 percent a year. Factory managers were ejected and replaced by committees of political cadres and workers. Discipline slackened, men left their machines to attend rallies, and production plummeted.

"Many workers thought the revolution meant they wouldn't have to work. It was hard to instill the idea that if a box broke, it was their loss and their responsibility, not someone else's," recalled Edgardo Cavíz, a self-taught man in his sixties who helped the U.P. government manage expropriated mining firms. "Allende had no one on his side but the workers, and they weren't prepared for what he gave them."[36]

Amid increased scarcity, leftist party connections became crucial for anyone wanting to obtain basic necessities. Food lines and rationing committees, called Price and Supply Boards (Juntas de Abastecimiento y Precios, JAPs), aroused extraordinary resentment; years later, mere mention of the JAPs or of *colas* (queues) still evoked a visceral reaction among women from all social levels who had to shop for their families at the time.

Carmen García, a mother of four from working-class Lo Prado, wept as she remembered having to "stand all night in the cold to get milk for the baby." She added, "I will never, ever forgive the Communists for that." Lucía Santa Cruz, an upper-class professional woman, recalled "going from store to store trying to find a bit of cooking oil or sugar. The sense of deprivation gave you a terrible feeling of uncertainty."[37]

As Allende's star faded, his legislative opponents became more emboldened. The U.P. coalition obtained eight additional seats in the March 1973 congressional races, but fell short of the majority it needed to implement its far-reaching programs through law. However, Allende's Christian Democratic and rightist opponents in the legislature also failed to get the necessary seats to impeach the president or force him to resign. Trapped, Allende mounted a desperate personal struggle to keep his government alive, pleading with workers to abandon strikes, inviting military officials to his residence to voice their grievances, and appealing to Christian Democratic opponents for compromise.

But the trust essential for negotiation was gone. The moderates on both sides of the political divide had dwindled to a handful. Conservatives openly plotted to overthrow the government, while leftist groups demanded that Allende surge ahead with the revolution and arm workers for its defense. Politics had become so divisive that friends stopped speaking and wedding parties deteriorated into raging arguments. A university official saw smoke billowing from Socialist party headquarters one day and rushed to call the fire department. His secretary, normally placid and sweet, grabbed the phone away. "Let them burn," she snarled.

A dramatic eleventh-hour call by Cardinal Raúl Silva Henríquez for dialogue between Allende and the Christian Democratic leader Patricio Aylwin gave many Chileans hope that a regime-saving compromise might be found. But Aylwin and his advisers suspected that Allende's reassuring words were a ruse to gain time to impose his will by force, while Allende could not accept the Christian Democratic demands that he virtually abdicate power by appointing military officers to mid-level government posts. Knowing that many Christian Democratic leaders had been in touch with the military, he feared that they sought a coup against him.

WHILE the politicians talked, the armed forces, convinced that leftists had infiltrated their ranks and built armed bunkers in expropriated farms and factories, grew increasingly restless and frustrated. Commanders were torn between their loyalty to the constitution and their instinct for self-defense. In a desperate gamble for survival, Allende named the four military commanders to his cabinet. But instead of cementing support from his political opponents, the move only aggravated tensions within the military.

When civilians began clamoring openly for a coup, they touched a chord of military pride. Hundreds of housewives, irate over food lines and convinced the government was planning to impose leftist indoctrination in schools, threw chicken feed at soldiers on parade. "We felt vilified and cornered; the people were calling us cowards," General Leigh recalled bitterly.[38]

By August, the war of nerves was at fever pitch. Rightist newspapers screamed that the "totalitarian nightmare" was at hand; leftist media exhorted workers to thwart a "fascist coup." Chanting U.P. supporters marched through the streets, and home owners barricaded their windows with timbers, expecting an armed rabble to invade. In a letter to General Carlos Prats, the army commander, a veteran politician described Chile as a Greek tragedy, with each character doing "precisely what is necessary to bring about the misfortune they are seeking to avoid."[39]

"You had to be there to understand it, the psychosis and panic of the moment. In our hearts we were all at war," explained Sergio Arellano Iturriaga, then a young lawyer and Christian Democratic activist whose father was a prominent general. "Incredible things were being said; political leaders were threatening violence and calling for mass mobilization. No one knew how many weapons there were, so it seemed as if one were facing a vast, invisible army."[40]

On the other side of this "Maginot line," Osvaldo Puccio Huidobro, a young firebrand from the MIR, yearned for action. "I wanted a coup; I thought it would bring matters to a head," he confessed years later. "I imagined myself as a leader in a liberated zone, fighting a revolutionary war in which the forces of good would sweep away the forces of evil forever." Instead, Puccio would soon be cowering in a basement, forced to eat his mustache by smirking soldiers, and then shipped off to a frozen prison camp.[41]

On August 22, a majority of the Chamber of Deputies declared that the government had engaged in unconstitutional behavior, and called on the military to "place an immediate end" to the state of affairs. "We had no choice. We were heading into either a military or a Marxist dictatorship. At that moment, a military government seemed the lesser evil," recounted Francisco Bulnes, a National party senator who helped draft the resolution. Like other conservative leaders, Bulnes had been warned he was on a list to be shot if a revolutionary regime took power—and he believed it.[42]

Clutching at straws, aides urged Allende to call a national referendum, but preparations for the coup had already begun. Hour by hour, the pressure intensified. On September 9, rightist newspapers trumpeted the alleged discovery of a vast guerrilla camp, and the Socialist senator Carlos Altamirano delivered a violent speech warning Allende's enemies that the left had mounted a "combative force which nothing and no one can contain."[43]

That night, high-ranking naval officers informed Leigh and Pinochet, who had just been named to replace Prats, that they were ready to move against Allende immediately and that there was no time to lose. Called away from his daughter's birthday party, the army general hastily added his signature to their handwritten pact, and the military "pronouncement" was under way.

ACROSS the emotionally exhausted nation, many Chileans reacted to the coup with relief. After months of extreme tension, people yearned for peace and order, for a return to daily routine unperturbed by cataclysmic events. "Life had become unbearable. You couldn't walk to work without worrying if the windows would be smashed or the streets barricaded," an airline clerk confessed to a customer in 1974.

For foes of the Popular Unity government, the "Eleventh" was also a day of deliverance from the forces of encroaching communism. The Supreme Court president sent a congratulatory message to the junta, while conservative Catholic bishops offered prayers of thanksgiving. Well-to-do families popped champagne corks and hung Chilean flags out their windows. At a busy intersection, a middle-aged woman in tweeds grabbed a foreigner's sleeve and blurted in broken English, "We are free now, do you understand? F-R-E-E!"

In Washington, officials cautiously waited to recognize the junta until twenty-two other countries had done so. But their few public comments belied relief at the overthrow of Allende and deliberate disingenuousness about the nature of the coup. "I don't think it is for us to judge what happened there," Jack Kubisch, the senior State Department official for Latin America, told a congressional hearing on September 20. "That is for Chileans themselves to decide."[44]

For disciples of Salvador Allende, September 11 was a day of numb mourning. Factory workers lit votive candles, and teary-eyed students gathered glumly around radios. Carmen Vivanco, a nitrate miner's daughter who had risen to become a Communist party leader and provincial governor's wife, tried to remain calm while her world crumbled. "There was gunfire, police, people running," recalled the petite, steely-eyed widow. "My husband suddenly seemed sick and old. It was the first time I had ever seen him cry."[45]

The coup also brought home to Allende's supporters how hated they were by much of society. Mourners described wandering in shock amid the din of celebration; a Socialist party member who ventured out to buy groceries was appalled at the comments of other shoppers. "I expected someone to express sympathy for Allende's death, but there wasn't one ounce of compassion," the woman recalled. "They were saying good riddance."

For its first victims, the repression unleashed by the coup came as a severe shock. Chileans had little notion of what a military takeover signified; it was not part of their history or vocabulary. Most people assumed that the armed forces would remain in power for a matter of months, then return control to the proper civilian authorities once order had been restored.

At first there seemed little to fear. The junta had promised to respect the rights of unarmed citizens. Trust in authority was a deeply ingrained habit, and if a problem arose, surely a call to a well-placed friend could resolve it. Professionals who had advised U.P. programs reasoned that they had nothing to worry about. When the radio began broadcasting lists of political figures who should report for questioning, the most common impulse was to obey.

Indeed, a number of individuals spent hours attempting to turn themselves in, reacting indignantly when confused guards sent them to yet another facility. Carlos Naudón, a television commentator and professor of international affairs, whose name had been read out, talked his way into the Ministry of Defense and was pleased to encounter a former student inside—a colonel who greeted him with a hearty embrace and apologized for having to detain him temporarily.

That night, Naudón realized he had made a terrible mistake. Soldiers with machine guns shoved him from a bus into the bleachers of Chile Stadium, where hundreds of prisoners milled nervously or slumped in despair. One young man shouted hysterically at a guard, who calmly drew a pistol and shot him dead. Naudón was shuttled among prison camps for months, before being suddenly freed without explanation.

It quickly became clear to those in custody that military officials viewed all U.P. supporters as traitors who deserved to pay for their sins. In a few accounts, soldiers or officers were described as sympathetic, but in testimony from a wide variety of detainees, military men seemed hysterically enraged. In one factory raid, workers testified that soldiers burst in "wanting to see blood," raped a secretary, and tortured an elderly doorman until he identified union leaders.[46]

More than seven thousand civilians were herded into the National Stadium, where, as many detainees later described, they were brutally interrogated in rooms beneath the bleachers. Some survivors watched fellow prisoners being marched out of sight, then heard bursts of heavy gunfire nearby, and never saw the men again. In Chile Stadium, Victor Jara, the protest balladeer, was seen covered with blood and cigarette burns. When his British wife recovered his body from the morgue, she saw that the revolutionary guitarist's hands had also been broken.[47]

Military authorities repeatedly denied all such accounts, asserting that detainees in the stadiums were well treated and even conducting a sanitized media tour. Asked about reports of Jara's death, the commander of the National Executive Secretariat of Detainees dismissed it as an "invention" of government opponents. "That person was never in the National Stadium, nor does he appear in our registers of those detained," the colonel insisted.[48]

On shipboard detention facilities, one progovernment magazine archly suggested that prisoners were enjoying sea breezes. But down in the holds, hellish scenes unfolded. Aboard the naval training schooner *Esmeralda*, Luis Vega, an Interior Ministry lawyer, described how a masked guard whipped a fellow prisoner, poured salt on his back, and forced Vega to grind it in with his feet.[49] On the merchant ship *Lebu,* a law student described a woman who had been raped and nearly drowned in excrement. "She looked out with unseeing, haunted eyes. She never made a sound, never ate. She just sat there dying."[50]

In the port of San Antonio, police began rounding up leftist militants several days before the coup, including students from the MIR like the fifteen-year-old Mariela Bacciarini, and detaining them in a local army barracks. Fifteen years later, the slender, nervous woman, eyes heavy with makeup and bitter lines etched around her mouth, smoked cigarette after cigarette in a rundown Santiago café and described what happened next.

"There were men in uniforms rushing everywhere, huge numbers of prisoners began to arrive, and I heard someone shout my father's name. They let me see him for three minutes. He could hardly stand . . ." The young woman's eyes filled with tears, and she wiped her mascara on a paper napkin. "He said his back was broken and they were going to kill him. I never saw him again."[51] Two months later her father, a local Socialist leader, was reported shot dead while trying to flee from an army truck.

THE new regime was more cautious in its treatment of high-ranking Popular Unity officials, most of whom were well known abroad. On October 4, *Qué Pasa* magazine published a list describing the whereabouts of leading U.P. figures: twenty-seven were reportedly being held at a military camp, twenty-five had sought asylum in embassies, fourteen were described as fugitives, ten were in "pending" circumstances, six were detained, three had been abroad at the time of the coup, and two were dead.[52]

Carlos Altamirano, the rabble-rousing Socialist who had confidently predicted that the workers would rise up and overthrow the "mutinous bourgeoisie," found himself alone and fleeing from military pursuers like a hunted animal. Ultimately, he was smuggled out of the country by an East German diplomat, who disguised himself as a traveling salesman and hid the terrified ex-senator under a pile of suitcases and pharmaceutical samples in his car.[53]

The architects of Allende's revolution who turned themselves in were spared torture and death, but more than fifty former senators, cabinet ministers, and academics were flown to Dawson Island, a military base in the Strait of Magellan, and informed they were "prisoners of war." For a year, these middle-aged professional men struggled to preserve dignity and sanity in an environment designed to destroy them: frozen barracks, gang labor, and calisthenics in the snow.

Most of these men were never charged with a crime, and authorities took pains to show the world they were being well treated, allowing several visits by the International Red Cross. Once out of the spotlight, though, they were treated as worthless pariahs. "Chile does not need lazy, idle intellectuals like you. Chile needs soldiers, and we will make you into soldiers, whatever it costs," one camp commander instructed grimly.[54]

To combat humiliation and abuse, the prisoners created a climate of respect and affection among themselves. Patricio Guijón conducted German classes, and the former education minister Edgardo Enríquez wore his necktie and freshly shined shoes each day. Still, wrote the former foreign minister Clodomiro Almeyda, it was depressing to "swim against a tide of hate from our own countrymen. I will never forget one sergeant who pointed a machine gun at several of us and said with a venom that was absolutely indescribable, 'God, how I hate you all.' "[55]

Hundreds of less prominent leftists were also transferred to remote military camps, where treatment ranged from humane to subhuman. At the northern desert camp of Pisagua, detainees were forced to crawl and lick the ground in front of military officials. And at Quiriquina Island, a navy training camp in Concepción harbor, they were made to run naked until they dropped and to endure elaborately staged, mock executions.

Camilo Cortés, a round little man of iron socialist convictions and religious faith, was arrested and taken to Quiriquina. Navy interrogators, demanding to know about secret arsenals at the giant steel mill where he worked, beat him unconscious. Fed up with his quiet defiance, they marched the Protestant lay preacher to a pile of sandbags at dawn. A firing squad pinned a target on his chest and took aim.

"I wanted to shout 'Viva Chile!' but I needed to urinate badly, and I didn't want them to think I was afraid. So I concentrated all my effort on not peeing as I died," recalled Cortés, half smiling at the absurdity of that moment fifteen years before. "There was a huge barrage of sound, then a sepulchral silence. I was sure I was dead. They had gone beyond the limits of bestiality."

Afterward Cortés survived to become the unofficial prison chaplain, offering communion from soda cans on a packing-crate altar and converting a number of Communist prisoners to Christianity. "Every time they came to take someone away for torture, we would tell them to be dignified, and we would sing, 'Not a leaf moves without His power,' " Cortés said, his eyes filling with tears. "In prison, your faith becomes real."[56]

At least two hundred leftist militants held in prison camps were shot while allegedly attempting to escape or after being condemned by military war councils. These legal procedures were so swift and one-sided that the Inter-American Human Rights Commission said they lacked "the most basic guarantees of due process."[57] In early 1990, mass graves were discovered near Pisagua containing a number of cadavers with their hands bound and bullet holes in their heads.

THE harshest treatment of all was reserved for the most vulnerable supporters of Allende: small-town peasant and labor leaders who had no international contacts and no place to hide from official and personal vengeance. Landowners called on troops in combat gear to clear out illegal squatters. Army and police detachments, aided by deputized farmers, swept through towns and farms in convoys, seizing and brutalizing peasants.

"The coup was like a landlord coming down on a drunken peasant, punishing his insolence with an immense cruelty," said Marco Antonio de la Parra, the psychiatrist. "In Chile we never could have imagined such cruelty before, but it could only have happened in a country that was already sick. The crimes were committed by one side, but the passions of the other side took away all their scruples and made anything possible."[58]

Near the town of Mulchén, about eighty miles from Concepción, nine peasants were massacred in a two-day vigilante spree; the crimes remained uninvestigated for years. In the nearby papermill town of Laja, nineteen labor leaders and leftist officials were arrested and placed in the local jail. One morning they vanished; police first said they had been transferred to an army base, but then denied they had ever been in custody. The men remained missing until 1979, when a church delegation exhumed their bones from a graveyard.

One prosperous farmer, asked in 1989 about violence against peasant leaders after the coup, grimaced in disapproval. "Yes, some of the hotheaded Marxists were killed and never heard from since. But you have to understand what the U.P. did to people," he added apologetically. "We were within a hair of becoming a dictatorship like Cuba. There was total disorder. Good or bad, the military saved us from that."

Rural violence was an intimate act: everyone knew the local authorities and tended to trust them. Mulchén's mayor, Alfredo Kunkar, escorted a Communist alderman to the police station, certain he would be unharmed. Inside, the man was beaten to death. Residents lived silently with the knowledge that certain neighbors had participated in the farm massacres. One Sunday in 1988, Kunkar and a friend were chatting with the authors when a church procession passed, chanting hymns. "You see that man with the Bible? He was one of them," murmured the friend.[59]

In the neighboring village of Santa Barbara, a widow named Norma Panes endured for years the insolent impunity of the landowners' sons who kidnapped and killed her husband. A sturdy woman with a shock of prematurely white hair, she rocked in a chair in her neatly swept, three-room bungalow, stroking a cat as she calmly related the story. Above her hung an old framed photograph of a lean, grinning figure in overalls and a strawhat.

"My husband was Miguel Cuevas Pincheira. He was a shoemaker and a Socialist," she began. "He loved to read, and people were always coming over to talk. His only vice was smoking." One night in October, a posse of masked men roared up in a caravan of jeeps. They had already been to a nearby farm and seized several peasant leaders. Bursting in the door, they began to beat her husband. "I knew their voices, I knew them all," Panes said quietly. "They cracked his head open, and it sounded like a watermelon splitting. They dragged him into a jeep, and then they were gone."

The next morning, Panes and the other wives began a desperate search of barracks and hospitals. No authority acknowledged that their husbands had been arrested, and in 1975 the Concepción appeals court rejected their habeas corpus petitions. The missing men were never found, and a military court ultimately acquitted the vigilante members of charges of illegal possession of firearms. Often, Panes saw them lounging in the village square. "They would snicker and curse when I came by," she said. "Once, one of them spit in my face."[60]

WHILE the wave of free-lance rural violence that followed the coup sprang from passionate, often personal hatreds, the harsh, punitive behavior of Chile's military establishment against the left sprang from a combination of fear, heavy ideological indoctrination, and a calculated institutional need to justify the imposition of military rule.

For months after the coup, a few armed revolutionary cells, especially underground MIR commandos, continued to launch sporadic armed attacks against the regime, and many military men clearly believed they faced a real threat. Their paranoia was reinforced by official reports of spectacular shoot-outs with "extremists," and by elaborate displays of confiscated weapons. Within six months, the regime reported seizing more than 100,000 pistols and revolvers, 12,000 combat rifles, 500 rocket launchers, and 70 antitank guns—enough to arm a massive uprising.

On September 11, General Leigh had vowed to "struggle against Marxism and to extirpate it to the last consequences." To a career soldier like Colonel Medina the task seemed a continuation of the patriotic military mission to which he had dedicated his life, as had his father and grandfather. "The residents begged us to get rid of the delinquents, and they had hidden enormous quantities of arms," he recalled grimly. "There was only one solution."[61]

Later, other officials insisted a swift crackdown had been necessary to prevent worse bloodshed. Crushing any incipient insurgency, they argued, saved lives on both sides—even if innocent people were swept into military nets in the process. Yet the scattered pockets of resistance were hopelessly outgunned by Chile's professional fighting forces. By the end of December, the military regime had lost only fifty-two soldiers, seventeen policemen, and twelve sailors to armed attacks or confrontations.[62]

Although it was soon clear that the threat of armed uprising had been vastly exaggerated, months of rhetorical provocation by the MIR and other radical groups also goaded the armed forces into a frenzied lust for battle. Chile was at war, the military had been unleashed to vent its frustrations, and the actual level of threat was largely irrelevant.

"We were very surprised there was not more resistance. Our casualties were very low. The left could not confront the power of the army; their weapons were laughably crude," recounted one retired colonel. "But if you are a professional soldier and you are attacked by a mortar or a slingshot, and you have a tank or a cannon, you let the enemy have it with all you've got. We were trained for war, and our job was to search out the enemy and destroy him."[63]

To a large extent, Pinochet and his commanders manufactured the war atmosphere to guarantee their control over an explosive political situation and to ensure public support. In the weeks after the coup, provincial commanders received orders to provide lists of "subversives" for interrogation. Often they regarded local U.P. officials as relatively harmless, but rightist civilian groups such as Patria y Libertad were quick to offer names, and officers desperate to please superiors simply passed them on.[64]

To intensify the sense of urgency and danger, military authorities developed a last-minute thesis that Allende and the left had been plotting to assassinate senior military officials and other prominent figures in mid-September. The evidence of this conspiracy was largely a fabrication, stitched together from assorted leftist party documents and false intelligence. The CIA, which maintained an active propaganda apparatus after the coup, assisted in preparing a document called the White Book, which detailed the alleged plot, known as Plan Z.[65]

The book was widely circulated in Washington in an effort to justify the coup, and in Chile Plan Z became a military obsession. Throughout the country, officers were ordered to discover by any means necessary the details of Plan Z and the location of hidden arsenals connected with it. In hundreds of barracks and police stations, prisoners were beaten and tortured in an attempt to extract confessions related to the diabolical plot.

In early October, General Sergio Arellano, commander of the Santiago army garrison, set off on a whirlwind helicopter tour of military installations in six northern cities. The official purpose of his trip, on special orders from Pinochet, was to review and in some cases "upgrade" prison sentences that had been handed down by military war councils in each city.

But the general's trip was also intended to stimulate the battle-field atmosphere and make certain that local commanders were pursuing leftists with vigor. According to Colonel Efraím Jaña, who greeted Arellano when he emerged from the big Puma helicopter in Talca, the general asked how many casualties his forces had sustained. When Jaña assured him the region had been secured in a peaceful manner, the general reacted angrily.

"Later, I understood," Jaña explained to the Chilean writer Patricia Verdugo. The colonel's attitude "did not square with the superior plans, which called for exacerbating military fury against the left," Jaña recounted. The situation in Talca was too peaceful, "just when they wanted many prisoners and people on trial to accuse them of Plan Z."[66]

For many of the local leftists who had been rounded up and charged with subversive activities, the outcome of Arellano's tour was fatal. Wherever the Puma landed, prisoners were removed from their cells and secretly executed, apparently by members of Arellano's crew. Some had not yet been tried; others, like the journalist Carlos Berger, were serving extremely brief sentences. In all, sixty-two people were killed and buried in unmarked graves.[67]

For years afterward, Arellano refused to defend himself against public condemnation for his role in the killings, but his son, acting as family spokesman, steadfastly maintained that the general had been unaware of the prisoners' fates at the time. Three of his crew members turned out to be agents of a new clandestine intelligence service that did not respond to the regular army chain of command, and Arellano's family suggested that they were acting on separate, secret orders.

Yet accounts such as Jaña's, coming after years of silence, were extremely damning to the retired general. In La Serena, Arellano checked off sixteen names on a list of condemned prisoners and then strolled through a garden with his military host while the victims were being killed. In Calama, he ordered a military tribunal convened for the next day, but while he was at dinner that night, twenty-six prisoners were taken into the desert and shot.[68]

DESPITE the sustained crackdown, most Chileans initially assumed that once order was restored, the armed forces would return to their barracks and relinquish power to civilian authorities. They did not realize that a military takeover could develop its own, irreversible dynamic, they failed to grasp the resentment against political elites that had festered within the armed forces for years—and they gravely underestimated the ambitions of General Pinochet.

As far as military officials were concerned, the blame for Chile's near-collapse lay not only with Allende but also with decades of corrupt and demagogic rule. The junta's "state of war" applied both to a specific military enemy and to an ideological and political adversary whose definition grew broader by the day. Having rescued their country from certain disaster, Pinochet and his colleagues saw an opportunity to set Chile on a new course of disciplined and efficient management, governed by military principles of duty, hard work, and patriotism.

One month after the coup, the junta president laid out this new vision in a solemn first "state of the nation" message. He described the coup as guided by "the hand of God," and pledged himself to the "heroic struggle" to "extirpate the root of evil from Chile." He vowed to bring about a "moral cleansing" of the nation, to build a new democracy "purified of vices," and to create a new constitution that would banish "politicking, sectarianism, and demagoguery from national life."[69]

Pinochet's impassioned address signaled the beginning of a new revolution in Chile, one with even more radical implications than the reformist utopia of Eduardo Frei or the socialist dream of Salvador Allende. Chile was now in the hands of a military establishment that believed civilian rule had failed and that viewed its mandate for leadership as open-ended. "We cannot give timetables or fix dates," Pinochet warned the nation. "Only when the country has reached social peace and economic development will our mission have ended."[70]

CHAPTER TWO

THE SOLDIERS

"Thy names, courageous soldiers
Who of Chile have been the backbone
We will carry engraved in our hearts
By our sons will they also be known
May they be the cry of death
We send forth marching to the fight
And echoing in the mouths of the strong
Make the tyrant tremble in his might."

—*Second verse, Chilean national anthem*

THE military men who seized control of Chile on September 11, 1973, were an enigma to most civilians. The holiday parades of goose-stepping foot soldiers and cavalrymen astride white horses, their pointed blue helmets crowned with silver eagles and flowing white tassels, seemed a relic of nineteenth-century wars, part of a harmless patriotic tradition of marches and melodies that made old men misty-eyed and small boys shout with glee.

But most parade watchers had never been inside the hermetic enclave of Chilean military life. They knew nothing of the rigid moral values, the vertical command system, and the powerful group mystique that lay behind those ceremonial drills. They could not imagine Chile's army, with its antiquated dress uniforms, as a tough, modern fighting force, capable of turning on its enemies with deadly precision.

During 150 years of constitutional rule, the military had remained generally aloof from public life, evolving in isolation from a society which regarded it with a mixture of fondness, bewilderment, and contempt. In the mid-1800s, civilian leaders kept the military small and poorly equipped to prevent it from threatening oligarchic democracy. As added insurance, presidents encouraged the development of a national guard composed of pliant citizen-soldiers.

When war broke out with Peru and Bolivia in 1879, Chile's ill-prepared armed forces fought with legendary heroism, and the army alone swelled from 2,500 to 25,000 men; yet their victory relied heavily on "gentlemen officers."[1] The government, realizing Chile needed an effective fighting force to defend its newly won territories, sought help from the Prussians, who had built the first professional army in the West.[2]

The Prussian army, created after the Napoleonic Wars and honed under a succession of military monarchs, was renowned for integrity and style as well as battlefield prowess. In 1885, the Chileans hired Emil Körner, a Prussian army captain and professor of military studies at Germany's prestigious Kriegsakademie. His staff drilled duty and discipline into newly recruited middle-class and provincial officers, the most promising of whom were sent to Prussia to train with the elite imperial guard.[3]

"The harshness of the system led to unspeakable treatment," one trainee reported,[4] but the results were dramatic. By 1914, the erratic army had been forged into a remarkable replica of the polished, severe German forces. "In my long career as a military officer, only in my fatherland have I seen the equal of Chilean soldiers," remarked the German ambassador in 1910, watching the corps of cadets goose-step through Santiago.[5]

Ironically, this modernization also eroded Chile's tradition of military subordination to civilian authority. The splendid new officers, schooled in the principle of promotion through merit, came to resent the political elite for pushing the advancement of upper-class officers and for operating a corrupt patronage system. When nitrate exports collapsed in World War I, officers were dismayed by the paralysis of Chile's legislature in the face of deepening social and economic crisis.

In 1924, these grievances drove junior officers to demand reforms, forcing the president to resign and placing a military junta in power for four months.[6] Seven years of political turmoil and elected strongman rule followed, culminating in a second, brief military intervention. Once fully competitive elections were restored in 1932, political leaders took great pains to rein in the armed forces, although remaining aloof from barracks affairs and providing a generous military budget.

With President Arturo Alessandri's blessing, armed civilian groups revived the nineteenth-century "republican militia" as a counterweight to military ambitions. Chastened by its ill-fated incursion into politics, the army retreated quietly to the barracks but continued to nurse grievances against a political establishment it regarded as corrupt and incompetent.

Civilian society, in turn, paid elaborate homage to military heroes, and high-ranking officers were given privileged access to the municipal opera and polo club. Yet soldiers were socially snubbed and the army was regarded as a fallback for slow or rebellious sons—a necessary but subservient institution manned by brutish, intellectually inferior beings.

"There was a palpable lack of understanding and contact between the two worlds. People loved parades, but politicians mocked us as little toy soldiers. We suffered great economic hardship, and it caused much resentment," recalled a retired colonel. Posted to the provinces, officers mingled with local dignitaries and sometimes married their daughters. "But in Santiago, we weren't taken into account."[7]

General Alfredo Mahn was one of the most prominent army leaders of the 1950s and 1960s, but his daughter Liliana grew up feeling excluded from society. Once a teacher humiliated her in class, calling her father a "dumb little soldier." Later, her friends were surprised to learn he was "a cultivated man, who read, listened to music, and knew how to converse," she recalled. "It was believed that soldiers thought with their feet or their horses."[8]

Cadets were sent off to the Santiago Military Academy as teenagers, while other young people remained at home until they married. Away from society, they strove to become more patriotic than the average citizen, more virtuous than civilian leaders, and more professional than soldiers in other Latin American armies.

Enduring hardship and hazing together, cadets formed bonds that endured for a lifetime. Long after retirement, officers still met regularly in private clubs, although their luncheons and card games were strictly social and their institutional influence disappeared. Old colonels and generals became a caste within a caste, cut off from both the civilian world, which made them feel uncomfortable, and from the military world, which was now closed to them.

The barracks were a secret, Spartan society designed to produce the ideal warrior. There everything was divided into good and evil, superiors and subordinates; and perfect obedience was the price for the privilege of command. There was no room for weakness or doubt, and surprise was to be avoided at all cost. Teams of officers would debate all options, but once the commander decided on a course of action, it was followed to the letter.

Chilean soldiers were constantly obliged to demonstrate loyalty to their institution. Once a year, each man raised his right hand and swore, "by God and this flag," to serve the fatherland. The mystical power of symbols was omnipresent: the flag, the uniform, and especially the company insignia were sacred objects to be defended with one's life.

Taught that martyrdom was the height of glory but denied the opportunity to march off to war, many a middle-aged military bureaucrat yearned for battles he would never see. "Dying for the fatherland" was "the greatest fulfillment to which a soldier can aspire," asserted Colonel Eugenio Covarrubias, who commanded the military academy in the mid-1980s, "It is the only thing I would have left to feel completely fulfilled."[9]

The rigid hierarchy of rank was reinforced by a thousand gestures and details. Officers were fawning with superiors and brutal with inferiors, as they passed down the tradition of iron vertical command. The most senior colonel felt the same heel-clicking tension in the presence of "my" general as the most junior cadet did, and rivals fretted over minute matters of protocol that signaled who was higher on the seniority ladder.

Frustrated but secure in his niche, the Chilean army man found civilian relationships anarchic. The endless debate and deal making seemed inefficient; the political skills of compromise and persuasion seemed mere weakness and bombast. "I remember a deep frustration among my colleagues—a tremendous resentment against civilian elites and a brewing sentiment that they were not good at governing," recalled one retired general.[10]

Yet the vast majority of Chilean officers had no desire to intervene in politics, and the decades following the 1931 intervention were characterized by strict respect for elected authority. From time to time, rogue coup movements did surface—the most serious being the so-called Straight Line movement of 1955, which sought to persuade President Carlos Ibañez to rule as a dictator with army backing—but they never achieved wide military support.

Instead, the dominant tone was set by generals like Mahn and René Schneider, who believed in the constitution and viewed the armed forces as subordinates of the civilian authorities. Some high-ranking officials became Masons and developed sympathies for the Radical party, but all were banned from voting in elections or from "deliberating" on national issues, and even senior officers were expected to refrain from expressing views in public.

"We had seminars on many subjects, but if you had opinions, you discussed them only inside the barracks," explained Alfredo Rehren, a retired colonel. "It was always passed down from the senior officers, not to mix in politics. You were trained to follow the rules unless you became completely fed up. It wasn't just written; it was engraved up here too," he said, tapping his temple.[11]

IN 1932, a spindly youth of sixteen named Augusto Pinochet entered this hermetic military world. His father, Augusto, a customs officer in Valparaiso, had hoped he would become a doctor, but his mother, Avelina, a much stronger influence, encouraged his childhood dream of joining the army. After being rejected twice by the National Military Academy (first for being too small, then for being too thin), Pinochet was accepted for the four-year officers' training course.[12]

An average student, he compensated by exhibiting unusual devotion to duty and a flair for spit-and-polish drills. Classmates recalled him as hardworking and imperious, but always ready with a joke. It was a "highly disciplined and predictable life," Pinochet later wrote, confessing that he and his fellows often "suffered moments of bitterness" on being severely corrected by superiors who "inculcated us with a sense of responsibility."[13]

Graduating in 1936 as a second lieutenant, Pinochet entered infantry school, where he further cultivated values of patriotism, public service, and respect for authority.[14] He came to view a military career as a self-sacrificing vocation, and in later years he referred to his presidency as an extension of this mission. A soldier must be "noble and assume great obligations," he wrote in 1983. "His first duty . . . is to renounce life and material possessions as the fatherland demands."[15]

Immersed in logistics and strategy, these young officers knew little of the intense political debates that consumed civilian society. Pinochet was aware of this divide, describing army barracks as "veritable watertight compartments." Neither in class nor in the mess hall, he wrote, "did I hear any discussion of a political nature."[16]

When world turmoil began to swirl in the 1930s, soldiers and officers were only dimly aware of it. Authoritarian regimes were taking power across the continent, Europe careened toward war, and the struggle between fascism and socialism marked Chile's 1938 elections. But the military, smarting from its failed foray into politics, remained on the sidelines.

After World War II broke out, Lieutenant Pinochet and his cohorts delighted in following the battles on wall maps. They rooted for the Germans and were "enchanted by Rommel," he later confessed, but had little sense of the issues. "We were interested only in the professional part, like a doctor who has a patient with a tumor," Pinochet explained.[17]

His first brush with politics came in 1939, when he was sent on a relief mission to Concepción after a devastating earthquake. There he met a number of Socialist militiamen, whom he described as swaggering, "two-bit thieves," but who also made him feel intellectually inferior. "When we had to have discussions with civilians, we appeared to lack culture," he recounted with embarrassment.[18]

The strong social and moral influence of the army over a soldier's life further reinforced the distance from civilian society. In the military caste, many officers' sons followed in their fathers' footsteps, and married young women from military families. Permission to marry was rarely granted before they reached lieutenant rank, however, and until the 1970s they could not marry a separated woman.

Pinochet, assigned as an officer to the military academy, was more exposed to the capital than were most of his contemporaries. There he met and courted the daughter of a Radical senator and future interior minister, Osvaldo Hiriart. Yet his marriage into a political family did not lessen his discomfort with the civilian world; indeed, there are indications that his prominent in-laws looked down upon him, reinforcing that resentment.

Lucía Hiriart was an ambitious young woman whom one relative described as "leading Augusto around by her little finger."[19] Yet for more than a decade, she and her growing brood (three daughters, two sons) followed him dutifully from outpost to outpost. In segregated housing complexes, military families socialized almost exclusively with each other and nursed their prejudices against the civilian elite that had turned politics into a national sport.

While Pinochet was serving at the military academy in 1945, his bitterness against civilian authority was further fueled by the abrupt, politically motivated transfer of the two top academy officials to other posts. In his memoirs, he described the incident as "a violent act" which made him realize that, at times, "the man of arms is defenseless before the actions of certain politicians." In fact, he was so upset that he asked to leave the academy, and returned to provincial commands.[20]

Despite their distaste for politics, Chilean officers were inevitably drawn into the conflict that accompanied the rise of the Communist left. When the party was outlawed in 1948, Captain Pinochet was first ordered north to command the Pisagua concentration camp, where more than four hundred party activists were banished; then he was sent south to take control of the Schwager coal mines, where Communist unions were fomenting a bitter strike.

At Pisagua, he encountered a former mayor and governor who had received him hospitably during military maneuvers; now, as his prisoners, they introduced him to Marx's *Manifesto* during long, rambling conversations. Initially, Pinochet was impressed by their commitment to social justice and their discipline under unpleasant conditions. In the coal region, where mining families lived in dire poverty, he also met a number of union activists who appeared dedicated to improving their lot.

Yet there were also several unsettling incidents, such as his discovery of a coal-town market woman who concealed leftist pamphlets in her breadbaskets. In Pisagua, a group of leftist congressmen led by Senator Allende appeared and demanded to inspect the facilities; Pinochet denied them entry and later remarked they had "only come to agitate" the prisoners.

In hindsight, Pinochet concluded that the sincere-seeming detainees were "masters of subterranean struggle" and agents in a "diabolical" scheme to foment hatred among the poor and infiltrate the middle class.[21] Communism was "not just another party," he wrote; it was a "system that turned everything upside down, without leaving any belief or faith."[22]

These ideas, refined during Pinochet's studies at the War Academy in 1949 to 1952 and then as an instructor there, were linked to the new doctrine of national security that spread across the continent with the rise of the cold war. During the 1950s, with the French conflicts in Vietnam and Algeria and the development of the NATO "containment" policy, anticommunism came to replace nationalism as the cardinal tenet of Latin America's military institutions. After the 1959 Cuban revolution, Chile established mutual defense treaties with Brazil and Argentina against the potential threat of a Soviet / Cuban plan to dominate South America.

Much of the theory and training behind this new military thrust came from the United States, where a generation of cold-war theorists held the reins of foreign and defense policy. Between 1950 and 1979, nearly seven thousand Chilean officers were sent for advanced instruction at the U.S. military-run School of the Americas, in Panama, or at other American bases, where national-security concepts and counterinsurgency techniques were taught. Gradually, after decades of coexisting with a wide spectrum of political parties, the army refocused its sights from external foes to domestic ideological adversaries.

The size of the army remained at roughly 45,000 men—smaller than that of Argentina or of Mexico—but the ratio of military to civilian population was among the highest in Latin America. Defense spending dropped gradually, from 25 percent of the national budget in 1940 to only 13 percent in 1970, but the lion's share continued to go to the army.[23]

Communism gave the Chilean armed forces a new focus for their Manichaean view of the world, and a new image of the enemy burrowed into the heart of society, purporting to champion the oppressed but bent on destroying the state. Military tracts evoked images of cancer or plague whose extraction required not only traditional military tools but political, economic, and psychological ones as well.

"I saw a fundamental change in the postwar period, when the United States provided the indoctrination of our institutions," recalled General Horacio Toro, one of the few military critics of the Pinochet regime. But he blamed U.S. indoctrination for the evolution of cold-war thinking in Chile, saying it ultimately "helped create an infernal anti-Marxist machine."[24]

MAJOR PINOCHET, continuing his career climb, entered the University of Chile law school in 1955, but his studies were aborted by a sudden posting to Ecuador, where Chilean officers were overseeing a military training project. His superior, General Anibal Mansilla, recalled him as displaying many qualities of a born commander: "Perseverance, valor to adopt decisions and take the consequences, courage to impose on his subordinates and discipline to respect his superiors." To know Pinochet, he added, "you must understand him first as a soldier."[25]

From there, Pinochet was sent to the northern deserts of Antofagasta, where he was promoted to regimental commander, then posted back to Santiago as associate director of the War Academy under General Mahn. There, the teenage Liliana Mahn recalled him as a "terse but affable, rather timid" man, "enormously respectful with his superiors," who offered her tea while she waited for her father.[26]

Friendship and esprit de corps notwithstanding, competition among aspiring officers was intense. Only a handful ever reached the rank of general; all others were required to retire after thirty years of service. Promotions were based on a formal set of criteria reviewed annually by a panel of generals. Their recommendations required approval by the Senate and the president, who could end any general's career by appointing a colleague of lower seniority as army commander.

Although academic study was crucial for a man to rise within the army, suspicion of intellectual achievement was deeply ingrained within the military establishment. In interviews, several army officers with graduate training acknowledged being torn between the desire to advance academically and the need to display the conformity of a "good soldier." Some said their careers had suffered because superiors saw them as too ambitious and cerebral.[27]

"I thrived on being challenged by my professors to question assumptions, but I recognize this might not be so good for the institution," said one officer, proud of his university degree but insistent on anonymity. "We are formed to fight and kill, not to reason and debate. I worry about my own instinct to question everything," he confessed. "Undivided loyalty to the institution comes above everything else."

Pinochet fit squarely into the desired military mold: he did just well enough to advance, but not so well as to arouse suspicion. He styled himself an intellectual, writing several books on geopolitical strategy at the War Academy, but he was never singled out as a leader. His record was competent and plodding, rather than brilliant.

To all who knew him, Pinochet seemed the archetypal army careerist: loyal, disciplined, and circumspect. There is no record of his having participated in the Straight Line movement in 1955, or of sharing his budding anti-Communist ideology with colleagues. "His ideological orientation was an enigma," said Mónica Madariaga, a younger cousin. "If he had any, he had not demonstrated it publicly."[28]

TENSION between military and civilian elites sharpened in the 1960s, just as Pinochet moved into higher army echelons. President Jorge Alessandri reduced military spending to promote economic recovery and development after a major earthquake. Military expenditures, which in 1957 had reached 3.2 percent of the gross national product, dropped to 2 percent in 1964, and the army was sharply cut back to 20,000 men.[29]

Some officers, wary of the left, welcomed the election of Frei, and Pinochet was among them. But Frei kept military budgets low to boost development and antipoverty projects.[30] The armed forces felt maligned and abandoned by progressive politicians, and in protest officers at the War Academy refused to cash their Christmas bonuses. In response, Frei retired outspoken officers and promoted others he believed loyal. Civil-military tensions mounted quickly.

On October 21, 1969, General Roberto Viaux, who had written Frei requesting an "urgent solution" to the army's problems, seized the Tacna tank regiment.[31] Top commanders sympathized with Viaux's demands, but they condemned his twenty-four hour armed protest as unacceptable. In his memoirs, General Prats wrote that the Frei government had "committed a grave historic error" by turning its back on the armed forces, yet he blasted Viaux's "thankless breach of military discipline" and warned that such actions could unleash a dynamic of rebelliousness that would be difficult to control.[32]

As the 1970 election approached, discontent grew in the ranks, but Chile's military leaders pledged to support whichever candidate won. The new army commander, General René Schneider, a leader of refined tastes and democratic convictions, was determined to keep his troops out of politics. But Viaux's protest had broken the half-century taboo against military intervention in politics, and shortly after Allende's election, Schneider himself became its first victim.

The CIA, having failed in its effort to undermine Allende's popular election, received frantic instructions from Director Richard Helms—himself under orders from Nixon—to stop his confirmation by the legislature. Agents in Santiago knew that Viaux and another group of officers had been plotting against their superiors, and they decided to encourage a military uprising in hopes it would abort Allende's confirmation. Secret meetings were held with the conspirators, and "sanitized" (unmarked) U.S. submachine guns were passed to one group of plotters.

Meanwhile, the other group concocted a muddled plan to kidnap General Schneider and provoke a coup, but the deed went tragically awry. On October 22, eight cars ambushed Schneider's limousine and a group of men tried to drag him out. When he fired back, he was shot and critically wounded. The crime appalled the nation and strengthened the hand of strict constitutional officers like Prats, who was named new army commander. General Viaux and a number of coconspirators were arrested and charged. Three days after the attack, with Schneider on his deathbed, the Congress voted to name Allende president.[33]

Pinochet, stationed in far northern Iquique, has asserted he knew nothing about the plotting. But on the night of Allende's election, the general wrote, he called together his subordinates and warned them Chile had embarked on a "grave path" towards communism. Then, with a touch of melodrama, he added, "My career is at an end. The problem of saving Chile will rest in your hands. May God help the fate of our fatherland."[34]

Instead, Pinochet was asked by Allende to command the Santiago garrison. Presiding over holiday parades, he saluted the president in his reviewing stand, but privately fumed while society grew "poisoned" with hatred and moral decay.[35] "With great bitterness we men of arms watched the road Chile had taken, and we felt the desperation of impotence," he wrote. "As a soldier sworn to protect the fatherland, I felt inhibited from acting, because the instigator of chaos was the very government . . . to which I owed obedience."[36]

If the general harbored such emotions, he kept them to himself, and was rewarded with promotion to the post of chief of the army general staff. During a three-week visit by Fidel Castro in 1971, Pinochet was required to accompany him in formal parades, and they were photographed saluting in tandem. General Prats was so convinced of Pinochet's loyalty that he asked him to develop contingency plans in case of an antigovernment uprising.

By mid-1973, the drumbeat of strikes, marches, and insurrectionary rhetoric was driving military paranoia and frustration to new heights. On June 29, a regiment of tanks advanced on La Moneda, firing wildly, but the rebellious gesture was quickly thwarted under Prats's orders. A few days later, a group of army, navy, and air force officials formed the "Committee of Fifteen" to discuss the growing political crisis, and sent Allende a list of twenty-nine demands.

Allende tried to deflect this criticism by naming Chile's military commanders to cabinet posts, but the officers' meetings increasingly took on the shape of a conspiracy. In the navy, Vice-Admiral José Toribio Merino conspired behind the back of his commander, Raúl Montero, an upright "gentleman of the sea." The air force general Nicanor Díaz joined in the plotting, as did senior army generals, including Sergio Arellano, Oscar Bonilla, Hermán Brady, Augusto Lutz, Sergio Nuño, and Javier Palacios.

The CIA, which had been tracking military unrest, fabricated evidence of Cuban military links to Allende and passed them on to Chilean officers, but stopped short of actively abetting a coup. A congressional investigation in 1975 found "no hard evidence of direct U.S. assistance" to the plotters, while U.S. officials strongly denied any involvement.[37] Henry Kissinger testified before Congress that "the CIA had nothing to do with the coup" unless "some madman" had been operating "without instructions."[38] CIA officials said their men had been told to monitor any plotting but "to avoid contacts or actions which might later be construed as supporting" a coup.[39]

Many on the Chilean left, however, believed that the United States was heavily involved. They pointed to Ambassador Nathaniel Davis's sudden trip to Washington only two days before the coup, the presence of U.S. ships and sailors in the Valparaiso area, and the disappearance of Charles Horman, a young American living in Santiago, shortly after the coup. A harrowing 1982 film about Horman, *Missing,* suggested U.S. embassy complicity in his arrest, and Horman's family sued the Nixon administration. But Ambassador Davis persuasively refuted these charges in his memoirs and countersued the filmmakers.[40]

Even without "direct" involvement, however, American attitudes and pressure helped set the stage for the coup, while CIA efforts to undermine Allende in the past—and ample foreknowledge that a coup was in the works—gave the conspiring generals extra confidence in tacit U.S. approval. As the congressional investigators noted, U.S. officials in Chile "may not always have succeeded in walking the thin line between monitoring indigenous coup plotting and actually stimulating it."[41]

General Prats, rapidly losing his battle to preserve the army's constitutional posture, was humiliated by a demonstration of officers' wives, who gathered outside his home on August 21, taunting him as a coward. The following day, the shattered commander submitted his resignation, saying it was his "soldier's duty" to avoid causing an institutional breakdown or "serving as a pretext" for an overthrow of the government.[42]

Throughout the crisis, Pinochet reassured Prats and Allende of his loyalty and refused to join the conspirators' debate, arguing that it was "prohibited." The plotters' skepticism intensified when Allende, desperate to replace Prats, turned to Pinochet. On August 23, he was sworn in as army commander, with orders to restore discipline among the officer corps. At first he attempted to obey, requesting the resignation of several generals who favored a coup. But when they refused to go, he hurriedly withdrew the order.[43]

Once the chain of command had snapped, Pinochet suddenly summoned his top officers and made them take an oath to remain loyal to the army, hinting that a coup might be necessary. But the conspirators, holding a flurry of meetings with coup-prone civilians, were still loath to confide in him. "In all this, no one had talked to Pinochet," recalled Díaz. "The idea existed that he opposed the coup. . . . We all believed it."[44]

Late on Saturday, September 8, Arellano visited Pinochet and attempted to secure his support for the plans, but was received with a "mixture of surprise and annoyance."[45] The next afternoon, Leigh drove to Pinochet's house, interrupting his daughter Jacqueline's birthday party, and began arguing for urgent military action.

At that moment, two navy officers arrived with a message from Admiral Merino in Valparaiso, asking both commanders to pledge support for a coup at dawn two days hence. On the back were two notes: "Gustavo: This is the last opportunity" and "Augusto: Do not fail to act with all the force of Santiago from the first moment. . . . Pepe." Leigh scribbled his agreement; then Pinochet did the same. If he failed to join the coup now, he might become its first victim.[46]

PINOCHET'S postcoup description of these events conveys a starkly different impression of his role, implying he became convinced of the need for action long before September 1973, while watching society move toward civil war and imposed Marxist rule. "If the extremists believed the moment of confrontation was coming, so did I," he wrote in 1980. "They wanted triumph to take total power; I wanted it to save Chile from communism."[47]

If few people knew about his plans, Pinochet explained, it was

because he had developed them in secrecy. Reports of leftist infiltration in the armed forces were widespread, and no one could be
totally trusted. When he had broached the idea of a "little coup"
to General Prats, his commander dismissed the idea. As a result,
he said, "I had to seek a formula so that all could be done in the
most discreet form possible."

Pinochet's secret plan was to transform the army's official
"internal security" preparations from a defensive strategy to an
offensive one. In *The Decisive Day,* his book about the coup, the
general described working on this plan at the War Academy, with
colleagues sworn to silence. "Plans, orders, dispositions, and a total
military preparation" were developed, he said, "all disguised beneath
a war game."[48]

Once, Pinochet recounted, Allende became suspicious and confronted him at a bizarre, predawn meeting, but the general allayed
his fears. Afterward, Pinochet reported gleefully, Allende reassured a colleague the general was a harmless "old man who thinks
only about military matters" and "isn't even capable of deceiving
his wife."[49]

Pinochet said he had planned to stage an uprising several days
after September 11, using military parades on the September 19
national holiday as an excuse to mobilize troops and distribute
arms. Years later, he acknowledged that Merino and Leigh had
surprised him with their own proposal, but added, "If I had not
been prepared, do you think it would have been possible to move
the troops in 24 hours?"[50]

Yet no officer has ever confirmed Pinochet's version, and the
evidence suggests he twisted past events to reflect more positively
on his role, disguising vacillation as slyness and creating an anticommunist hero out of a cautious, apolitical opportunist.[51]

LONG before Chile's new junta leader had the leisure to rewrite
history, he was faced with the immediate problem of how to establish command over an army in revolt. His reputation for cautious
deference and his last-minute entry into the conspiracy made it
essential for him to outdo the leading plotters in anticommunist
ardor. Moreover, Pinochet had headed the army for less than three
weeks and was far from secure about his ability to control the
institution.

The great majority of officers and troops eagerly followed their
superiors into battle against the left, but a few senior officers were

known to sympathize with Allende, and Pinochet feared that some army units might disobey orders. He was especially uncertain of the situation in Talca and Calama, where his inspection tours had unearthed officers of suspiciously "progressive" mentality.[52]

The most effective way to ensure discipline was to generate fear of reprisal against those who did not pursue subversives with ruthless dispatch. The "state of internal war" declared by the junta was aimed, as much as anything else, at guaranteeing military compliance with a violent takeover of the elected government. Under "battlefield" conditions, anyone who failed to follow orders risked being demoted, arrested, or worse.

Colonel Renato Cantuarias, commander of a mountain training school where Pinochet sent his family for shelter during the coup, was taken to the Military Academy on September 12 and died there mysteriously a week later. According to several reports, including that of a cousin who was Allende's minister of mines, the colonel was forced to shoot himself as punishment for refusing to order the bombing of a copper mine.[53]

Major Iván Lavandero, while processing detainees in the National Stadium, was persuaded to release a group of Uruguayan prisoners by the Swedish ambassador, Harald Edelstam, a Popular Unity sympathizer who helped hundreds of Chileans and foreigners reach asylum. When a colonel directing stadium interrogations found out, according to Edelstam, he ordered the major executed immediately by firing squad.[54]

Within days of the coup, a group of left-leaning air force officers was arrested, harshly interrogated, and eventually tried before war tribunals. They had been in secret contact with aides to Allende and members of the MIR, and claimed their intent was to warn the government of a pending coup. But they were accused and convicted of aiding leftist forces to infiltrate the military. The senior officer, General Alberto Bachelet, fell ill and died in prison; the rest were forced into exile.

"They convicted me of treason, and I kept thinking, what had I done to betray my country except to respect the elected government?" recalled the ex-captain Patricio Carbacho, a portly engineer, sipping coffee in his Maryland kitchen sixteen years later. In prison, he was interrogated and tortured by his former colleagues, then forced to watch helplessly while his mentor, Bachelet, died in his cell without medical treatment.[55]

To make officers capable of turning on each other with such fury, military commanders had to intensify their fear and hatred of communism—to convince them that an invading enemy had plotted to destroy them as well as the Chilean "way of life." According to Carbacho, air force squads were told by superiors soon after the coup that leftist forces had mined military parade grounds with explosives and drawn up death lists of military men and their families.

"We had been taught to trust the word of higher officers, so we had no reason to doubt them. What they said created great anxiety and mistrust among us; it created the desire to go out and kill those animals," Carbacho recalled. "This explains the transformation of an army that respected civilian leadership into one that could treat prisoners like the Vietnamese. Anyone who acted with humanity was a traitor. Anyone who supported the government was serving a foreign enemy."[56]

The most elaborate instrument of this internal propaganda crusade was Plan Z. There is little doubt that it was a fabrication; Pinochet himself made no mention of it in his memoirs, and the lack of evidence aroused enough skepticism that officials soon dropped it from their litany of Marxist-inspired danger narrowly averted by the coup.[57]

But for months the alleged plot served a critical purpose: it transformed the armed forces into an instrument of ideological warfare, united by hatred, fear, and a conspiracy of silence about postcoup atrocities. The orders were to find out about Plan Z at all costs, and any officer who appeared squeamish was suspect himself. The reported executions of Colonel Cantuarias and Major Lavandero sent an especially vivid warning through the army grapevine.[58]

"They hit you and pressured you so much that you began to ask yourself if you were involved in the plan or not," recounted Mario O'Ryan, a low-ranking air force officer who was detained in October. He imagined the hatred planted in his fellow officers, told that even a "normal" military buddy like himself could turn out to be a "diabolical Marxist" intent on killing them and their families.[59]

General Arellano's helicopter tour in October was clearly aimed at making sure that "progressive" commanding officers displayed proper belligerence. Colonel Jaña was imprisoned for three years for failing to carry out antileftist raids with sufficient vigor. The officer who replaced him, Colonel Olagier Benavente, was left terrified. "The fear General Arellano provoked in us spread throughout Chile like a torrent," he recounted. "I realized we had to be much harsher if we wanted to survive."[60]

IRONICALLY, an even greater threat to Pinochet came from the anticommunist generals who had upstaged him on September 11. The coup had broken two military principles: vertical command and noninterference in politics. Although the breakdown in loyalty had brought Pinochet to power, he knew he must restore it in order to maintain authority. This meant moving against the architects of the coup and promoting officers known for strict adherence to institutional discipline.

Bonilla and Arellano, both more dashing and respected than Pinochet, emerged as "heroes" of the coup with new sources of power: Bonilla as interior minister and Arellano as commander of the Santiago garrison. Other coup leaders began expressing their opinions on issues ranging from poverty to social injustice, and Bonilla and Lutz met secretly to share their concern about the growing ambitions of Pinochet and the secret police.

But the new junta members had grander ideas. They now wielded exclusive control over executive, legislative, and constitutional powers—and they used them to enact laws that gave each commander sweeping authority over all promotions and retirements in his branch. Thus, Pinochet was able to retire fifteen of the army's twenty-five generals by April of 1974, including the four closest to him in seniority. Within three years, almost all generals who had played leading roles in the coup were gone.

In July 1974, Pinochet abruptly removed Bonilla from the Interior Ministry and named him defense minister, a far less influential position; at the same time, he transferred Lutz to a military post in remote Punta Arenas. "This was a key turning point, the beginning of the development of Pinochet's personal power," observed a former aide.[61]

Within six months, moreover, both generals met a mysterious death. In October, Lutz fell ill at a party and was flown to the military hospital in Santiago, where he died after a series of faulty diagnoses and operations. In January 1975, while returning from a vacation in the countryside, Bonilla was killed in a suspicious helicopter crash, in which the pilot attempted to take off in a heavy fog. In both cases, the results of official inquiries were kept secret.

A more complicated fate awaited Arellano, a popular officer nicknamed the Wolf, who was viewed in the army as a potential regime leader. His image was tarnished by the executions that coincided with his helicopter tour, and his family thought Pinochet had orchestrated the killings to undermine his stature. "My father believed that Pinochet betrayed the cause of the coup and destroyed democracy," contended Arellano's son. The new junta leader, he added, was "pathologically obsessed with eliminating rivals."[62]

In 1975, Pinochet offered Arellano the dubious reward of a distant ambassadorship, and the furious general resigned on the spot. After his retirement, his request for an army hearing on the executions was denied, and his only comfort was the support of loyal subordinates and peers. "He lives on that," his son said years later.[63] With Arellano's downfall, Pinochet's most serious army rival was neutralized.

The junta president's paranoia extended beyond Chile's borders to Argentina, where his former commander, Carlos Prats, had moved shortly after the coup. Although retired and living abroad, Prats was still highly respected among the officer corps and maintained close ties with domestic opponents of the regime. He was also writing his memoirs, rumored to criticize Pinochet.

On September 30, 1974, General Prats and his wife, Sofia, were blown to pieces by a car bomb outside their Buenos Aires apartment. Three independent investigations linked the killings to Chilean intelligence agents, and although the Pinochet regime denied all involvement, it made no real effort to investigate the crime.[64] Even in death, the distinguished general drew Pinochet's remarkable hostility; he was denied a military funeral, and police agents harassed mourners at the private burial.

"The authorities ordered army people not to attend the mass and checked everyone's identification," recalled Prats's daughter Sofía, a soft-voiced woman in her forties. "No one helped us find out what had happened; my sister and I had to do everything ourselves. We asked for an audience with Pinochet to request an Argentine investigation, but he thought we had come to thank him for his help in bringing back the body. It was a very disagreeable encounter."[65]

In 1989, Pinochet called Prat's death "vile and perverse" and denied any knowledge of the crime, exclaiming, "God knows who killed him!" The Prats family had made him a "scapegoat," he charged, claiming that sections of Prats's memoirs criticizing him had been "added on" by others after his death.[66]

THE most significant legal step taken by the junta to achieve total military dominance was Decree Law 527, which granted each commander an indefinite term in office, ending only in the case of "resignation, death, or incapacity." With their tenure open-ended, the commanders now held absolute control over the careers of subordinate officers. Such measures set Chile on a course radically different from that of neighboring regimes, which respected traditional retirement rules and regularly rotated their leaders.

Even more than his peers, Pinochet realized the enormous potential of his double office as army commander in chief and president. With no civilian legislature, executive, or independent military review board to contradict him, he was able to pervert the normal process of army career advancement and replace it with one man's whim.[67]

Whenever he felt threatened by an independent officer, Pinochet ordered him retired or transferred to a distant garrison or embassy. At the same time, he promoted loyalists who were required to sign undated resignations upon becoming generals. The commander also created several new high-level ranks to keep favored generals past retirement age, and gave himself the unique title of captain general, further emphasizing the distance between him and all other officers.[68]

As he built his power base, Pinochet surrounded himself with self-effacing aides like General René Escauriaza, who became known as "the general of the shadows," laboring with selfless efficiency and cajoling his mercurial boss with well-timed quips. In 1979, he was often forced to mediate during quarrelsome, smoke-filled cabinet meetings, exacerbating a chronic lung ailment. During one debate, he began coughing uncontrollably. That night, the forty-seven-year-old officer died, and Pinochet decreed a day of mourning.[69]

Such self-abnegating service was often rewarded with lucrative positions on state corporations or commissions. Yet Pinochet could also turn on his confidants when it suited his purposes. General Sergio Covarrubias, an aide crucial to the building of Pinochet's executive power, was eased out of sensitive posts when he became too visible, and sent into "exile"—first as commander in the far southern city of Punta Arenas, then to Chile's UN delegation in New York.

As Pinochet retired younger generals, the increasing age difference between the commander and his subordinates placed them at an even greater disadvantage.[70] Although he became a father figure to some aides, they never dared consider him a friend. "I have known my General Pinochet for 42 years, since I was a recruit and he was a lieutenant instructor," recounted Lieutenant General Julio Canessa, one of his closest aides. "I have known him deeply as a subordinate, and it is not the custom in the army for a subordinate to say he is the friend of a superior."[71]

UNDER dictatorship, the army's authoritarian nature was accentuated. Relationships became more cold and formal, and a more palpable thread of fear bound the chain of command, with hard-liners tending to rise in influence. In meetings, Pinochet encouraged wide debate, but all officers had to speak in formal terms of address and in reverse order of seniority—and the general's word was always final.

Officers known to be clever or independent minded were systematically held back; the last thing Pinochet wanted was to be intellectually upstaged. To advance, senior officers had to stifle their creativity and initiative. "I know it sounds ridiculous, but I practically have to get permission to move a plant in my office," confided one widely-read colonel. "You can disagree to a point, but when the boss decides on Plan B, you have to obey, or it hurts your career."[72]

One iconoclastic officer who lasted only four years under Pinochet was General Toro, an intense, bespectacled man descended from four generations of generals. At first he was assigned a key role on the junta's advisory staff, but in 1977 he infuriated Pinochet by expressing, both privately and publicly, his concern about human rights and excess executive power. Abruptly forced to retire, he was barred from all military facilities and shunned by his colleagues.

"I was always willing to speak my mind, and that's what led to my ostracism. I would bring up human rights, but no one wanted to hear about them. The unconditional loyalists didn't like me," explained Toro, a lonely crusader in a small, borrowed office, in 1989. "I didn't want to become just another bureaucrat, but if I had kept quiet, today I would be a major general in the institution of my forefathers."

A soldier who believed his army had been perverted by dictatorship and fanaticism, Toro said he feared many of his peers had "lost their core values." "Military honor comes not from battle but from a sense of service to the nation. Authoritarian governments remove honor and replace them with blind loyalty," he said sadly. "My colleagues are trapped by the system, and they are afraid to talk freely."[73]

For officers who played by the rules, dictatorship provided

unprecedented rewards. Under Pinochet, the armed forces became larger and richer than at any other time in the twentieth century. Defense spending soared by 30 percent in 1974, and within a decade it had reached 4.6 percent of the gross domestic product, not including funds for the secret police. By 1989, colonels were earning 191,000 pesos a month and captains 146,000 pesos—far more than the 50,000 earned by a veteran high school teacher or a civil engineer.[74]

Between 1973 and 1980, the number of military troops swelled from 60,000 to 88,000 with the army growing a full 65 percent, to 53,000 soldiers. In 1975, Chile had the highest ratio of men of arms to working-age adults of any Latin American country except Cuba.[75]

In part, these increases were justified by the revived threat of foreign military confrontations after a century of regional peace. Peru, under the control of the left-leaning General Juan Velasco Alvarado, briefly threatened to invade in 1974. Three years later, after the military seized power in Argentina, an old border dispute over the far southern Beagle Islands escalated into a tense stand-off, with both defense forces on full alert, until the issue was resolved by papal mediation.

The advent of unprecedented domestic power infused the military establishment with a new sense of self-importance, pride, and social ambition. Colonels and generals assigned to diplomatic posts acquired worldly tastes and returned with duty-free Mercedes or BMWs. High-ranking officers built spacious homes in newly developed suburbs, and their wives and daughters began to shop in fashionable stores. And, as a financial scandal eventually revealed in 1990, a number of high-ranking officers reportedly profited from illegal investment operations set up within the military itself.[76]

With the enhanced stature of a military career, middle-class families began to look less askance at sending their college-age sons for officer training. Applications to military academies rose substantially, the quality of applicants improved, and competition became so fierce that some secondary schools even instituted preparation courses for entrance exams.

Yet military rule did not narrow the traditional gap between civilian and uniformed society. Instead, secrecy and fear of outsiders became more pronounced. Even senior officers were anxious and reticent in speaking with visitors, since a careless remark could jeopardize their careers. During an easygoing chat with one colonel, a foreign professor reached into his briefcase for a notebook. The officer's cordial tone vanished. "Take one note and I'll sue you," he snapped.

On a formal level, relations with the American military establishment became cooler and more distant as well, partly as a result of the congressional ban on U.S. military aid that was adopted in 1974 as a form of protest against human rights abuses, then expanded to include arms sales and credit two years later.[77] Personal and professional relationships continued, however; U.S. and Chilean military officials collaborated on plans to use Chile-owned Easter Island as an emergency landing site for the American space shuttle, and U.S. ships joined Chilean navy vessels in annual exercises off the Pacific coast.

Some U.S. military policymakers argued that the ban on aid deprived the United States of a valuable source of "leverage" with the Chilean armed forces. At times, though, cordial signals from the Pentagon clashed awkwardly with the stated U.S. policy of prodding Pinochet to become less repressive. In 1985, General Robert Schweitzer embarrassed the Reagan administration by presenting Pinochet with a ceremonial sword, praising him for freeing Chile from communism, and suggesting that foreign press reports had deliberately distorted the truth about his regime.[78] U.S. officials were forced to counter the effects of the incident by sending other military officers with a different message, confusing supporters as well as opponents of the military government.

In Chile, political affinity between uniformed officials and the progovernment civilian elite seldom translated into friendship. To ensure loyalty and cohesion, Pinochet frowned on his men's fraternizing with civilians. Businessmen and conservative politicians would chat with high-ranking officers at receptions—then leave wondering what they "really" thought.

Moreover, decades of cultural isolation could not be overcome on command. Despite higher incomes and ambitions, officers and their wives were still snubbed socially by civilians. In self-defense, the new military elite created its own high society—self-conscious, haughty, and adamantly antidemocratic. Prominent military and civilian figures rarely socialized, and some attempts ended in disaster.

One upper-class woman, married to a conservative lawyer, described an excruciating luncheon with the wife of an army official who kept "dropping names and talking about her special privileges," then complained that "civilians had ruined the country and weren't fit to run things." The lawyer's wife said she left thinking, "We'd better get rid of these military people fast." Later, she added wryly, the officer's wife called their hostess "and said I had confirmed all her prejudices about civilians."[79]

For average Chileans, the image of the patriotic soldier deteriorated rapidly with the onslaught of repression against political parties, labor unions, and students. For years, people in working-class areas vividly recalled the combat troops breaking down doors and seizing neighbors in the wake of the coup. Riot police with clubs and water cannons became a familiar presence in daily life, and the midnight rap on the door became a symbol of dread to hundreds of thousands of Chileans.

Long after 1973, the arrogance of military power made itself felt in a thousand ways. Military motorcades often careened through traffic at high speed, leaving tie-ups and accidents in their wake. When special ceremonies were held at the Military Academy, which was located near a major intersection, armed soldiers would order rush-hour traffic to a halt and block the lanes for thirty or forty-five minutes, oblivious to the silently fuming commuters, while military officials and their guests strolled to their cars and departed along the cleared route.

AS military rule became entrenched, the anticommunist fears that had unleashed the coup developed into a strong, unifying ideology that bound the armed forces to Pinochet. The junta commanders portrayed their mission as morally, even divinely, inspired. Most soldiers became convinced they had saved Chile from catastrophe and that they alone stood as guardians of the nation's values against the forces of subversion.

Although only 107 members of the armed forces and police were killed during the first two years of military rule, there was no letup in the campaign of "psychological warfare" aimed at keeping the armed forces alert to the Marxist threat.[80] According to General Toro, officers were subjected to "an intense and penetrating fog" of propaganda, which "created a strong current that is anticivilian and antidemocratic."[81]

In 1974, the Superior Academy of National Security was created to train officers in anticommunist ideology and strategy, and students were warned to remain vigilant. "Subversion can act behind the kindness of a lady . . . or the innocence of a child," explained Colonel Eugenio Covarrubias a decade later. Such enemies must be attacked with subterfuge and ruthlessness, he said. "One feels more joy than sorrow in destroying something which is destroying what we are."[82]

Gradually, the notion of a brief interregnum was replaced by a new definition of the military as a permanent, purifying, and protective force. Officers came to believe they had replaced 150 years of corrupt, weak civilian rule with a firm foundation of peace and order; some suggested that Chile was neither economically nor civically advanced enough to handle democracy. But the armed forces, secure in their mandate and united behind their president, had a special, open-ended mission to fulfill.

At 8:00 A.M. on August 23, 1975, a marching band struck up a patriotic tune outside Pinochet's residence in suburban Las Condes, and a row of generals lined up to salute and embrace the general on a special occasion. At 11:30, army officers from garrisons across the nation and officials from other branches gathered at the Military Academy stadium to offer him their testimony of loyalty and support.

"On the second anniversary of your designation as commander in chief, you find the army bound together, cohesive as steel in its professional aspects, and united in its human aspects," declared General Hermán Brady, now the minister of defense. "My General, we are with our commander in chief. My General, we are with our army. My General, we are with our fatherland."

Pinochet, completing the ritual, answered; "This institution and its sister institutions . . . are struggling to attain the goals we set on September 11, 1973. Many are the actions which from the outside try to produce a vertical break in our institutions. But they must know that the cohesion of the armed forces . . . will not permit this breakdown. Because that would mean a suicidal act, and we, who have the responsibility for the fatherland, will never permit such an outcome."[83]

CHAPTER THREE

THE DICTATOR

"I wasn't looking for this job. Destiny gave it to me."
—*General Pinochet, 1984*[1]

THE ceremony was planned with stealthy precision. First, General Pinochet secretly ordered a new presidential sash and clasp designed with the emblem of General Bernardo O'Higgins, the father of Chile's independence, replacing the original objects that had been destroyed in the La Moneda bombing. Then an army aide called the president of the Supreme Court and asked him to preside. The palace press was notified and a small guest list prepared.

Ten days earlier, on June 17, 1974, Pinochet had persuaded the three other junta members to sign Decree Law 527, making him the chief executive, by arguing that this would add "efficiency" and coherence to the government. The decree gave him the title of Supreme Chief of the Nation, a flourish dreamed up by Mónica Madariaga, his chief legal aide. Pinochet's colleagues had conceded to these changes with some skepticism; General Leigh, with open indignation. But none realized the ambitious junta president was planning his virtual coronation.

As the ceremony was about to begin, an enraged Leigh confronted Pinochet in an upstairs office of the Diego Portales building. "You think you're God!" he snapped. Equally furious, Pinochet smashed his fist on a glass tabletop, which splintered with the impact. The collegial rule of the junta had been shattered. Moments later, the four men marched into the Blue Salon, grim-faced, while the cameras whirred and the invited dignitaries applauded.

The event lasted exactly twelve minutes, but it sealed Pinochet's personal and legal dominance over the military government. Justice Enrique Urrutia Manzano placed the tricolored sash across his shoulders, and the general thanked the judge for an honor he had "never imagined, much less sought." Then he read a short statement. "I will exercise the principle of authority with energy and justice," he vowed. "He who from this day exercises the Supreme Command of the Nation" will have "no other motive" than a soldier's love of country.[2]

AT first, it appeared Chile's military government would take a very different shape, more like that of the "collegial" regimes run by groups of officers in Brazil, Uruguay, and Argentina in the 1970s. On the day of the coup, Pinochet was named president of the junta purely as a matter of protocol, since he headed the oldest and largest military branch. The presidency was to rotate by "gentlemen's agreement" among the four commanders, a plan Pinochet heartily endorsed.

"I don't want to appear to be an irreplaceable person. I have no aspiration but to serve my country," Pinochet asserted. "Today it is me, tomorrow it will be Admiral Merino, then General Leigh, and so on." Moreover, he pledged that "as soon as the country recuperates, the junta will turn over the government to whomever the people desire."[3]

For a time, the branch commanders did function as equals, debating issues and approving all measures through unanimous consent. To make sure no member was slighted, ceremonies were held in rooms with doorways wide enough that all four men could enter abreast. To streamline governmental administration, the members divided up areas for study and policy planning: security to Pinochet, social welfare to General Leigh, economy to Admiral Merino, and agriculture to General Mendoza.

If anyone seemed likely to emerge as the junta's natural leader, it was the fifty-three-year-old Leigh, a man of keen intellect, strong personality, and wide popularity among his officers. But the taciturn Pinochet, thrust into a position of absolute command after forty years of saluting his superiors, soon began to reveal an ambition for power that his colleagues had never imagined he possessed. Behind the façade of absolute unity, he began maneuvering to gain control.

Expertly wielding the privileges of his double title as army commander and junta president, he always spoke last in formal junta discussions, and surrounded himself with well-informed aides who enabled him to overwhelm his colleagues with detailed knowledge of issues. With a keen sense for the symbolic power of pomp and protocol, Pinochet also worked to create a public image of aloof superiority over his colleagues—sometimes stooping to astonishing pettiness.

After Leigh was applauded while attending an opera performance at the elegant Municipal Theater, Pinochet declared the presidential box off-limits to him and the other two commanders. He also decided that instead of walking into ceremonies together, they should enter first and he would follow alone. Although top government appointments were meant to be made by the entire junta, he began announcing key positions during solo tours in the provinces. "Details, but that's how the steamroller started," recalled Leigh.[4]

Soon, Pinochet was working to make the distinction more substantive. With support from conservative legal experts, who argued that the state needed a clear separation of power to function effectively, he urged his colleagues to make him the chief executive, while they would act as the legislature. The other commanders were uneasy with the plan, but only Leigh dared to protest, and he finally conceded for the sake of preserving junta unity. "On legal matters they were in over their heads; we simply ate them up," Madariaga recalled in 1985. "I now realize I was helping to create a monster."[5]

Decree Law 527 was the perfect tool for a budding autocrat: Pinochet now had full executive powers, while retaining a vote on the junta, which was required to adopt all measures unanimously. Thus, he could issue decrees that his colleagues had no power to veto. Although each commander was entitled to his own advisory staff, Pinochet established a personal, ministry-level staff under Colonel Covarrubias, which gained control of the paper flow and signature routing for regime orders. By late 1974, it had become the "brain and heart of political power."[6]

From Supreme Chief of the Nation, it was a short, if tense, leap to President of the Republic. For weeks, Pinochet pressed his colleagues to provide him with this added title, insisting it would give the regime greater legitimacy at home and abroad. Leigh resisted, arguing that it would create an excess concentration of power. Finally, in December, Merino and Mendoza gave in and signed the new decree, admonishing Leigh not to create a public impression of divisiveness. Seething, he added his signature, and the notion of a rotating, "collegial" junta was abandoned forever.

"We had real power at the beginning," but "as advisers and courtesans began to appear, we ... were systematically displaced until we had no influence whatever in executive matters," Leigh recalled bitterly in 1979. Even though the armed forces had dismissed the constitution in 1973, he said, "Pinochet grabbed all the powers of the constitutional president" until his colleagues were "left at the margin of the governmental process."[7]

For all his titles, Pinochet's claims to legitimacy grew harder to sustain as time passed. Abroad, political repression drew sharp condemnation from former allies and the United Nations; at home, Catholic church officials broke with the government, critics like Leigh pressed for a timetable for the return to civilian rule, and some aides privately described Pinochet's edicts as "Amin One" and "Amin Two," referring to the Ugandan dictator Idi Amin.

The president was stung by the attacks, and devastated when the UN, on December 16, 1977, sharply condemned Chile for human rights abuses by a vote of 96 to 14. Determined to prove his enemies wrong, Pinochet decided to call a national referendum on his rule. His colleagues and staff were appalled, and Leigh wrote him a letter saying that such an act smacked of "personalistic regimes" and would sully the honor of the armed forces. Merino penned a similar protest, although he withdrew it under pressure. Prominent Chileans, from Cardinal Raúl Silva Henríquez to all three living presidents, strongly urged Pinochet to reconsider, but he flatly refused.

In a sharp response to Leigh, Pinochet retorted that the decision was the "exclusive prerogative" of the chief of state, and he called the air force commander a "traitor" for circulating letters critical of his plan. The people, he insisted, must choose between the champion of Chile's honor and her foreign detractors.[8]

The referendum was prepared under state-of-siege conditions, with no voter registration and no critical press coverage. The elderly state comptroller, Héctor Humeres, notified regime officials he would not certify the referendum as legal, but Pinochet refused to be stopped by an officious bureaucrat. Upon learning that Humeres was due to retire, he ordered the civil service to rush the paperwork through in one day. By nightfall, Pinochet had named a loyal aide, Sergio Fernández, to replace him, and the referendum decree was promptly endorsed.

At the polls on January 4, 1978, voters were handed a ballot with a Chilean flag for "yes," and a black box for "no," in answer to the following statement: "Faced with international aggression launched against our fatherland, I support President Pinochet in his defense of the dignity of Chile and reaffirm the legitimacy of the government. . . ." Votes were tallied inside the Interior Ministry, with blank ballots counted as "yes." At nightfall the government claimed victory, and Pinochet crowed, "Mr. Politicians, this is the end of you! Today there is a new Chile."[9]

As Leigh watched Pinochet bask in this dubious mandate for one-man rule, his endurance snapped. He brooded for weeks, then finally went to the press. In an interview with an Italian newspaper that was reprinted in Chile, he proposed his own timetable for the return to political "normality." Shortly before this, Pinochet was informed that a group of air force officers had contemplated launching a coup against him. Leigh's interview was the last straw. Furious, the president demanded Merino's and Mendoza's help in forcing him to resign.

When the air force general reported to work at the Ministry of Defense on Monday, July 24, he was flabbergasted to find the doors locked and army combat troops stationed outside. At the same time, he learned, troops had surrounded key air bases, immobilizing his planes. Storming up to Pinochet's office, Leigh found his three colleagues waiting with a decree removing him from the junta. Citing the well-being of the nation and the unity of the regime, they asked him to sign it. Stunned and angry, Leigh refused. But Pinochet produced a trump card: an executive decree declaring him "incompetent" to remain as a junta member.

Leigh was literally trapped in the ministry; his aides were stopped by soldiers with orders to shoot trespassers; his telephone lines were cut. That afternoon, Pinochet named General Fernando Matthei, the ninth in line after Leigh, to succeed him. As a matter of protocol, the eight generals in between automatically submitted their retirements. And, in a dramatic gesture of loyalty to Leigh, nine of the ten generals below Matthei resigned from the air force that day. "Their sacrifice gave me the most intense emotion of my entire military life," he confessed later.[10] Matthei was immediately sworn in, and at 4 P.M. Leigh walked down the ministry steps, stepped into his waiting military car, and never returned.[11]

Pinochet's preeminence on the junta was now undisputed. The obstreperous member had been removed, and the army commander seemed unfazed by the display of loyalty to his arch-rival.

"If some said I wouldn't dare make changes in the air force, you've now seen it," he gloated to reporters.[12]

Leigh's replacement, moreover, quickly demonstrated proper respect for the president. "I believe General Pinochet is fully aware of his value, his courage, his management capacity, and the tremendous power he has at this moment," Matthei said in early August. "No one can stop him in what he seeks to achieve: to carry ahead the process of institutionalization he proposed. He has always said so: it is not that I WANT power; I HAVE it, and I will make use of it to give Chile a true normality."[13]

GENERAL PINOCHET was now in a position to begin implementing his political vision for Chile: a society of order and progress in which the shrill, destructive clash of ideologies and partisan rivalries would be replaced by harmonious, vertical relations among individuals, civic groups, and the state.

Although the Marxist left bore the brunt of physical repression under Pinochet, contempt for all civilian politics was deeply rooted in his military psyche, and his concept of "the enemy" extended to anyone who represented Chile's traditional order. To the general, liberal democracy was a showcase for irresponsible, selfish demagogues that had proven itself a failure. He often vowed to purge the system of "partisan vices" and asserted he would never relinquish control to the same political elite that had allowed Chile to slip into communist clutches.

"The politicians wanted us to clean the house (and) let them occupy it again," but Chile needed a new political system and mentality, Pinochet said in 1975—something it might take "a generation" of military rule to achieve.[14] Four years later, his tune was unchanged. "We are not a vacuum cleaner that swept out Marxism to give back power to those Mr. Politicians," he snapped.[15]

There was more than a hint of social revenge in the general's outbursts against "partisan oligarchs" and "privileged minorities"—and in his bullying treatment of elite civilian institutions. He placed battalion commanders in charge of universities that probably would have rejected them as students, sent distinguished former senators into exile on a whim, and imposed a "recess" on all political parties—including conservative groups—that lasted nearly fifteen years.

Much of Pinochet's vitriol was aimed at the Christian Democrats, partly because their deal making had permitted Allende's election and partly because their stature, size, and links to the Catholic church represented the only real political threat to his power. Although he did not dare attack them physically, he dissolved the party in 1977, on a pretext of the discovery of "subversive documents" in a party leader's luggage, and sent two prominent Christian Democrats into exile, without time to pack a toothbrush or make a telephone call, for criticizing the regime.

As a military man, moreover, Pinochet had little respect for the arts of democracy: compromise was surrender, debate was inefficient, and dissent was anarchy. "I'm a soldier. . . . For me what is white is white and what is black is black," he once stated.[16] In an essay on politics, he wrote that man, like the planets, must submit himself to structure, since "nature shows us basic order and hierarchy are necessary" for the perfect functioning of the cosmos.[17]

Named for a Roman emperor, Augusto Pinochet expressed frank admiration for authoritarian rulers. One of his few trips abroad after the coup was to attend Franco's 1975 funeral in Madrid, and in 1981 he praised the late dictator as "a leader who had the courage to rescue Spain from chaos and the capacity to convert it into a modern nation."[18]

Compared with other modern military strongmen, Pinochet lacked the charisma and oratorical powers of Argentina's Juan Peron, the heroic stature of de Gaulle, or the political machine of Franco. Yet as one former military colleague put it, Pinochet "thinks of himself as the Franco of Chile."[19] And in time, he came to dominate Chile as no head of state had done before, amassing a degree of personal and institutional control unrivaled by contemporary military regimes anywhere else in Latin America.

To build a new, apolitical order, he turned for inspiration to Diego Portales, a powerful Chilean statesman of the 1830s and a driving force behind the strong, autocratic central government— the "Portalian Republic"—that emerged from the chaotic aftermath of Chile's revolt against the Spanish crown. Brutal but honorable, Portales disdained partisan politics and believed that the best government was an "impersonal" semidictatorship with limited concessions to popular representation.[20]

Pinochet's studied emulation of Portales was evident in the calls for discipline, efficiency, and the "principle of authority" that peppered his speeches. He posed for official photographs with an oil portrait of Portales behind his shoulder, named the regime's principal office building in his honor, and encouraged the cult of a "Portalian ethos" among his aides.

Looking abroad, Pinochet was attracted to the political model of Franco's Spain as well as the formula proposed by Juan María Bordaberry of Uruguay, who was president when the armed forces seized power there in 1973 and remained on as titular head of state. Bordaberry envisioned a permanent military state with a designated civilian leader and periodic referenda to consult the populace. Pinochet, searching for the ideal form of semidemocratic rule, maintained an active correspondence with him in Montevideo.[21]

In 1977, prodded by aides who were anxious to set the regime on firmer legal footing, Pinochet made a dramatic first effort to outline his new political vision for Chile. On the night of July 9, he mounted the hillside ramparts of an old war memorial, with flaming torches illuminating a cascade of patriotic banners, and addressed a rapt audience of several thousand young people from conservative and government-sponsored youth groups.

"Our duty is to give form to a new democracy that will be authoritarian, protected, integrating, technically modern, and with authentic social participation," Pinochet declared. The "classic liberal state, naive and spineless," must be replaced with one willing to "use strong and vigorous authority to defend the citizens from demogoguery and violence."[22]

The speech also outlined a five-year transition to controlled democracy beginning in 1980—the first time Pinochet had made a public commitment to phase out military rule. But that pledge, made as a result of pressure from Leigh and other regime moderates, was soon forgotten. Instead, buoyed by the successful referendum of 1978, the president pressed ahead with the legal centerpiece of his revolutionary scheme: a new constitution.

At the time, Chile was governed by the 1925 constitution, a charter for liberal democracy which had succeeded the long-standing constitution of 1833. Pinochet regarded it as an anachronistic relic of more innocent times, inadequate in a world where "violence and terrorism reign" and communism "infiltrates the very bases of government."[23] What he wanted was a charter that would confer short-term juridical legitimacy on military rule and create a permanent legacy of strong executive authority.

Virtually since the coup, a government legal commission had been quietly studying constitutional reforms; now Pinochet injected the panel with a new sense of urgency and provided members with a set of presidential "guidelines." In mid-1978, the group produced a highly authoritarian charter that banned Marxist groups, created a powerful executive and a partly appointed Congress, and gave the armed forces a permanent legal channel for influencing important government policy decisions.

The document was then sent to the Council of State, an advisory group headed by former President Alessandri. But instead of rubber-stamping the plan, Alessandri changed it to feature an elected Congress and presidential elections in 1985. Greatly displeased, the general ordered aides to revamp the charter secretly and include provisions to extend his rule sixteen more years. When they objected, he agreed to a slightly less imperious formula: a first eight-year term, followed by a referendum for which he and the other commanders would choose a sole candidate for another eight years. Pinochet was pointedly exempted from a ban on reelection.

Upon reading the final version, the distraught Alessandri protested privately to Pinochet that it "violated the fundamental spirit" of the original draft, and resigned from the Council of State. But the general was unfazed; amid great fanfare, he called for a constitutional plebiscite on September 11, 1980—always his lucky day of the year.

A group of Christian Democrats tried to organize in opposition, but they were harassed, banned from television, and limited to one indoor rally, where former President Frei blasted the constitution as an "illegitimate" attempt to prolong Pinochet's power.[24] Government propaganda, in contrast, was massive and hyperbolic. Posters urged Chileans to vote "yes" to freedom from communist chaos and tyranny, and official youth and women's groups held rallies across the country.

Polling conditions were little improved from those in 1978: there was no voter registration, and government officials and proregime businessmen were sent to man the booths in poor neighborhoods. The ballot was disarmingly simple: "New Political Constitution: Yes or No." Several hours after the polls closed, authorities announced that 67 percent of 6.2 million voters had chosen "yes."[25]

It is probable that a majority of voters did endorse the constitution, but widespread allegations of fraud suggest the margin was much smaller. One research group found that in nine regions the official turnout was higher than the entire population. Some voters were confused by the document, which one jurist called "convoluted and Machiavellian."[26] Others voted against their conscience in order to give the government a legal base. "It seemed like a lesser evil, to provide some legitimacy and order," recalled one former conservative senator. "We never thought it would lead to sixteen years of Pinochet."[27]

For the general, the procedural details hardly mattered. The results crowned his regime with the legitimacy it had lacked, and he exulted in them shamelessly. "For a second time, we have defeated the totalitarians!" he declared. "We have shown the world how democratic this nation is, that it needs no one to come give it lessons."[28]

On March 11, 1981, Pinochet was sworn in as president for the next eight years, and the new constitution went into effect. Six hours of parades and ceremonies were capped with a blessing from Cardinal Silva, reluctantly delivered over the protest of most of Chile's bishops. As an extra flourish, Pinochet took up official quarters in La Moneda. Home to Chile's presidents since 1846, it had been expensively renovated to erase the stigma of the 1973 bombing. Stepping onto the balcony to thank his supporters, Pinochet was radiant. "I feel in my spirit the emotion and the demanding call of history," he said. "May God illumine me for the difficult task of guiding our beloved nation."[29]

THE new resident of La Moneda had little in common with any of the previous occupants—perhaps least of all with his immediate predecessor. Under Allende, the palace had been a chaotic, bohemian hive of smoke-filled, shirt-sleeved meetings that often lasted until dawn. Under Pinochet, it became a severe, efficient command post, where aides conferred in whispers as they hurried along the corridors, then clicked sharply to attention at the president's approach.

Barking out orders in the elegant gloom of colonial antiques and chandeliers, Pinochet was a study in contradictions: the messianic potentate who reveled in the trappings of absolute power, and the austere military man who maintained a near-spartan personal regimen. A fitness fanatic, he ate simply and sparingly, never touched liquor, and preferred herb teas to coffee. Hardworking and punctual to a fault, he maintained a rigorous domestic travel schedule of speeches and ceremonies; on vacations, he set his watch for thirty-minute sunbaths and carried a Dictaphone during country rambles.[30]

Robustly built, with a salt-and-pepper mustache and ice-blue eyes, Pinochet enjoyed projecting an aura of toughness. He dressed impeccably as a civilian, sporting a pearl tie tack and ruby ring, but when serious business was at hand, he invariably appeared in uniform. In public, he often wore dark glasses that gave him a stern, sinister demeanor—until aides persuaded him to project a more open image. One former aide described him as a "veritable tank."[31]

In 1981, Pinochet offered this detailed account of his demanding daily regimen: "I get up every day between 5:30 and 5:50.... Then I normally do gymnastics for 15 minutes.... At 7 or 7:15 I am en route to work.... I arrive [by] 7:30 at La Moneda. First I receive information from the chief of intelligence, then from the press.... At 8 I eat breakfast with some group or person, always a working breakfast. At 9 I have an interview with the chief of the presidential staff and then I meet with ministers....

"At 11:30 I begin audiences until 1:15. At that hour I lunch with some group, also a working lunch. I rest an hour to take up activities again at 4.... At 4:30 I go to sign reports.... Then I dedicate myself to studying matters for the next day.... I leave La Moneda between 8 and 9 p.m. and arrive at my house, when there is no social activity on the program ... I prepare documents for the next day. At 10 I am in bed, reading ... philosophy, history, politics. I read for fifteen minutes. Sometimes I go overboard, and the next day I pay the consequences...."[32]

In his mind, Pinochet was an indefatigable public servant, a soldier sacrificing himself for the fatherland. One of his first acts as junta president was to offer a public accounting of his financial worth. He had little in common with Third World tyrants like Anastasio Somoza of Nicaragua or Ferdinand Marcos in the Philippines, who lived off the spoils of a cowed crony state.

Although Pinochet did not use the office of president to enrich himself, he was less scrupulous about the financial dealings of his close relatives. One son-in-law, Julio Ponce Lerou, parlayed posts in the state economic bureaucracy into profitable partnerships in public enterprises sold cheaply to private investors. And Pinochet's oldest son, Augusto, was in 1990 discovered to have received checks from the army worth nearly $3 million for acting as agent to a munitions manufacturer in which he owned stock—an arrangement apparently condoned by his father.[33]

Despite his own austere life-style, Pinochet savored the perquisites of his military presidency and utilized them to maximum effect. Where previous presidents had driven modest sedans or even strolled to work, Pinochet was whisked between appointments in caravans of gold, bulletproof Mercedes. He often presided over elaborate ceremonies, exuding an aura of formidable majesty in his Prussian uniform, high-peaked cap, and, in colder weather, a floor-length gray cape.

His most controversial indulgence was the construction in 1984 of an ultramodern, fortress-like mansion for Chile's presidents. Perched on a hillside overlooking the suburb of Lo Curro, it featured a three-level underground bunker and living space for an army of servants. The project's estimated cost of $12 million at a time of nationwide recession, and the radical departure from Chile's modest public traditions, caused such a scandal that Pinochet was forced to abandon plans to move in, and the house remained empty.[34]

At about the same time, he built a private suburban home called Melocotón (Peach Tree), which also aroused controversy when allegations arose that the Pinochet family had acquired the publicly owned property at far below value. The Council of State, whose duties included protecting the state patrimony, found evidence of fraud but took no action. "It was an open-and-shut case, but we really had no choice," recalled one member. "In the past, we could be removed only by the Senate. Under the new laws, Pinochet could fire all of us."[35]

Pinochet's personality could change at a moment's notice. He was a generous friend, a doting grandfather, a charming gentleman, and a witty raconteur, popular with the attractive women invariably chosen to cover the palace by progovernment media. There was a sly, mischievous streak in the aging general, who delighted in trotting up steep stairs on his summer estate while aides half his age puffed along behind. He astonished one interviewer by impishly offering to divulge his boyhood pranks, and teased several women journalists by saying, "Every day I lift 150-pound weights. Let's see; could any of you do that?"[36]

Yet when his authority was defied or his actions were criticized, he became a blustering, vengeful martinet, exploding in rage and pounding his fist, his face reddened and his eyes flecked with angry yellow. All but the thickest-skinned subordinates quaked before his tantrums, and his arguments with defiant peers like Leigh left a trail of shattered glass, shredded papers, and vicious insults. "It is very different to know him intimately than to see him disguised as a kindly grandfather," Leigh remarked.[37]

Pinochet's autocratic tendencies sharpened as he grew entrenched in power. Once ensconced in La Moneda, he became physically more remote, surrounding himself with layers of military aides and insisting that even top civilian officials request audiences in advance. He often spoke of the responsibility and "solitude of command," asserting he cared not a whit what outsiders thought of him. "We are making a government to move the country ahead, not to be likable," he said.[38]

He was an avid reader who boasted of accumulating a 30,000-volume library as president, but his literary tastes ran to European military histories, Machiavelli's *The Prince,* Sun-tzu's fourth-century Chinese classic, *The Art of War,* and the works of Karl von Clausewitz, the leading Prussian military theorist. He also made it a point to read Marxist works—but only as a way of gaining insight into his ideological adversaries.[39] In many ways, he remained a crude, simple soldier who spoke with a lisping country accent, never mastered a foreign language, and never overcame his instinctive suspicion of intellectuals.

However much he might admire other warrior-politicians, though, Pinochet could not bear to be thought of as a dictator. Indeed, the very word provoked a strong visceral reaction in him. In a 1983 television address, he railed at critics who accused him of operating "a fascist dictatorship": "This is not a fascist government; it is a government that tries to protect the country from totalitarianism!" Later he asserted, "Neither my moral nor spiritual formation permits me to be a dictator. . . . If I were a dictator, you can be certain many things would have happened. . . ."[40]

At times, Pinochet seemed bemused by his tyrannical image, blaming it on an unintentionally stern countenance. "My wife tells me that when I talk I always seem angry. It's because my conformation is like that," he once explained.[41] Yet he often reacted with extreme sensitivity to any slight or mockery, once ordering every copy of a magazine seized after it printed a cartoon cover of him. Although commonly referred to as Pinocho, Spanish for the puppet Pinocchio, he insisted his position was sacrosanct. "It is a profound error to ridicule my image," he lectured an interviewer. "The Chilean people always respect the figure of the president."[42]

Once the 1980 constitution was in place, Pinochet frequently insisted that Chile was a democracy with the "majoritarian backing" of the citizenry. "I never asked for this job; I am here because the people want me to stay on," he said in 1984.[43] When critics complained of press censorship, he pointed to the proliferation of high-priced magazines. When opponents protested the lack of dialogue, he ticked off his frequent breakfasts with "union leaders,

volunteer women, workers," and so on.[44] The separation of powers posed no problem, either. "The executive is here, independent;
the legislature is there; the judicial power has total independence,"
he contended. "So, this is a dictatorship?"[45]

His attitude toward the public was ambivalent and emotional.
Although he often professed indifference to popular opinion, he
basked in the cheers of crowds at official rallies, seeming not to
care that they were handpicked from government volunteer groups
or low-income housing projects. After delivering his customary
anniversary speech on September 11, 1982, Pinochet strode happily through a crowd of applauding citizens bussed from working-
class districts. Then, turning impulsively, he tossed a single gray
glove to the crowd.[46]

Pinochet's image as a paternalistic provider of order and security had a strong appeal to women, and he took pains to cultivate
their support—especially among the volunteer groups headed by
his wife and other junta members' spouses. He was also keenly
interested in youth, which he envisioned as pure and ripe for mold-
ing into a new, patriotic elite. "It is indispensable to stimulate the
development of a new civil generation, impregnated with [moral]
values," he urged students at the University of Chile in 1979.[47]

Finally, Pinochet believed he had a special relationship with the
poor, whose misery he dreamed of eradicating—even while his harsh
economic policies were throwing hundreds of thousands out of
work. He often inaugurated low-income housing projects and
sometimes waxed dangerously effusive when imagining all he would
do for the underprivileged. On the night of the 1980 plebiscite, he
vowed to provide a million new jobs, 900,000 new houses, a car
and telephone for every seven citizens, and a television for every
five—a pledge he would be far from fulfilling nine years later.[48]

But even though Pinochet constantly reminded critics that "the
people" had supported him in 1978 and 1980, he never really trusted
them. He discouraged the formation of progovernment political
movements, for fear that they would spin out of his control. Instead,
he relied primarily on his own convictions and instincts to steer
him on the right course. "He is a leader who never vacilates. He is
supremely confident; he feels he can achieve impossible goals and
conquer all adversity," observed Jaime Guzmán, a former close
aide.[49]

The largest chink in Pinochet's claim to legitimacy and popular
support was the regime's poor human rights record, yet he flatly
refused to acknowledge the problem. Indeed, he was vehemently

unrepentant about political repression, arguing that a "vigorous hand" was needed to defend the nation against Marxist wiles. "If you have gangrene in an arm, you have to cut it off, right?" he demanded.[50]

When faced with criticism for human rights abuses, he responded with either defensive sarcasm, flat denial, or an impassioned anti-communist tirade, insisting that he had liberated Chile from a totalitarian nightmare, that "15,000 foreign guerrillas" had been poised to seize power, and that human rights were "an annoyance invented by the communists."[51] Once, he barred a UN human rights commission from the country, asking "How many commissions did they send to Cuba, the USSR, Vietnam?"[52]

The general's speeches were often laced with bellicose rhetoric, and his obsessive anticommunism drove him to acts of senseless pique—such as deporting prominent lawyers and former legislators on a whim—that made his more even-tempered advisers wince. As far as he was concerned, there was little relevant distinction between Eurosocialism and Stalinism, and in later years the general dismissed Mikhail Gorbachev's *perestroika* policy as a "nicely prepared morsel which many will eat, but I will not be one of them."[53]

For all his paranoid excess, Pinochet successfully brandished the Red menace as a cudgel to keep his opponents off guard, rally his supporters, and justify his prolonged tenure in power. Each time foreign governments or human rights groups condemned his regime for repression, he wrapped himself in a mantle of nationalism, depicting his critics as tools of a vast Soviet-backed conspiracy against Chile and himself as a martyr for the anticommunist cause.

The general's attitude toward the United States alternated between indignant fury and exaggerated indifference. Having assumed power with strong tacit support from the Nixon White House, he was stung by the drumbeat of congressional criticism and enraged by the Carter administration's blunt condemnation of dictatorial rule. In 1976, when U.S. economic aid was reduced to $27.5 million as punishment for human rights violations, Pinochet haughtily rejected a grant for that amount, saying he was proving "the dignity of Chile to the entire world."[54]

Yet when Republican administrations tried a more subtle approach, such as the "quiet diplomacy" of ambassadors under Presidents Ford and Reagan, Pinochet ignored the message and boasted of wholehearted U.S. support. If an official was sent to admonish him, Pinochet invariably responded with a lecture about the Marxist threat, telling one U.S. diplomat he was "the number one communist target in the world."[55]

Pinochet's least favorite American was undoubtedly Senator Edward M. Kennedy, the Massachusetts liberal who waged a decade-long crusade in Congress to punish his dictatorship for its human rights abuses. When Kennedy visited Santiago in January 1986, officials snubbed him as "an enemy of Chile," and a proregime mob carrying posters of Mary Jo Kopechne, the secretary who drowned in the senator's car in 1969, attacked his motorcade with stones and rotten eggs while police stood by.[56]

In contrast, the government offered an intimate, highly publicized welcome six months later to the rightist senator Jesse Helms, Republican of North Carolina, one of Pinochet's few enthusiastic apologists in Washington. After a long private talk with the general, Helms gratified the regime by publicly excoriating his American critics. Back home Helms might be viewed as an eccentric extremist, but to an isolated state in search of external legitimacy, he was a powerful and sorely needed emissary to the world.[57]

Although Pinochet tended to brush off most allegations of abuse, he professed disbelieving horror when asked point-blank about the most heinous crimes committed under his rule. In 1989, presented with descriptions of tortures used in his prisons, he remarked that they sounded like "things of the Inquisition, not of today." Asked about the executions of prisoners after the coup, he exploded in indignation. "I'm a soldier, not one of the SS troops. How could I accept someone telling me they had shot a prisoner?"[58]

Pinochet's dual personality—the messianic crusader and the disingenuous manipulator—emerged most sharply in his avowals of religious enlightenment. Although Chilean Catholic church officials led the crusade against human rights abuses during his regime, the president claimed to have a mandate from heaven, suggesting repeatedly that the "hand of providence" had guided the coup and destined him to rule Chile. "I am a man fighting for a just cause: the fight between Christianity and spiritualism on the one hand, and Marxism and materialism on the other," he asserted in 1984. "I get my strength from God."[59]

WHETHER they viewed him as a monster who disfigured a proud democratic tradition or as a hero who freed the nation from the Marxist yoke, few Chileans would deny that Pinochet evolved into a leader of remarkable forcefulness and impact. He possessed an uncanny instinct for survival, and reportedly lived by Sun-tzu's list of attributes for the perfect general: "clairvoyance, a strategy carefully supported by long-reach plans, a sense of opportunity, and the ability to perceive human factors."[60]

Drawing heavily on his military training, he approached each policy issue or political problem with the same exhaustive, strategic analysis a field commander would use to plan his next battle. First, he sought out multiple points of view and urged his aides to debate while he listened in silence, sometimes for hours at a time. Then, having pondered all possible contingencies and scenarios, he announced his course of action. Anyone who objected, or tried to squeeze in an extra point, was cut off coldly.[61]

To consolidate and maintain control of the government, he relied on the expertise and energy of a sprawling civilian staff and a smaller corps of loyal military aides. One week after the coup, he broadcast a welcome to "high-level technicians who come to collaborate for the benefit of the fatherland, leaving aside their political tendencies."[62] Dozens of conservative young professionals responded to this appeal, evolving into a stable of efficient, buttoned-down bureaucrats who exhibited few qualms about serving an authoritarian regime.

There were ideologues like Jaime Guzmán, a brilliant, ascetic jurist and devout conservative Catholic who helped shape a new institutional framework for Pinochet's "protected democracy." There were technical wizards like Sergio de Castro, a low-key but inspired economist eager to test his bold academic theories under the regime's powerful imprimatur. There were political commissars like Sergio Fernández, always willing to take on a new ministerial post to further Pinochet's ambitions; and sharp legal factotums like Mónica Madariaga, who helped construct an imposing juridical rationale for dictatorial rule.

Many of these aides admired Pinochet for his strong leadership, quick grasp of issues, and dedication to Chile's future. He made them feel as if they were part of an elite corps of political and economic missionaries, and in turn they devoted long hours to the cause, at relatively little pay. "None of us were typical bureaucrats who wanted to stay in government forever," recalled Cristián Larroulet, a longtime economic planner for the regime. "We wanted to help rebuild a country that had arrived at total anarchic division. We felt we were part of a revolution."[63]

Nevertheless, the general never totally trusted his civilian aides and often used military loyalists to keep tabs on them. Rolf Lüders, appointed minister of economics and finance in 1982, believed he had a broad mandate to revamp these ministries, although Pinochet named a colonel as his deputy. "I never thought about it at the time," Lüders recalled, "but later I realized that was how he controlled everything."[64] In 1983, shortly after Mónica Madariaga was named education minister, two army officers came to call and told her she was making certain mistakes. "I suddenly knew I had a shadow cabinet," she recalled.[65]

Pinochet also kept his aides off balance by assigning overlapping tasks to different teams—often without telling one what the other was doing—and by abruptly rotating individuals in and out of positions. Few men lasted more than a year or two in the tense, high-stakes atmosphere of absolute power; during one period of economic crisis in 1982–84, Pinochet replaced the treasury minister thrice and the economics minister four times. Even senior cabinet officials seldom knew where they stood; at any moment their telephones might ring with a presidential request for information, advice—or their immediate resignation.

With spies planted throughout the bureaucracy, Pinochet possessed multiple, mysterious channels of information, which he dispensed in strategic bits so that no aide felt totally secure. A minister might rush to his office with a piece of fresh bureaucratic gossip or political news, only to hear it from Pinochet's lips as he entered. "He plays at surprise and is capable of unhinging even the most cautious of his collaborators with an ironic glance or enigmatic smile," wrote one Chilean journalist in 1987.[66]

Pinochet's parceling out of information and duties also sheltered civilian aides from what was happening in the darker corners of the regime. One former economic aide, asked how he had felt about the torture and disappearances taking place while he mapped out anti-inflation policies, replied, "I never dealt with politics; I was only perfecting economic laws. President Pinochet created compartments: the cavalry, the artillery, the economists. The key to our success was the division of labor."[67]

A shrewd judge of human nature, Pinochet often removed problematic individuals from the center of action by playing to their vanity. In 1977, when three former conservative senators on the junta advisory commission raised concerns about political repression, he promptly named them ambassadors to Peru, Colombia, and the United Nations, respectively.

But if someone made the president look foolish, however unwittingly, he was severely chastised or unceremoniously sacked. One

economics minister was banished from Pinochet's office for circulating an unflattering joke about the boss. Mónica Madariaga, on
a provincial tour with the president, made the mistake of delivering a more eloquent speech than his—and found herself on the
next plane back to Santiago.

In early 1980, Foreign Minister Hernán Cubillos and his under
secretary, General Sergio Covarrubias, meticulously planned a
presidential trip to Asia, intended to bolster Pinochet's stature in
a hostile world. The climax was to be a state visit to Manila, with
lavish banquets and even an honorary degree awaiting Pinochet.
But the unpredictable Marcos apparently decided a warm welcome for the Chilean dictator would reflect poorly on him. While
Pinochet's delegation was in midroute over the Pacific, Marcos
canceled their meeting, and Pinochet abruptly returned home.
Blamed for the diplomatic disaster, Cubillos was fired within days,
and Covarrubias languished in obscure posts.[68]

The internal politics of the Philippine incident reflected a much
deeper "personnel" problem that dogged Pinochet constantly: the
struggle between regime moderates like Cubillos and nationalist
hard-liners, such as Pablo Rodríguez of Fatherland and Liberty,
the ultraright, fascist-style group that had been founded to combat
Allende. Pinochet needed the support of both groups, and he often
played to their competing ambitions. This time Cubillos got the
ax, but more often Pinochet snubbed the demands of the hard-
liners by consistently naming their adversaries to important economic posts.

Indeed, there was only one group of civilian aides to whom Pinochet tended to defer: the "Chicago Boys," a team of U.S.-trained
technocrats who dazzled him with a bold scheme for transforming
the economy. Impressed by their scientific aura and zeal to serve
the nation, the general tolerated challenges from these brash economists that would have cost other men their careers.

Although Pinochet had great respect for competence and expertise, he valued one quality above all others: unconditional loyalty.
He viewed the world as divided between allies and enemies, and
could be breathtakingly cruel to anyone he thought had "betrayed"
him. In the 1980s, Federico Willoughby, an early aide who had
become an opponent of military rule, was stricken with kidney
disease and nearly died. At a dinner speech at a posh men's club,
Pinochet coolly suggested Willoughby would be better off dead.[69]

Sometimes, the president's preference for "unconditionals"
clouded his normally sound judgment in making appointments. In

1977, he named Renato Damiliano, a childhood friend, justice minister; within less than six weeks, Damiliano was forced to resign after making a speech implying that Catholic church officials were "devotees of Marx and Lenin." At about the same time, Edmundo Ruiz, a chum of Pinochet's intelligence chief, Colonel Manuel Contreras, was named housing minister. During a series of formal presentations by cabinet members, Ruiz distinguished himself by stating, "The Housing Ministry builds houses, gentlemen. I have spoken."[70]

On even rarer occasions, Pinochet's stubbornness combined with obsessive loyalty to produce policy disasters. In 1982, he clung for months to the radical monetary policies favored by Finance Minister Sergio de Castro, supporting his protégé and ignoring cries of alarm from business groups, military colleagues, and other cabinet members. By the time he finally relented, the currency had collapsed, nearly taking the economy with it.

ALTHOUGH civilians held many influential posts in Pinochet's government, there was never any question that he and the junta were in full command of the nation. After the fall of Leigh, relations with the junta stabilized and an unspoken hierarchy developed, with Pinochet clearly holding sway over the other three commanders. Only Admiral Merino, who had known Pinochet for years and shared his wry sense of humor, influenced him during critical moments.

A caustic, hard-drinking old salt, Merino was prone to outrageous off-the-cuff remarks, and often suggested he would rather be sailing or playing golf than running the country. But he was also an impassioned anticommunist who regarded Marxists as satanic, soulless "humanoids," and who proudly preserved his September 9, 1973, note to Leigh and Pinochet launching the coup, framed in a double-sided glass case.[71] The same age as Pinochet, he was the only junta member who dared call him Augusto or use the familiar *tu* form of address. He rarely crossed the president, but soothed the general's temper at many critical moments.

General Matthei, a thoughtful and laconic air force veteran, began his junta career at the age of fifty-one under cloudy circumstances that made him appear a power-hungry opportunist. He described that moment as "the bitterest" of his existence, however, and insisted he had accepted the post only to serve his country in a moment of crisis.[72] Despite his deference to Pinochet, the devout Lutheran proved one of the most progressive junta members, often hinting at the need for regime liberalization as Pinochet lingered in power. Yet, like Merino, he remained an unwavering apologist for the regime's violent war against the left.[73]

The Carabinero commander, General Mendoza, was a devoted horseman and self-described "simple man of simple tastes."[74] A dutiful yes-man to Pinochet, he habitually shrugged off questions about police abuse with disingenuous sarcasm. In 1985, he was forced to resign after a number of Carabinero officials were implicated in the gruesome beheading of three communists. Yet even as the disgraced general ceded his junta seat to his respected second-in-command, General Rodolfo Stange, he found cause for flippancy. "I'm leaving because it struck my fancy," Mendoza said.[75]

The advent of military rule brought a steady stream of senior officers into public office, and Pinochet, who personally appointed all high-level officials, often entrusted sensitive government jobs to army subordinates. Between 1973 and 1986, of the 118 individuals who served as agency heads, 52 were military men, nearly half from the army. All provincial governorships were held by military officers, and two-thirds of them were army officers as well.[76]

But the expanding role of the military in public life never constituted a government by the armed forces in Chile, as it did in the "collegial" military regimes of Brazil or Argentina. While harnessing the armed forces to his political agenda, Pinochet was determined not to let the officer corps become influenced by politics. Aided by the army's tradition of subservience to executive authority, he enforced the distinction between military and government duties with rigorous formality.[77]

As president, Pinochet met with agency heads in La Moneda on certain days of the week; as commander in chief, he dealt with military matters at the Ministry of Defense on other days. During their assignments in government posts, officers took leave from their military units and reported only to their agency superiors.

"In eleven years in government, I never received a single instruction from the army about my government work or vice versa. The two chains of command were exclusively separated, except at the very top," recalled General Luis Danús, who served Pinochet in a series of advisory and economic jobs. "Most officers had no vocation for government; they saw it as a sacrifice and wanted to go back to their [military] institutions as soon as possible."[78]

On the other hand, officers serving in governmental posts remained acutely conscious of rank in dealing with other military bureaucrats. During an interview with a visitor, a colonel in a natty tweed jacket was cordially explaining his work as under secretary at an important ministry. The telephone interrupted, and the colonel harshly ordered a subordinate to tend to an emergency in the field. A few minutes later the phone rang again, but this time it was his agency superior. The colonel tensed, and his voice became ingratiating. "Yes, My General, it will be arranged as you wish," he said. When he hung up and turned back to his guest, his face relaxed visibly.[79]

Ever concerned about potential threats to his dominance, Pinochet tended to keep military men out of the most important cabinet-level positions, such as justice, finance, and interior. Many senior officers, concerned about social unrest and raised in a state-dominated system, strongly opposed the free-market schemes of Pinochet's economic advisers. But persistent critics were shifted to other jobs, and almost all officers were rotated back to the barracks after a year or two, with insufficient time to stake out an independent policy.

In fact, most officers preferred it that way. They missed the rigors of field training and commands and worried about damaging their chances for promotion if they dropped out of military life for too long. Those who lingered in government were privately mocked by their uniformed colleagues as "general managers" who had gone soft. One attractive general in his fifties, who spent years as a regime diplomat in three-piece suits, confided after being retired that he deeply regretted never having commanded a regiment. He had seen the world and tasted power, but he had failed to meet the principal challenge for which he had trained since youth.

"The military man who says he would prefer to stay in government functions is not a good military man," explained Brigadier General Luis Patricio Serré, one of Pinochet's longest-serving aides. "If tomorrow I am told that I have to return to the command of a military unit, I will go happily because that is my reason for being. If I felt any hesitation whatsoever, I would go immediately to my commander and turn in my stripes." Despite their lengthy tenure in power, Serré insisted, "the military institutions are not part of the political process" and their members "do not express opinions about it."[80]

The ideal military servant of the regime was a professional officer like General Alejandro Medina: well educated and opinionated, yet utterly loyal to the government's ideological mission—and to his commander in chief. Over a fourteen-year period, Pinochet asked Medina to serve in an astonishing variety of capacities: health minister, university rector, military judge, junta adviser, division commander, riot-control coordinator, war academy director, and paratroop trainer.

"I always had the luck to be in the right place at the right time, and the confidence of my superiors," explained Medina, puffing on his pipe in an office filled with books on terrorism and national security. On one wall was an ornate, framed copy of a prayer: "To you, God all-powerful, who helped with infinite wisdom to unsheathe the sword and wield it to recover the liberty of this fatherland . . . help this people today, with faith in you, seek their best destiny." It was signed by the author, General Augusto Pinochet.

Medina regarded each of his government jobs as "linked by a common theme: to promote an integrated scheme of national security and development." But he also displayed the vital contradictions of a sophisticated officer serving a personalistic regime. While devoted to Pinochet, he criticized some of his civilian aides as palace bootlickers, obsessed with power and pet economic theories. And while arguing for a permanent military role in national policy, he insisted the armed forces must remain professional and nonpartisan. "I don't like to see the army dragged into politics," he said. "What must come first for us is the institution and the nation."[81]

Nevertheless, the armed forces were inevitably changed by the years of military rule, and many officers came to view their institution as a fourth branch of government—superior to the hurly-burly of partisan politics but morally authorized to intervene in national policy. "We realize our executive role will lessen in the future, but we want to remain a part of the intelligentsia, to work for progress with prominent civilians," explained General Medina. "We do not want ever again to be used as cheap slaves or substitute police."[82]

Indeed, the 1980 constitution guaranteed the armed forces a permanent role in national policy through an advisory body called the National Security Council, which had the right to "represent" military opinions on major issues to the president. Although the extent of the council's legal power was unclear, the new charter appeared implicitly to legitimize the right of the armed forces to overthrow a future civilian government if it failed to heed the views they "represented."

In one speech to an assembly of army officers, Pinochet promised they would never again be "marginalized" from public affairs or relegated to "obscure passivity." With their right to speak up now enshrined in law, he said, a "historical void" would be corrected and their "political function" would become permanent.[83] To some officers, this pledge evoked even grander visions, with Pinochet as the inspiring example. "Before 1973, the highest ambition of a young soldier was to become a general," commented a former air force officer in 1989. "Today, he imagines he might one day become president."[84]

BY the mid-1980s, the aging dictator's command began to slip. Pressure for democratic change was building, spurred by economic recession, and student protests erupted on a number of campuses. Stung by the attacks and enraged by the challenge to his authority, Pinochet attempted to dismiss the unrest as instigated by leftist malcontents, and continued to insist that "decent" Chileans supported him.

When critics suggested he had remained in power too long, the general reacted with a defensive shrug. "Why would I want to cling to power? It's no fun," he said, complaining that he was unable to go shopping or attend public events like a regular citizen.[85] But to many observers, Pinochet's personal ambition seemed to have become intertwined with his notion of the benevolent state. He referred to "my borders" with Argentina or "my pockets" as the source of government welfare for the poor. Sometimes he used the royal "we"; at other times he spoke of himself as "The President of the Republic," using the imperious third person.

The longer Pinochet remained in power, the more isolated and paranoid he became. Trusting virtually no one except his wife and a few close aides, he grew dependent on ambitious sycophants like Sergio Fernández, the interior minister who reassured him he was popular and irreplaceable. As Federico Willoughby put it, he became "enclosed in a praetorian guard that exists to satisfy him" and "defend him against any distinct influence."[86]

Despite his assertions of a heavenly mandate to rule, Pinochet was especially insecure about his physical safety, and fear of assassination was one reason he clung to the military presidency, with its retinue of bodyguards and spies. He surrounded himself with elaborate security measures against real and imagined enemies: the bulletproof Mercedes and the fortified mansions were more than pretentious vanities; and he had a labyrinthine bunker with heavily guarded entrance ramps constructed underneath La Moneda.

"Pinochet has a great love for Chile and has sacrificed a great deal for it, but he has confused the good of the country with his own power," one former aide mused sadly in 1987. "He no longer wants to project the regime, he wants to project himself. I fear he has become like a bull going to the red cloth, that he may have a dangerous identification with leaders like Napoleon, who finished badly but fought to the end."[87]

By late 1985, the pressure on Pinochet to permit political liberalization was acute. Democratic politicians were demanding he negotiate reforms to the constitution, and protesters were calling for his resignation day after day. In the streets of Santiago, students battling riot police and choking on tear gas heralded the regime's certain demise with an infectious chant: "It's going to fall! It's going to fall!"

But the old warrior was far from defeated. On his seventieth birthday, he called in press photographers while he lifted weights, performed calisthenics and jogged around his driveway in a baby-blue track suit. The defiant image was splashed across the next morning's papers, making it clear the still-robust president had no intention of retiring.

And, when his own junta colleagues asked for a private tea at Pinochet's Melocotón residence to discuss possible constitutional reforms, the general launched a preemptive strike. Calling a sudden meeting of top-level officials in advance of the scheduled tea, he motioned for an army aide to read from a document. It was the defense statement of an admiral on trial for torture and murder in Argentina's "dirty war" against leftist subversion.

"I have not come here to defend myself," Admiral Emilio Massera's defiant testimony began. "I am here being tried for having won a just war. If we had lost it, we would not be here, neither you nor I, because the judges of this high chamber would have been exchanged for turbulent popular tribunals, and a fierce and irreconcilable Argentina would have been substituted for the old fatherland. But here we are, because we won the military war but lost the psychological war. . . . The winners are being judged by the losers, and I ask myself, which side are my judges on?"[88]

The maneuver was pure Pinochet, and so was the message: no concession to the enemy, no acknowledgement of error, no retreat from the official plan. The men of September 11 must stand together and defend their patriotic mission against all attack. The gathered junta members and cabinet officials knew they had been disarmed. The meeting adjourned abruptly, and the tea at Melocotón was never mentioned again.

CHAPTER FOUR

ARMY OF
THE SHADOWS

"We will fight in the shadows so that our children
can live in the sunlight."

—*private motto of the DINA*

CLAUDIO HUEPE, a brash young Christian Democratic politician, was enjoying dinner in a candlelit Santiago supper club in late 1974. Suddenly the house musicians struck up the national anthem, and a tableful of rowdy, military-looking men demanded that all the customers rise and sing. Huepe, annoyed and indignant, remained seated.

"To me, the song had become a symbol of oppression, but everyone around us stood up," he recalled. "The air was vibrating with hostility. Several men came over and swore at me, calling me a communist, so I swore back." Within minutes, Huepe was being hustled off to a police station, still more angry than worried. "They started asking questions; saying I had threatened the government. I had no idea what was going on. I didn't know what a dictatorship was."

Huepe had never heard of the DINA, but for the next week, he received a mild taste of its formidable powers. He was grilled about his travels and acquaintances, and thrown into a cell with an elderly man who was trembling from electric shock. Finally freed unharmed, he was never charged with a crime and never told who had ordered his arrest. But he had seen a name on the police blotter that first night, and the frightened eyes of the rookie who showed it to him: Colonel Manuel Contreras Sepúlveda.[1]

WITHIN weeks of the coup, a secret war was launched against Marxist "subversion" and enemies of the regime. Colonel Contreras, a decorated army engineer, had been placed in charge of military operations in the port area of San Antonio, where he converted the Tejas Verdes engineering barracks into an interrogation center for local leftists. Soon he convinced Pinochet, his former military school instructor, that the regime needed a single agency to coordinate a nationwide ideological purge—and that he was the man to head it.

Officially, the National Directorate of Intelligence (Dirección de Inteligencia Nacional, or DINA) was created on June 18, 1974, by a junta decree which assigned it to "produce the intelligence necessary to formulate policies and planning, and to adopt measures to procure the safeguarding of National Security and development of the country." But in three secret articles the decree also gave the DINA authority to arrest suspects, as well as to demand collaboration from all public agencies.[2]

In practice, the Chilean gestapo had already established an efficient clandestine service. The CIA, which had scaled down its other Chile operations after the coup, provided technical and training assistance under the retired army general Vernon Walters, deputy CIA director for foreign liaisons.[3] Contreras selected several hundred men from all branches of the armed services and assembled them at Tejas Verdes, where he offered them a "privileged place" in a crusade aimed at the "total extermination of Marxism" and promised them "carte blanche" to carry out any orders they received.[4]

Their specific mission was to infiltrate Marxist parties, eliminate their leaders, and uproot leftist thought from Chilean society. Their techniques, learned at Tejas Verdes and other barracks, were those of institutional terror: to spy, deceive, kidnap, interrogate, torture, and break the human spirit. Their secret symbol was a clenched, armored fist.

The DINA's first priority was the MIR, which had vowed to resist military rule until death. After the coup, surviving MIR leaders like Miguel Enríquez formed small commandos that moved among safe houses, plotting guerrilla strategies and staging bank robberies to finance their operations. At the same time, the DINA worked to penetrate their network of political cells. Late at night, heavily armed agents would burst through the door of a safe house, dragging the occupants into unmarked sedans and vanishing into the dark.

The combatants in this shadow war were symbiotic, mirror images of society's extremes: obsessed with a cause, prepared for violence, sworn to secrecy, organized in cells, and known by code names. Enríquez, a physician who vowed to transform society through insurrection, found his counterpart in Contreras, a soldier determined to eradicate the scourge of communism. But the terms of combat were hopelessly one-sided, and the MIR's challenge to the military state was suicidal.

One night in late 1974, Contreras's men silently surrounded a shabby house where Enríquez and his companions were sleeping. Gunfire erupted, and people began running from the house; when it was over, Enríquez lay dead in the street. After that, the MIR unraveled as more cadres fell into DINA hands. Four captives, briefly presented on television, urged their comrades to admit ideological and military defeat. As reports spread of kidnapping and torture in DINA dungeons, hundreds of desperate leftists sought refuge in European or Latin American embassies, whose grounds had been converted into refugee camps after the coup.

The only institutions that came to the aid of these terrified Chileans were the churches. The Catholic archbishopric of Santiago, in conjunction with Protestant and Jewish leaders, established two organizations—the National Committee to Aid Refugees and the Committee of Cooperation for Peace—to provide free legal support to victims of persecution and social assistance to their families.

On a more secretive level, religious volunteers concocted schemes to sneak fugitives into closely watched embassies. Bishop Helmut Frenz of the Lutheran church delivered meals to refugees inside diplomatic compounds, accompanied by "aides" in clerical garb, then drove back out alone.[5] Claudio González, director of a Protestant social services agency, parked his "repair" truck beside embassies while fugitives hidden in the back scrambled up a ladder and over the garden wall. "Desperation made us resourceful," he recalled with a grin.[6]

Catholic officials were deeply ambivalent about military rule. A number of bishops were strong anti-Marxists who hailed the coup as an act of national liberation and ignored the severe repression that followed. The archbishop of Valparaíso asserted that any bloodshed was outweighed by Chile's salvation as a "free and sovereign nation"; the bishop of Linares compared the coup to Chile's fight for independence from Spain and praised Pinochet for bringing "more hope, more beauty" to the nation.[7]

Cardinal Silva, Chile's highest Catholic official, was more critical but still reluctant to alienate regime officials, with whom he tried to maintain correct relations. He agreed to bless the new authorities, although not in the traditional cathedral setting, and he offered them "the same collaboration" the church had provided Allende. As repression spread, however, Silva grew increasingly outspoken in his defense of human rights.

Contreras, who viewed the cardinal as his one true rival for power, worked to undermine Silva and tar church human rights activities as Marxist infiltrated. After one confrontation in which DINA agents left a wounded man at the door of the Committee for Peace, Silva personally showed Pinochet medical reports of his torture marks and asked that the DINA be dissolved. But his plea had no impact, and religious sanctuary remained no barrier for secret police intent on pursuing their quarry.

On October 15, 1975, the DINA closed in on a rural MIR safe house, but Pascal Allende, the late president's nephew, and a wounded colleague sought refuge in a Catholic parish house. Contreras's men tracked them to a residence for priests and opened fire on the entrance, killing the maid. The two fugitives were ultimately slipped into diplomatic compounds, but the British woman doctor who treated them was imprisoned and tortured, and the MIR seemed to have reached a pathetic denouement.

Flush with triumph, Contreras's shadow army expanded rapidly, acquiring dozens of secret detention centers, developing a complex command structure, and deploying up to four thousand agents—as well as a vast network of informants. Their crusade was joined by other intelligence services in the loose "Joint Anti-Subversive Command," which turned its attention to the Socialist and Communist parties.

While some members of these parties were hardened military cadres, the majority were academics, labor leaders, students, and politicians who sought to keep their organizations alive in defiance of the regime. Any meeting of more than two people was risky, so colleagues made contact in crowded soccer stadiums or while taking long walks.

"It was a bleak, terrifying time," recalled "Germán Correa, a young Socialist militant who plunged into underground party work after the coup. As other members began to fall into DINA hands,

Correa and his colleagues hardened themselves against grief and forced themselves to forget names and addresses in case they, too, were caught. "We became numb like soldiers, or doctors," he said. Fifteen years later, Correa still carried scars from his underground existence: an inability to express emotion, and a hopeless memory for names.[8]

For Patricio Hales, a twenty-six-year-old architect and budding politician in the Communist party, the coup meant the end of a promising public life and the beginning of a secret existence focused exclusively on survival. "People were being captured or shot, and bodies were floating down the river. Our top priority was saving lives, and we had to keep moving in the shadows," recalled the intense, emotional man. "Many people left the party because they were just too afraid of being killed."[9]

In 1976, more than a hundred Communist party members, including seventy-eight midlevel officials, were seized; they were never seen alive again.[10] Most were kidnapped from their homes late at night, but occasionally the secret police emerged briefly from the shadows to snatch a victim. On a busy Santiago street one day, a man began screaming, "I am Carlos Contreras Maluje! Don't let the DINA take me!" As pedestrians froze and a policeman watched warily, men with machine guns leaped from a Fiat sedan and yanked the young Communist inside; he never reappeared.[11]

BY the most conservative count of the Catholic legal aid office, 668 prisoners vanished between 1973 and 1978, but the actual figure was probably close to 1,000. This was far below the estimated 9,000 people who disappeared in Argentina during that regime's "dirty war" against the left in the late 1970s. But the rumors of people vanishing made the DINA seem omnipresent and omnipotent. "To disappear" evokes images of "magic intervention by mysterious forces," wrote a team of Chilean psychologists. "It suggests the inexplicable, the irrevocable, an absolute loss of knowledge."[12]

The harrowing experiences of these men and women died with them, but hundreds of other DINA prisoners lived to tell their stories—and to describe a nightmarish world of military barracks, abandoned convents, even a colonial villa that had been refurbished to include cells and interrogation rooms. To enter one of these secret prisons, survivors said, was to descend into hallucinatory hell.

In November of 1973, the sixteen-year-old Mariela Bacciarini arrived at Tejas Verdes. Guards tied a hood over her head and threw her into a damp cell, where she could hear the faint screams of a friend, calling for her mother. Then she was led down a passage into a hot room, still wearing the hood. "I felt hands tearing off my clothes and forcing me onto a metal bed," she recalled. "They tied my wrists and ankles to the corners. I felt horrible pains on my tongue, in my vagina. They asked the names of everyone I knew, they shouted obscene things. Far away, I heard the sound of a piano playing."[13]

An equally notorious DINA facility was the Villa Grimaldi, an uninhabited country mansion where groups of prisoners were confined for days in metal closets. In 1975, Humberto Vergara spent one week as a prisoner there. Fifteen years later, the shy man in his late fifties could not speak of the experience without trembling.

"It was like a palace, with marble stairways and an indoor swimming pool. They put four of us inside a container no bigger than a table. In the dark, we could hear screams all day and sobbing all night. It was how I had imagined hell would be," recalled Vergara, a peasant union official. Inside the box, he said, "we were cramped together, never allowed to wash. The heat and the stench were unbearable. The guards would splash in the pool and pass by the cells, saying they were going to kill this one or castrate that one. I don't know if you call that torture, but it was horrible."[14]

The most frequent forms of torture used by the DINA and other intelligence agencies were electric shock on sensitive body parts such as genitals and temples ("the grill"), repeated dunking in excrement or filthy water ("the submarine"), prolonged suspension with the body twisted around a pole ("the parrot's perch"), cigarette burns, close confinement, exposure to blinding light or deafening noise, and sleep deprivation.[15]

An equally effective method of coercing confessions and collaboration was extreme psychological pressure. People were forced to watch their spouses being tortured or listen to tapes of their children screaming. Otto Trujillo, an air force intelligence agent tried for murder, described to a judge how he and his colleagues recorded voices of prisoners' children and spliced them with cries of agony. "That is the worst; it is what generally makes people burst," he said.[16]

Both men and women were stripped and sexually humiliated in order to destroy their morale—and entertain their captors. One man described how he and a group of prisoners were forced to bend over naked, while guards insulted them in foul slang and pretended to rape them. "I had always protected my intimacy greatly; for me this was the most brutal degradation possible," he said. "I felt I was no longer a man; I wanted to die."[17]

To make their prisoners feel politically isolated, agents used false confessions and other gimmicks to convince them they had been betrayed by their colleagues. Building webs of lies, they created doubt, guilt, anger, and fear—and let them fester until the victim grew emotionally dependent on his destroyers. They gave the impression of such vast knowledge that it seemed pointless to resist. What a prisoner imagined, alone in the dark and awaiting the next torture session, became even more terrifying than what was real.

ONLY the toughest, most committed prisoners could endure such ordeals, which were aimed at destroying their will and, by extension, undermining the cohesion of the Marxist left. For true political cadres, the ultimate goal was to reveal the least possible amount of information, or to plant false intelligence that would both ease torture and hinder infiltration of their organization.

Occasionally, a prisoner's resistance evoked grudging respect from the men assigned to break him. Andrés Valenzuela, a former air force intelligence agent, said he came to admire a Communist Youth leader for his courage under interrogation. "He never said a word although he was tortured very hard for almost four months. He is one of the people we considered the enemy that I admired for his bravery," Valenzuela acknowledged with chagrin. "He died for his convictions."[18]

Many prisoners, however, eventually cooperated, and some were squeezed until they became full-fledged collaborators, devoid of morals and reduced to betraying colleagues for a few more days of life. The most notorious was Miguel Estay, a Communist known as El Fanta, who broke under torture and agreed to reveal the names of eighty-four party members; later he reportedly helped capture a number of the Communist party leaders who disappeared in 1976.

Once they had been "turned," prisoners were often sent out to mingle with their old contacts, then picked up again and pumped for information. Because party cell structures were so compartmentalized for security reasons, it was nearly impossible to confirm someone's identity, and trust was steadily eroded. "There was a tremendous fear of betrayal," recalled Patricio Hales. "You never knew if someone was an informant, and you had to keep track of who had fallen, who had been released, and what they might have revealed."[19]

These prisoner-collaborators were ostracized as contemptible traitors by their former colleagues, yet they were among the most pathetic victims of Chile's security apparatus—psychologically destroyed and universally despised. The torturer "imposes on his victim an extreme dilemma: let himself be mistreated and exposed to intolerable pain . . . or transform himself into the executioner of his own beliefs and companions," wrote the team of Chilean psychologists. "This second alternative saves the person from physical suffering, but destroys a fundamental part of himself."[20]

WHO were the soldiers on the other side of this subterranean war? How did a civilized nation produce an underworld of spies and sadists? How did a military establishment steeped in traditions of honor and law lend itself to a secret terror campaign? Hitler's Germany had shown that members of a sophisticated Western society, sufficiently indoctrinated to dehumanize and hate, could relish barbarous acts. Many authoritarian situations in other cultures and eras had drawn bullies and fanatics to the fringes of power.

But in Pinochet's Chile the secret police represented the psychotic edge of a society whose democratic values had collapsed. Like the thugs of Fatherland and Liberty, they acted out the rage and fear that had festered inside thousands of citizens as the Marxist left gained power. Once initiated into the secret police netherworld, they were bound by the mystique of an anticommunist brotherhood. And once their hands were dirtied, complicity enmeshed them in a system of state terror.

Most of Contreras's men were low-profile army officers, known within the agency by code names, who said little if called to testify in court and nothing to the press. Indeed, the only detailed, inside account of intelligence work in Pinochet's Chile came not from the DINA but from the former air force officer Andrés Valenzuela, who served for a decade with a notorious antisubversive squad.

In 1985, Valenzuela described his sojourn in a dark, lawless world where truth and lies were interchangeable weapons, where ideological crusading masked a ·crude quest for power, where bombings and gun battles were staged to justify an expanding antisubversive war. He also exposed the depth of rivalry between the DINA and other security agencies, and described the murders of several communist informants and an air force private who had attempted to "defect" to the DINA.

His most revealing description, though, was of his own initial horror at participating in torture—and how it gradually faded to numb indifference. "At first you cry, hiding it so no one knows. Then later you feel sorrow but you no longer cry. And finally, without wanting to, you begin to get used to it," he said. "You no longer feel anything."[21]

Only one known DINA agent ever willingly defected to confess his role in the shadow war. Armando Fernández Larios was an ambitious young army officer whose life had been shaped by values of honor, duty, and patriotism. As a lieutenant of twenty-three, he had entered La Moneda under General Palacios, and later presented his commander with a blood-stained handkerchief as a memento of those heroic moments.

Selected to join the DINA in 1974, Fernández saw the assignment as an exciting challenge. He was one of the three secret police officers sent with General Arellano on the northern helicopter tour; his own role on that trip has never been established. But life in the DINA changed him; the "temptation to play James Bond," his lawyer later explained, overcame the values he had been taught as the son of an air force colonel.

It was an arrogant, impatient young captain who sauntered into see his aging father in 1974 and shrugged off his pleas to return to regular army duty. "Look, Armando, I know you," the old man said. "I know your loyalty to your superiors. One day, you are going to be in jail, and none of those superiors are going to protect you." Fernández was not listening. "My father knows nothing," he told himself.[22]

The dominant influence on such young officers was Manuel ("Mamo") Contreras, a man whose pudgy build and Cheshire cat smile belied a powerful personality. Contreras described himself as being "forged in the heat of mystique, of unity, of comradeship, of common ideals, of love of fatherland," and other soldierly qualities.[23] Seized by puritanical zeal after the coup, he had ordered troops in San Antonio to shave the heads of long-haired men and arrest couples caught kissing in public.

Whenever the DINA was accused of human rights abuses, Contreras blamed the far left or the CIA. Although he had developed close ties with the U.S. agency, once visiting General Walters in

Washington, CIA-DINA relations cooled after 1975, with the sensational congressional revelations of past CIA exploits and the election of President Carter.[24] Contreras was left deeply suspicious, although the two agencies still shared an anticommunist mission, and CIA officials continued to assist DINA agents in visiting the United States.

For Contreras, the crusade against Marxism justified all actions, twisting his military virtues into snarling fanaticism. One of the prisoners brought to Tejas Verdes, a Socialist shipyard manager who had chatted with Contreras at receptions, remembered him as a "terse but gentlemanly" officer. But once they met inside the prison gates, Contreras flew into a rage, shouting anticommunist obscenities. When the prisoner insisted he was only a Socialist, the colonel became apoplectic. "It was hatred, pure hatred," the man recalled.[25]

With time, the combination of power and immersion in a seamy underworld also corroded military norms within the DINA. Contreras's aides became personal lackeys; call girls were recruited for undercover work and late-night revelry. But the colonel cultivated a refined image, moving into an elegant office and shedding his uniform for business suits. While his men tortured prisoners in distant cells, Contreras was ensconced among European antiques, chatting on his hot line to the president.[26]

EACH time the shadow army snatched up a new victim and vanished, it left behind other casualties: the families who were helpless to intervene and frantic to find out where their loved ones had been taken. Hundreds of wives and mothers embarked on fruitless rounds of police stations and barracks, and some kept up the search literally for years, chasing tips and living in emotional limbo, unable to mourn the dead as long as there remained a faint hope of life.

After security agents seized Ana Molina's son, a Communist Youth member, she set out each morning from her shabby row house in La Cisterna and plunged into a surreal maze of military bureaucracy, clutching at scraps of information and begging for help at the gates of DINA camps, while her other children came home to an empty house with no supper. Long after dark, their mother would arrive, lock herself in the bathroom, and weep.

"There were witnesses who had sworn they saw him inside Tres Alamos, but each day the guards told us something different. One lieutenant finally acknowledged he was there, and I almost fainted from joy," recalled the frail, nervous woman of sixty-five. "But when I came back, they told me he had never been detained at all. I never saw the lieutenant again, and I never found my son."[27]

Angel and Edita Castro, a middle-class couple with the vague, idealistic views of many older Allende supporters, had paid little attention when their daughter Cecilia and her husband, caught up in the more extreme passions of their generation, joined the MIR. "We didn't know much about what she was doing," Edita explained over tea in their modest apartment. "She always said they were working to help the poor."[28]

One night, a dozen armed men burst into their house and threatened to kill their granddaughter Valentina if they did not reveal Cecilia's whereabouts. "Angel wanted to say nothing, but I thought we had to protect Valentina," recalled Edita, beginning to weep. "Finally, I took them to the house, and the kids came out with their hands up. I will always remember the look on Angel's face. As they took Cecilia away, I cried, 'Chichi, we didn't have any choice.' . . . I can hardly bear to think about that moment."

After months of torment—chasing rumors that Cecilia had been seen in one DINA camp or another, filing court petitions, calling on once influential friends—the Castros finally gave up hope. Angel seemed to fade away, his family, profession, and sense of purpose destroyed by forces beyond his control. Edita struggled with the indignity of their reduced circumstances, bursting into tears when she lost her last piece of family jewelry—but then shaking herself, saying, "How could I cry over that after losing my daughter?"[29]

Like hundreds of other women, Ana Molina and Edita Castro found solace in the Association of Relatives of the Detained-Disappeared, a group formed under the aegis of Cardinal Silva. Meeting regularly in church offices, members shared stories of their legal travails and sewed *arpilleras*, colorful quilted squares with political themes, to raise funds.

Within the church, sharp tensions had developed over the proper role of Catholic leaders under dictatorship. Despite widening evidence of torture and disappearances, prominent bishops still praised Pinochet for "liberating" the nation, and the Episcopal conference issued only vague, cautious critiques. In deed, however, the church remained the focal point of assistance to victims of repression, sponsoring legal and social aid offices across the country.

Gradually, the family groups acquired a testimonial mission that brought meaning to a personal loss that most of society refused to acknowledge. The women's public debut was a hunger strike in

1978; after that, they staged regular protests outside churches and courts, brandishing cardboard human silhouettes and snapshots captioned by the question "Where Are They?" Usually, riot police broke up the demonstrations with tear gas or hauled the women into paddy wagons.

Such commitment was exhausting, and such public martyrdom tended to reinforce pain instead of letting it heal. The disappeared could never die, and the cause of human rights could not let them. The most ideologically driven members frowned on widows who found new men or mothers who decided to devote more time to their living children. Over the years, membership dwindled to a small, dedicated core of women, heading resolutely into the streets with their snapshots and grief held high.

THE DINA's intimidating power reached beyond victims and their families, into the roots of society itself. With a network of spies and informants in factories, universities, political parties, and social organizations, the DINA sowed mistrust among colleagues, neighbors, and friends. The secret police tentacles also wound through the government itself: dossiers were gathered on employees and telephones were tapped.

Liliana Mahn, who served as state tourism director for four years before quitting the regime, described how her agency was purged under DINA scrutiny. "There was no one hired, not a clerk or a secretary, who did not have to pass through the DINA person in the ministry," she said. Initially content to serve as a glamorous saleswoman for Pinochet's Chile, Mahn grew disgusted by the bullying behavior of military and DINA officials. "At first it all seemed infantile," she recalled, "but by the end I found it unbearable."[30]

Many army officers were uncomfortable with the growth of Contreras's parallel army, which cast an unsavory light on the armed forces. They resented and feared Contreras, who became Pinochet's close confidant and breakfasted with him daily. Yet only a few high-ranking officers attempted to challenge his power. General Arellano protested to Pinochet that the DINA was becoming "a true gestapo," to no avail.[31] General Bonilla, whom Federico Willoughby called "the only man who could have stopped Contreras,"[32] was dead within two years of the coup.

Despite their common mandate, the DINA had little respect for Chile's other security services. If competing authorities stood in their way, Contreras and his men went to elaborate lengths to deceive and discredit them. In October 1974, DINA agents posing as army officers removed a prisoner from the Santiago penitentiary; from there, all traces of the man vanished. The DINA asserted he had been kidnaped by the MIR, and when the warden, Captain Jorge Ortiz, refused to corroborate their story, the DINA accused him of conspiring with the MIR, and he was interrogated by the military courts. "Each time they called me, I didn't know if I would come back alive," he confessed years later. "But I realized I had to cling to the truth." As punishment, Ortiz was retired early.[33]

Officials of other intelligence services criticized Contreras's methods and complained when he rode roughshod over their own agents—again, to no avail. General Odlanier Mena, the army intelligence chief, caught the DINA spying on his own men and demanded that the junta president choose between him and Contreras. Soon afterward, Mena was named ambassador to Panama.[34]

As his influence on Pinochet increased, Contreras formed close relationships with members of his family, especially Lucía Hiriart. But his ambition to create a permanent police state alarmed some of Pinochet's top civilian aides, who were working to steer the government toward institutional legitimacy. One of them, Jaime Guzmán, described Contreras in 1987 as an obsessed, "amoral individual," and said he feared that if Pinochet lost control of the DINA, he too would become its victim.

"Contreras operated virtually like a cogovernor; he ran an entire world that no one wanted to get involved in," recalled Willoughby. But no one had the nerve or influence to stop the "sordid machine," he added.[35] Contreras's grip on the president was too strong, and the power he offered was too tempting. The DINA had files on thousands of Chileans—and Pinochet had access to them all.

By 1976, the DINA chief's ambitions had soared to new heights. Taking control of a number of business enterprises sold by the government, he created a web of import-export firms to finance his operations. He also schemed to build an international network of political police, through a structure he called Plan Condor. Contreras's men forged ties to neofascist terrorist groups in Italy, antisubversive squads in Brazil and Argentina, and violent Cuban exiles in Miami. "He wanted to create a veritable KGB. He saw himself as the leader of anticommunism in all of Latin America," said Willoughby.

Most of Contreras's international schemes, however, were aimed at neutralizing Chilean exiles who were vocal and influential critics of Pinochet. Eugene Propper, a U.S. federal prosecutor who spent two years investigating the DINA, described one of its agents, the U.S.-born Michael Vernon Townley, attempting to bomb an exile conference in Mexico in 1975, and plotting with Cuban and Italian terrorists to eliminate a list of leftist Chilean politicians living abroad.[36]

In September 1974, General Carlos Prats, whom some regime officials suspected of plotting to overthrow them, was assassinated with his wife outside their apartment in Buenos Aires. The crime was linked to Argentine intelligence agents under orders from the DINA. Thirteen months later, Bernardo Leighton, a distinguished Christian Democrat who had condemned the coup, was shot with his wife in Rome. Both were gravely injured but survived. This time, investigations pointed to an Italian fascist group—again reportedly acting on DINA orders.[37]

"I never had an enemy in my life. Adversaries, yes, but we treated each other with respect." The eighty-year-old Leighton paused between words, his memory slowed by the bullet that had lodged in his neck fourteen years before. The walls of his modest Santiago house were crammed with portraits from half a century of public service; on his desk was a tiny Chilean flag, rescued by a legislative colleague after the coup.

His wife, Anita, leaned heavily on a cane because of the spinal damage she had suffered, but her blue eyes were animated. "It is still so vivid, the feeling of being engulfed in darkness, the rush of noise and lights, the pain," she said. "People were very kind to us when we came home; taxi drivers refused to charge us. But there was never a word of sympathy from the government. They said Bernardo was organizing people to overthrow Pinochet." She shook her head in wonder, repeating his phrase tenderly. "He never had an enemy in his life."[38]

The attacks on Prats and Leighton disturbed many Chilean officials, but there was no hard evidence of DINA involvement, and the agency's role in combating domestic subversion was still viewed as crucial in government circles. But on September 21, 1976, Contreras's agents committed an international crime so audacious that neither the DINA nor the regime could escape the ensuing scandal.

It was a rainy morning in Washington, D.C., and forty-four-year-old Orlando Letelier was driving to work in his Chevrolet. A foreign minister and ambassador to the United States for Allende, he had been imprisoned for a year after the coup and then fled to

Washington, becoming one of Pinochet's most vociferous exile critics and operating out of the Institute for Policy Studies, a left-leaning research organization. High on the list of the regime's enemies, he had just been stripped of his Chilean citizenship.

That day he had two passengers: Ronni Moffit, his twenty-five-year-old American assistant, and her husband, Michael. At 9:38 A.M., as the car rounded Sheridan Circle in the heart of the embassy district, a remote-control bomb exploded under his seat. Chunks of metal hurtled skyward; Letelier's legs were blown off, and he bled to death in minutes. A passing doctor tried in vain to save Ronni Moffit, while her dazed husband wandered in circles shouting a Spanish acronym that detectives at the scene could not understand: "La DINA, La DINA."[39]

The Pinochet regime vehemently denied all connection to the crime and offered to collaborate with U.S. investigators. Many American officials were suspicious of Letelier's leftist background and skeptical that Pinochet's men would have risked such an attack in the pristine, heavily policed U.S. capital. But after a twenty-two-month investigation, Propper, the prosecutor, and FBI agents pieced together an intricate criminal conspiracy that had been plotted at the highest levels of Chile's secret police.

Michael Townley, the DINA's explosives expert, had built and planted the bomb with assistance from a group of right-wing Cuban-American exiles. Armando Fernández, the swaggering army captain, had been sent to spy on Letelier in preparation for the murder, accompanied by a mysterious woman using the alias Liliana Walker. Both were traveling on false passports obtained from the Foreign Ministry, and operating on orders from Colonel Pedro Espinoza, the DINA's operations chief.[40]

Townley had come to Chile in the 1960s, the rebellious son of an international businessman. Drawn to Santiago's right-wing fringe during the Allende era, he had found thrills as a bomb builder and clandestine radio operator for Fatherland and Liberty. He had also sought to work with the CIA, which initially considered using him as an operative, but never pursued the contact. Townley did become a U.S. embassy informant, however, and often bragged of CIA connections to his friends.[41]

After the coup, the highly skilled and morally indifferent operative found a niche in the DINA, becoming a favorite of Contreras and working from a luxurious home.[42] The Letelier bombing was his most ambitious assignment, involving an elaborate charade of false passports and the shipping of explosive components. For

Townley, the mission was a success. Asked by a U.S. judge in 1979 if he had any remorse about Letelier's death, the blue-eyed hit man shook his head. "He was a soldier, and I was a soldier," he said evenly. "I received an order, and I carried out the order to the best of my ability."[43]

Townley's loyalty to the DINA and Contreras, whom he called "my colonel," was so intense that he initially refused to cooperate with U.S. investigators without permission from his superiors. Yet his obedience was tinged with terror: he also testified that after the killing, he had feared he would be made to "disappear."[44] By 1979, his devotion had turned to venom, and he accused Contreras of becoming "mentally disturbed" at the prospect of seeing his "messianic dream" collapse.[45]

To many Chilean officials, the scandal was ultimate proof that Contreras had gone too far. The navy and air force withdrew their officers from the DINA, while civilian aides warned Pinochet that its criminal adventures could undermine his own accomplishments. In late 1977, a shaken and angry president removed Contreras from his post, although promoting him to general at the same time. He also dissolved the DINA and replaced it with a new, more circumscribed agency called the National Information Center (Central Nacional de Informaciones, or CNI).

Several months later, Townley was turned over to U.S. authorities and tried in federal court in Washington, D.C., where he recounted his exploits in chilling detail. Ultimately, he and three of the Cubans were convicted in the bombing, and he served three years in American prisons. Meanwhile, the State Department demanded the extraditions of Fernández, Espinoza, and Contreras, and all three men were confined to a military hospital for fourteen months while the case proceeded.

But the former DINA chief was far from defeated. He concocted multiple cover stories to explain his agents' visits to Washington, dismissed Townley as a foreign communist agent, and stymied an army investigation into the case.[46] During 1977 and 1978, three Foreign Ministry officials connected with issuing false passports for Contreras's men died mysteriously. Guillermo Osorio, the director of protocol, was reported to have committed suicide, but army officials prohibited an autopsy and Osorio's family remained convinced he had been murdered for acknowledging his role to U.S. prosecutors.[47]

Contreras also insinuated that the CIA was behind the murder. He threatened to expose its links to the DINA unless the investigation was dropped, asserting that the agency had helped his agents travel to Washington.[48] American diplomats confirmed that the CIA had known of the visit in advance, yet failed to inform Propper after the killing.[49] U.S. prosecutors found "not one scintilla of evidence" that the CIA was involved in the assassination, but Letelier's family remained suspicious, given the CIA's ties to Townley and anti-Castro Cubans, the revelations of previous CIA plotting in Chile, the agency's slowness to cooperate with Propper, and its promotion of the theory that Letelier had been slain by Marxist enemies.[50]

The bombing provoked condemnation from the United Nations and spurred several members of the U.S. Congress, notably Senator Kennedy and Representative Thomas Harkin, Democrat of Iowa, to redouble efforts at banning all U.S. aid to Chile. Since 1974, their proposals had been opposed by the Ford administration and Republican legislators, but in 1976 the full Congress banned military aid to Chile and approved Harkin's legislation, aimed at Pinochet, that prohibited all nonhumanitarian aid to governments displaying a "consistent pattern of gross violations" of human rights.[51]

After President Carter was elected that November, the tone of U.S. policy toward Chile changed abruptly. For the first time, U.S. officials began voting for UN resolutions condemning Pinochet and against multilateral loans to Chile. Relations deteriorated further in 1979, when the Chilean Supreme Court refused to extradite the three DINA men and they were released. The State Department accused Chile of condoning "international terrorism," the U.S. ambassador was recalled twice, private commercial credits were cut, and the navy was withdrawn from annual exercises with Chile.[52] But these measures had little impact on Pinochet, who warned the United States to "leave us alone" after his triumph in the 1980 plebiscite and seemed to take comfort from the nationalistic rhetoric which U.S. actions helped engender.[53]

While the Letelier case languished for years, Armando Fernández was brooding in fear and frustration. He had not thought much about the purpose of his spying assignment in Washington, and when he learned of the assassination, the brash young agent's world fell apart. Drawn into a web of criminal deceit, he tried to resign from the army and flee abroad, but was closely watched by the DINA. Finally, in 1987, with the collusion of U.S. diplomats and FBI agents, he slipped into Brazil and flew to Washington, where he presented himself to the judge who had tried Townley.

In court, Fernández portrayed the anguish of a man torn between the tradition of military honor and the demand for obedience from superiors who forced him to lie, even to the Supreme Court. He recounted how Pinochet had urged him to "be a good soldier" and suffer in silence, and how Contreras had halted the army's investigation by hinting that his orders had come "from the chief"— the only evidence to date that Pinochet knew of the murder plot in advance.[54]

Fernández said he hoped his confession would "teach fellow officers they should not blindly obey orders, and that superiors should not abuse the loyalty of their young subordinates." He also sent a long resignation letter to the army high command, explaining his actions. But the greatest burden on his conscience was having shamed his late father's name. To clear it, he told the judge, was worth spending a lifetime in prison. "I think my father is going to be very happy," he added.[55]

AT first, Chile's new intelligence agency appeared to represent a fundamental change from the DINA. Its mandate was to focus on "collecting and processing" information, and the new director, General Mena, was a by-the-books professional who had long disdained Contreras's crude methods.[56] Vowing to act within the law, Mena fired hundreds of DINA agents, recruited trained technicians, and curbed overseas spying.[57] Human rights groups reported a marked decrease in torture and a virtual halt to disappearances. But Mena's intentions, backed by "soft-line" officials like Foreign Minister Hernán Cubillos, were gradually thwarted by several powerful forces.

One was Contreras, who launched a behind-the-scenes war against the soft-liners he despised. Although his name was no longer on the door, his stamp remained on the network he had created. Hundreds of former DINA men resigned from the CNI as a sign of loyalty to their former chief, while others remained as spies to keep sensitive information from Mena.[58] As extra insurance, Contreras had thousands of intelligence files purged or shipped to Europe before he left his post.[59]

As this internal war intensified, torture charges against secret police agents began to recur. In 1980, a journalism student (and alleged MIRista) named Eduardo Jara was kidnapped by a group calling itself the Command to Avenge Martyrs, and abandoned to die of torture wounds. For once, the conservative establishment did not look the other way. *Qué Pasa* magazine called the crime a "grave threat" to the government and "another form of terrorism." Jara's death would "weigh over Chile," the editors warned, "capable of destroying everything the country has struggled for since September 11, 1973."[60]

Blaming the case on the Carabineros, Mena insisted his agency's hands were clean, asserting that new rules required CNI recruits to have a "firm ethical formation" and that officials maintained control over agents' activities. "There are no delinquents in the Central," he vowed.[61] But Mena's reformist impulse was being thwarted by a second problem: a surge in left-wing guerrilla activities. A number of exiled MIR leaders, who had received military training abroad, slipped back into Chile and began assaulting banks and police stations. Growing bolder, they gunned down an army intelligence officer named Roger Vergara in mid-July.

The assault galvanized Contreras and the hard-liners into action. Alvaro Puga, a right-wing columnist, lamented the passing of the DINA era, when surely the agency's "preventive work" would have kept the Vergara assassination from occurring.[62] Mena was trapped between his determination to fight a clean war and pressure to fight an efficient one. Pinochet abruptly replaced him with General Humberto Gordon, who maintained good relations with Contreras—and launched an all-out campaign to infiltrate and destroy the radical left.

THE rebirth of the MIR revived a guerrilla conflict between foes who shared a fanatical war mentality. Friends and relatives of the returned MIRistas described them as thoughtful, serious men dedicated to seeking justice against dictatorship. But according to one account, none of Vergara's attackers asked why they were to kill him; "they viewed themselves as soldiers in a cause and obeyed orders without discussion."[63]

As the deadly game intensified, the tactics grew dirtier and the players harder to tell apart. Both sides staged bombings to discredit the other; police informants were arrested and beaten for show. As in 1974, the MIR's cause was hopeless. A rudimentary rural combat-training camp was easily discovered and destroyed; a network of urban safe houses was infiltrated and a number of their occupants killed in late-night "armed confrontations."[64]

In August 1983, after the military governor of Santiago was assassinated, intelligence squads surrounded two MIR safe houses and opened fire with machine guns mounted on jeeps, killing all inhabitants. "The intent and the order were simply to liquidate the residents," stated Andrés Valenzuela, the air force agent, who was there.[65]

In January 1982, Enrique Reyes, a MIRista who had sneaked into Chile after guerrilla training in Nicaragua and Algeria, was gunned down as he left his apartment. "My boys ran into the street screaming. Then the CNI burst in, tearing up the walls and looking for guns," recalled Reyes's wife, Patricia Garzo. "They took me to a secret prison and kept beating me and asking me questions. I resisted for a long time, but when they said they were going to torture the boys, I broke down and signed a paper."

Imprisoned for two years, Garzo insisted that she knew little about her husband's activities, but she shared his revolutionary beliefs and justification of violence against the regime. One of her sons, badly traumatized by his father's death, refused to speak for a year. "The police called Enrique a delinquent, but it's not true," Garzo insisted. "He was fighting for our ideals."[66]

IF the fanatical inspiration of MIR leaders survived eight years of repression, that of Manuel Contreras survived political disgrace and bureaucratic purges, gaining new force with the revival of ideological warfare. Beneath the façade of legalism, CNI agents received the same kind of military brainwashing that Contreras had introduced at Tejas Verdes.

In 1981, an ex-CNI agent named Gabriel Hernández, condemned to death in a bank robbery and murder in the northern city of Calama, defended himself on grounds that he had been acting as a robot on orders from a CNI superior. "His behavior was the result of psychological training" aimed at ensuring the "fulfillment of orders without question, without moral value, under fear of death," Hernández's lawyer argued.[67]

The Calama crimes also exposed a seamy side of the intelligence netherworld. The convicted agents, both former members of criminal gangs, hinted that the robbery was intended to finance overseas CNI operations. Yet evidence was ignored, police investigators were hampered, and the case was closed before it reached higher into the secret police hierarchy. "We are being sacrificed to hide the true background of these tragic events," Hernández said before he was executed.[68]

General Gordon reacted to the scandal indignantly, saying he was tired of being called a torturer and an assassin. "I have tried to do the best possible," he said. "I have made changes. We are not all going to pay because of some deranged people."[69] Gordon eventually fired over three thousand agents, more than half of whom, according to one report, had police records or court charges pending against them.

But, as Hernández's defense suggested, it was the institution that was deranged. In the secret police world, there was no relevant distinction between the "professional" military officer and the "delinquent" right-wing thug. Moreover, it was never clear how much control officials actually exercised over their men. A number of political murders were blamed on mysterious right-wing squads, but often evidence pointed to intelligence agencies.

Especially scandalous abuses provoked new feuding among security forces. In 1984, General Matthei withdrew all air force men from CNI postings after its agents blew up a woman in order to create an "extremist bombing." In March of 1985, a teacher, an artist, and a sociologist who belonged to the Communist party were kidnapped and found beside a rural highway with their heads nearly severed. The grisly execution was linked to a Carabineros squad, and the CNI provided supporting evidence of the crime.[70]

Despite their embarrassing excesses, the secret police remained a central, privileged component of Pinochet's war against enemies both real and imagined. Throughout the 1980s, as the spread of antigovernment protests coincided with the growth of urban guerrilla groups, intelligence organs responded with a campaign of infiltration, harassment, and intimidation. In their methods, they were more circumspect than the DINA, but they did not always discriminate between democratic opponents and armed rebels.

Officially, the CNI's mission was to safeguard decent citizens against left-wing violence. When reporters asked Pinochet about CNI abuses, he snapped, "Thanks to the CNI, you sleep tranquilly."[71] But to the regime's ideological warriors, anyone who challenged official policies was an enemy. During 1981, an economist critical of Pinochet's free-market model was kidnapped and severely beaten, two members of the Chilean Human Rights Commission were seized and tortured, and the chief lawyer for the Catholic church legal aid office found bags of dismembered cats in his yard.

On February 25, 1982, Tucapel Jiménez, a centrist labor leader, was found shot and slashed to death in his car. The crime was linked to the CNI by a terrified munitions clerk who sought asylum in the French embassy, then testified in a Paris court that he had issued the murder weapons to four CNI agents. The men were freed for lack of evidence, but testimony at their trial revealed the outlines of a CNI plan to destroy opposition labor groups with help from right-wing unions.[72]

The secret police also devoted extensive efforts to intimidating and discrediting the university protest movement, planting informants and harassing student groups. Many youths were drawn to street protests, and a handful joined new urban guerrilla movements such as the Manuel Rodríguez Patriotic Front, an offshoot of the Communist party, which the CNI made assiduous efforts to infiltrate.

Carlos Rojas Mazzinghi, a young CNI collaborator who deserted in 1986, gave a chilling account of spying on student leaders, beating up protesters, and planting bombs. If picked up by the police, he gave them a certain telephone number—and was released within minutes. Growing exhausted and disgusted by his work, he decided to go to the press despite his terror of reprisal. "I had something inside that did not let me live," he said.[73]

To counter criticism, the CNI continued to refine its methods of extracting information, leaving fewer scars and concentrating on psychological techniques.[74] One woman, forced to lie next to a mutilated corpse, was told it was that of her lover.[75] Pablo Yuri Guerrero, a student seized with an alleged arsenal in his car, testified that his captors created a "sensation of terror" and built a "sinister and surreal climate" of darkness and violence in order to "annihilate [his] personality."[76]

In 1986, a new surge in left-wing terrorism deflected attention once again from the sins of the secret police—even while drawing their harshest response since Contreras's heyday. In August, agents discovered an elaborate scheme in which cadres from the Patriotic Front, posing as fishermen in the coastal village of Vallenar, had been receiving large quantities of weapons from Cuban ships on the high seas, then stockpiling them inside abandoned mine shafts.

Meanwhile, a squad of two dozen commandos was preparing the Patriotic Front's "final offensive" against the regime. Ensconced in a safe house near the highway that led to Pinochet's suburban mansion, Melocotón, they practiced military drills, memorized maps, and planned a flawless assault and getaway. At dusk on September 7, as Pinochet's motorcade of bulletproof Mercedes sped along the highway, a barrage of machine-gun and rocket fire exploded from a deserted ridge. Several cars were hit and five bodyguards killed, but Pinochet's driver instantly reversed course and sped safely back to Melocotón.[77]

The attackers escaped, but Pinochet's men launched a furious, vengeful assault on the left. Under cover of a newly declared state of siege, CNI agents seized and brutally interrogated hundreds of activists, while unidentified armed squads kidnapped four known Marxists and left their bullet-riddled corpses dumped beside deserted roads. Several men detained at the time later described sadistic treatment at the hands of the CNI. Sergio Buschmann, the forty-five-year-old actor who masterminded the arms importation plot, testified that CNI interrogators shut rats inside his mouth for hours. Dr. Pedro Marín, accused of running a secret clinic for the Patriotic Front, charged that he was brutally sodomized on a torture table.[78]

The CNI's campaign against the Patriotic Front continued through 1987, in a series of nighttime assaults on safe houses that left twelve members dead. This time, agents claimed to be acting under orders from a military prosecutor, but the assertion proved false.[79] According to the Chilean Human Rights Commission, the case proved that the CNI possessed "autonomous powers" of repression and was not subject to "any effective civilian control." Such a structure, the commission said, "represents the maximum synthesis of the National Security State."[80]

THE prolonged tenure of a vast security apparatus, with periodic purges of "bad seeds" and rotation of military personnel, created a sizable population of ex-spies with skills and values alien to a democratic society. These men often remained at the fringes of the intelligence community, collaborating with their former associates and inhabiting a hermetic demimonde of fast money, violence, and right-wing politics.

In this world, Contreras remained king, with continued access to Pinochet, a network of informants, and a storehouse of information on thousands of Chileans. He also presided over a far-flung business empire and a private security agency that employed numerous former DINA agents. In 1980, it was discovered that a firm linked to Contreras had fraudulently obtained $6 million in tax refunds by filing false receipts for exported copper. Some of the fake invoices bore names of individuals who had "disappeared."[81]

There were many rumors of current and former agents being involved in other unsavory ventures, from money laundering to cocaine distribution, and occasional spats between members of the secret police fraternity led to glimpses of violent, high-rolling life-styles. At a party in 1988, Manuel Contreras's twenty-six-year-old son emptied his pistol into a CNI officer after a drunken quarrel. The murder set off a volley of cross-charges among CNI-linked families, and young Contreras was charged—although never convicted—under the arms control laws used to condemn hundreds of leftists.

The man who most symbolized the ultimate decadence of Pinochet's intelligence forces was Julio Alvaro Corbalán, alias Alvaro Valenzuela, a dashing army major who rose to become chief of CNI operations. As Corbalán, he pursued a lavish bohemian nightlife and was feted by hard-line conservatives as the hope of ultranationalist politics. As Valenzuela, he was a quick-tempered military man who called himself "the boss of repression."[82]

In a society magazine interview, Corbalán boasted of the talents he had dedicated to the "defense of Western and Christian principles." Asked about his alleged role in one-sided "shoot-outs" with leftist groups, he struck back with sarcasm. "Do you think it is possible to go to the house of a terrorist . . . ring the bell and ask him to please turn himself in?" he asked. "Is it possible to combat cancer or AIDS with aspirin?"[83]

With the revolutionary left in disarray after the failed attack on Pinochet, it was harder to justify such "dirty war" tactics. Men like Corbalán became a liability to a regime trying to legitimize itself. Rightist civilian leaders grew embarrassed by the CNI's involvement in politics, and a group of CNI agents published an anonymous letter charging that Corbalán's opulent life-style was "making a mockery" of the agency. Finally, Chile's "chief of repression" was fired.

In July of 1989, the predawn slaying of a flamboyant business-man named Aurelio Sichel intensified speculation about a Mafia-style criminal world linked to the secret police; Sichel had co-owned a glitzy steak house with an ex-CNI agent, and rumors circulated that it had been a cover for laundered funds used in drug or arms smuggling. No witnesses came forward and no serious investigation was pursued, however; the case became mired in legal technicalities and was nearly forgotten.

But a year later, after Pinochet had left power and the CNI had been disbanded, a financial scandal erupted that explained Sichel's murder and exposed a web of corruption involving numerous current and former security agents—including Corbalán and several men linked to some of the most notorious abuses of the Pinochet regime. Suddenly, after years of shrugging off charges of human rights violations in the name of a patriotic, antisubversive crusade, Chile's intelligence community was shaken to the core.

The case came to light in August 1990, when an army captain charged with passing bad checks confessed to being part of a secret investment firm known as La Cutufa. It developed that the military men who ran La Cutufa had persuaded hundreds of officers and civilian friends to invest—and then absconded with the money. Sichel's widow declared he had been murdered after threatening to expose the operation; his former CNI partner was extradited from Paraguay and gave closed testimony implicating dozens of colleagues. By year's end, court investigations produced strong allegations that La Cutufa had been used to launder money from arms dealing, drug smuggling, and valuables looted from the homes and offices of CNI detainees.[84]

The accusations also devastated the Chilean army, shattering its reputation for incorruptibility. Many of those implicated were former or active-duty officers, and an internal investigation led to the "voluntary" retirement of six generals, including two former intelligence chiefs, an ex–inspector general of the army, and a former head of the general staff. After years of defiant denials, La Cutufa proved what critics had long asserted: that granting broad immunity to intelligence organizations created a parallel power capable of corrupting even a proud military institution.[85]

Yet even as their mandate faded and their heroes were disgraced, Chile's shadow warriors remained convinced of the righteousness of their cause. Least repentant of all was Contreras, who became secretary-general of the association of retired generals and admirals, and reminisced about the DINA years with frank nostalgia. One day, he vowed in 1989, the men who had labored in the dark to combat communism would occupy a proud place in Chilean history. Asked if he had any regrets, Contreras nodded faintly. "Yes, I regret not having been tougher on the Marxists."[86]

CHAPTER FIVE

THE LAW

"Those who excel in the art of war cultivate above
all their own justice, and protect their laws and
institutions. In that form they make their
government invincible."

—*Sun-tzu,* The Art of War, A.D. *320,*
passage underlined in Pinochet's copy[1]

"The disappeared are driving me crazy."

—*Israel Bórquez, Supreme Court president,*
asked in 1978 about 660 missing prisoners[2]

THE dignified, slightly balding lawyer paced back and forth across
the small, shabby office, his fists clenched and his voice trembling.
He had remained silent for years, haunted by remorse but frightened of reprisal, ever since leaving his job as a prosecutor for the
Pinochet regime. Now he begged fiercely that his name not be
revealed, for the safety of his children. But once he began to speak,
a torrent of rage and shame and anguish poured forth.

Soon after the coup, he and other attorneys had been assigned
to the war councils convened to judge leftist detainees. "We believed
in the letter of the law, and we tried to do our jobs well, but the
whole system seemed to have gone insane. People were tried for
war crimes even though we weren't at war," he recalled. "Everyone wanted to show they were tough, and no one would stand up
to the military judges." Whenever he could, he hurried the sen-
tencing paperwork, because "that was a prisoner's life insurance.
Otherwise, he might disappear."

During his years as a prosecutor for the military justice system, he also watched the civilian courts he admired become corrupted by fear and privilege. The DINA routinely ignored court orders, while judges repeatedly rejected petitions to protect prisoners who were likely to face torture. "For years, there was practically no justice in this country," the lawyer said. "Terrible things happened, and the courts washed their hands." Gesturing toward his shelves of legal volumes, he gave a bitter laugh. "I used to believe in these books, but not any more."

Why had he remained with the system for so long? "We all went along with it, because we were afraid of losing our jobs," the former prosecutor confessed. "Maybe I could have done more to help people, but they would just have gotten rid of me." His eyes were tormented as he searched for words. "You have to understand, the country was full of hatred. Where did so much hatred come from? I ask myself that every day. But in one way or another, we all became part of it. Nobody escaped."[3]

FOR years, such a denunciation would have shocked anyone familiar with Chile's public institutions. The republic had long stood as a bastion of civilized, "legalistic" behavior in a region of tyrants and revolutionaries; its officials prided themselves on scrupulous attention to constitutional norms and legal procedures. Law was the most prestigious profession, and judges, although not highly paid, enjoyed considerable status in a legally conscious society.

During the tumultuous thousand days of Allende's government, Chile's judicial establishment brandished these principles with special fervor, clashing repeatedly with Popular Unity officials. Many judges felt that Allende had flouted property laws and abused executive authority in his drive to build socialism; in turn, the president and his followers viewed judges as reactionaries, upholding "bourgeois legality" in a futile attempt to stop "inevitable" changes in society.

When peasants and workers took over estates and factories, the courts sided with their owners and ordered police to drive out the invaders, only to be vetoed by the interior minister. Thousands of arrest orders issued by the courts were ignored for political reasons. In one nasty exchange of letters in 1973, the Supreme Court warned Allende that executive interference was threatening the "imminent breakdown of the judicial system."[4] Allende retorted that the judges were ignoring the "process of transformation" and the popular demand for social justice, while placing the law "at the service of those interests" affected by change.[5]

For many Popular Unity disciples, judges were the last line of capitalistic defense against impending socialist order; a symbol of the privileged elite whose time had passed. Courts became targets of countless noisy demonstrations and insults by the pro-Allende yellow press: one sneering tabloid headline called the Supreme Court justices "Old Men Full of S——."[6] By mid-1973, civil communications between the executive and judiciary had broken down completely.

Stung by this unprecedented defiance of law and judicial authority, judges welcomed the military coup. Like many other Chileans, they were too convinced of looming economic chaos and ideological enslavement to question the violent overthrow of an elected government. On September 12, the Supreme Court's president, Enrique Urrutia, expressed his "delight" at the junta's pledge to "respect and enforce" judicial decisions.[7] In 1975, while the DINA's persecution of leftists raged unabated, the chief justice delivered a speech asserting that the nation enjoyed a perfect state of legal order and civic rights.

In turn, Pinochet and his men paid careful homage to the dignity and prestige of the judiciary—especially the Supreme Court, whose seventeen members were assigned state cars and chauffeurs. Instead of trying to change the courts, as the impatient U.P. leaders had done, the regime played to judges' vanity and conservatism, thus ensuring the collaboration of all but a few, stubborn iconoclasts. "During the administration of Salvador Allende, the president insulted the courts; his press insulted us every day," recounted Urrutia's successor, José María Eyzaguirre, in 1978. In contrast, he said, "the current government has never insulted the courts."[8]

Yet under Pinochet, judges relinquished much broader authority than Allende had ever dreamed of asking them to yield. Trained in a European legal system that stressed literal interpretation of law and deference to law-making bodies, judges automatically accepted the four-man junta as Chile's new source of executive and legislative authority. While remaining nominally independent, they were far more vulnerable to interference from a powerful military executive, and the intimidating chill of dictatorship affected even august, white-haired gentlemen named to the bench for life.

THE perversion of the justice system began with the war tribu—
nals. In case of foreign invasion or domestic anarchy, the law permitted the executive to invoke certain emergency powers, including the use of military tribunals to judge political crimes. The
Supreme Court, convinced that the extreme left constituted an active
threat to national peace and order, accepted the regime's assertion
that a "state of war" existed, and made no objection to the establishment of an autonomous military justice system free from all
civilian oversight.

Within weeks of the coup, war tribunals were functioning in
cities and towns throughout the country. An estimated six thousand Chileans were tried by these bodies during the first three years
of military rule, for crimes that ranged from the distribution of
subversive leaflets to treason. Approximately two hundred were
sentenced to death and executed.

Lawyers who represented defendants said there was little pretense of dispensing justice. Charges were based on anonymous
accusations or confessions extracted under torture, prisoners were
given only a few hours to prepare a defense, and sentences were
meted out by military men with no legal experience.

"The sessions had a martial atmosphere, with the officers armed
and dressed for combat. People were accused of treason and espi-
onage under the wartime military justice code, which none of us
knew anything about," recounted the lawyer Hernán Montealegre.
One war council in Temuco convicted twenty-five alleged MIRistas to prison terms of up to twenty years, with a single court-
appointed lawyer given less than twenty-four hours to review all
their cases.[9]

One group of Socialists, who had vaguely discussed attacking a
police station during the coup but then fled unarmed to the foothills, were captured and charged with "unconsummated assault on
a police station with Marxist aims." One evening, Montealegre
was notified to present a defense for one of the defendants, whom
he had never met, by 9:00 A.M. the next day. Working through the
night, the lawyer rushed to the war council with a bold argument
that the charge was illegal because no such crime existed. "I was
able to get him a long prison sentence, which was lucky," he said.
"His friends had been condemned to death and shot."[10]

According to defense lawyers, some civilian prosecutors were
helpful and professional, but seemed caught up in a massive machine
over which they had no control. One rumpled, small-town lawyer
who volunteered to help process prisoners described his job thus:

"The colonels ran everything; I just took statements to see who was against the regime and who could be set free. Sometimes if I freed someone, the military intelligence men would come back and say I couldn't. I guess I was naive," he added. "I thought they knew what they were doing."[11]

The largest, most elaborate war trial was that of nearly one hundred air force officers charged with subversion and treason. Some probably had been involved in efforts by the MIR to infiltrate the armed forces; after being sent into exile, several of the convicted men became guerrilla trainers and secretly returned to Chile to join the insurrectionary struggle against Pinochet. But other officers, like Captain Patricio Carbacho, were merely trying to monitor a possible coup and warn Allende if an uprising seemed imminent.

Years later, Carbacho described being brought to court in chains and forced to file between heavily armed soldiers, while helicopters circled overhead, in order to visit the bathroom in another building. He recognized some of the guards and tried to make conversation, but most were "terrified because they had been told we were dangerous criminals." His former colleagues, now sitting in judgment, also saw him as the enemy. "A whole web of imaginary conspiracy had been created. The real purpose of the trial was to make an example of us and to test the loyalty of the officers on the war council," Carbacho said. "They passed with flying colors."[12]

In defending some of the air force men at a second trial, Montealegre argued they could not be tried for wartime crimes, because no legal state of war had existed. "No one in Chile had studied these issues, so it became a fascinating challenge," he recalled. "When I made my case, the council members paid great attention and eventually decided I was right. They were honorable men, not brutes. It was a major breakthrough." A short time later, however, the council's decision was reversed under pressure from General Leigh.[13]

LIKE the judicial establishment, most Chilean lawyers had little sympathy for accused leftists and were unwilling to represent them in court. Provincial chambers of commerce forbade their associates to defend "extremists," while members of the National Lawyers' Association pressed their president, the prominent jurist and Christian Democrat Alejandro Silva Bascuñan, to step down because he was "not inspired by the values of the new government." Many of his colleagues, Silva reflected years later, "did not really believe in democracy. They simply gave in."[14]

The exception was a small group of attorneys, many of them Christian Democrats, who volunteered to defend leftist prisoners and victims of persecution. About fifty such lawyers, working principally through the Committee of Cooperation for Peace, plunged into the harrowing task of tracking down prisoners, taking testimony from hysterical relatives, and representing defendants before war councils. In two years, the committee staff handled more than seven thousand cases and filed 2,342 habeas corpus petitions.[15]

As the committee grew in size and scope, a number of Marxist professionals joined the staff, and the regime began to harass and terrorize its members. In 1975, the attorney José Zalaquett was sent into exile, and Montealegre was seized and tortured. In a letter to Cardinal Silva, Pinochet charged that the committee was being manipulated by "enemies of the fatherland" and urged him to dissolve it. Although Silva formally refused, he too feared that the committee had exceeded proper political bounds, and he departed for consultations in Rome while Contreras stepped up his terror campaign against committee associates.[16]

The cardinal's retreat was only strategic, however; in January of 1976, much to Pinochet's annoyance, he announced that the peace committee would be replaced by a new legal aid agency, the Vicaría de la Solidaridad (Vicariate of Solidarity), under the full protection and control of the archdiocese. Silva, by then referred to as the "Red cardinal" in government circles, warned Pinochet he would hide fugitives under his own bed and formally broke relations with the regime.[17] The Vicaría, under the leadership of dedicated priests and lawyers, went on to become one of the most effective human rights organizations in Latin America.[18]

A handful of "establishment" lawyers like Eugenio Velasco, a law school dean and diplomat who had ardently opposed Allende, were driven to defend human rights victims by sheer outrage. One day in 1974, a trembling woman appeared at Velasco's law office and related how a squad of armed men had broken into her house, dragged her husband off into the night, raped her in front of the children, and seared a crude hammer and sickle symbol into her breast with a heated screw driver, screaming anticommunist obscenities. When she pulled aside her blouse to reveal the bloody brand, Velasco took the case.

"I had to do it. People kept coming to me, saying no one else would defend them, because they were leftists. Some of my colleagues were frightened, some said I was crazy, that all the stories were invented by the communists. They had no idea of the magnitude of the atrocities being committed," recalled the nervous, impeccable gentleman, years later. He described how the woman fainted while telling her story in court, how the judges blanched while inspecting photographs of her wounds—and how nothing ever came of the case.[19]

Throughout the court system, the work of human rights lawyers was regarded with suspicion and hostility. According to Jaime Castillo, a former justice minister under President Frei who represented hundreds of prisoners and missing leftists, "judges almost always reacted negatively to us; they were servile and afraid, and so bitter against the Popular Unity." The devout Catholic and Christian Democrat added, "I didn't share the political views of many of the people I defended; I did it to balance an injustice."[20]

In mid-1976, Velasco and Castillo were seized and forced onto a plane for Argentina without even a chance to telephone home. The regime accused them of "endangering internal state security" because of statements about human rights abuses they had made to delegates from the Organization of American States. The audacious move sparked an outpouring of protest from diverse groups and individuals, including former President Frei, who joined 295 prominent Chileans in a letter asking the Supreme Court to rescind the expulsion order, and asserting that abuses of power threatened to "destroy the most valuable part of the national soul."[21]

But most members of the legal establishment remained cowed or indifferent, and some proved themselves eager converts to the authoritarian cause. A former law school colleague of Velasco's, Hugo Rosende, argued the government's case, calling the expulsion vital to national security and sneering at critics as rabble-rousing publicity seekers.[22] Velasco's onetime student aide, Ambrosio Rodríguez, assisted Rosende in preparing the brief against his former mentor and called Castillo a "fanatic" and "terrorist."[23]

The Supreme Court's response was even more disillusioning to both men, who had great respect for the institution. Denying the lawyers' petition to return home, the high court ruled that the "efficacy" of the regime's emergency powers must be preserved and that the government need not produce any evidence that Velasco and Castillo were "dangerous subversives." All critical media coverage of the case was banned, while the official newspaper *El*

Cronista reported that the two lawyers were enjoying a life of luxury abroad.

Castillo returned from exile in 1978 but was later expelled again; Velasco was forced to remain abroad for a decade, unable to practice law and living in modest circumstances. In a bitter memoir from exile, he wondered, "Had we been deeply mistaken when we felt pride in our tradition of respect for the law, for the will of the majority, for all ideas? Had we been living a gigantic farce in which many professed those principles only because of pressure from the cultural and social environment?" Even judges who boasted of "giving their lives to public service and the defense of democracy," he added, "today bow before the dictator and render him homage."[24]

THE military takeover exposed Chile's distinguished juridical tradition as a charade of eloquent phrases and prodigious paperwork. With a handful of exceptions, judges turned a blind eye to abuses by security forces and docilely collaborated as the law was transformed from a shield for individual rights into a weapon of persecution. Evidence of kidnapping and torture at the hands of police agents or rightist vigilantes was summarily rejected, while officials' versions of events were accepted without question.

When lawyers from the Vicaría filed habeas corpus petitions on behalf of "disappeared" prisoners, many judges dismissed them as a form of political harassment. If the court made a routine query to military authorities, officials often suggested that the missing individual had "left his wife" or "fled the country"—explanations judges found far more palatable than the hair-raising tales of midnight kidnappings recounted by distraught relatives. Between 1973 and 1983, the Supreme Court rejected all but 10 of 5,400 habeas corpus petitions filed by the Vicaría.[25]

"I believe some of the cases were real, but often you'd find the person had just gotten drunk or gone off looking for work. Later he might reappear, but the Vicaría would pretend he hadn't," asserted one veteran member of a provincial appeals court in 1989, clearly still uncomfortable with the subject of human rights. That particular court rejected scores of habeas corpus petitions between 1973 and 1978, and in many instances, the missing individuals were never seen alive again.[26]

Often, judges requesting information on the whereabouts of prisoners would simply be told the person was not in custody, and would accept this as fact even if there were numerous witnesses to the detention. In the town of Laja, where nineteen prisoners vanished from the police station in October 1973, local judges rejected family habeas corpus petitions after authorities denied that the men had been arrested, despite glaring contradictions in their testimony and statements from relatives who had visited the detainees in jail.[27] Six years later, church investigators unearthed the bodies from a cemetery where they had been secretly buried.

Even when the numbers of unsolved disappearances grew into the hundreds, the higher courts retained their legalistic approach and their faith in official explanations. In 1975, Judge Enrique Zurita Camps, named to investigate 131 disappearances, told an interviewer, "The authorities have held that the persons being sought were not detained, and there is no reason to suppose this is not the truth."[28] In 1976, when Vicaría lawyers sent the Supreme Court a massive report of legal abuses, including more than 220 disappearances, the justices responded with a terse letter saying most of the points were "without cause."[29]

Judges were especially reluctant to challenge the DINA and other secret police agencies, which virtually always denied any detentions and refused to provide further information on national-security grounds. In theory, Chilean courts had nearly unlimited power to obtain information if a person's life or safety was at risk, and they were required to rule on habeas corpus petitions within twenty-four hours. In practice, they meekly accepted the DINA's refusal to collaborate.

In March of 1975, Colonel Contreras informed the Santiago Appeals Court that all requests for information concerning the DINA should be directed to the Interior Ministry or the National Service of Detainees. Two weeks later, the Supreme Court announced that, "given the situation in which the country finds itself," it was "convenient" to follow this procedure, and instructed all lower courts to follow suit.[30] Thus, the urgent matter of protecting lives became mired in elaborate, time-consuming paper trails, while many prisoners were tortured and killed.

Periodically, the Interior Ministry would deny that a person had been detained, then discover an "unfortunate administrative error" or a back-dated detention decree if the prisoner turned up in DINA hands. A man named Julián Ricci was seized in December 1974, but the ministry repeatedly asserted he had not been detained until three months later, when army officials acknowledged he was in a prison camp. Suddenly, the ministry announced it had ordered his arrest in December after all, citing a typographical error as the cause of confusion.[31]

While the ponderous legal machinery ground on, families of victims were driven frantic with fear and frustration. But even desperate personal pleas to judges met with skepticism or bureaucratic foot-dragging. In 1976 Estela Ortiz, whose father, a Communist party leader and history professor, had been missing for months, received a tip from a government source that he was alive in a DINA prison camp. She rushed to the Supreme Court and begged for an audience.

"After a long wait, I finally got in to see one of the justices. I felt like an ant in front of an elephant, filled with such terrible hope of saving my father," recounted Ortiz, a pretty mother of three. Her jaw clenched and her eyes hardened at the memory. "He put in a call to someone at the DINA, who of course told him it wasn't true. I pleaded with him to go visit the camp; I was almost hysterical, but he said no, he was leaving on vacation to South Africa the next day. We never heard anything more about my father again."[32]

Occasionally, a judge would attempt to defy the DINA's wall of silence or exercise his right to enter a secret police facility without warning, but efforts to discover the whereabouts of disappeared persons virtually always failed. In 1979, when several bound and mutilated bodies appeared in the Maipo River delta, Judge Servando Jordán forced Contreras and two other DINA officials to testify in court, but found insufficient evidence to bring charges against them.

Supreme Court members made periodic inspections of secret police facilities, but they usually gave officials advance notice and kept their findings secret. After visiting several DINA camps in 1975, Justice Urrutia pronounced conditions "satisfactory" and said he had received no complaints of mistreatment. His successor, Justice Eyzaguirre, made little comment about his prison visits and suggested that civilian courts had no jurisdiction over the DINA, because it was a special "military organism."[33]

The cavalier attitude of Chilean justice officials hardly encouraged aggressive judicial action. In 1978, the bodies of fifteen peasants, missing since their arrest after the coup, were discovered stuffed in an abandoned lime quarry oven in the Lonquén hills. Justice Minister Mónica Madariaga, asked about the case, answered airily, "What is the truth of Lonquén? Did they not eliminate themselves?" Asked whether she believed that the DINA had committed abuses, she retorted, certainly, "just like Scotland Yard."[34]

A far more formidable figure was Hugo Rosende, the tall, scowling man who was named justice minister in 1983. An ardent Catholic and anticommunist intellectual, Rosende was extremely close to Pinochet and wielded vast behind-the-scenes influence in expanding the regime's emergency powers and intimidating the Supreme Court. "He was even more dangerous than Contreras," said one conservative lawyer, "because he made repression respectable."

By 1978, when the Vicaría painstakingly documented 613 unsolved disappearances and most conservative bishops had joined in the demand for their investigation, the high court still refused to pursue the problem as a whole, asserting that each case was being handled by local courts. Had judges acted with more alacrity, the Inter-American Human Rights Commission asserted in 1985, "the disappearance of persons . . . would not have reached the dimensions it did." By their "grave negligence," rote application of law and deliberate "self-limitation," the commission concluded, the courts helped ensure that "the state of law does not currently exist in Chile."[35]

THE failure of Chile's distinguished judicial system to meet the challenge of dictatorship stemmed partly from judges' innate conservatism, exacerbated by the trauma of the Popular Unity years, and partly from a system of legal training that confined them to a literal interpretation of the law and taught them to apply it without regard to the motives of the lawmakers or the political context of the times.

Although few judges would admit to ideological prejudice, they easily adopted the phraseology of Chile's military rulers, in which leftists became "terrorists" or "bandits" deserving of "severe punitive sanctions," as Justice Eyzaguirre put it in 1976.[36] "A judge may think he's being objective, but he sees each case through a filter of experience and prejudice," observed one iconoclastic appeals court judge, speaking on condition of anonymity. "When the prisoner is a communist, at some level he represents not a human being but three years of Allende."[37]

Occasionally, a judge would unintentionally reveal the kind of bias that had crept into years of court rulings. One provincial jurist, asked in 1989 about local vigilante killings after the coup, blamed "leftist agitators" for stirring up peasants and leaving them vulnerable to reprisal. "You have to understand, this was the countryside. From time immemorial, we sat at the table and the maid didn't," the judge explained with a smile. "People did not want that hierarchy to change."[38]

A few prominent judges were deeply dismayed by their colleagues' attitudes, but even in the late 1980s they were not willing to criticize them publicly. One white-haired appeals court member said he had seen "terrible things" done to prisoners while serving in a provincial court. "But when I got to Santiago and told my colleagues, they said I was being political. It was astonishing to see how they had adopted ideological criteria," he recalled. "They were nice people, but they had been so brainwashed by hatred that they simply didn't believe me."[39]

The courts' reluctance to take aggressive action against the regime's abuses had equally deep roots in the formalistic legal philosophy taught in Chile's law schools, following the country's Civil Code tradition. Adhering to the precepts of European positivist doctrine that aimed at building the perfect society through enlightened legal codes, Chile's judges were trained to believe that, "when the sense of the law is clear, you cannot ignore its literal tenor on the pretext of interpreting its spirit."[40]

In Chile, it was heresy to think that the law could be interpreted more broadly to fit higher principles of justice or to respond to changing social realities. "Here, there has always been the notion that the law solves everything. It is not just respect; it is exaggerated fetishism for the law," noted Judge Germán Hermosilla, who became a quiet but determined champion of judicial reform after winning the presidency of the National Magistrates' Association in 1986.[41]

The dispute between Allende and the Supreme Court had hinged on two sharply opposed concepts of the role of judges. Allende contended that all laws were subject to interpretation and that the courts were refusing to adapt to the "new realities" of Chilean society.[42] The justices retorted that if the executive did not like the laws, it should seek to change them. But with no majority in Congress, Allende was unable to do so, and his judicial adversaries could always find a legal text that stymied his controversial initiatives.

With the coup, the impasse between executive and legislature was neatly resolved, and the regime needed only four signatures to create or change the law. Instead of defying the juridical order, the junta used it to construct an elaborate façade of legitimacy around dictatorial rule. From their first days in power, the commanders issued a stream of decree laws, duly debated and signed, that granted the regime a widening range of repressive powers—from the right to censor news and rescind citizenship to the authority to hold prisoners "incomunicado" without charge for five days or banish dissidents to remote villages for three months at a time.

"We thought we were embarked on a mission that was best for the country. I really believed we were fighting for freedom," recalled Mónica Madariaga, whose typewriter in a tiny cubicle near Pinochet's office cranked out drafts for hundreds of early regime laws.[43]

The courts, which had balked so indignantly at the "illegitimacy" of Allende's elected government, immediately accepted the new authoritarian law-making process. Although many of the regime's executive actions and decree laws clearly defied existing statutes and the 1925 constitution, the veneer of legal formality gave timid, mediocre, or conservative judges a perfect rationale for avoiding sensitive issues. If military officials swore someone had not been detained and a string of witnesses contradicted them, for example, the law permitted a judge to reject the case for lack of conclusive proof.

"Most judges were neither cowards nor heroes. They simply kept on applying the law as they always had, even though the circumstances had changed," observed one veteran appeals court judge with a reputation for independence. "Society expected them to put a brake on executive power, but just as in Nazi Germany or [Fascist] Italy, the courts were not prepared to confront an institutional crisis. The world had turned upside down, but the machinery kept functioning."[44]

Having initially persuaded the judicial establishment that a "state of war" existed in Chile, the regime continued to invoke emergency legal powers long after any threat of armed resistance was quashed. In a series of decrees, the government created a complex hierarchy of "states of exception," which could be declared by the government in cases of internal disturbance, "latent subversion," or public calamity. The grounds were extremely subjective, including the potential existence of not yet organized "seditious forces."

"It would be a very grave error to think that this latent civil war ended immediately after the military pronouncement," warned Sergio Fernández, the interior minister, in a June 1978 speech.

Admitting for the first time that the regime was responsible for some deaths and disappearances, he argued that it was a necessary cost of the battle against communism. "To have tried to carry out this combat with the methods of a normal period would have meant succumbing to subversion."[45]

The courts never questioned these actions, not even after the pretense of belligerent conditions had become a thin legal fiction and the emergency powers had become concentrated in the hands of the president. Several "states of exception" were renewed continually for a full fifteen years, while the most repressive category, "state of siege," remained in effect until December of 1977 and was briefly invoked twice more, permitting Pinochet to order arbitrary arrests, censor the press, and suspend a wide range of civil liberties.[46]

One of the few significant challenges to the regime's emergency laws came from Renán Fuentealba, a former Christian Democratic senator, who was sent into exile in 1976 for hinting at human rights abuses to foreign reporters. His lawyers argued before the Supreme Court that expulsion without trial violated the 1925 constitution. But while the case was pending, the junta issued a sweeping new decree law which said that any previous decrees found to conflict with the 1925 charter would retroactively be considered constitutional amendments. "We called that the Varsol law," Madariaga recalled sheepishly, referring to a household detergent.[47] With the law scoured of any untidiness, the high court denied Fuentealba's appeal.[48]

On several occasions, when facing severe foreign pressure on human rights abuses, the regime issued decrees that appeared to amplify the rights of prisoners and defendants. In May 1975, officials declared that anyone detained under state-of-siege provisions must be turned over to civilian authorities within five days. In 1976, the junta created one new law requiring all prisoners to be examined by a doctor, and another limiting detention to certain publicly identified facilities. But these formalities were routinely ignored or falsified by security forces—and virtually never enforced by the courts.

In another attempt to reassure international and domestic critics, the regime commissioned a panel of lawyers to draw up four "constitutional acts" in 1976, which declared support for basic concepts of law, democracy, and "Christian humanism"; set forth essential civic rights and duties; and described the various states of emergency that could be declared.[49] These acts were announced with great solemnity, yet officials had no qualms about "adjust-ing" them to meet particular repressive needs. Within two years, Constitutional Act no. 4 was amended twice: once to suspend in "emergency" situations the newly guaranteed right to habeas cor-pus, and again to legalize the shutdown of Christian Democratic–run Radio Balmaceda.[50]

The regime also found ways to avoid the requirement that all new laws be approved in advance by the comptroller general. Twisting a little-used provision that exempted certain minor stat-utes from comptroller review, officials declared a wide variety of laws exempt, especially those dealing with state security. "This was very technical but decisive, and it produced the self-weaken-ing of another institution that could have exercised some control," explained Enrique Silva Cimma, a senior opposition leader and legal scholar who served as comptroller before the coup.[51]

When military officials wanted to promulgate an especially con-troversial law, they simply made it secret. According to a study by Roberto Garretón, chief lawyer for the Vicaría, the regime created ninety-eight secret or partly secret laws between 1973 and 1985, including those granting broad police powers to the DINA. Ga-rretón and others argued that such statutes were illegal, since the Civil Code required all laws to be "published." But military authorities fulfilled this technical requirement by posting secret laws in limited editions of the Official Daily Record, which were dis-tributed to select high-level officials.[52]

Even political problems as delicate as torture and disappear-ances found a neat legal solution in Decree Law 2191, a master-piece of euphemistic phrasing. On April 19, 1978, the government announced that since Chile's "internal commotion" had subsided and a state of "peace and order" reigned, it had decided to grant amnesty to all "authors, accomplices, or concealers" of politically connected crimes committed since the coup, including those con-demned by military tribunals. The goal of the measure, officials claimed, was to "leave hatreds behind" and foment national reuni-fication.[53]

The principal effect of the law, however, was to absolve military and police officials from responsibility in the abuse and deaths of thousands of Chileans. In case after case, including the massacres in Laja and Mulchén, painstakingly gathered evidence was erased from the record and the matter closed. According to General Leigh, Pinochet had rushed the junta members into signing the law with-out time to consider it carefully. While meeting afterwards with a legal aide, Leigh later recalled, "We realized I had signed a bar-barity."[54]

Some opposition lawyers argued that the regime could not decree an amnesty law and still assert the country had been in a "state of war," since in that case it would be subject to the 1949 Geneva accords that prohibited amnesty for wartime crimes, including the execution of prisoners. "There was no war in Chile. This is a juridical monstrosity," Garretón contended in 1989.[55] But the Supreme Court flatly rejected that argument in the Lonquén case, stating that national law took precedence and that no one could be held accountable for the murder of the peasant activists and their relatives.

The amnesty law did lead to pardons for several hundred leftist prisoners, but most were sent directly into exile after having served several years in prison, whereas virtually none of the soldiers or security agents who had participated in torture and executions were even brought to trial. Four and a half years of crimes by the Pinochet regime were legally erased, and their perpetrators were absolved without being conclusively identified. For thousands of victims' families, the need to know the truth, let alone to see justice done, was flatly denied.

THE ultimate enforcers and role models of Chile's justice system were the seventeen life-term members of the Supreme Court, who dominated the rest of the judiciary "like a feudal power," as one appeals court judge put it. These aging, mostly conservative justices did much more than merely review cases; they oversaw an entire system of rank and promotion, and they could suspend a judge's pay or reduce his performance grade for insubordination or other sins.

As with many other Chilean institutions, the courts' tendency toward an authoritarian internal structure intensified under military rule. No longer subject to democratic oversight, the Supreme Court began to mirror the harsh vertical command lines of the military. Reprimands were meted out to the few judges who refused to be accomplices to persecution, and their example further fostered conformity and caution among lower courts.

"There is a panic of the Supreme Court. A judge knows that if he is too independent, it can hurt his career," noted Judge Hermosilla, adding that most "find it easier to take a comfortable attitude, rather than be tenacious about investigating cases."[56] Sergio

Dunlop, an appeals court judge, was censured for "lack of respect" after he mildly criticized the antiquated court retirement system. Leaving the bench in 1983, he bitterly condemned the judiciary as a career for paper pushers willing to "remain prudently silent." Those who cannot "fall on their knees" are better off quitting, he said.[57]

The personality and ideology of each Supreme Court president set the nation's judicial tone for his three-year term of office. The most ardent conservative was Israel Bórquez, who replaced Eyzaguirre in 1978 and soon afterward made headlines with his exasperated remark "The disappeared are driving me crazy. I don't believe they exist."[58]

In the ultimate display of deference to the authoritarian state, Bórquez took the lead in denying U.S. extradition requests for Contreras and his two agents in the Letelier slaying, citing insufficient proof of DINA involvement. In office, he was criticized for promoting pliant, poor-quality judges. Under his tenure, "the reign of mediocrity began," charged Judge José Cánovas, and a judicial career lost the "solidity, prestige, and respect it had once deserved."[59] The regime, on the other hand, was so pleased with Bórquez that it issued a special decree extending his presidency by two years.

A few high court justices risked occasional mild, dissenting opinions against repression and manipulation of the law, but most simply deferred to the wishes of the regime. Neither ideologues nor iconoclasts, they sought the path of least resistance or, in the case of an honorable but cowed justice like Eyzaguirre, argued privately that it was better to maintain the institutional integrity of the judicial system than risk its being dismantled like the legislature.[60]

One highly regarded justice, who hesitantly consented to an anonymous interview in his musty, velvet-curtained chamber, expressed strong concern over the excessive power of military courts, complained about the lack of an independent judicial investigative service, and called the problem of disappearances "extremely grave." But when asked about the high court's role in protecting human rights, he seemed to misunderstand the question and responded in strict, legalistic terms.

"We often felt we were not competent to deal with human rights. Perhaps we are partly to blame, but how could we apply a law that didn't exist?" the wizened judge explained earnestly. "I am a great admirer of the law, and I believe a judge's task is to apply the law, not to interpret it."[61]

The only chief justice regarded as truly independent was Rafael Retamal, a diminutive, white-haired man who eventually replaced Bórquez. An outspoken defender of judicial autonomy, Retamal often issued stinging solo dissents from rulings that favored the regime, and once pointedly declined an invitation to dine with Pinochet in La Moneda, for which he was publicly shunned by his brethren. Critics suggested that Retamal was a hypocrite, since he arranged sinecures for numerous relatives in Pinochet's judiciary. But admirers considered him a slim beacon of hope in a corrupt and cynical system, and they persuaded him to remain on the court long after he had grown weary and disillusioned.

For two years, the aging judge struggled to force the CNI to reveal the names of agents charged in torture cases—and failed. Equally frustrating were his long, fruitless debates with colleagues, such as the arduous session in which Retamal persuaded a panel of fellow justices to allow *Apsi* magazine to publish political news, against the regime's wishes. When he returned to court the following week, the others had mysteriously reversed their opinions. After their meeting ended, the old man "slumped in a chair and wept," recalled a former aide. "He said there is no longer any reason or justice in Chile."[62]

IN a handful of instances, lower-court judges defied the weight of tradition and authority to pursue cases of human rights abuse, but their efforts were ultimately doomed. In 1983, Appeals Court Judge Carlos Cerda, a brilliant legal thinker and political maverick, undertook an intensive investigation of the disappearances of twelve Communist party leaders in 1976; ultimately, he charged thirty-eight members of the air force and Carabineros, including General Leigh. But after numerous appeals the case was closed by the Supreme Court, and all defendants were absolved under the 1978 amnesty law. When Judge Cerda continued with his investigation, he was censured by the high court.[63]

An equally determined—and vain—pursuit of justice was attempted by Judge José Cánovas in the gruesome murders of three well-known Communist party members, who were kidnapped in March 1985 and found nearly decapitated beside a rural road. After a lengthy investigation and several attempts to turn the case over to military courts, the judge charged seventeen police intelligence agents and officials. The scandal led to the resignation of General César Mendoza, the Carabineros representative on the junta, but the Supreme Court ultimately freed all major defendants for lack of evidence.[64]

Judge Cánovas, a ghostly-looking, taciturn man, avoided the limelight and never discussed his views while on the bench. After retiring in 1987, however, he published a dry but devastating memoir that depicted a judicial system corrupted by military rule, where the secret police defied the courts with impunity and where the most important criteria for being named a judge were "personal ties to a high-ranking military officer" and ideological approval by the intelligence services.[65] The regime's attitude toward his own court, he added, was one of "total disdain."[66]

Only one sitting judge, René García Villegas, dared publicly condemn the abuses of the secret police. A slight, mild-mannered man in his seventies with sharp, sea-green eyes, he was the son of a small-town schoolteacher who attended public law school and rose slowly through the ranks of provincial courts. By chance, he was transferred in 1985 to a criminal court in a Santiago district that included the CNI facility on Borgoño Street. Soon he began receiving complaints of torture from prisoners' families, and he pressed the CNI and military prosecutors to allow him to visit or question them, to little avail.

"When the cases first started coming to me, I was faced with the alternative of doing my duty or not. I knew I was putting myself under the horses' hooves, but I felt a strong commitment to the vows I took as a judge. My duty was to do justice," explained García in 1989 over coffee in his modest, formally arranged parlor. His eyes, brooding but mischievous, glinted across the room. "I received no cooperation at all," he said. "I couldn't get the prisoners examined; I couldn't get any ministry to acknowledge it had jurisdiction over the CNI."[67]

After months of bureaucratic resistance, García was able to indict eight unnamed CNI agents in the abuse of Yuri Guerrero, and to hear accounts of torture from prisoners accused in connection with the illegal arsenals and attempted assassination of Pinochet. But he was unable to identify specific agents, and so he decided to speak out publicly. In September 1988, a videotape of García describing systematic abuse of prisoners was televised by government opponents. He was instantly reprimanded by the Supreme Court and suspended from the bench.

"They accused me of participating in politics, but the truth is they were afraid of offending the government," García said. His colleagues reacted as he expected: three stepped forward to protest his punishment, a few more sent discreet messages, but that was all. "Some are afraid of losing their jobs; some still believe the stories of torture are communist fantasies. I cannot judge them," he said gently. "I try to avoid ideology, look at each case, and do what is right. That is my vocation. If you took it away from me, I would be like a bird with a broken wing." Six months after the interview, he was expelled from the bench for good.

DESPITE a willingness to collaborate that bordered on abject, the civilian courts were still suspect to Pinochet and his colleagues. Chile's rulers were much more comfortable with the military courts, whose members answered exclusively to the executive and shared the ideological mission of their commanders. As a result, the regime continued to expand the scope and authority of the military courts, long after it suspended the use of wartime military tribunals in 1976.

Ordinarily responsible for judging military infractions such as desertion or common crimes involving military personnel, these courts were given broad new jurisdiction over any crime linked to political subversion, from graffiti spraying to murder, through the laws of internal state security and weapons control. Periodically, these laws were amplified to provide stiffer sentences for a widening array of offenses, transforming the military courts into a pillar of legitimized political repression.

Civilian judges routinely declared themselves juridically "incompetent" to handle cases involving military or police defendants. In the Lonquén case, Judge Adolfo Bañados undertook an exhaustive investigation and demonstrated that the police version of how fifteen prisoners had died in a mysterious nocturnal ambush was patently false. But then Bañados declared himself incompetent to pursue the case, and a military court promptly closed it, citing the 1978 amnesty law.

With the Supreme Court relinquishing all control over military justice, a defendant's ultimate recourse was the martial courts, military appeals courts which comprised three military officers and two civilian judges—and often issued three-to-two rulings. Not surprisingly, the martial courts showed consistent leniency toward regime agents charged with abuse, and unstinting harshness toward civilians accused of violating the military justice code. If a ruling displeased their superiors, moreover, military members could be removed or retired for "disloyalty."

"Military tribunals are never independent, even less so when the president is military," observed Roberto Garretón. "These men are not impartial; they are fulfilling a military function. They are in a war against Marxism, and they are judging their enemies."[68]

Military courts functioned in near-total secrecy, but in 1979 the death of a leftist chemistry teacher named Federico Alvarez Santibáñez provided a rare public glimpse into the complicity between military courts and the secret police. Seized from his home, Alvarez was brought before a military judge after five days in CNI custody, so badly injured that he could barely stand or see. The judge, handed a police doctor's statement that Alvarez was in good health and a declaration signed by the prisoner that he had not suffered "physical duress," denied him medical aid and ordered him back to prison. The next morning, he was rushed to a hospital, dying.

The incident was investigated by a special prosecutor, who found that the victim's skull had been fractured from severe beatings and that a CNI doctor had helped to "cover up" the crime. But a martial court ordered the case closed, saying there were "no founded presumptions that certain persons participated in said crime." The junta, anxious to leave no loose ends, rushed through a decree law making all CNI employes "members of the armed forces," and thus protecting its doctors from prosecution in civilian court.[69]

The jurisdiction of military courts continued to widen in the 1980s. They were used principally for cases of antigovernment violence, but officials kept expanding the limits of what constituted an attack against the regime. Journalists were sent to prison for printing cartoons of military officials. In 1983, Enrique Silva Cimma was accused of "injury to the armed forces" after suggesting on television that regime agents were responsible for the murder of the labor leader Tucapel Jiménez. "The penalty was sixty days, but it took four years of appeals until I was absolved," he recalled. "And right after that, the junta raised the penalty to ten years!"[70]

The regime also kept broadening the definition of who could be charged as a terrorist. In 1979, it decreed that any member of an "illicit association" could be tried for a crime committed by another member. Antiterrorist statutes were revised so that the Military Justice Code would apply to anyone who "organizes, belongs to, finances, endows, aids, instructs, incites, or induces" the activities of armed opposition groups or "militarily organized parties"—a category so inclusive that dozens of people could be charged in an attack by three gunmen on a policeman.[71]

And in 1981, responding to an upsurge in leftist guerrilla activ-

ity, the regime reestablished war councils to judge all crimes resulting in the death or injury of a member of the armed forces. Human
rights lawyers argued that to reestablish the councils in peacetime
was a "juridical fiction," but in 1984, when three leftists were
swiftly condemned to death for the murder of the army general
Carol Urzúa, the Supreme Court rejected a defense appeal that
contended that the use of war councils was "inapplicable."[72]

The wide authority of the military courts gave enormous power
to military prosecutors, who collaborated closely with the secret
police and often flatly refused to cooperate with civilian judges. In
1983, Judge Cánovas learned that a woman informant alleged to
have helped the DINA capture dozens of disappeared leftists was
in custody, and he asked to question her. Instead, the military
prosecutor released her, saying he thought Cánovas's call was a
hoax. The woman was never seen alive again.[73]

An especially zealous prosecutor was Colonel Fernando Torres
Silva, who pursued an equally ruthless crusade against underground leftists and the Vicaría, especially after its lawyers provided medical aid to a man wounded while allegedly attempting
to blow up a bakery. Sarcastic and evasive with the press, Torres
was notorious for blocking civilian judges' requests to visit prisoners who had complained of torture or who had been taken to
military hospitals.

By 1988, Torres's abusive practices provoked pointed international criticism. Fernando Volio, the customarily circumspect United
Nations special rapporteur for Chile, charged that under Torres's
influence, Chile's already harsh military justice system had been
perverted into "an odious and unjust instrument" of repression.[74]
But Pinochet, clearly pleased with the colonel's work, promoted
him to the post of army auditor general.

THE final brick in the regime's legal edifice was the 1980 constitution. After years of building piecemeal legal control over the
country, Pinochet needed to establish a comprehensive body of
laws that would legitimize his rule and enshrine his authoritarian
powers in a manner more befitting Chile's legalistic traditions.

The preparation was long, tortuous, and marked by repeated
disputes within the regime's Constitutional Commission. Moderate conservatives, named to give the process a legitimate air, hoped
to build upon Chile's traditional democratic precepts. But Pino-

chet's ideological loyalists were determined to create a revolutionary charter for modern authoritarian rule. Before the task was
completed, three of the more moderate members resigned, in part
because they felt their work was being improperly used to create
the "constitutional acts," and in part to protest the regime's 1977
decision to dissolve all political parties.

"Some of the members acted like spokesmen for the government, and the rest of us were cornered," recalled Alejandro Silva
Bascuñan, one of two commission members who quit over the ban
on parties. "I'm proud of the work I did, but they delayed the most
sensitive issues until after we left, and then they added things that
we never would have approved."[75]

The final proposal, reworked by Pinochet's aides after passing
muster with the Council of State, was a masterpiece of legal obfus-
cation that appeared to guarantee a wide variety of civil liberties
and protections. All "illegitimate" forms of punishment and forced
confessions were prohibited; prisoners must be held in "public
places"; defendants were presumed innocent and guaranteed a legal
defense. Police raids on private homes required legal authoriza-
tion, and the rights to collective bargaining, free association, and
expression were guaranteed, with certain exceptions.[76]

But scattered among the noble-sounding clauses were ones that
substantially weakened these protections by subjecting them to vague
"national security" restrictions, and strengthened or formalized
repressive powers that had been exercised through decree laws.
The military courts were declared permanently exempt from
Supreme Court oversight when dealing with "terrorist" crimes.

Moreover, the "transitory articles" added by Pinochet's aides
greatly expanded the general's powers through 1989, freeing him
to declare states of emergency and impose drastic curbs on individual rights. Under Transitory Article 24, he could invoke such vague
grounds as the "danger of disturbance to internal peace." During
renewable six-month periods, he could order individuals to be held
without charge for five days, and extend that to twenty days if
"grave terrorist acts" occurred meanwhile.

The regime gained a number of permanent repressive powers
too. The right to habeas corpus was revoked during states of siege.
Civic and labor leaders were prohibited from belonging to political parties and from "intervening in activities alien to their specific
goals." But the most notorious permanent statute was Article 8,
which outlawed any group advocating violence, "doctrines that

offend the family," or a concept of society that was "totalitarian" or "based on class conflict."[77]

By such a vague definition, even groups that sought to liberalize divorce laws might be considered illegal.[78] Anyone convicted under Article 8 was banned from holding public office, high-level education and media jobs, or leadership roles in special-interest groups for five years. Finally, the state could exile anyone with a "reputation" of being involved in Marxist or antifamily causes, with no appeal allowed.[79]

So sweeping were these powers, so minimal the citizen's recourse against them, and so tenuous the conditions for imposing them that the Inter-American Human Rights Commission charged that these laws "gravely injure the international order in matters of protecting human rights."[80]

In Chile, few people were fully aware of the repressive measures contained in the proposed constitution, and the regime went to elaborate lengths to make sure most would remain uninformed. In preparing for a national referendum on the constitution, the government promoted it heavily as a charter for freedom and fatherland, while harassing and limiting press coverage of Christian Democratic groups that attempted to focus attention on the fine print.

On September 11, 1980, when 6.2 million voters marked their ballots and officials announced that 67 percent had endorsed the new charter, Pinochet's legal triumph seemed complete.[81] For the next eight years, the regime invoked the charter each time an oppressive legal measure was criticized, pointed to its popular approval as proof of the armed forces' legitimate right to rule, and insisted on following the letter of the law that established a slow, tightly controlled transition to civilian government.

Nevertheless, it has since been widely agreed not only that many positive votes were generated fraudulently but also that many Chileans who voted in favor of the constitution were confused about what the densely written document said. Indeed, prominent legal analysts have argued for years over the meaning of many obscure clauses.

"The constitution did represent some progress, because it set forth an institutional base and a transition timetable, but it was a cryptic document. The immense majority of people voted without understanding what they were voting for, in a general hope of improving things," José Luis Cea, a leading scholar in constitutional law at the Catholic University, said in 1989. "Even we experts didn't fully understand the transitional articles. They were brilliant, convoluted, and Machiavellian. Today we are still discovering tricks and secret provisions, and we may find more yet."[82]

CHAPTER SIX

THE CULTURE
OF FEAR

"Terrified of chaos, we had all prayed for a strong
system, for a powerful hand that would stem the
angry human river overflowing its banks. This fear
of chaos is perhaps the most permanent of our
feelings."
                            —*Nadezhda Mandelstam,*
                            Hope against Hope[1]

NO tomb in the hillside graveyard at Viña del Mar bore Salvador Allende's name, but mourners who gathered on the tenth anniversary of his death knew just where to place their red carnations.
Many had made other, furtive pilgrimages to the cemetery in the
seaside town near Valparaiso, rendering quick homage and dis-
persing before the Carabineros moved in. This time, authorities
decided not to prohibit the vigil, and by noon more than a thousand people had gathered, clambering atop family crypts and
tombstones adorned with stone angels.

"Comrade Salvador Allende?" the roll-call query echoed through
the cemetery. "Present!" came the thundering response. Then the
eulogies began—poetic, pained, fierce. "On the day of your assassination, a seed was sown. Now we come with a firm will to unite
and overcome," vowed a slender young man. Students shouted
slogans across the grave tops, and a white-haired woman stood
weeping, a black rose pinned to her lapel. "I will wear this every
day until the memory of Allende brings back democracy," she said.

In Santiago, one hundred miles inland, the regime and its supporters were commemorating the same anniversary—but the tone
was one of triumph rather than of mourning, and the date symbolized the beginning, not the destruction, of a dream. Pinochet,
regal in his white dress tunic, reminded a glittering audience that
the armed forces had "saved Chile from totalitarian tyranny," and
recited a list of his regime's accomplishments, from reducing infant
mortality to building a major highway through the south of Chile.

Along O'Higgins Avenue, military bands were followed by phalanxes of bureaucrats and women volunteers in pastel uniforms.
"Everything they say abroad about Chile is a lie," snapped a well-
dressed matron carrying a Pinochet poster, striding off before a
visitor could reply. Several telephone operators recoiled in repug-
nance when asked their feelings about Allende's death. "Mourn
him?! He was a monster who wanted to brainwash our children,"
spat out one woman. "I am a good Catholic, but I hope he burns
in hell!"

EVEN after a decade, the wounds were still raw; the hatred still
festered. Chileans remained fixated on the Popular Unity debacle
and the coup as if time had stood still. One side grimly savored
the triumph over Marxism but remained obsessed with the fear
that it could return. When military bands struck up the national
anthem at parades, they sang the second verse praising Chile's
"courageous soldiers" with defiant pride. The other side was in
permanent mourning, anguished by failure and scornful of everything Pinochet represented. When the anthem was played at soccer
games, they booed during the second verse.

Chile had long been divided by enclaves of clan, class, and party,
but it had masked these divisions with a veneer of civility. Within
their circles, people were generous and gracious, making social
rituals of visits to grandparents and hospitalized friends. But Chilean society was also ingrown and insecure. Even successful people
were quick to dismiss others' merits, and individuals were marked
for life by family names and party affiliations. It was a country of
parallel subcultures that never touched, of parochial worlds whose
members rarely ventured beyond their familiar, if often claustro-
phobic, confines.

By September of 1973, the façade of civility had fallen away,
exposing society's most primitive fears and permitting democracy
to degenerate into a screaming match. Polite relations between social

classes soured into sullen suspicion, and emotions were heightened by a polemical tabloid war. Friends hurled unforgivable insults at each other and never spoke again. In the all-consuming debate, everyone had to take sides, turning relatives, friends, and entire categories of fellow citizens into enemies.

If the Popular Unity years drew the battle lines, the military takeover hardened them. Chileans needed to come to grips with the collapse of their much vaunted democracy and learn how to rebuild it. But no healing process was permitted, no objective assessment of blame. Instead, people were insulated by curfews, cut off from debate, and forced to rely on biased information sources that only reinforced their mutual terror and contempt.

Retreating into their subcultures, the shell-shocked combatants nursed their grievances and relived the coup through a thousand private prisms. Society divided between winners and losers, and for years there was literally no communication between them. Thus, it was possible to believe anything about anyone on the other side.

"Our history was halted and put between parentheses," reflected the playwright and psychiatrist Marco Antonio de la Parra in 1988. Fear and inability to face the truth made Chileans "create tiny islands" inside their houses and communities, where they became prisoners of opposing myths about the coup—myths which "grew, flourished, and remain to this day."[2]

THE world of the winners was small and powerful: that of the moneyed elite and striving middle class. In tree-lined communities like Providencia and Las Condes, life returned to normal within weeks, and military rule was virtually invisible. Schools reopened; staples reappeared on supermarket shelves. Newsstands bristled with fashion and skiing magazines, and society pages announced the weddings of couples with Basque and British surnames—a reassuring sign that the bonds and values of the elite were passing to a new generation.

In gratitude to the armed forces, civic and business groups opened donation drives for "national reconstruction." A suburban mothers' club donated twelve wedding rings; sugar refinery employees gathered 1.3 million escudos; and the Association of Racehorse Owners presented authorities with a check for 15 million.[3] The enthusiasm spilled into orchestrated public events, such as the 1974 Festival of Song in Valparaiso, where thousands of voices joined in chorus after chorus of an anthem that began, "Free, we are free . . ."

Occasionally a prominent citizen would come face to face with the indignity of military rule. One distinguished lawyer recounted with horror how, after parking in an illegal zone, he was forced into a paddy wagon and manhandled by several policemen, who snickered when he threatened to call their commander. Conservative congressmen who had strongly backed the coup were indignant to find their offices locked and their papers dumped in boxes outside.

Because many sons and daughters of the upper and middle classes had been caught up in Allende's revolution, quite a few affluent Chileans had to face disturbing news that a nephew or godchild had been arrested. Desperate relatives would ask a lawyer or politician to make some gesture to the authorities, and a call would go out to an old military crony or ministry official. Sometimes it made a difference, but usually the reply was a curt dismissal or sheepish admission of impotence.

Pilar Armanet, a university professor from a family long active in conservative politics, recalled her younger sister being picked up by the DINA and her parents assuming their connections would save her. "Former senators called, even a Supreme Court judge," Armanet said—all to no avail. "These were people who had always managed things, whose names were on street signs and wine bottles, and they could do nothing."[4] The girl was eventually released but forced to leave the country.

Just as often, influential relatives turned their backs on accused leftists, believing that the young hotheads deserved a scare. Brought up to trust authority, people assumed that anyone truly "innocent" would not be mistreated. Jorge Ovalle, a centrist lawyer and legal adviser to the junta, persuaded a friend's nervous son not to flee the country. "I told him the government wouldn't persecute him for his ideas, and I believed it," Ovalle recalled bitterly. Several days later, the youth was seized by armed men; he was never seen again.[5]

The anti-Marxist fervor ravaged friendships and family relations; marriages collapsed and sons were disinherited. Hernán Gutiérrez, ambassador to Colombia at the time of the coup, received a call in Bogotá from an acquaintance in Santiago, warning him that the man's own son was an "escaped extremist" and might be heading across the border.

But the vast majority of affluent and comfortable families were never touched by repression. Nightly curfew, an inconvenience that sent diners careening down highways to reach home by 11:00 P.M., also insulated "nice" people from the manhunts and raids taking place in the dark. "If you were trapped at home, it was easy to deny what you couldn't see," said Elizabeth Lira, a psychologist and human rights activist.[6]

Even after such restrictions were lifted, the well-to-do remained isolated. Women circulated in districts where private schools and shopping malls were located; men commuted in fast cars to downtown offices or new suburban complexes. "We created ghettos that lasted for years," said Lucía Santa Cruz, the conservative journalist. "There were schools for children of dissidents and schools for children of the establishment. There was absolutely no contact with people who thought differently; they became phantoms who had no face."[7]

Abdicating moral and political leadership, the conservative elite gladly ceded control to military authorities. People were afraid of what their "special" society had unleashed, and they no longer trusted their institutions. Convinced that a Soviet-style revolution had been imminent, they longed only for order. Decent, educated people were poisoned by irrational hatred that permitted them to regard leftists as inhuman.

"During the U.P., my dad put up bars on the house because he was afraid the communists would come and rape us. My mother kept saying it was like World War Two. So when the coup came and people were detained, we were all in favor of it," recalled Anita Cortés, a thirty-year-old advertising executive. "None of us believed what happened at the National Stadium," where thousands of Chileans were detained after the coup and hundreds tortured. "Even today, some people in my office still think all communists deserve to die."[8]

Affluent women harbored an especially visceral wrath, and interviews would take a nasty turn when the subject of Allende came up. Even after fifteen years there was a testy, defensive edge. "You weren't here then; you never had to stand in line, so you can't possibly understand how we feel," a visitor would be informed. At one pro-Pinochet rally, an elegant woman stabbed a lacquered fingernail at a foreigner and warned, "If the Russian *rotos* [rabble] try to take over again, we'll have another eleventh, just like the first one."

For years, "human rights" was a synonym for Marxist propaganda among the elite, and the few prominent individuals who spoke out against repression were shunned. Jaime Castillo confided, "I have friends from infancy who have not greeted me in public since 1973. They call me a traitor to my class."[9] Even after incidents like the Letelier murder received worldwide publicity, many affluent Chileans simply refused to believe that the government was involved. "People who benefited from the coup wanted desperately to believe the government," observed Lira. "It takes a long time to accept horrible facts, because once you know, you cannot remain indifferent."

Since there was little official recognition of human rights abuses, it was possible for sheltered and incurious Chileans to remain ignorant of gruesome cases years after they had become household words in other social sectors and abroad. At a conference in Washington in 1989, a group of Americans discussing a new book about General Arellano's helicopter tour were joined by a Chilean economist and former Pinochet cabinet member, who politely asked them to explain what the incident was about. In 1990, when the bodies of prisoners shot at the Pisagua concentration camp were unearthed and shown on television, a conservative intellectual confided that his influential parents and their friends "couldn't believe this had really happened in Chile."

Some well-to-do citizens, initially horrified by reports of repression, were soon seduced by the comfort and order of authoritarianism. Across dinner tables and tennis courts, people agreed that Chile wasn't "ready for democracy," and few were willing to face the opprobrium of employers and peers just to salve a troubled conscience. One banker confided that for years he hid his concern for human rights in order to avoid jeopardizing his social and professional position. "In meetings, I often said things I didn't believe, so as not to go against the tide," he confessed. "The truth is, we were all afraid."

While genteel Chileans kept a discreet distance from dictatorship, less scrupulous social climbers gravitated toward the new centers of power. Mediocre figures who would never have risen in a democracy were named judges, deans, and mayors, replacing purged leftists and Christian Democrats. The arrogance of power made petty tyrants of minor bureaucrats and created a new cult of authoritarian privilege. Narrow access to the top exacerbated the old tendency to discredit and criticize.

For some social climbers, it became important to have a friend in the secret police, and good military connections assured that if trouble arose—a drunk-driving charge, a questionable political connection from college days—the matter could be quietly resolved. Desire to prove loyalty to the regime also tempted people to spy on each other, and small-town officials eagerly composed lists of "suspect" individuals for the authorities. "There was a mad scramble to turn people in. Everyone wanted to ingratiate themselves, to show they were on the front lines," recalled a lawyer who quit government service in disgust.[10]

It took years for Chile's elite to peek out of its ghettos and inch toward "national reconciliation." Lucía Santa Cruz took a first, bold step across the divide by choosing a Christian Democratic doctor. But in 1984 her children begged her not to go to a conference with Communist leaders, afraid she would be killed. "I never taught them that," she said sadly. "Today kids pick up fear at school. It's in the atmosphere."

ON the other side of this invisible barricade, the world of the left crumbled in despair and defeat. A generation of workers, students, and intellectuals had lost its leaders and its illusions. Racked by paranoia and guilt, banned from public life and hunted like criminals, survivors mourned alone or in small groups. Many drifted in psychological exile, unable to accept the death of Allende's revolution or adjust to life under military rule.

"It was like the death of a son, the end of a world," recalled Manuel Antonio Garretón, a leftist academic who was ejected from his position as a vice-rector at the Catholic University. "Everyone reacted differently. Some sank into terrible depressions; some became paralyzed with fear. My remedy was to stay as active as possible, talking on the telephone constantly and writing as much as I could."[11]

Fear of persecution was exacerbated by isolation and lack of reliable news. As Popular Unity supporters exchanged arrest reports in crude telephone codes, rumors fueled wild estimates of repression; many believed for years that tens of thousands had been massacred. Terrified of being labeled "subversive," young people burned revolutionary posters and shaved off their beards. In one popular joke, a white rabbit hopped desperately away from some elephant hunters, crying, "How can I convince them I'm not an elephant?"

The Allende era had been an intensely public experience, with an endless stream of political activity and cafés bustling until dawn. The coup brought down a swift steel curtain on this frenzied drama.

Bookstalls closed, nightlife vanished, and radio stations replaced Andean protest ballads with Mexican *mariachis* and American pop songs. Santiago became a tense, subdued city where commuters rode buses in silence and restaurant conversations were held in murmurs.

Authorities swiftly suppressed all traces of political life. Public meetings were banned and newspapers and magazines shut down. Teams of volunteers scrubbed graffiti off the walls. Military officers were placed in charge of universities, sociology and political science texts were seized from libraries, and thousands of teachers and students were dismissed.

"The first years of dictatorship were like putting society in a straitjacket or a psychiatric ward. We were confused and anguished, docile and waiting to take orders," observed Marco Antonio de la Parra. "At first it was a relief, but as with any prolonged hospitalization, people regressed; they became more dependent and fearful. A long-term paralysis set in."[12]

Brooding in darkened parlors and cramped prison cells, former activists debated why their revolution had fallen apart. Suddenly, the subtle distinctions of theory that had splintered the left into enemy camps seemed absurdly trivial. Socialists who had cursed Christian Democrats as "fascists" belatedly discovered what the word really meant; middle-class progressives found they were no "better" than shantytown communists as far as the regime was concerned.

Under extreme duress, ideological differences were cast aside, and shared suffering forged bonds of moral support. María Teresa Lladser, a university instructor, had been excoriated by a colleague as insufficiently radical in the superheated precoup atmosphere. The next time she saw him, many of their co-workers had been arrested and both were in danger of losing their jobs. "He looked like a frightened child. We put our arms around each other and wept," she recalled.[13]

Just as often, however, the atmosphere of fear and failure undermined relationships between people who had struggled side by side for years. A network of proregime spies and informants reached into factories and campuses, sowing mistrust among co-workers, neighbors, and friends. The thought that someone was watching made many Chileans avoid organized activities and shun acquaintances who had been picked up by the police.

Labor and political activists rarely dared visit each other's houses; instead, they would meet on street corners or in parks. "The myth of the omnipresent security apparatus became so great that no one wanted to take risks," recalled Carlos Gálvez, a longtime Socialist labor organizer and telephone company accountant. "You would confide only in people you were absolutely sure of, and even then there was always a seed of doubt."[14]

In working-class neighborhoods, residents grew accustomed to the sight of soldiers ransacking homes or rounding up all adult males for questioning. In some neighborhoods, repression reinforced political ties among the vanquished; in others, it sowed hostility and suspicion as families became identified as "extremists" or "Pinochetistas." Rumors spread that community telephones were tapped, and neighbors stopped speaking to each other. In 1983, when the first national protests broke out, residents banging pots and pans in disapproval of the regime were astonished when their next-door neighbors joined them.

René Escobar, a Socialist bookkeeper in Allende's forestry development agency, was imprisoned and then blacklisted from professional work after the coup, so he and some friends opened a shoemaking workshop in his house in San Miguel. But his neighbors repeatedly informed the authorities that they were manufacturing guns. "The troops raided us three times; they took all the history and philosophy books my father had left me," the grizzled man of sixty recalled with pain. "One officer suggested we move away, but I had been a leader of the neighborhood since 1957. Why should I be forced to leave?"[15]

Many people who had been active in politics for years simply went into hibernation. Edgardo Cavíz moved from La Florida, the lower-middle-class suburb where he had been a local Popular Unity leader, to the opposite end of Santiago. There he became a recluse, working in meat-packing plants and avoiding contact with his neighbors. "I spent years swearing at the television set," he confided in 1989.[16]

For thousands of people who emerged from prisons or experiences of torture, the sense of isolation was especially overwhelming. The government denied what had happened to them, society refused to acknowledge it, and even intimate friends often shrank from knowing the details. Sexual torture produced shame and withdrawal, ruining marital relations. Many victims retreated into a tormented internal exile, haunted by nightmares but pretending to be normal for fear of alienating those around them.

Guillermo, a shy man who spent two years in a prison camp and several more in exile, went to work in a downtown business office when he returned, and never told his story to a single colleague. "It is like having two existences; it is emotionally exhausting," he said, speaking softly with his door closed. "I feel so much repressed rage, but I still don't dare tell people I was a prisoner. I haven't yet broken the stigma. One day it will all come out, but for now I feel I have to keep it a secret."[17]

THE most wrenching form of segregation was exile itself. Within two years of the coup, more than fourteen thousand Chileans and their families had received diplomatic asylum, been expelled directly from prison, or moved abroad for fear of persecution. By 1979, the official exile figure had doubled, and some estimates placed it far higher.[18] Several countries were especially receptive to large numbers of refugees: Sweden and France accepted more than five thousand and three thousand, respectively, and many thousands poured back and forth across the border with Argentina during the period of military rule.[19]

The Pinochet government painted the exodus in rosy tones, describing former Allende "bosses" as enjoying luxurious sojourns in Europe and prisoners being "liberated" to live abroad. A number of exiles did receive academic scholarships from the World University Service, and a handful entered such elite institutions as Harvard or the Sorbonne. Many exiled artists were active in promoting foreign opposition to Pinochet, and some built international followings. Isabel Allende, the former president's second cousin, wrote surreal political novels in Venezuela; the Inti-Illimani folksong group galvanized audiences in Italy.

For dedicated leftists, exile became a full-time political activity. In Moscow, Chileans beamed a radio program to Latin America that grew into a nightly ritual to news-starved Santiago listeners. In East Berlin, Ricardo Núñez lived a frantic existence as secretary-general of the Chilean Socialist party. "We worked fourteen hours a day, maintaining contact with Chile, checking on the fate of prisoners, building links with human rights groups, denouncing the crimes of the junta, and reflecting on our own past mistakes," Núñez recalled in 1989.[20]

Political work abroad was dangerous. Exiles in Europe and Latin America were harassed by DINA agents, sometimes working with local security services (Argentina, Brazil) or right-wing extremist groups (Italy, United States). Those who gave testimony of torture at the United Nations were denounced as traitors. The attacks on

Bernardo Leighton and Orlando Letelier sent panic through exile communities. A few hundred committed revolutionaries sought out a dangerous existence, joining the Sandinista army in Nicaragua, guerrilla forces in Argentina, or training camps in Cuba, Eastern Europe, and northern Africa to prepare for a clandestine return to Chile.

The experience of most exiles, however, was neither thrilling nor glamorous. Crusaders torn from lives of intense activity and purpose were cast into anonymity and dependence; torture victims arrived in cities where life was maddeningly normal and indifferent; professionals were forced to work on assembly lines. Most social activities revolved around fellow exiles, who continually debated why the U.P. had collapsed or who idealized the revolution they had left behind, along with Chile's snowcapped mountains and spicy empanada pastries.

"The exile lives in a world of the past, in a permanent state of bereavement," said Liliana Muñoz, a Chilean psychologist who moved to England after the coup and wrote a doctoral thesis based on interviews with other exiles. Many described feelings of rage, helplessness, guilt, loneliness, and grief over leaving home. Watching the Andes recede out the airplane window, one woman told Muñoz she felt "as if an umbilical cord had been cut." Once settled in England, she recounted, "I felt my mind becoming empty. I thought I was slowly dying."[21]

Exile imposed extraordinary burdens on marriages, and a large percentage of couples separated. One woman, tortured and expelled to France, waited for her husband to be released from prison while she scrubbed floors in a Paris warehouse—only to learn he had fallen in love with someone else. After attempting to commit suicide, she married a Frenchman and cut all ties with her native land.

Some host countries were hospitable and sympathetic, but even in affluent cultures, daily life could be alienating. Few uprooted peasant or union leaders were able to master complex new languages or rise beyond menial labor. Jaime Troncoso Valdés, a Socialist who helped organize exiles in Sweden, said not more than fifty families became fully integrated into Swedish society. "They never learned the language, so they became mute," he said. "The tie with Chile was all that kept them going."[22]

Ardent leftists were often disillusioned by their first real taste of socialism, whether the blandness of Scandinavia or the heavy-handed climate of Eastern Europe. Almost all who moved to Romania, an especially oppressive regime, soon resettled elsewhere. For Soledad, a Socialist who spent fourteen years in Sweden, it was the boredom of utopia that drove her mad.

"We had our basic needs met, but we were cut off from our professions, our plans, our purpose; we became parasites in a paternalistic state," she recalled in 1989. "Imagine the change from being at the heart of national politics to working in a meat-packing plant where people are discussing soap operas! It was like a womb; everything was provided, but there was no spontaneity. I learned that paradise is never perfect."[23]

Most exiles were not allowed to return to Chile for at least a full decade after the coup; many of their passports were marked with an *L* (for *listado,* or "listed") to signify they could not be granted an entry visa. The 1980 constitution banned all returnees who might promote Marxist or "antifamily" doctrines, or whose presence might "act against the interests of Chile." Not until two years later did the government begin publishing lists, a few hundred names at a time, of those eligible to return.

Sometimes the rationale for such restrictions was absurdly cruel. Luis Tejeda, an elderly Communist lawyer from Mulchén known for his eloquent, unpaid defenses of the poor, was forced to leave Chile virtually penniless. Falling ill in Europe, he asked for permission to return but was repeatedly turned down. Badly burned in a Vienna hotel fire, the old man died without seeing Chile again.[24]

By the time the exile ban was substantially eased, many families had lost the desire to return. Life in affluent welfare states was undeniably pleasant, whereas Chile's future seemed uncertain. Children made foreign friends and stopped speaking Spanish; many resented their parents' obsession with Chile or developed a cultural identity crisis of their own.

"My memories of Chile were of my mother crying, men in uniforms searching for my father. In France I wanted to put the violence behind me. I wanted to become French," recalled Luciano, a sober man of twenty-six. But in 1988 he decided to return home alone, and went to live in a group house for single returnees. "I had to come back and face this mythical country, where they said the wine was richer, the land greener," he explained. "I had to find out if I was still Chilean."[25]

Many families found that the return to Chile was like a second exile. After the initial euphoria of airport welcomes, it wasn't so easy to find a niche or to adjust to fifteen years of change. Old friends who had stayed behind were both envious and superior, noble intentions vanished in a thicket of mundane problems, and the ideological toughness that had helped them survive overseas seemed anachronistic.

Camilo Cortés, removed from prison in 1977 and forced onto a plane, landed at Kennedy Airport with five dollars in his pocket. Slowly, he built a meaningful life caring for elderly Hispanics in a Connecticut nursing home, and when he and his wife learned they were free to return in 1988, they were deeply torn. "We had dreamed of Chile every day, but we had grown so close to the old people," the stout little pastor recalled, pacing his tiny parlor in Talcahuano. "One lady gave us a doll that meant everything to her; she had no one else but us. Now that we're back, we keep wondering, have we come home or have we left it?"[26]

THE fear and the hostility that divided Chilean society were deliberately exploited by the regime to justify the coup, counter foreign criticism, and foster domestic acceptance of prolonged military control. At first, Chile's new leaders appeared to encourage reconciliation, speaking of the need for a "healing process" and pledging there would be "no winners and losers"; just citizens united to rebuild the nation. In fact, however, they worked assiduously to keep the wounds open.

Official propaganda stressed the violence and chaos of the Allende years and depicted the coup as a glorious act of liberation. One brochure showed people waiting in bread lines while Allende stashed whisky and pornography in private hideaways. Another book contrasted scenes of Chile past and present, with hyperbolic captions. Yesterday there had been scarcity, "chaos, ambulances, violence"; today there was order, plenty, and "a new morality." Yesterday workers and students had been turned into "puppets of international communism"; today they were happy and hardworking.

For months after the coup, authorities warned that "nests of extremists" remained at large and staged elaborate displays of captured weapons. The most ambitious effort to justify the coup was Plan Z, the alleged plot to "exterminate" the right. Although the conspiracy was never proven, many Chileans found it plausible after months of listening to intoxicated MIRistas exhort the masses to insurrection. A social worker said her cousin confessed years later that "she thought I had Plan Z hidden in my desk"; a lawyer's maid told him she, too, was on the death list. Apocryphal or not, Plan Z became a fearful symbol of what might have been.

Reminding citizens constantly that a state of war existed, the regime portrayed measures restricting civil liberties as necessary to safeguard order. Women were encouraged to accept curfews as a patriotic sacrifice—with the added benefit of keeping husbands home at night. One edict requested all citizens to make the "patriotic contribution" of turning in any foreign "extremists" and "fanaticized Chileans" they spotted. "Denounce them," it urged. "Contribute to cleansing your homeland of undesirables."[27]

As criticism of human rights abuses intensified overseas, so did the regime's diatribe against foreign interference and Marxist expansionism. Stung by criticism from the international press and the United Nations, Pinochet condemned both as tools of a vast Red conspiracy. The official response to all reports of torture and disappearance was to dismiss them as leftist fabrications. When a British doctor, Sheila Cassidy, told the UN she had been tortured in a Chilean prison, regime officials called it a "product of her imagination."[28]

Under the tutelage of the secret police, propaganda took on a more sinister aspect. In a scheme aimed at refuting charges of "disappearances" in 1975, Chilean agents planted accounts in the Brazilian and Argentine press that 119 MIRistas had sneaked out of Chile and been killed in guerrilla-linked violence. Santiago tabloids trumpeted the story with glee, but the reports were vague and unconfirmed, and the two foreign newspaper editions that printed them proved to be elaborate hoaxes. Moreover, many of the listed individuals had been seen in Chilean police custody.

"We were certain they were all former prisoners. The names were copied from our own lists, with the same misspellings," said the lawyer Hernán Montealegre, who tracked down the fraudulent newspapers in Buenos Aries and Curitiba, Brazil, and discovered that secret police from all three countries had been involved in the plot. "It was a chilling thing, totally concocted to trick the international press," he said.[29]

In another effort to undermine the credibility of human rights groups, the government compiled a list of allegedly disappeared people who, it said, were either alive or had died of natural causes. Sergio Diez, Chile's envoy to the United Nations, read out the list in triumph—and indeed, several individuals had been mistakenly identified as missing. But three years later the bodies of seven people he had listed as dead of natural causes—with medical examiners' certificates to prove it—were discovered in the lime ovens of Lonquén.[30]

A CRUCIAL accessory to propaganda was the establishment press, which for years served as an eager mouthpiece for most regime policies, published unquestioning versions of the official "truth," and ignored or ridiculed opposition points of view. Any criticism was gentle, between the lines, and couched in terms of correcting mistakes in order to preserve the grander aims of Pinochet and his men.

The printed word in Chile was dominated by *El Mercurio,* the conservative morning newspaper founded in 1900. During the U.P., its owner, Augustín Edwards, an eccentric millionaire, moved to Connecticut and collaborated with the Nixon administration to undermine Allende. With aid from the CIA, *El Mercurio* perfected such techniques as juxtaposing photos of Allende with scenes of slaughtered animals.[31] "We did everything we could to provoke a coup," boasted the paper's former editor, Arturo Fontaine.[32]

Once Pinochet was in power, covert American funding was dropped, but *El Mercurio* became a bastion of support for the regime, full of flowery references to "His Excellency" and lectures on the benefits of military rule. Edwards, returning to Chile in 1979, breakfasted weekly with the president. The editors criticized several scandalous cases of repression, including the Letelier murder, but they made no effort to investigate most military abuses, while dutifully printing official descriptions of crimes by "extremist delinquents."

The paper also fervently promoted the regime's neoconservative economic policies, becoming a daily bible of free-market solutions. Ironically, Edwards's fortunes fell steadily and the paper became deeply indebted to the Chilean State Bank, giving the regime extra leverage. In 1982, when Fontaine criticized the rigidly fixed exchange rate and the murder of Tucapel Jiménez, Edwards fired him and hired a new team of Pinochet devotees.[33]

"Our idea was to be critical collaborators, to be loyal to the government but to warn them about especially bad things," recalled Fontaine. But even mild criticism provoked tirades from La Moneda, and the staff was split between moderates and hard-liners. When the showdown came, the former editor said, "suddenly I was out and the paper was an open plaza occupied by enemy troops. Edwards opted for total submission."[34]

Another pillar of the pro-Pinochet press was *Qué Pasa,* a sophisticated weekly magazine that combined glowing official profiles with cautious criticism. After several years of unabashed regime boosterism and bleak retrospectives on the U.P., the editors aligned with moderate conservatives against Colonel Contreras, whose abusive tactics they saw as a threat to economic progress.[35]

Their style was subtle. A 1975 puff piece about a detention camp where inmates picnicked under trees was followed by a "letter to the editor" proposing a similar tour of the notorious, secret DINA camp next door. But with the announcement of the 119 dead MIRistas, *Qué Pasa*'s tone changed. An indignant editorial head-lined "Are 119 Chileans Missing?" cast doubt on the official reports and asserted that even "extremists" had rights as human beings. "That was a watershed for us," the magazine's founder, Hernán Cubillos, confided years later.[36]

Despite often fawning coverage, the conservative press faced a constant battle with unpredictable, petty censorship—and more violent forms of intimidation. At *Ercilla,* another proregime mag-azine, an issue exploring university problems was seized and burned. In 1977, when *Qué Pasa* published the testimony of a teenager who had been kidnapped by the DINA, the editor, Jaime Martí-nez, was seized in his car by two armed men and barely escaped.

The tameness of the establishment media was also a product of laziness and self-defense. "It was easy to write from official bulle-tins, to fill an apparent journalistic role," explained Martínez. "Those covering the government tended to become friends with the authorities and lose their sense of aggression." In constantly second-guessing what the government would permit, editors also practiced an insidious form of self-censorship, squelching stories about Pinochet's family and referring to the armed forces only in respectful tones. "We were reacting to the extreme nature of jour-nalism during the U.P.," reflected Martínez, "but perhaps we passed to the other extreme."[37]

A far more important propaganda tool was television. Only a handful of Chileans could afford magazines; about 700,000 read a daily paper.[38] But by 1982, with heavy tariffs on foreign tele-visions virtually eliminated, nearly 78 percent of all households owned a set—the one part of Pinochet's 1980 election-night prom-ise that was fulfilled.[39] This was the ideal medium for a modern authoritarian government: it kept people home, created a direct link between the individual and the state, filtered reality through an appealing prism, and encouraged consumption instead of thought.[40]

Under Pinochet, state-controlled TV was crammed with soap operas, military parades, and soccer games. No political debate was allowed, and the most popular show was a variety special called "Giant Saturdays." Station managers were replaced by retired military officers or right-wing journalists like Gonzalo Eguiguren, who believed his mission at TV Chile was to "serenify spirits" and unite citizens behind the regime.[41] News was a placebo of official announcements, with periodic exposés of leftist violence accompanied by ominous music. In 1983, while economic crisis and street protests raged, a typical newscast featured ministers cutting ribbons on housing projects and Pinochet receiving visitors.[42]

One channel, operated by the Catholic University, attempted to maintain editorial independence. Raúl Hasbún, an iconoclastic priest who ran the station at the time of the coup, refused orders to submit staff and scripts for approval by the university's military rector, protesting "the canonization of audacity and fear." But Hasbún was fired for his outburst, and the station retreated to tame programming for many years.[43]

WHILE progovernment media played cat-and-mouse with La Moneda, the voice of opposition was silenced. All Popular Unity periodicals and radio stations were seized after the coup, and for four years the only critical journalism came from small private publications such as *Mensaje*, a journal of the Jesuit community. One centrist newsweekly, the Christian Democrat–affiliated *Hoy*, was permitted to publish in 1977, and other dissident magazines appeared after 1981. But the first opposition newspaper did not win approval until 1986, and two more years passed before antigovernment views could be heard on television.

While attempting to monopolize information, the government was careful to conduct most of its antimedia attacks within legal bounds. In 1977, the regime decreed that all new publications would require prior approval, but the government communications director reassured an interviewer that all proposals would be passed as long as they "do not act against Christian morals and do not violate the political recess." Aside from emergency restrictions, he added, "I can affirm categorically that in this country freedom of the press exists."[44]

Other decrees, however, gave authorities even more sweeping censorship powers. The law of internal state security allowed officials to suspend any publication if they felt its reportage "tends to create alarm or unhappiness" or defied limits decreed for "reasons of internal order." In 1979, when *Hoy* printed interviews with two exiled Socialist leaders, it was suspended for two months on grounds of defying the regime's legitimacy.[45] "We were trying to bring back civilized debate, but we were the first thorn in the side of the regime, and we were totally alone," recalled Emilio Filippi, the founding editor.[46]

In the early 1980s, the government permitted a number of opposition magazines to open. But new publications like *Apsi* and *Análisis*, which investigated abuses and attacked economic policy, faced constant harassment. When protests erupted·in 1983, the media were barred from "promoting news related to terrorist or extremist acts." In 1984, all opposition magazines were suspended under the renewed state of siege, and by 1986 more than thirty journalists had been prosecuted and some jailed for "offending the armed forces."

The odyssey of one magazine, *Apsi,* illustrates the contest of wills that raged as journalists attempted to report the news and officials to control it. An international bulletin that started with three hundred subscribers and a volunteer staff, *Apsi* spent months in court, arguing without success for the right to cover domestic events. Undaunted, the editors tested the limits of the regime's tolerance, publishing foreign news cables about Chile and printing blank spaces when articles were censored.

"Before we could inform, we had to win the struggle to exist. After that, it was a constant, dangerous ballet," recalled the associate editor, Sergio Marras. Some aggressive exposés provoked no formal reprisal, including cover stories on torture and Pinochet's Melocotón mansion. But in 1987, when *Apsi* published a humor issue with a caricature of Pinochet as Louis XIV on the cover, Marras and the chief editor were charged as "intellectual extremists" and jailed for two months.[47]

Another embattled medium was radio, on which millions relied for news. Radio Cooperativa, a Christian Democrat–owned station, was shut down repeatedly for broadcasting news of protests and strikes and nearly driven bankrupt by official pressure against advertisers. "They tried to asphyxiate us, but we survived because we had credibility," recalled Genaro Arriagada, Cooperativa's president. "We had no money, no ads, and the largest listening audience in Chile!"[48]

Attacks on press freedom elicited mild, pro forma protests from the establishment media, but little public clamor followed. The rightist elite dismissed dissident journals as propaganda organs, and many ordinary Chileans found the reassuring tone of official news a blessing after the vicious media wars of the U.P. In 1982, when aggressive press probing led to the release of an accused murderer, Supreme Court Justice Bórquez made a well-received speech demanding greater curbs on the media.[49]

The 1986 death-squad kidnapping and murder of José Carrasco, foreign-news editor at *Análisis,* aroused instant condemnation among regime opponents at home and abroad. But because the crime followed the ambush of Pinochet's motorcade, and Carrasco was a member of the MIR, the impact was muted. "Most journalists killed during this period have also been leftist political actors," pointed out Martínez. "This regime reacted harshly against all its enemies, no matter what their profession."

INTELLECTUAL repression affected all forms of expression, including books, theater, and films. Some early attempts at literary censorship were laughable: José Ortega y Gasset's *The Revolt of the Masses,* one of Pinochet's favorite works of philosophy, was confiscated; authorities imprisoned the author of a novel called *The Assassins of the Suicide,* until they discovered that it had been published months before Allende's death.[50] Later, book banning became more systematic, but not always linked to literary content. In 1977, the works of the acclaimed Latin American novelists Gabriel García Marquez and Mario Vargas Llosa were prohibited—because the writers had verbally criticized the Pinochet regime.

Restrictions on publishing domestic books were severe, and requirements were confusing and labyrinthine. Few drafts were rejected outright, but many were allowed to languish in the bureaucracy, and some sensitive works, such as a legal history of the Lonquén case, were impounded for months. Aconcagua Press, a small dissident publishing house run by Claudio Orrego and Genaro Arriagada, was sued for printing books with critical essays on state economic policy and human rights. In turn, Arriagada blasted an official "culture of banality" aimed at making people isolated and apathetic.[51]

Only a few establishment intellectuals spoke out against censorship. Luis Sánchez Latorre, president of the national Society of Writers, charged that repression of ideas had brought Chile to a "state of abysmal somnambulism."[52] But most men of arts and letters were reluctant to offend the authorities, while those with official sinecures found elaborate rationale for censorship. Enrique Campos, state director of libraries, insisted that official controls were "the price we must pay for not having reached the level of political and social maturity that the ideal of free coexistence demands."[53]

Foreign films were heavily censored and replaced with innocuous action films from Hollywood, although the review board sometimes missed its mark: *Fiddler on the Roof* and *Day of the Jackal* were banned for depicting military abuses and regicide, but *The Conformist*, a more subtle indictment of fascism, was approved. And when *One Flew over the Cuckoo's Nest*, a riveting portrayal of institutional authoritarianism, arrived in 1975, it was sold out in Santiago cinemas for weeks.

The theater also suffered; a 20 percent surtax was put on all plays considered "noncultural," including Beckett's *Waiting for Godot*, and controversial productions were harassed. *Leaves of Parra*, a protest play staged in a circus tent, was shut down on the pretext that it violated sanitation codes. After a businessman donated special bathrooms for the facility, the tent mysteriously burned down.

Yet many inspired young playwrights were spawned by dictatorship, and theater soon emerged as a powerful if elite source of protest. In 1976, David Benavente's *Pedro, Juan and Diego* portrayed the humiliation of state antipoverty programs. By the 1980s, Santiago stages were bristling with abstract condemnations of military rule. Marco Antonio de la Parra's *The Raw, the Cooked, the Rotten* created a surreal authoritarian microcosm whose characters, waiters in an empty restaurant, were obsessed with order and death.

"From a total vacuum, there was an explosion of culture at the margin of official life," recalled de la Parra, whose plays were first performed at the University of Chile medical school while he was a student. Rather than rail against dictatorship, he explored the passive response of ordinary Chileans, the self-pity of the left, and the banal world of the torturer. In one drama, *The Secret Obscenity of Every Day*, the theme of torture was a continuous, existential joke.

IT was relatively easy for the regime to suppress the cultural legacy of the Allende years, but Chile's new leaders had a more ambitious goal in mind. They sought to create a new culture based on values of patriotism, order, hard work, godliness, and respect for authority—to build a harmonious society where social classes and political parties would not compete but cooperate for the common good.

Shortly after the coup, Pinochet vowed to spearhead a "moral cleansing" and "change in mentality" throughout society, and soon a government information office was diffusing the new values through press releases and seminars with civic groups. "We are on a campaign of habits," explained the office director, an army colonel. "Little by little [civilian leaders] will be totally imbued with the thinking of the government, so it can reach the entire population. . . ."[54]

To critics, the regime's hidden agenda was to create a "culture of authoritarianism" in which each citizen would conform to the dictates of those in power, never questioning their ultimate purpose. The government and its supporters, contended the sociologist José Joaquín Brunner, sought to mold a society of "good workers, good citizens, and good patriots," and to replace the purged leftist intelligentsia with a new elite of apolitical, professional achievers.[55]

On an elite level, the regime attempted to create an "official" artistic culture. State publishing houses and cultural institutes produced lavish books on Chilean military history and anti-Allende documentary films. The society pages of *El Mercurio* featured gala fund-raisers for the Municipal Theater and other worthy causes, glittering with wives of military and civilian officials.

The major thrust of the cultural crusade, however, was aimed at a less upscale market. Its core was a panoply of civic groups whose mission was to channel official values to ordinary citizens— and popular energy into regime projects. The Feminine Voluntary Enlistment, the National Secretariat of Youth, and the Councils of Neighbors all promoted the norms of a conservative, vertical society, training midlevel leaders to become role models for members at large.[56]

One of the most ambitious efforts to change the Chilean mentality was aimed at women. Traditionally preoccupied with order and stability, wives and mothers had been a key element of support for the coup. "The Chilean woman suffered . . . the most terrible consequences of the regime of the Popular Unity," Pinochet asserted in one speech. "Thus she was transformed into a solid foundation of my government, which liberated her from the nightmare."[57]

It was First Lady Lucía Hiriart, however, who took up the banner of feminine support for military rule, reigning over a network of forty-nine charities anchored by the National Secretariat of Women and the national Mothers' Centers (Centros de Madres, or CEMA). These agencies, managed by wives of military officials, mirrored the official chain of command, and their parallel army of volunteer housewives, dressed in neat, smock-like "uniforms," grew to a force of over twenty thousand.

On one level, the goal was strictly charitable: ladies in lilac or pink helping the elderly or teaching poor women a craft. But there was a second, parallel goal: to promote and reward loyalty to the regime; to inculcate anticommunist and "family" values; and to replace an egalitarian model of civic participation with a vertical one. "Women must think of Chile and forget about politics," explained a general's wife shortly after the coup; her friends in the volunteer movement spoke of helping women to "listen to the authorities" and find new meaning in the "function God gave us."[58]

Critics charged that these programs preyed on needy women, demanding political loyalty in exchange for social services and seeking to convert housewives into vessels for official ideology by preaching conservatism and passivity.[59] "Women belong to CEMA, but they don't participate. The institution assists them, it does not represent them," wrote the sociologists Norbert Lechner and Susana Levy.[60]

Officials claimed that CEMA had been far more manipulated under Allende, but in fact the new forms of control were much stronger. Where CEMA had once aimed to organize and represent women, it now became a paternalistic structure. The proceeds of its handicraft sales were not made public, army officers worked in top CEMA management, and computerized files helped mobilize members for political purposes.[61]

Program leaders proudly acknowledged that their mission was more than philanthropic. In 1988, Eliana Trabuco, a general's widow and official of the Women's Secretariat, explained that it was crucial to restore the "values of family and fatherland" lost during the U.P. Yet she reacted indignantly when asked about the first lady's parallel army. "People abroad have put a lot of emphasis on our uniforms, but you can't go into a poor neighborhood dressed like this," she said, indicating her tweed suit. "A uniform lessens the distance."[62]

Strongly Catholic and antifeminist, volunteer leaders sought to stimulate women's "self-development"—but never to the point of challenging male authority at home or in government. The ideal homemaker should be aware of her civic and patriotic duty, but obedient as a wife, mother, and citizen. "Men are the ones with power; women should project themselves through their children," explained one volunteer.[63]

At critical moments, thousands of CEMA members could be marshaled to appear at proregime rallies, cheering and waving banners. During antiregime protests in 1984, Lucía Hiriart exhorted volunteers to wage a "holy war" against a renewed Marxist threat. "You cannot fail in the moments when the fatherland needs you, when the peace of homes is threatened!" she cried. In 1987, with CEMA boasting 215,000 members, she called on its leaders to "carry the political offensive" and help her husband win a new term in power.[64]

Many women expressed gratitude to CEMA for teaching them skills and easing their access to social services; a small core became fervent Pinochetistas. But in private, many members confessed they resented the high-handedness of the "ladies of colors," and others joined "alternative" mothers' centers that served as focal points of community opposition to the regime. The cult of devotion to Lucía Hiriart was not always what it seemed either; one CEMA member from Nuñoa confided that whenever the volunteers left, she and her friends turned the first lady's portrait to the wall.

Other efforts to create a proregime culture met with similar, limited success. First, officials underestimated the strength of Chile's democratic and ideological roots and failed to realize that forcing people to attend parades might arouse more resentment than patriotic fervor. Flattered by a few cheerleaders, they mistook others' compliance for enthusiasm and dismissed as "extremist" the alternative community groups that nurtured seeds of dissent among the poor.

Second, the regime's mistrust of mass politics blocked efforts to organize "civic-military movements," such as those proposed by aides like Federico Willoughby and supporters like Pablo Rodríguez of Fatherland and Liberty. Regime hard-liners feared they would prove uncontrollable, while moderates worried about creating the appearance of totalitarian rule. Even though Pinochet periodically urged followers to form such a movement, each attempt withered for lack of an official imprimatur.

Finally, the regime's message was hollow: its rhetorical values did not square with the suspicious, fearful society created by military rule. There could be no true civic "healing" or patriotic "rebuilding" as long as Pinochet's anticommunist harangues, repressive actions, and designs on permanent power kept the nation divided and afraid.

"I grew up believing all our myths: that Chileans were patriotic, dignified, literate. For years, I never questioned my values," recounted Liliana Mahn, the former tourist director, during a long, thoughtful conversation in her tasteful suburban home. "It wasn't until I traveled and saw military Chile from afar that I realized what was happening: the abuse of power, the self-censorship, the mediocre people who rose because they were unconditional loyalists. Unless all our myths were false, that is not what Chilean values were all about."[65]

MOST ordinary Chileans were neither Marxists nor Pinochetists; they were dubious spectators caught in a system they had not chosen. Military rule made them uneasy, but instinct told them to take the path of least resistance. Fearful of confrontation with authorities, shell-shocked by the upheaval of the Allende years, and faced with moral choices for which democracy had not prepared them, most Chileans ducked and kept quiet, praying they would survive the storm.

Like all dictatorships, Pinochet's made spies of the unscrupulous, sycophants of the ambitious, and conformists of the majority. For every teenager who threw a rock, there were a hundred bank customers who watched in silence while a general cut to the head of the line. Even after years of military rule, Chileans remained far more concerned about economic issues than about human rights, and opposed to public protests. In one 1985 poll, 80 percent of the respondents disapproved of spraying graffiti or blocking traffic; the most widely accepted form of complaint was "taking petitions to the authorities."[66]

In part, Chile's strong legalistic traditions explained this reluctance to speak out. In a nation of dignified, middle-class mores, people tended to defer to authority. But there was also an unconscious process of adaptation to authoritarian rule; a protective instinct learned over time and through experience. Drivers crawled past police checkpoints; government opponents made sure to hang out Chilean flags on national holidays. In a military state, it was wise not to call attention to oneself.

"When the government put security guards on campuses, it made me so angry," recalled Josiane Bonnefoy, a graduate student at the Catholic University. "If you walked on the grass, they would blow whistles at you. But people didn't resist; they complained among themselves, but they obeyed. That's how it happens," she added. "You accept things little by little, and finally you end up submitted to them."[67]

Work relationships became more hierarchical, and managers frowned on any sign of sympathy with the opposition. One day in 1983, as protesters swept through Santiago's office district, a law firm secretary helped a visitor who was choking from tear gas take shelter in her office. "The partners won't be back from lunch for an hour, so we're safe," she explained, pointing to a signed portrait of Pinochet.

Life was especially precarious for public employees, who were scrutinized for any hint of dissidence and pressured to attend progovernment functions. On September 11, 1983, several thousand men from a state day-labor program were being herded into buses to attend the regime's tenth-anniversary parade. Instead, they started chanting antigovernment slogans and milling in the street; police fired tear gas into the crowd, and one man was shot dead.[68]

In provincial towns, where appointed officials held absolute power to hire and fire, pressure to conform was extreme. One village butcher named Domingo, a longtime Radical party member, described with shame how he and his family had become grudging participants in government parades and campaigns. "I was against the coup, so they made it hard for me. The bank wouldn't give me credit; the city sent inspectors to my shop," he recounted. "My daughter went to rallies so she wouldn't lose her teaching job, and I ended up going too," he said with disgust. "I had to defend my family."

After the coup, Domingo saw tragedy befall many friends. A Communist watchmaker was murdered; a Socialist school principal was fired and eventually died an alcoholic. By the time Chile's political climate relaxed, the gray-haired meatcutter had lost his nerve. "People asked me to help, but I was afraid," he confessed. "There was one man, a sawmill owner, who did speak out. I always admired him, but I never dared associate with him. Fear was a sickness we all caught."[69]

Sometimes, victims of persecution made political compromises to survive; others shut out the past and let themselves be seduced by the system. Even human rights work was not free of petty greed. Hernán Montealegre described how some attorneys had charged steep fees to desperate, imprisoned leftists. Norma Panes, the Santa Barbara woman who spent years seeking justice for her husband's

murder, said another widow in the case accepted a job and romantic attentions from a local official.[70]

For middle-class people who had struggled to achieve security
and respectability, the plight of wayward leftist children was a
heavy cross to bear. One man had clawed his way to a modest
niche in the state bureaucracy. His son, a medical student, was
tortured and imprisoned after the coup. The distraught father never
dared breathe a word of this nightmare at the office, but every
Sunday he drove to visit his son in a damp prison; and every Monday he was back at work for the military state, a little more withdrawn and embittered.

The ultimate moral choice—that of a witness to abuse—was
dealt to relatively few Chileans, yet its stark images haunted the
nation's conscience for years. How many people, briskly walking
to work in suits and ties, saw Carlos Maluje scream for help as he
was dragged away by the DINA on a crowded boulevard in 1976?
What did respectable passersby feel as they watched riot police
clubbing students or hurried away from clouds of tear gas, hand-
kerchiefs pressed over their mouths?

One night in 1984, a taxicab was careening down Recoleta Avenue between a phalanx of advancing riot police and a mass of
shouting students. Reaching the safety of a downtown hotel, the
gray-haired driver, Renato Gómez, turned to his passengers with
a look of anguish. "What has happened to this country? I used to
be so proud to live in a democracy, and now I feel my honor and
dignity have been violated," he burst out. "There is such malignancy, such power. Dictatorships put people to sleep, and the only
ones brave enough to fight it are the youth. Today, I am ashamed
to be a Chilean."

To Marco Antonio de la Parra, the evasion of moral choice made
dictatorship possible—and years later it remained a disquieting
challenge to the full recovery of Chile's civic values. "I worry more
about the fascist within than the fascist without," he said in 1989.
"How many of us could become torturers? Pinochet could not
have happened if the society were not already sick," he added.
"We became used to being in the cuckoo's nest, and we couldn't
escape. The fear has lessened now, but how little would it take to
bring it back?"

CHAPTER SEVEN

THE TECHNOCRATS

"We are tenacious, obstinate and very honest. We are convinced that things must be done just once. Perhaps that is why we are called cold."

—*Francisco Javier Labbé, vice-dean, economics faculty, University of Chile*

"They elevated their economic theory to the level of religion, neglecting the fact that the economy is at the service of man, not the other way around."

—*Pedro Calvo, Christian Democratic economist*[1]

ON the night of September 11, 1973, while gunfire echoed sporadically through the deserted streets of Santiago, the Lord Cochrane publishing house, owned by Augustín Edwards, was bustling with activity. Long after midnight, the mimeo machines whirred, churning out copies of a document known to insiders as "the brick." Its authors had waited a long time for this moment, and they wanted their product delivered bright and early to every military official in the new government.[2]

The brick was a 500-page blueprint for reversing Allende's economic policies; the product of months of study by opposition economists under the sponsorship of the Society to Promote Manufacturing (Sociedad de Fomento Fabril, or SOFOFA), Chile's major industrial lobby. SOFOFA's president, Orlando Sáenz, had set up the group, with funding from foreign corporations, as part of a "war plan" to destabilize the U.P. and outline policies for a "replacement government."[3]

"We were in low spirits because of what was happening to Chile, so we got together two evenings a week to talk about the problems," recalled Sergio de Castro, longtime dean of the Catholic University's economics faculty and chief architect of the document. "We wrote a booklet, but we didn't see it had any future. It was something for our nerves, a kind of therapy."[4] But by March 1973, recounted Sáenz, "the government was weakening, so we decided to go on the offensive."[5]

Through its links to *El Mercurio,* the group launched an aggressive public attack on Allende's economic policies and established private contacts with navy officials. Edwards, a yachtsman, and several of his managers, including the former naval officer Roberto Kelly, had often chummed with navy officials in an informal association called the Nautical Fraternity of the Pacific. As the possibility of a coup increased, Kelly circulated the SOFOFA group's findings among his navy associates.[6]

When the new junta convened on September 12, one of its most pressing concerns was the grim state of the economy. Inflation had soared to 900 percent, essential goods were in severe shortage, and the black-market currency rate was thirty times the official value. International reserves had been depleted, and the government deficit equaled a staggering 24.7 percent of the gross domestic product.[7] More than six hundred state-run enterprises, employing over 5 percent of the work force, were losing $500 million a year.[8]

When the junta members divided up areas for policy responsibility, Admiral Merino agreed to take charge of the economy. He immediately summoned Kelly to his office and said, "Bring me names."[9] After years of secluded study at the fringe of national politics, and months of frustration under Allende, the authors of the "brick" were finally poised at the edge of power.

FOR a generation, they had been out of step with their time: stuffed shirts in a revolutionary era, acolytes of private profit when the cause of the downtrodden was in fashion. They were sons of the Chilean right; middle- and upper-class students at the Catholic University in the 1950s and 1960s, who shared a conservative religious background, a visceral rejection of socialism, and a contempt for Chile's freewheeling, mass democracy.

When the tide of reform swept the nation's campuses and leftist parties dominated the student movement, these buttoned-down, slick-haired conservatives banded together to form a counter-movement. Rejecting the interference of partisan politics in university life, they championed purely student or *gremial* (guild) issues. In 1969, the *gremialistas* won control of the student federation—and held on to it through the Allende years.

Among the most active *gremialistas* were those influenced by the monetarist school of economics at the University of Chicago. Between 1956 and 1961, at least 150 promising students received fellowships to Chicago through a U.S. government–sponsored program; many, including de Castro, returned to teach at their alma mater. Although the economist Milton Friedman was most widely identified with this school of thought, his colleague Arnold Harberger became the students' "spiritual father" and visited Santiago to select new candidates.[10]

The "Chicago Boys" returned to Chile with a new vision of economic science, based on the principle that market forces and careful control of the money supply were the keys to sound economic policy. Under rigorous tutelage, they acquired a firm theoretical certainty, which one alumnus described as "a belief that economic events have a rational explanation, and that thus economic analysis has a great capacity to interpret" other aspects of society.[11]

Beyond their antagonism to socialist policies, the Chicago Boys were convinced Chile's economy had been smothered for decades by an overblown welfare state, and they dreamed of replacing it with a pure free-market model. Such precepts contrasted sharply with the Marxist cure for underdevelopment that inflamed Chile's intellectual vanguard at the time. They were also at odds with the prevailing beliefs of Latin American economists, who viewed market forces as keeping poor nations in thrall to wealthy ones and the state as the chief engine of development. Even businessmen, pampered by subsidies and protective tariffs, regarded the free-marketers with suspicion.

But within weeks of the military coup, these outcasts were being called to fill dozens of government posts: Sergio de Castro and Pablo Baraona as advisers to the economics minister, Sergio Undurraga as aide to the finance minister. Roberto Kelly became head of the Office of National Planning (Oficina de Planificación Nacional, or ODEPLAN) and recruited a research team from the next generation of Catholic University technocrats.

The free-market economists soon discovered they had considerable competition, however. Admiral Lorenzo Gottuzo, the new finance minister, immediately sought out his old friend Sergio Molina, a Christian Democrat and former finance minister to Frei, to become his chief aide. But the Chicago Boys reacted quickly, and by the time Molina, who was traveling abroad, reached Gottuzo's office on September 18, the minister politely brushed him off. "His tone had changed completely," Molina recalled. "It was clear he had been told I was too close to the Christian Democrats."[12]

A few Christian Democratic economists did play central roles in setting policy, but rightist officials constantly schemed to keep others out of government, and the party's strained relations with the armed forces worsened as repression escalated. By mid-1974, the Christian Democrats had broken with the regime and requested any members in high government posts to choose between the party and the junta. Two men—Alvaro Bardón and Jorge Cauas—took the latter option, but the party's potential for exerting any influence on economic policy was gone.[13]

A stronger challenge to the free-market advocates came from businessmen and conservative politicians who opposed Allende's policies but wanted to retain a strong interventionist state. Their views were echoed by influential military aides like Colonel Contreras and by officers named to manage the state development agency, who believed national security required public control of major economic assets.

Pinochet and his colleagues, not yet committed to an economic policy, called in advisers with conflicting views and listened to their debates with attentive skepticism. Fernando Léniz, an executive from *El Mercurio* who became economics minister in 1974, said he spent 90 percent of his time "trying to explain to the generals and the country what a free market was. This was a totally new experiment, and there was huge resistance."[14]

One of the sharpest early battles erupted over the issues of price controls and currency devaluation. Chile's foreign exchange rates were confusing and badly distorted, with hundreds of rates for a variety of imports. Three weeks after the coup, the free-market aides persuaded Admiral Gottuzo to drastically devalue the escudo and establish a single exchange rate of 280 per dollar. To the junta's alarm, the increased cost of foreign goods sent domestic prices skyward.

On October 2, an array of advisers was summoned before the commanders, including Hugo Araneda, a financial lawyer and a

Military Academy colleague of Pinochet who vehemently opposed devaluation. The debate was stormy. Araneda argued that inflation was like a runaway team of horses; unless slowed gently, it could overturn the entire wagon. Merino exploded at Gottuzo, saying the junta "cannot be increasing prices. We will be accused of killing the people with hunger." Finally, de Castro rose to defend the measure, offering a dazzling tour de force of free-market economics.[15]

Still unconvinced, the junta consulted the distinguished economist Raúl Sáez, a key figure in the Alliance for Progress who had helped design Chile's state-sponsored industrialization program in the 1940s. This time, however, Sáez declared himself in favor of de Castro's strategy, and the military commanders concurred. Within days, goods reappeared on store shelves, but prices shot up even more dramatically; the scarcity of consumer items had been replaced by a scarcity of money.[16]

Under the influence of Sáez and Léniz, the government pursued a pragmatic, gradualist economic reform policy during most of 1974. State spending was reduced, tariffs above 200 percent were eliminated, and the fiscal deficit was brought down to 11 percent of the gross domestic product. At year's end, though, inflation still hovered at 375 percent, while real wages dropped sharply and unemployment rose to unprecedented levels. The central budget showed a 32 percent shortfall. Chile's problems were compounded by skyrocketing international oil prices and the resulting world recession, which led to a sharp drop in the country's copper earnings.[17]

The Chicago Boys argued that more drastic reforms were needed, and their position was reinforced by Milton Friedman himself, who paid a high-profile visit to Santiago in March 1975. At the University of Chile, he told students the economy needed a "shock treatment" and deep spending cuts. In a talk with Pinochet, he counseled the general to ignore his poor image abroad, focus on curing the "disease" of statism, and take sharp action against inflation.[18]

Shortly afterward, Kelly went to see Pinochet and warned him bluntly that Chile's military "saviors" could turn out to be its economic "undertakers." The general ordered an emergency plan prepared and decided to centralize economic policy in the hands of Cauas, a low-key former World Bank official who had been named finance minister in December. The junta quickly approved a decree law giving Cauas broad economic authority, and Pinochet replaced Léniz with de Castro. The balance of power was shifting rapidly.[19]

During a weekend meeting at the presidential retreat in Viña del Mar, Pinochet watched his intellectual gladiators clash over the proposed "shock plan." Sáez and several army aides warned that drastic measures would radically alter the economic system; Cauas countered that inflation had to be broken at all costs. When the marathon session ended, Pinochet's conversion to free-market economics was complete.

THE Chicago Boys' rise to power was clearly enhanced by the crisis. Their penchant for quick, tough action appealed to the military commanders, and their harsh proposals—no longer counterbalanced by Christian Democratic influence at high levels—seemed just the surgery to rescue Chile from economic catastrophe. As Admiral Gotuzzo declared, "The dog's tail must be cut off in one chop."[20]

Other factors also contributed to the free-marketers' conquest of the junta, especially their scientific expertise and nonpartisan approach. The commanders were impressed by the way de Castro and his colleagues demolished opponents' arguments. "They made us feel like insects," recounted Mónica Madariaga.[21] The Chicago-trained economists also seemed impervious to political pressure and motivated by a higher interest in the common good. Detached and austere, they exuded an air of self-sacrifice that resonated among officers trained to die for their country.

Pinochet was especially intrigued by the Chicago Boys' self-described "revolutionary" aims to transform the economy and break with the orthodoxies of the past. The general yearned to be identified with a historic act of national renewal, and he decided these bold technocrats held the key to a new, prosperous future that would forever distinguish his rule. In return, Pinochet was willing to guarantee them protection from all political pressure. "Public opinion was very much against [us], so we needed a strong personality to maintain the policy," de Castro recalled in 1979. "It was our luck that President Pinochet understood and had the character to withstand criticism."[22]

Finally, the junta hoped the Chicago Boys could win badly needed financial assistance from a world that had condemned and isolated Chile for human rights abuses. Seven of the nine men who served Pinochet as finance ministers held advanced degrees from U.S. universities, and they seemed ideal envoys to the urbane world of international finance.[23]

Over the years, this situation often created schizophrenic U.S.-Chilean relations: while the gruff dictator was shunned by officials in Washington, his sophisticated aides were being praised by bankers in New York. Indeed, the funds that poured into Chile from private American and European banks during the Pinochet era—and from multilateral lending institutions with voting support from U.S. officials—compensated many times over for the gradual cutoff of economic aid from the U.S. government and other industrialized democracies.[24]

Encouraged by the junta's strong embrace of free-market tenets, Western lending institutions that had shunned Allende turned on the spigot again. Foreign lenders agreed to refinance Chile's foreign debt on unusually generous terms, and after U.S. aid was banned by Congress in 1976, the pace of loans from the World Bank and the Inter-American Development Bank steadily increased. Between 1976 and early 1986, these institutions made forty-six loans to Chile worth over $3.1 billion, ranging from $6 million for a municipal sewer system to $280 million for a mammoth hydroelectric power plant.[25]

During the Ford presidency (1974–76) and the first Reagan term (1980–84), the United States voted consistently in favor of multilateral loans; during the Carter administration (1976–80), it voted against them. In both cases, bank officials approved all the loans on grounds of need and creditworthiness, stressing their desire to avoid "politicizing" the decision process. Most European and Latin American democracies, moreover, voted along with the majority.

Legislative critics like Kennedy and Harkin argued in vain that the United States, which carried preponderant voting weight in the multilateral banks, was helping to prop up financially an abusive dictatorship. In 1979, they also failed to force the U.S. government to curtail or disclose private U.S. bank loans to Chile, then reported to total over $2 billion since the coup. Even for the liberal Carter administration, incensed over Chile's refusal to extradite the alleged killers of Orlando Letelier, this was too intrusive a step to risk.[26]

ON April 24, 1975, the quiet, bald-pated Cauas appeared on television and announced that an emergency plan to halt inflation and spur growth would be imposed "at any cost." This was the first dose of shock treatment, and the effects were dramatic. Public spending was cut by another 27 percent in 1975, and within four years it had dropped to nearly half the 1973 level in relation to the gross national product.[27] Public investment was also slashed: between 1974 and 1979, it fell 13.9 percent.[28]

Drastic measures were taken to reduce the supply of money: the Central Bank mint was "put under lock and key," and huge bundles of escudo notes were burned.[29] To stimulate a private capital market, officials freed interest rates charged to banks, deregulated the banking system, and created incentives for foreign investment.[30] Import tariffs were further reduced to an average of 30 percent in 1976, then dropped to a uniform 10 percent by 1979.[31] Officials freed prices on more than two thousand goods, excluding "essential" items like petroleum.

The double-barreled attempt to curb inflation and streamline industry, just when the economy was weakened by external forces, had a painfully high cost. The GNP fell 13 percent—the greatest drop since the 1930s.[32] Industrial production plummeted 28 percent, unemployment soared to 16.8 percent in 1976, and purchasing power plunged to 40 percent of the 1970 level.[33] But all these effects were anticipated. "This path was chosen because it is the only one that goes directly to the sickness," explained Cauas.[34]

Although the mild-mannered minister served as spokesman for the "shock treatment" policy, its undisputed intellectual architect was de Castro. A brusque, austere academic in his midforties, he cared little for wealth, honors, or culture; his chief leisure activity was a hard game of rugby. Pursuing his theories with iron-willed drive, he was unruffled by criticism and coolly dismissive of all detractors.[35]

De Castro was so sure of himself that he even argued with Pinochet, to the astonishment of his colleagues and the bemused annoyance of the general. In one notorious incident, Pinochet cut off a long-winded economic debate and reminded his aides that he was the one with Chile's "pot by the handle." De Castro promptly retorted that if the economy continued to decline, Pinochet would be left "holding just the handle." The general was so furious at the upstart economist, recalled Sáenz, that "we had to mount a major operation to save his job."[36]

Once Pinochet was convinced and the moderates were defeated, however, de Castro's star rose quickly. After replacing Léniz in April 1975, he placed his disciples in key posts—Alvaro Bardón as head of the Central Bank, Pablo Baraona as his own top aide—and easily outmaneuvered the weaker Cauas. In the late 1976, Pi-

The Coup. Soldiers on the roof of the Ministry of Defense observe the bombing of La Moneda palace on September 11, 1973. Anonymous photo from private archive.

The Parade. Prussian-trained soldiers march in front of La Moneda, 1984. Photo by Marco Ugarte.

The Strategist. 1986 photo by
Miguel Angel Larrea.

The general, undated.
Photo by Jose Agurto.

The King. Cartoon of Pinochet as Luis XIV,
which resulted in all issues of *Apsi* magazine
being seized and editors imprisoned, 1987.
Drawing by Guillo.

The Disappeared. Relatives hold placards
with photographs of victims missing after
being detained by the secret police, 1989.
Photo by Pamela Constable.

Carabineros beat protesters,
1984. Photo by Marco
Ugarte.

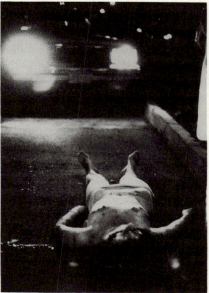

Bullet-riddled corpse of a
woman after a series of raids
on leftist safe houses, 1986.
Photo by Miguel Angel
Larrea.

The Mall. Affluent shoppers browse amid boutiques in a gleaming new suburban mall in Santiago, 1986. Photo by Julio Pereira.

Persian Market. Jobless men pawn plumbing fixtures at a flea market, where many poor Santiago residents shop, 1986. Photo by Pamela Constable.

ABOVE. Children in the improverished coastal and mining town of Lota,
1989. Photo by Pamela Constable.

Guanaco. Protesters being hosed by a water-cannon truck, nicknamed after a South American spitting llama, 1983. Photo by Miguel Angel Larrea.

The Patriotic Front. Young members of an urban guerrilla group drill with home-made weapons, undated. Photo by José Agurto.

OPPOSITE. A boy plays by a graffiti-covered wall in La Victoria slum, showing Pinochet as Nazi pig, 1984. Photo by Miguel Angel Larrea.

The Yes. Women from the poor neighborhood of Conchalí gather for a pro-Pinochet rally, 1988. Photo by José Agurto.

The No. Young volunteers rally for the No vote in the 1988 plebiscite. Photo by Marco Ugarte.

The Triumph. Celebrating
crowds hug an embarrassed
policeman after the No vote
victory, October 5, 1988.
Photo by Marco Ugarte.

Patricio Aylwin, opposition candidate for president, greets miners in 1989. Photo by Reuters; Helmut Rosas.

Hernán Büchi, regime candidate for president, speaks at a rally in Valparaiso, 1989. Photo by Arturo Valenzuela.

Families in the poor neighborhood of Conchalí supporting
opposition candidates, 1989.
Photo by Pamela Constable.

Patricio Aylwin is elected
president of Chile, December
15, 1989. Photo by Reuters.

nochet appointed de Castro finance minister, and from this pos
de Castro launched a five-year crusade to build a free-market mode
far more daring than anything Cauas had imagined.

De Castro's goal was not only to reverse three years of socialist
policy but also to erase a "half century of errors" in state-driven
economic planning. Since the Great Depression, governments had
used tariffs and subsidies, wage and price controls, and restrictions
on private capital as tools to regulate the economy and reduce
dependence on imports. After 1939, the Chilean Development
Corporation (Corporación de Fomento, or CORFO) pioneered in
building subsidized steel, chemical, and textile industries, transforming Chile from an agricultural to a manufacturing economy
in twenty-five years.[37]

In their determination to remake history, the Chicago Boys would
not acknowledge such historical contributions; instead, they asserted
that state policies had produced little more than stagnant growth,
heavy deficits, and a private sector that was inefficient, strangled
by inflation, and too diversified to take advantage of specialization
or the economies of scale.[38] "Our experience shows this is the way
to stay poor forever," de Castro stated in 1979.[39]

By the same token, the neoconservatives would not admit that
some of the measures enacted by both Frei and Allende made their
own task of economic transformation much easier. Land reform
and industrial expropriations had weakened the business elite,
unintentionally giving Chile's new authoritarian regime far more
autonomy to restructure the private sector than its counterparts in
Argentina, Brazil, or Uruguay. Moreover, Frei's massive tree-
planting program stimulated timber exports in the 1980s, while
Allende's copper nationalization gave Pinochet critical revenues to
cover social and military spending.

Yet the Chicago Boys were no less idealistic than Allende's
Marxist cadres or Frei's communitarian disciples. De Castro and
his cohorts were just as certain they possessed the truth, and just
as frantic to change all the rules at once.[40] The state must give way
to the market; populism must be replaced by expertise and ideological conflict by economic competition. Only by shrinking government and steamlining enterprise, they believed, could Chile
become a developed nation. And only economic growth could cure
poverty—even if that meant extra hardship while waiting for the
chorreo, or trickle-down, to occur.

"In this country everyone, businessmen and employees, was
educated in weakness. In order to educate them to strength it is

necessary to pay the price of temporary unemployment, of bankruptcies," asserted Baraona in 1977, amid a wave of business failures.[41]

A number of high-ranking military men expressed concerns about the social impact of such policies. Within the junta, General Leigh attempted to check the power of the Chicago Boys, but once he was gone, they enjoyed full support at the top. "Let fall those who must fall," Admiral Merino said when asked about the high bankruptcy rate. "Such is the jungle of . . . economic life. A jungle of savage beasts, where he who can kill the one next to him, kills him. That is reality."[42]

PINOCHET'S free-market team inspired a generation of devoted disciples. Many were younger members of the *gremialista* movement, and some had ties to conservative Catholic groups such as Opus Dei. Recruited by Roberto Kelly, they were sent off to Chicago in return for a commitment of several years in public service.[43] At ODEPLAN, they designed dozens of blueprints for economic reforms and issued devastating cost-benefit analyses of pet development projects requested by local officials. They spread through the bureaucracy like an army of eager auditors, establishing tight fiscal controls and enabling the junta to gain firm command over the massive state apparatus.[44]

The shining light of ODEPLAN was Miguel Kast, a young, German-born economist who entered government in 1975. Persuasive and indefatigable, Kast was a mystical Catholic who saw his work as a moral mission—and would stop at nothing to achieve it. He enlisted dozens of students and friends in his campaign against poverty and inefficiency, persuading them to put promising private careers in abeyance and toil at low wages to improve sewer or health insurance costs. In 1983, Kast's untimely death of cancer at the age of thirty-five elevated him to near-sainthood among regime collaborators.[45]

"Miguel was a motivator who captured us and imparted the ideal of service. We became part of a crusade to build a modern, efficient economy and to combat poverty," recalled Cristián Larroulet, a campus *gremialista* leader who was lured into ODEPLAN by Kast and spent the next decade as a government economic aide. "To us, it was a revolution. We had terrible salaries, but a great deal of mystique."[46]

Despite such idealism, the Chicago Boys seemed oblivious to the contradiction of relying on a repressive state to enforce the promotion of economic freedom. They often clashed with Colonel Contreras, but their quarrel had more to do with the DINA chief's preference for populist policies than with his abusive police methods, and Pinochet kept them well insulated from the dark side of dictatorship.

Enclosed in their specialized world, the economists were contemptuous of partisan politics, and they believed that democracy was a luxury that poor societies could not necessarily afford. For them, military rule offered an opportunity to solve problems and apply unpopular policies for long-term public benefit—and they were in no hurry to see it end.

"You are the president we need for many years," Kast wrote to Pinochet in 1982.[47] Bardón argued that democracy had failed to solve any of Chile's basic social or economic problems and that, since the coup, most Chileans had come to appreciate the security and opportunities offered by military rule. "I honestly feel that the people who are unhappy are a minority of intellectuals," he added.[48]

To these men, the only kind of freedom that mattered was individual economic freedom, which de Castro argued was best guaranteed by an "authoritarian government" with its "impersonal" method of exercising power.[49] Yet their definition of economic freedom was highly selective: businessmen were "free" to move capital and raise prices, but workers were not "free" to present collective demands or strike for better working conditions. Indeed, Chileans could be imprisoned or exiled for protesting policies aimed at making them economically "free."

In a democracy, the Chicago Boys would not have survived public pressure; under dictatorship, they had no need to account for their actions. Bardón argued that if the regime had consulted business or labor leaders before enacting radical reforms, the "establishment" and the "union dictatorship" would have totally opposed them.[50] Yet he seemed bewildered by charges that he and his colleagues were antidemocratic. "I don't understand what political power the economic team could have," he said. "We are making a policy in order to lose power, so how can we be concentrating it?"[51]

AS the effects of the world recession diminished, the economy responded vigorously to the Chicago Boys' prescriptions. By 1979, the fiscal deficit had been eliminated, and annual growth rates were averaging 6.5 percent.[52] The negative balance of payments abroad, which had reached nearly $800 million, was trimmed to $344 million, and the foreign debt was renegotiated. Inflation had dropped to 65 percent by 1977, and production climbed 8 percent in 1978, reducing unemployment.

To counter inflationary pressures, authorities ended the policy of currency devaluations. Exports surged from 13 percent to 33 percent of the GNP.[53] A dynamic capital market was encouraged, the value of corporate stocks rose substantially, and new firms were permitted to extend credit. "The critical situation has been overcome," de Castro crowed. "We are in a process of expansion and takeoff."[54]

Under the tutelage of the Chicago Boys, the Chilean state became much more efficient. In ten years, the number of public employees was reduced from 700,000 to 550,000, while the state's proportion of the GNP remained about the same, meaning that it was producing as much value with far fewer hands.[55] The tax system was streamlined and the web of economic regulations simplified.

In its campaign to pare the fat off public administration, the economic team also attacked the bloated roster of state enterprises and properties. Officials set about divesting more than 400 of 620 state-owned businesses, many of which had been confiscated under Allende, returning some to their owners and auctioning off others at bargain prices.[56] They also returned between 30 and 40 percent of all expropriated land to private hands, mostly small farmers. By 1979, the fiscal deficit had become a surplus.[57]

General Luis Danús, the head of CORFO, supported the privatization process, but some senior officers believed that strategic industries should remain in state hands. In 1979, the economic planners tried to sell off the state copper-mining consortium, which they viewed as an unmanageable "monster." But its vice-president, Colonel Gastón Fréz, argued that to abandon this critical commodity to private whims was "antipatriotic," and threatened to resign from the army.[58] Pinochet quickly ordered his aides to leave the monster intact.[59]

By 1980, only twenty-three strategic industries, including mining, energy, and communications, remained in state hands; yet, because they were among Chile's largest enterprises, the state continued to control about 75 percent of national production.[60] Indeed, while the Chicago Boys' aggressive efforts drastically reduced the government's property and payroll, it still wielded more economic power than in 1965.[61]

THESE early reforms were only the first phase in Pinochet's plan to transform Chile's political economy. Beginning in 1979, a second generation of aides began pushing beyond "monetarism" into a more profound "liberalization" of society. They drew their philosophical inspiration more from Friedrich von Hayek, the Austrian Nobel laureate in economics and champion of unbridled capitalism, than from Friedman's technical contributions to monetary theory.

Miguel Kast was one of the driving forces behind the new thrust; under his leadership, ODEPLAN produced studies aimed at a complete privatization of medical care, social security, and even labor relations. Another was Jaime Guzmán, the conservative idealogue, who abandoned his early corporatist and integralist views to embrace neoliberalism after reading Hayek and the American Catholic thinker Michael Novak.[62]

José Piñera, an energetic, Harvard-trained economist who hailed from a family of clergymen and diplomats close to the Christian Democrats, envisioned an even broader agenda of neoliberal change for society. Working out of a corporate research center, he attracted the attention of Roberto Kelly and was invited to address the junta in mid-1978. His performance was so impressive that by Christmas, at the age of thirty, Piñera was minister of labor.[63]

Piñera and his colleagues promoted a new definition of freedom: one that replaced both traditional democracy and egalitarian socialism with a more individualistic, consumer's notion of economic choice. According to this view, once economic freedoms had led to abundance for all, voters would "shop" for parties that maximized their economic interests and shun those that made tired appeals to ideology.

Pinochet was especially taken with the argument that the regime must "modernize" the nation.[64] First, he was sensitive to charges that a free-market system could be imposed only by dictatorial means, and he hoped economic modernization might lessen the need for repression. Second, he wanted to be remembered for something grander than economic stabilization, and neoliberalism seemed to coincide with his dream of creating a prosperous nation free from ideological conflict. "It wasn't hard to convince Pinochet, because he felt he was making history," recalled Piñera. "He wanted to be ahead of both Reagan and Thatcher."[65]

Soon Pinochet was espousing a global vision of Chile, with the free market anchoring a sweeping "new institutionality." In his sixth-anniversary speech, a joint product of Piñera and Guzmán, the president asserted that democracy was "not an end in itself" but a process in building a truly "free society." He also announced ambitious plans to "modernize" seven areas of policy: labor, social security, education, health, justice, agriculture, and regional administration.[66]

As labor minister, Piñera focused first on creating a new "relationship" between owners and workers. His Labor Plan, hastily sketched in the final days of 1978, reestablished limited collective bargaining but conceived of labor as a commodity that should be subject to market forces, not protected. The new laws were widely condemned by labor leaders for placing sharp restrictions on rights to organize and strike.[67]

From there, the economic team moved on to new areas, designing plans to promote choice among public service "consumers." State health insurance was supplanted by private health maintenance organizations called Instituciones de Salud Previsional (ISAPRES), and the social security system was shifted to a scheme in which workers paid into individual, capitalized accounts administered by private firms. As officials cast a widening net for "inefficient" activities to turn over to the private sector, everything from kindergartens to cemeteries and community swimming pools was put out for bid.[68]

At CORFO, officials continued selling off state assets and divided twenty-seven "strategic" agencies such as the electric company into smaller, self-financing subsidiaries. The flood of transactions aroused criticism that many properties were being sold at prices far below their worth.[69] Alejandro Foxley, a leading opposition economist, calculated that the average sale was subsidized by about 30 percent of the firm's value and that most transactions were extremely advantageous to the buyers.[70] Many of the sales were made to a handful of wealthy investment groups, especially those controlled by Edwards, Manuel Cruzat, and Javier Vial.

Despite their claims to independence, the architects of Chile's economic model were closely linked to the investors who benefited most from privatization and the new, deregulated business climate. Piñera and Cauas came from positions with Cruzat; Rolf Lüders, minister of finance and economics in 1982–83, came from the Vial group. Many executives of Edwards-owned companies rotated through the regime; after 1982, Sergio de Castro went to work for Edwards and helped the near-bankrupt *El Mercurio* obtain a mammoth, $53 million government loan.[71]

By 1980, five conglomerates, led by the Cruzat and Vial groups, controlled more than half the assets of Chile's 250 major private enterprises. By 1982, the banks built or purchased by those two groups alone accounted for 42 percent of all banking capital in Chile, and 60 percent of all credit.[72] Moreover, the companies they created to administer the new health and pension funds came to control half the savings of Chile's work force.[73]

Officials denied that their policies were aimed at benefiting the few, arguing that they sought to remove the privileges provided by the old client state. "I don't know any important economic groups that have been formed under the shelter of this policy," asserted de Castro.[74] "Everyone is getting exactly the same treatment. If people are earning money, it is because they are productive and efficient."[75] Bardón asserted that the government had taken the "moral path" by reducing subsidies for the affluent. "To do well in business," he boasted, "it is no longer necessary to be a friend of the finance minister or the vice-president of CORFO."[76]

If the free-market model made a few people wealthier than the vast majority, the economic team viewed this as an inevitable part of creating a prosperous economy. Convinced that an upward redistribution of wealth was essential to increase savings and promote growth, they were untroubled by the extra advantage this gave to larger, more powerful enterprises. Viewing recession as necessary to stabilize and liberalize the economy, they accepted as a given that the burden would be disproportionately borne by workers.[77] "Either we want a country with no rich people or a country with no poor ones," stated Piñera. "Personally, I prefer a thousand times a country without poor than a country without rich."[78]

The note of alarm sounded by critics was drowned in a widening chorus of praise for the economic team. In the United States, where the conservative Ronald Reagan had taken office as president in 1981 and neoconservatism was in its heyday, business magazines hailed Chile's "Brave New World of Reaganomics," and the World Bank issued glowing reports on Chile's responsible fiscal policies.[79]

Under Reagan, an ardent anticommunist and free-enterprise advocate, the hostile U.S.-Chile relations of the Carter era quickly thawed. The president's first emissary to Pinochet was Jeane Kirkpatrick, the new U.S. ambassador to the United Nations, who had argued that rightist dictatorships should be supported as allies against Third World totalitarian movements.[80] During a four-day visit to Santiago in 1981, she met with Pinochet, praised his economic policies, and said the administration hoped to "completely normalize" relations with Chile "in order to work together in a pleasant way."[81]

Later that year, Reagan named James Theberge, a conservative academic, as his ambassador to Chile. Testifying before Congress in 1974, Theberge had defended U.S. policy toward Allende and presented a paper called "Kremlin's Hand in Allende's Chile."[82] Now, as Reagan's man in Santiago, he set out to "devote all of [his] energies" to improving U.S. ties to Pinochet's government.[83] Disdaining opposition leaders, he hobnobbed with pro-regime businessmen, pronounced Chile "on the road to a Western-style democracy," and pressed for a restoration of U.S. economic and military aid.[84]

On the surface, Chile was experiencing an economic miracle, enjoying 32 percent growth in four years and an average inflation below 50 percent.[85] A consumer boom exploded as savings and loan companies vied for customers, and shops were flooded with imported goods. New ventures in agricultural exports, from timber to kiwi fruit, were flourishing. Officials were so confident of Chile's successful integration into the world economy that on June 29, 1979, the Central Bank approved fixing the Chilean peso at 39 to the dollar for six months; later, they extended that policy indefinitely.[86]

"It was a period of euphoria. We were convinced we were on our way to becoming another Korea or Taiwan: we felt rich, we wanted to consume, we took on great debts," recalled Rolf Lüders. "The support of the [International Monetary] Fund and the World Bank were crucial to us. They were very enthusiastic because our team thought the way they did; we were following their prescriptions more closely than any other country."[87]

For months, the economists reveled in triumph. Piñera promised an assembly of labor leaders that, "in ten more years, Chile will be a developed country."[88] And de Castro told a delegation of Japanese businessmen that by 1990 Chile's per capita income would reach $3,500 a year, "placing us at the vanguard of Latin America."[89] Three days later, riding a wave of economic optimism, voters approved the new constitution, and the victory of Pinochet's economic visionaries seemed complete.

WHAT few citizens knew, and what officials could not admit, was that the "Chilean miracle" was partly an illusion. Built on unrealistic economic assumptions and a fragile edifice of debt, high interest rates, and speculation, it was highly susceptible to world market downturns and excessively dependent on the fortunes of a few conglomerates whose intricate financial activities were virtually unsupervised.

The boom had also relied heavily on foreign loans and investment, while domestic savings had remained low for a full decade after the coup. From an annual average of 17 percent of the GNP between 1963 and 1973, Chilean savings fell to an average of 12 percent for the next ten years—a level far too low to sustain solid, long-term growth.[90]

As overseas borrowing increased, Chile's foreign debt more than doubled, from $6.7 billion to $15.6 billion, between 1978 and 1981.[91] In just two years, the portion of export earnings spent on foreign-debt interest payments rose from 37 percent to 60 percent.[92] But the mass inflow of money and goods masked underlying structural imbalances, as well as the high-risk practices of major entrepreneurs.

When the early twinges of a new world recession were felt, the government dismissed the problem as temporary and continued letting the economy expand on dollar credit. And when the huge Sugar Refining Company of Viña del Mar (known as CRAV) unexpectedly declared bankruptcy in 1981, de Castro assured foreign lenders that the incident was a passing cloud in a bright economic picture, and he insisted on maintaining the fixed exchange rate of 39 pesos to the dollar.

As the currency became more distorted, domestic producers were overwhelmed by cheap imported goods, and middle-class families could suddenly afford color televisions and trips to Europe—while foreign visitors found themselves paying $400 restaurant tabs. Between 1978 and 1981, imports surged from $3.2 billion to $7.3 billion, while exports suddenly fell 8 percent, to a level of $3.8 billion, dramatically widening the trade gap.[93]

The Chicago Boys assumed they could weather the crisis by borrowing still more; eventually, they believed, the market would make "automatic adjustments," bringing down domestic wages and production costs while making imports more expensive.[94] Long after the 39-peso dollar had become an asphyxiating burden to the nation, Sergio de Castro stubbornly clung to his theories, while proposing a series of deflationary measures—such as lowering the minimum wage and military expenses—that proved politically impossible.

Even the boosterish *El Mercurio* warned that de Castro's "excessive inflexibility" could undermine the free-market model itself.[95] But the finance minister, sheltered from public pressure by the unwavering support of Pinochet, would not budge. The military cocoon, which had allowed the Chicago Boys to make tough decisions needed to stabilize the economy, now shielded them from their own errors. Pinochet's doubts were growing, but he remained loyal to de Castro for months as the crisis deepened, ignoring advice from political and military advisers to let the peso fall.

Finally, in April 1982, the president relented, asking de Castro to resign and placing Generals Fréz and Danús in the regime's top economic posts. Two months later, he called them to his office and said grimly, "Gentlemen, I have decided to devalue." That night, Danús stunned the nation with a terse televised announcement that the peso would be dropped 18 percent.[96] Miguel Kast, who had just flown to West Germany to assure bankers the peso would remain fixed, learned the news in a 2 A.M. overseas call from his wife.[97]

After three years of military protection, the cornerstone of de Castro's theoretical edifice had been dislodged by his more pragmatic uniformed masters. But the turnaround was far too late and abrupt. While easing pressures on some firms, it was a harsh blow to Chileans who had borrowed heavily in dollars, from whisky importers to taxi drivers who had purchased cabs on credit. The Central Bank was besieged by a run on dollars, paying out as much as $22 million per day.[98]

The impact of these extreme policy swings was aggravated by a new wave of shocks from abroad: a sharp drop in world copper prices, an increase in oil costs, and the U.S. Federal Reserve Board's decision to raise the prime lending rate, which sent interest rates in Chile up to 16.5 percent.[99] During 1982, the Chilean economy shrank by 14.2 percent—the steepest decline registered by any Latin American country during a year of regionwide recession.

An especially difficult problem was the huge debt assumed by the large conglomerates, often with lax accounting and insufficient colateral. The powerful Vial and Cruzat groups were badly exposed, having borrowed heavily from banks they controlled to finance high-risk ventures. In their rush to privatize the economy, the Chicago Boys had ignored the need for regulatory oversight. De Castro had finally moved to tighten banking rules in September 1981, but the damage was done. By year's end, bad loans made up 25 percent of the total capital and reserves of Chilean banks.

That November, the state was forced to intervene in four insolvent banks and four finance companies; to prevent panic, officials also decided to cover their debts, at a cost of $300 million. These measures veered sharply from free-market tenets, which held that troubled businesses must be allowed to fail. But now philosophical deviation seemed a lesser evil than the collapse of the entire banking system.

The situation provoked intense debate within the government. Some officials were furious with the irresponsibility and greed of the financial groups; others asserted there was nothing wrong with speculation and continued to blame the recession. Critics heralded the demise of the free-market model; defenders insisted that the state had moved only to prevent a wider collapse and that other banks should not expect similar protection. "The government acted wisely in *defense* of a model of free economy," argued the editors of *Realidad,* a journal founded by Jaime Guzmán.[100]

Despite the government bailout, it was clear Chile's financial system was collapsing. The unpaid debts of Vial and Cruzat alone accounted for 46 percent of all private banking reserves—and their ability to repay seemed deeply in doubt. As he had done in the 1975 crisis, Pinochet replaced his finance and economics ministers with one man—Rolf Lüders, the capable former right-hand aide to the Vial group—and asked him to take charge of a massive emergency cleanup.

Taking office in August 1982, Lüders made a preliminary study of Chile's private banks. He discovered that at least $2.5 billion in debts, equal to 10 percent of the GNP, were uncollectible. It would be "immoral" for the government to rescue the big conglomerates, he said, but it could not risk a broader collapse. He proposed an intermediate step: to intervene in the insolvent banks, letting the larger, more indebted ones fail and rescuing the smaller ones. "It was arbitrary, but the other alternatives were worse. I saw no choice," Lüders recalled in 1989.[101]

On the night of January 13, 1983, the tall, Germanic minister appeared on television. Sternly criticizing the behavior of the conglomerates, he announced that the state was intervening in a number of Chile's largest banks. Three institutions, whose debts were triple their assets, were to be liquidated. Five others were to be taken over, and two more would be placed under observation. Early the next morning, state-appointed intervenors entered each institution, and guards barred the doors to long lines of frantic depositors forming outside.

Officials pledged that Chileans' savings accounts were safe, and they eventually covered nearly half the $2.5 billion to $4.0 billion in estimated domestic losses from all intervened banks.[102] Yet the takeover itself was extraordinary punishment to mete out to the business interests most closely identified with the Chicago Boys. Invoking the same expropriation law used by Allende, officials seized numerous enterprises linked to the failed banks and appointed 150 intervenors to determine which were worth saving and which should be allowed to fail.

The severity of the measure was even more startling because of the close personal relationships involved. Bardón and Baraona had headed two of the intervened banks. Cauas, then president of the Bank of Santiago, was forced to submit to a briefcase search. Lüders, having helped Javier Vial build his empire, proceeded to destroy it—although he was dismissed from government soon after the bank interventions, and later he followed his former boss to prison on fraud charges.

Overnight, foreign lenders' confidence collapsed and economic policy floundered in internal bickering. The International Monetary Fund imposed draconian conditions in return for new loans, while overseas creditors demanded that the regime guarantee the entire private foreign debt of the companies that had been taken over—about $7.7 billion—or risk jeopardizing their agreements for new loans. The desperate officials had no choice but to sign, thus fully protecting foreign banks while passing the burden on to domestic taxpayers. During the boom, Chile's economic gains had been privatized; now, in the crunch, the country's losses were socialized.[103]

The miracle had cracked, undermined by a rigid application of monetarist dogma. Instead of withdrawing from the economy, the state had seized control of 70 percent of the banks and a large chunk of the nation's private enterprise. Instead of stimulating competition, deregulation had led to a frenzy of speculation and a staggering foreign debt of over $20 billion. While helping to control inflation, the fixed exchange rate had dangerously overvalued the peso. And while making some industries more efficient, abrupt exposure to foreign goods had driven others into the ground, creating the highest urban unemployment on the continent.[104]

Public patience was at a breaking point, and anger swelled at the powerful men in uniforms and business suits who had failed to deliver on their pledge to bring order and prosperity to the nation. On May 11, 1983, a strike called by opposition labor leaders erupted into a nationwide protest by students, workers, and housewives—the most serious challenge to a decade of military rule.

The crisis forced Pinochet to make the most dramatic about-face of his dictatorship, one that seemed to repudiate everything the Chicago Boys had stood for. Hoping to defuse the growing protest movement and keep the rightist elite from losing faith, the general named Sergio Onofre Jarpa, a veteran National party leader, his interior minister. Jarpa's assignment was twofold: to open a dialogue with Pinochet's political opponents and to reassure businessmen that the regime would not abandon them.

These efforts encountered strong opposition from the free-market economists, who feared that their long labor to mold a new economic system was about to be sacrificed to populist demands. Indeed, spurred by continued public protests and Jarpa's private maneuvering, Pinochet eased most of the remaining Chicago Boys from policy-making positions and replaced them with individuals linked to the traditional, prostatist business world. "Many people were fired; we were no longer consulted," recalled Larroulet, who resigned from the government in 1984. "It was our lowest moment."

For finance minister, Pinochet chose Luis Escobar Cerda, an international businessman and former minister for the Alessandri government. The economics portfolio went to Modesto Collados, a construction industry leader and opponent of the Chicago Boys. Escobar moved quickly, raising some tariffs, placing new ones on luxury items, and devaluing the peso again. A blunt man, he made it clear his priority was putting more Chileans to work and "more beans in the cooking pot."[105] The theoreticians had presided over the collapse of the economy; now it was time for the pragmatists to save the government.

CHAPTER EIGHT

THE RICH

"This country doesn't need a single new idea. It
needs people who can get things done."

—*Máximo Pacheco, general manager,
Andean Leasing Corporation*

LEONEL GARCÍA, white-haired and tweed-coated, moved com-
fortably through the rhythmic din of the Nibsa valve and faucet
factory, patting his machines with pride, nodding to the men in
blue overalls, pausing in the foundry shed—a smoky inferno where
crucibles of silver liquid glowed through a dark haze, acrid with
the smell of oil and hot metal. Upstairs in García's cluttered office,
amid the tacked-up cartoons and order slips, was a framed photograph of President Pinochet.

The factory had endured a long and painful odyssey, mirroring
the trauma and transformation of thousands of Chilean businesses
that faced unionization, expropriation, two recessions, radical
swings of economic policy, and near-fatal foreign competition—
all within two decades.

Nibsa, founded just after World War II, had been a typical creation of state policies aimed at ending dependence on foreign goods,
protected by high tariffs and bolstered with loans and technical
aid from CORFO. Corruption was rare in Chile, but manufacturers were represented on regulatory commissions, and they cultivated friendships with bureaucrats who helped them secure a niche
in the rentier state.[1] "The strategy of the business community was
always to court whoever was in power, because that was the way
to prosper," said García.[2]

Despite the dominant public role in the economy, the authorities made little effort to prevent the concentration of industrial wealth in the hands of a few powerful Chilean families, such as the Edwardses and Mattes, and foreign firms like Anaconda copper and IT&T, which controlled 38 percent of all manufacturing assets by the mid-1960s.[3]

With the election of Frei, this relationship deteriorated as the state began to champion social change; after Allende came to power, strikes and factory takeovers multiplied as Marxist and Christian Democratic parties vied for power within the union movement. "Everything became politicized. The workers were turned into our enemies, and we were called bloodsuckers," García remembered with a grimace. "It was extremely painful."

In 1970, Nibsa was seized in a government expropriation drive that eventually placed 421 businesses in state hands.[4] An administrative team headed by Popular Unity militants took over, and the plant became a showcase for delegations from Cuba and the East bloc. The company's board of directors, desperate to preserve official goodwill, agreed to the new conditions, and for a few months García was allowed to remain.

But relations soured steadily until one day, in October 1971, García was fired. "After twenty-six years, they gave me fifteen minutes to leave," he said bitterly. "I had been very critical, but they were making terrible mistakes. The factory was my world. I had to defend it." After that, he recounted, things went downhill. Machines were poorly maintained, production fell, orders were canceled.

The disillusioned industrialist moved for several years to Bolivia, where a rightist military regime was more receptive to private enterprise. But when the coup came, García rushed home to take charge of his "liberated" plant, which the new government helped him buy back on generous terms. He dismissed politically "suspect" workers but kept on the old-timers, who had hung a Chilean flag out the factory window on September 11.

NO group of Chileans supported the coup as strongly as did the business community, which felt its very survival to be at stake. Business groups, with covert aid from the Nixon administration, unleashed a crusade of economic sabotage against Allende: grocers hoarded food, truck owners refused to deliver it, and business-led strikes paralyzed the country twice. Trade associations like SOFOFA produced scathing editorials and pressed the armed forces to take action.

"At first we tried to coexist with Allende, to give him the benefit of the doubt, but by the end of 1971 we realized he wanted to implant a dictatorship of the proletariat. From then on, our vow was to destabilize the government," said Orlando Sáenz, president of SOFOFA at the time. "We didn't know precisely when the explosion would come, but we kept putting more wood and paper on the fire. Eventually, they were bound to ignite."[5]

When the tinderbox did explode and the armed forces stepped in, the business community reacted with uniform relief. Lobbying groups pledged "unconditional support" for the new authorities and vied to collect donations for "national reconstruction." The Chamber of Construction begged the junta to "remain as long as necessary to banish the evils" that had been "fertilized" by abuses of democracy.[6]

Beyond this effusive endorsement, however, businessmen lapsed back into their customary passivity. With the crisis ended, they were happy to return to their private affairs and let military authorities tend to the problems of government. Reassured by the junta's vow to respect private property, some big-business leaders were also enthralled by the free-market theories being promoted in official circles, which they saw as a chance to reduce bureaucratic interference and become more dynamic.

"We industrialists accept this challenge . . . in which only the most efficient will survive," declared Raúl Sahli, the new SOFOFA head. "We must change our mentality."[7] Jorge Yarur Banna, the king of Chilean textiles, echoed this position. "I have waited my entire life for this paternalism to end, for the state to stop defending us so much," he said.[8]

But small merchants and manufacturers, more dependent and vulnerable, assumed that the state would resume its normal, sheltering function in their lives. Some, like Rafael Cumsille of the retail business association and León Vilarín of the truck owners, dreamed of becoming equal partners with the military. They expected to be rewarded for their role in overthrowing Allende—not made targets of radical economic reform.

From the beginning, however, it was clear the junta had no intention of extending special privileges to interest groups. Soon after the coup, a group of sausage manufacturers called on Sergio de Castro to negotiate higher price ceilings. Instead, barely glancing at their cost-analysis study, he told them they were free to charge any prices they wished. Stunned, the meat makers presented a second, more "reasonable" request. Again, de Castro insisted there were no limits. Several days later, the junta abolished the entire price-control system.[9]

When small-business groups chafed nervously at the new economic order, they were reprimanded both by big-business leaders and by government officials. "For years you have demanded the role you are now being granted; so play it!" Fernando Léniz challenged a convention of industrialists in 1974. Jorge Fontaine, president of the Confederation of Production, noted, "Some sectors are bolder, but others wait to have everything clarified for them. They are going to miss the train."[10]

While economic officials were exhorting businessmen to become tougher and more efficient, a few military officials, notably General Leigh, chastised them for being selfish and socially irresponsible. At one assembly, Leigh scolded a group of five hundred leading businessmen like a schoolmaster, saying they had been blinded by "egotism" and the "spirit of profit." "They dive into their own affairs and don't see anything beyond," he charged.[11]

But businessmen responded deferentially to any criticism emanating from the new rulers. The freshness of their trauma kept them loyal to their liberators, and even the most prominent businessmen were reluctant to offend the military, for fear of being labeled dissidents or traitors. Despite their high-profile role in opposing Allende, business leaders found they had little personal influence on military officials or their high-powered economic aides.

Thus, instead of examining and debating economic policy, business associations like SOFOFA abandoned their function as defenders of industry.[12] Regime loyalists, placed in charge of lobbying groups, served as "veritable ambassadors" for the government. "Unfortunately, few of us saw clearly that a massacre was coming," reflected Domingo Durán of the National Agricultural Association.[13]

BY 1976, the massacre was in full force. Buffeted by the combination of world recession and economic shock treatment, industrial production plummeted 23 percent. Auto parts and construction were badly hurt, and shoe production dropped from thirty to ten million pairs.[14] Textile mills, long protected by 200 percent duties on clothing, were devastated by a flood of cheap Asian shirts and socks. In 1975, cloth production fell 31.4 percent, several major mills failed, and all others were reduced to half capacity.[15]

Officials promised that the "tough medicine" would soon be over, so factories tried to avoid firing workers by shortening shifts or cutting wages. But as the recession stretched into 1977, a record 214 firms went bankrupt—including such major employers as Andes steel and Ferriloza aluminum—and thousands of jobs were lost.[16] In manufacturing, the work force declined from a peak of 776,000 in 1973 to 523,000; in construction, the number of jobs fell from 253,000 to 135,000.[17]

"It was like suffering a second expropriation. We had to cut back from 500 to 190 people, which is hard when someone has been with you for thirty years," recalled Roberto Fantuzzi, manager of his family cookware factory. "The Chicago Boys raised the interest rates to usurious levels and started importing everything. It was a crime. The banks started pressuring to take us over; there was an atmosphere of trickery and desperation. But we scrimped and fought back, and we survived."[18]

Some manufacturers saw the recession as an opportunity to streamline operations, but others suffered by failing to adapt to the new rules. Impervious to pleas for a softer landing, officials yanked protective tariffs out from under producers, and even businessmen who agreed that reform was needed feared that such swift and brutal change would destroy the very industries it was meant to strengthen.

"From the point of view of diminishing inflation . . . the measures are positive. But it seems to me a horror that an industry which took twenty years to build must disappear," observed Enrique Cantolla, a spokesman for electronics manufacturers.[19] Loath to condemn the economic model, most business leaders blamed bureaucratic zeal or delays. In 1976, after giving a bleak industry report, one Confederation of Production official added that they were "fierce partisans" of regime policies, "loyally" attempting to solve certain problems.[20]

A few groups gave full vent to their anger: the truck owners published a newspaper advertisement entitled "Unqualified Ingratitude," asserting that price deregulation was destroying a sector that had been crucial to the overthrow of Allende. But even such dramatic complaints were ignored. In 1982, a leading textile owner recounted bitterly that when his colleagues protested the drop in tariffs and other punitive measures, they were labeled as "whiney, pessimistic, and inefficient."[21]

THE economic recovery that began in 1977, and swelled to a full-fledged boom by 1980, muted such murmurs of discontent.[22] The losers—generally smaller, unknown firms—were forgotten; the winners—mostly larger, better-capitalized corporations—adapted and thrived in the new competitive environment. Several major textile mills began importing cloth and using their own distribution systems to sell it.

Because businessmen tended to focus on short-term, narrow interests rather than on broader economic trends, they rode the wave of artificial prosperity without worrying much about the structural distortions it was causing. Like the junta members, they were dazzled by the Chicago Boys' expertise, self-confidence, and coherent ideology. The economy was growing more than 7 percent a year, so the technocrats must be right.

The atmosphere of success was buoyed by the flood of imported consumer goods and the easy access to credit. By 1979, the government had eliminated barriers on most foreign products except furs and gems; between 1977 and 1980, spending on consumer imports more than doubled, to $1.2 billion.[23] Santiago stores were crammed with French cosmetics, Japanese radios, and Italian refrigerators. Over two million TV sets were imported between 1976 and 1981, and Scotch whisky, first mass-marketed in 1976, became so popular that sales within three years reached $11.9 million.[24]

To make this smorgasbord especially tempting, consumers were offered the novel enticement of credit cards. The first Chilean card, Diners' Club, was made available in 1979, and within one year more than fourteen thousand had been issued.[25] Appliance stores advertised easy credit, and first-time customers paid little attention to the interest rates. "It is the moment of fantasy for the laborer, the office worker, the housewife, the student, even the retiree who gazes in the display window with longing eyes," observed the journalist María Olivia Monckeberg.[26]

Free-market enthusiasts rhapsodized about a "revolution" in buying habits, but critics warned that the credit boom was luring people to spend beyond their means and widening the gap between haves and have-nots. In 1980, 100 percent of the foreign color TVs, 98 percent of the cars, and 94 percent of the whisky were bought by the wealthiest 20 percent of the population, whereas the poorest 20 percent bought virtually no imports at all.[27]

Among affluent urbanites, a fast new status-symbol culture emerged, departing markedly from Chile's tradition of upper-class modesty. Peugeots were replaced by flashy BMWs, shopping malls and condominiums sprouted in the affluent suburbs, and lavish residential developments crept up the Andean foothills. The use of computers, virtually banned by tariffs until 1975, caught on quickly, and Chile burst into the information age.

"Suddenly everything was credit, public relations, and technology. Chile became a cross between Hong Kong and Coconut Grove," recalled Marco Antonio de la Parra, who worked as a publicity agent during the boom era. "Among the poor, people were waiting outside factories for someone to be fired. But in advertising, people were earning spectacular salaries, buying cars, becoming overwhelmed in debt. It was empty and neurotic, but it was addictive."[28]

Beneath this façade of affluence lay a revolution in business and banking practices, stimulated by the deregulation of lending laws, the flood of petrodollars, and the opening of capital markets to foreign investors. Savings and loan companies and mutual funds were established, and the stock exchange, a leisurely gentlemen's club, was jolted to life. During the first half of 1980, the value of Colcura Timber shares rose 880 percent, that of the CRAV rose 490 percent, and trading reached a record eight billion pesos ($200 million).[29]

The growth of high finance generated a new breed of entrepreneur known as the *cuesco cabrera,* a rough equivalent of "yuppie." These eager young deal makers spoke a language different from that of Chile's traditional manager, with his proverbial eyeshade and adding machine; and their razzle-dazzle style made the trials of grubby hubcap or underwear factories seem déclassé. Whole fortunes were being manufactured out of paper, and every moment wasted was potential profit lost.

Suddenly, society was no longer sneering at businessmen as leeches; instead, it seemed to be looking up to them as glamorous figures. "It is no longer a political crime to praise free enterprise; it is no longer a sin to value the market," enthused José Piñera. "A genuine mental opening has been produced to the economic practices and forms that have achieved the free development of Western nations."[30]

The most flamboyant practitioner of this new kind of capitalism was Javier Vial. An energetic developer, he had spent two decades building a portfolio of investments, and when the financial system opened up, he and his partners borrowed from U.S. banks to expand rapidly. Using the BHC bank as a base and operating through holding companies, they purchased a number of "privatized" state enterprises, and by 1979 the Vial empire was worth at least $436 million.[31]

Unlike Chile's traditional captains of industry, Vial was brash and passionate. He raced horses and sports cars, wore expensive but ill-matching clothes, built the tallest skyscraper in Santiago, and constantly sought new ways to expand. Yet Vial never seemed to take business too seriously. "He entertains himself like a child, investing and moving his capital from one place to another," observed one writer.[32]

Style and timing were the keys to Vial's success. At one meeting in Manhattan's Plaza Hotel, he held 250 bankers and businessmen spellbound with his pitch for investing in Chile. "The American banks were flooded with money and eager to lend. We had the right foreign contacts, and we knew how to put together attractive projects," explained Vial in 1983, ensconced in his elegant penthouse office overlooking Santiago from the Santa María Tower. "In a market economy the speculator plays a key role. The name of the game is to buy low and sell high."[33]

Manuel Cruzat, Vial's chief competitor, was his exact opposite—a reclusive, austere homebody who rarely appeared at social functions, and a severe, highly educated perfectionist who ran his enterprises like an army.[34] Yet, in his discreet way, he was building an even vaster empire in the protective shadow of military rule. Cruzat and his partner, Fernando Larraín, borrowed heavily to acquire enterprises from CORFO, and by 1978 they controlled eighty-five firms, with assets of nearly one billion dollars, including the mammoth Chilean Petroleum Corporation.[35]

Some of these investments were solid, traditional firms, but many were speculative ventures in forestry and fisheries, mutual funds and real estate. In the aggressive new style of the day, Cruzat's aides launched sophisticated advertising campaigns to attract depositors to their bank and market Diet Pepsi to young consumers. As the economic miracle unfolded, the value of Cruzat-Larraín's assets multiplied; from 1976 to 1982, earnings from their timber operations alone doubled, to $104 million.[36] What few outsiders knew, however, was that both Cruzat and Vial were making loans to their own high-risk business ventures, building a tangled and precarious web of debt.

WHILE some entrepreneurs thrived in the new, competitive environment, others remained deeply suspicious of the free-market model. A few leaders of depressed industries, notably Roberto and Angel Fantuzzi of the Metallurgic Industry Association, publicly criticized the Chicago Boys when few others dared. At the height of the boom, they formed the Committee to Defend Chilean Products and painted their trucks with signs that said, "If you want your husband to be unemployed, buy imports."

The Fantuzzis saw themselves as struggling to preserve a solid, traditional way of doing business—early-rising, hardworking, paternalistic—against an encroaching modern style that was less humane and more ephemeral. "Some of my friends left their factories and joined the new financial world, but to us the firm was like a son; just because there are problems, you don't abandon it," Roberto explained.

Small-business groups also complained that Chile's recovery had left them behind. Rafael Cumsille of the merchants' association charged that "cold technicians" were imposing "suicidal measures." Juan Jara, leader of the taxicab owners federation, spoke out against the concentration of wealth among regime allies. "The moment has come to say enough, to rescue government from the hands of a privileged group," he urged in April 1980. But official reaction was swift: Jara was arrested and charged with insulting the authorities.[37]

Traditional agriculture was hard hit by the elimination of tariffs and price supports, and farm lobbyists invoked numerous arguments—ranging from national security to the "laws of nature"—to exempt themselves from the full Chicago treatment.[38] As usual, however, officials were not swayed: one Economics Ministry aide coolly informed dairy farmers they could "store their grain" or "eat their cows."[39]

The depression in conventional crop-growing was tempered by the boom in experimental agriculture, especially fruits that could be shipped to northern countries with opposite growing seasons. Between 1975 and 1980, fruit export earnings surged from $30 million to $136 million. In 1979, Chile shipped 7.8 million boxes of apples and 9.5 million crates of grapes to the United States, Canada, Germany, and forty-seven other countries.[40] The face of Chilean agriculture was changing rapidly, and the harvest of profits was just beginning.

Among the powerful urban lobbies, there was little sympathy for those who had failed to adapt to the new conditions. "Why should we ask the government to defend inefficient industries?" shrugged Domingo Arteaga of the Confederation of Production.[41] Yet such attitudes were also a result of constant pressure from La Moneda. According to some accounts, Pinochet held a virtual veto over nominations for SOFOFA officials and insisted on unconditional loyalists for its top posts. "They didn't just want supporters; they wanted total yes-men," charged Sáenz, who left SOFOFA soon after the coup.

As they neared the 1980 plebiscite, business leaders threw their weight behind the "yes" vote for Pinochet's continued rule. Casting the referendum as a choice between economic freedom and socialist apocalypse, industry spokesmen warned of shortages, paralyzed investments, and "general anarchy" if the "no" vote won. Critics suggested that their greater fear was that of losing the benefits of a laissez-faire economic policy—and that the free-market model could not stand "a drop of democracy," because it was an "economic fiction" imposed by the power of Pinochet.[42]

With the regime triumphant at the polls and the economy expanding rapidly, no one in the business community wanted to admit how thin that fiction really was. But in May 1981, with the collapse of CRAV, it became clear that falling commodity prices and punitive tariffs were not the only problem. CRAV's president, Jorge Ross, who had been speculating in sugar futures while building an empire of investments, suddenly found himself overextended and $300 million in debt. The government suspended trading in CRAV stocks, and stockholders' blue-chip savings were suddenly worthless.[43]

If there was a message here for other high-rolling entrepreneurs, they appeared to ignore it, while influential businessmen issued statements of confidence in government economic policies. But export firms were being squeezed as inflation rose and the dollar remained fixed, while firms that had borrowed heavily in dollars to finance imported goods or machines were hurt by rising foreign interest rates.

By 1982, the dimensions of the crisis were undeniable and the private sector was facing its worst battering since the Great Depression. Industrial production plunged 21 percent, and 810 companies went bankrupt, five times more than during the 1975 recession. Between 1980 and 1983, a total of 2,151 enterprises declared themselves insolvent; they ranged from family-owned machine shops to major employers like the Santa Carolina vineyards and the Manufactureras Chilenas de Algodón, a complex of three large cotton mills.[44]

For thousands of small businessmen and managers, the sense of failure was often unbearable. Many were forced to take semi-skilled jobs, and taxi driving became a widespread form of disguised middle-class unemployment. At the height of the crisis, one could hail a cab on any corner in Santiago and be picked up by a driver in tweed jacket and tie, invariably with a tale of dignity destroyed and dreams evaporated.

One middle-aged cabbie, asked about his previous work, said he had once owned a small plastics factory, prospering enough to send his children to private schools and take his wife on vacations abroad. With the inundation of cheap Asian toys, the factory went bankrupt in 1978. Undaunted, the owner mortgaged his house to set up a shoe factory. But in 1983 he was caught by the peso devaluation; his debts quadrupled and his business failed again. "We had to sell the house, and my wife went to work as a salesclerk," he confessed, breaking into tears. "This car is all we have left."

As bitterness against the government spread among small businessmen, a few groups attempted to spark a serious protest movement. Under the leadership of Carlos Podlech, a former army captain, the wheat growers called for radical changes in policy and joined forces with the truckers and retailers, holding rallies in provincial cities, blocking farm foreclosures, and issuing bold manifestos. "It is our duty as citizens to defend our productive assets," warned one declaration.[45]

In response, the regime moved to divide and decapitate the protesters: several groups were offered individual aid packages, and the police moved in on illegal farmers' rallies. In December 1982, Podlech was seized and forced into exile in Brazil—the only prominent businessman to be so harshly treated in sixteen years of military rule.[46] The movement had been crushed.

Among urban business leaders, only well-known mavericks spoke out at first. "It is not we who failed; it is the theoreticians," charged Angel Fantuzzi. Out of 500 metal manufacturers, he said, 150 had "fallen by the wayside, destroyed."[47] Looking back years later, he compared the Chicago Boys to "religious fanatics." "If you tried to tell them there were people behind the numbers, you crashed against a wall of technocratics," he recalled. "They never heard the voice of suffering."[48]

Another dissident was Orlando Sáenz, who noted dryly that the

"euphoric architects of the Chilean miracle have now confronted
Chile with what seems to be the worst economic disaster in its
history." Flush with foreign loans, "the country went on a binge
of new-model cars, multicolored perfume bottles, little machines
that dance and sing," he added. "Now begins the long and frustrating process of paying for the binge."[49]

Most business leaders were still reluctant to criticize the regime,
underscoring Pinochet's grip on an elite that remained obsessed by
fears of a return to leftist electoral politics. But gradually, they too
joined the clamor for relief from rigid free-market policies. And
when the capitalist old guard finally spoke out after months of
strained silence, Pinochet had little choice but to listen.

In April 1982, a pivotal stockholders' meeting was called at the
mammoth Paper and Cardboard Manufacturing Company (Com-
pañía Manufacturera de Papeles y Cartones, or CMPC), Chile's
second-largest private corporation, where production costs had risen
80 percent in three years. Former President Jorge Alessandri, who
had headed the firm for years, sharply criticized the fixed exchange
rate and other aspects of Sergio de Castro's policies. The next week,
Pinochet asked the finance minister to resign, and three months
later he devalued the peso.[50]

Military authorities were also growing belatedly alarmed over
the practices of the high-flying financial groups, whose banks were
badly overexposed in questionable insider loans. By 1982, the BHC
bank owned by Vial had lent 28 percent of its money to Vial-
linked ventures. And the Bank of Santiago, owned by Cruzat, had
invested 44 percent of its available credit in Cruzat-connected
projects.[51]

Desperate to find someone to blame for the crisis, policymakers
found a vulnerable target in Vial, whose dollar-debt burden soared
with devaluation. In an effort to "deconcentrate" private debts,
officials pressured Vial to sell his lapsed loans to the government
at a fraction of their worth. When he refused, protesting he was
being punished for practicing just what the Chicago Boys had
preached, they forced him from the presidency of the Bank of Chile,
which he controlled through a number of firms that were deeply
in debt to the bank.

Then, with the bank takeovers of January 1983, the Pinochet
regime broke completely with the conglomerates it had fostered
for nearly a decade. By liquidating Vial's BHC bank, taking over
the Bank of Chile, and intervening in two Cruzat-owned banks,
the government cut off the oxygen these highly leveraged behe-

moths needed to survive. In the ensuing months, both the Vial and the Cruzat empires were dismantled, with many of their "paper" companies declared bankrupt and many of their operations sold off by the state.

The spectacular collapse of these entrepreneurs symbolized the end of Chile's first fling with modern, high-stakes finance. Cruzat, well connected and willing to cooperate, was spared further punishment, but Vial suffered the full weight of official wrath.[52] In a court case that required three years and twenty thousand pages of documents, the government charged Vial and his partners in an elaborate scheme that set up a series of straw corporations with the same borrowed funds. Forced to abandon his gleaming skyscraper, Vial served nine months in prison for fraud.[53]

Years later, in a modest office that bore few traces of his former affluence except a massive antique desk with lion-paw feet, Vial looked back on his defeat with the aplomb of an inveterate gambler. "There's no question, I was made a scapegoat, but I don't hate anyone for it," he insisted. "When the crisis came, the law of the jungle took over: some people won, and some people lost. But it has been the greatness of this government to make people efficient, and the economic groups learned a lesson too; instead of competing savagely, they are cooperating more now."[54]

Some of the smaller speculators who drowned in the debacle of 1982–83 shared Vial's philosophical attitude toward losing quickly gained riches. While critical of the Chicago Boys and foreign banks for encouraging their schemes, they also accepted part of the blame. One executive whose construction firm went bankrupt, costing five hundred jobs, said the crisis stemmed from "overvalued assets, high interest rates, a zeal for biting off more than one could chew, a certain irresponsibility, an intense demand for profits by the banks, and a tremendous hurry to make up of the lost years of the Popular Unity."[55]

Most victims, though, were small investors caught up in a whirlwind they were ill equipped to handle. Iván and Sofía Solimano, a couple who ran a travel agency, borrowed funds to expand their business at the peak of the tourist boom. Suddenly they were hopelessly in debt, fleeing from creditors, and bankrupt. "For three years, we were kings of the block; we didn't listen when people said the boom couldn't last," explained Sofía, a slender, thoughtful woman of fifty-five. "When you start to succeed, you become irrational; you want to believe. Then one day you wake up and realize none of it was real."[56]

Many Chileans, moreover, were double victims of arbitrary fiscal-policy changes and shoddy big-business practices. More than 131,000 people, lured by advertisements offering windfall profits, had invested in mutual funds controlled by Vial and Cruzat. In the end, customers forfeited up to 80 percent of their deposits. "With one stroke, I am losing the effort of twenty years, saved peso by peso," fumed Jorge Brito, a sixty-six-year-old retiree waiting in line for his partial refund.[57]

THE collapse galvanized business associations out of their long silence. Alarmed by the eruption of protests, they realized that Chile's recovery demanded both a more pragmatic approach to economic policy and a gradual restoration of political freedoms. Replacing complacent leaders with tough infighters like Ernesto Ayala, they pressed for an emergency plan that included higher tariffs, a lower exchange rate, and a more flexible schedule for repaying the foreign debt.[58]

By naming Luis Escobar finance minister and Modesto Collados economics minister in early 1984, Pinochet reached out to reassure the alienated business community that the regime was listening. During the next year, a flurry of expansionary measures reversed Chile's economic free-fall, industry breathed more freely with higher import tariffs, and the GNP grew by 6 percent.

But Escobar soon encountered formidable opposition. Foreign bankers and the International Monetary Fund made it clear no further loans would be forthcoming if rapid economic expansion tipped the balance of Chile's foreign accounts, thus violating its pact for foreign-debt renegotiation. At home, the hapless minister also ran afoul of unexpected enemies: the very business community that had initially seemed so relieved by his appointment.

Led by a new breed of entrepreneurs who had become strong believers in the market economy, Chile's most influential businessmen soon decided they did not want an old-school conservative making policy after all. Despite their public fall from grace, the Chicago Boys had converted a substantial portion of the private sector to their belief in full freedom for the marketplace. Now that the banking system had come under total state control, business leaders began to fear a return to state-centered economic policy—or even to Allende-style socialism, should Pinochet fall.

Sensing the chance for a comeback, some former economic officials launched a merciless campaign against Escobar, and business leaders joined them in protesting his proposals to raise taxes and confront the IMF. José Piñera, now publishing an economics journal, accused the minister of undermining the free-market model through populist promises and deals with special interests.[59] Escobar retorted that Piñera was obsessed with becoming president, "or at least minister of finance. I would recommend he wait. How old is he? Less than forty. I am already fifty-seven. He will have many other opportunities later to save the country."[60]

Despite his frank and feisty style, Escobar was no match for the Chicago Boys at the politics of authoritarian rule. Schooled in free-wheeling democratic politics, the former "Alessandrista" failed to grasp that his most important audience was not twelve million citizens, or thousands of small-business owners, but four uniformed men. Pinochet and Merino were especially skeptical, viewing Escobar as weak and susceptible to political pressure.[61] Despite their tactical retreat, the junta menbers were still committed to the free-market model; by publicly attacking it, Escobar only aroused their wrath.

IN late 1984, with street protests brought under control but economic policy mired in internal disputes, Pinochet began searching for a new economic team more compatible with his views. The name that kept surfacing was that of Hernán Büchi, a young engineer with a business degree from Columbia University who came from a military family. After joining the government in 1975, he had worked his way up through a series of subcabinet posts, earning a reputation as a gifted, tireless problem solver. Named superintendant of banks in the thick of the banking crisis, he emerged as a clear-headed, reasonable figure in a chaotic and contentious climate.[62]

When Büchi was named finance minister, in February 1985, business leaders heaved a sigh of relief. Although a disciple of free-market economics, he was more flexible and realistic than his predecessors—and untainted by association with Chicago. Despite his shaggy blond locks and somewhat eccentric life-style, the thirty-nine-year-old minister was the ultimate servant of the authoritarian state: brilliant yet deferential to the junta, precise in his management style, and austere to the point of asceticism in his personal habits.

Despite the economic downturn of 1982, Büchi's predecessors had built a more efficient, streamlined state and spawned a new entrepreneurial class unafraid of economic challenges. Upon taking office, the young minister set out energetically to restore the broad lines of the free-market model: stimulating private enterprise, reducing the state's role, and opening up the economy to world markets. Unhampered by the ideological rigidity of a Sergio de Castro, he did not hesitate to use state powers to boost the market economy when necessary. Business and banking were regulated more tightly, and price-support systems were developed for agricultural staples such as wheat, which were sensitive to public pressure and world price fluctuations.

The men Büchi brought into government were, like himself, less mystical and more pragmatic than the purists of de Castro's era. "In the early days we all believed too much in science. With Hernán, we learned the art of the possible," reflected Cristián Larroulet, who returned to government as Büchi's senior aide.[63] Like Miguel Kast, Büchi set an example of austerity and hard work, letting ministry rugs remain threadbare and offering meager fare at receptions. "His abstemiousness affected the whole system. The notion of a lean public sector, where nothing was wasted and there were no free rides, spread throughout," recalled one American economist who visited Santiago often.[64]

The return to fiscal conservatism was reassuring to foreign lenders. In 1983, Chile had come close to defaulting on the $19 billion foreign debt, but within a year Büchi had reestablished Chile's credibility with the banks and signed a $1.9 billion refinancing deal. He also lowered the debt by pioneering in creative mechanisms such as "debt-equity swaps," in which the state traded chunks of discounted debt to banks or foreign capitalists in exchange for investment in Chile.[65]

The international finance agencies soon rewarded Chile with massive amounts of credit for recovery and development, including three $250 million "structural adjustment" loans from the World Bank. These loans were opposed by a number of Western democracies to protest renewed repression, and in 1986 the normally supportive Reagan administration abstained on one loan vote until Pinochet lifted a new state of siege. Generally, however, lenders confined their evaluation to issues of fiscal management. Between 1985 and 1987 alone, the World Bank approved more than $1.2 billion in loans to Chile.[66]

"In 1983, we had the worst debt problem in Latin America, but we put our house in order in a professional, disciplined way, instead of following the populist policies of our neighbors," asserted Hernán Somerville, a jaunty, impeccably tailored man who served as chief debt negotiator. In four years of dealing with international lenders, he added, "I never faced a single political question. The money flowed in because we managed things well. No one ever said change your government and then come back."[67]

Revitalized by fresh flows of foreign credit, investors expanded into new fields of export products, such as winter fruits. The long-dominant mining and manufacturing sectors ceded further ground to new enterprises: financial services, information technology, agribusiness. By 1986, services alone, from restaurants to security guard companies, accounted for half the GNP.[68]

A few industrial groups, notably the transport owners and Rafael Cumsille's retail business association, continued to condemn the government for not doing more to help small entrepreneurs recover. To a remarkable extent, though, the mentality of Chilean businessmen had changed. With the economy growing at over 5 percent a year, even die-hard protectionists discovered that by becoming more effecient and responsive to demand, they could prosper without state intervention. More adventurous entrepreneurs, meanwhile, had learned new lessons from the 1983 collapse: irresponsible speculation and borrowing did not pay.

One by one, traditional manufacturers adapted to the new, self-sufficient climate. Yarur textiles, once nearly destroyed by Asian imports, joined forces with two other mills to produce high-quality cloth for export. An old Fiat assembly plant was converted into a modern refrigeration facility for fruit. Fantuzzi aluminum purchased faster machines and diversified from pots and pans into street-lamp covers and wagon bodies for American toy stores. Nibsa computerized its engineering department and cut back on labor.

"The people who went bankrupt were those who failed to modernize. They can blame no one but themselves," asserted Leonel García, who by 1986 was producing eighty tons of high-grade valves a month, mostly for export, with one-third the number of workers he had once employed to make fewer, inferior products for domestic use. His profits were healthy, and his purpose in life had been redeemed. "We must admit that our industries were inefficient and needed to be pushed," he said. "Now we have entered a whole new era."

The boom in computer technology resurged after the 1983 collapse. Within three years, sales of personal computers were climbing toward $100 million a year, and many banks offered twenty-four-hour automatic tellers. The SONDA computer company, founded in 1974, played a pioneering role in automating banks and copper production. By 1986, with five hundred workers, $30 million in sales, and a new, glass-paneled headquarters, SONDA was bidding on a contract to computerize banks in Beijing.

Andrés Navarro, a young engineer who founded SONDA, said his education in the United States and exposure to business practices there convinced him that "technology was the way to improve productivity and create wealth." He described himself as part of a "new generation of businessmen that want to be independent. We criticize those who are capitalists in success and socialists in failure. We want to have both rights and responsibilities."[69]

Outside the capital, a green revolution was also rapidly expanding. Fruit exports, aided by modern grafting and irrigation techniques, increased 600 percent between 1980 and 1986, when Chile shipped almost $500 million worth of grapes, peaches, apples, kiwis, and berries to North America and Europe.[70] Timber plantations covered over one million hectares in 1986, and companies moved from exporting raw boards to exporting finished furniture.[71] Copper still accounted for 40 percent of all export earnings, but Chile was becoming much less dependent on a single commodity, while rapid provincial development reduced the stream of unskilled workers into the capital.[72]

Under Büchi's leadership, the government aggressively revived the privatization schemes of the 1970s, selling off firms that had been taken over in 1983 and public enterprises that had been profitably developed under military rule, including the telephone company (Entel), various electric utilities, the national sugar refinery (Iansa), and Pacific Steel.

This time, the transactions were handled more prudently, with the government requiring sound private financing through domestic banks or foreign investors. The sole touch of scandal stemmed from the coziness with which some regime officials involved in privatization policy—notably Pinochet's son-in-law Julio Ponce Leroú—became executives and partners in newly privatized firms.

To spread corporate ownership more widely and foster an entrepreneurial spirit among the public, the government designed an innovative plan for "popular capitalism," issuing shares of stock in public corporations and, in some cases, giving their employees the chance to purchase them. At Chilectra Metropolitana, workers purchased 27 percent of the stock; at Pacific Steel, they bought 31 percent.[73]

Officials also encouraged foreign investment, principally through relaxed rules on joint ventures and debt-for-equity swaps. Saudi bankers purchased timber and pasture land; American banks bought sugar mill and electric company stocks. Through a joint venture, New Zealand's Carter Holt Harvey group bought a controlling interest in the Chilean Petroleum Company and invested in coal mines and kiwis; the Australian billionaire Alan Bond purchased 36 percent of the telephone company.[74]

Critics warned that the invasion of capital was eating away the nation's patrimony, including such "strategic" industries such as energy and communications.[75] They also charged that once again, low sale prices were robbing state coffers to the benefit of anonymous foreign investors and domestic conglomerates.[76] Raúl Sáez and Orlando Sáenz formed the Committee to Defend the National Heritage, alleging that Chilean and foreign interests were conspiring to transform the state into an economically helpless dwarf.[77]

But officials dismissed these concerns as old-fashioned, arguing that the state lost more by subsidizing inefficient firms than by selling them cheaply, and that as long as new blood was being pumped into the economy, the source of the transfusions didn't matter. Gradually, with firm support from Pinochet and rapidly widening acceptance in the business community, Büchi's pragmatic version of free-market economics began to show results, launching Chile on a period of sure and steady growth.

THE collapse and rebirth of the economy led to a significant shift in the concentration of domestic wealth. Vial and Cruzat were replaced by other, more solidly financed conglomerates, especially one headed by Anacleto Angelini, who joined forces with the New Zealanders to buy Copec and thirty-six affiliated firms, and one founded by Eliodoro Matte Ossa, the paper baron. By the late 1980s, the Angelini and Matte groups alone controlled more than $5 billion in assets.[78]

Matte's giant CMPC, founded in 1920 with substantial state aid, was a spectacular example of corporate transformation under the free-market model. Although its financial power was eclipsed by Cruzat and Vial until 1983, its forestry interests thrived under the regime's export-promotion policies, and after the collapse of its flashier rivals, CMPC assumed a dominant role in the shaping of a new entrepreneurial mentality.

The voice of prudence that kept CMPC from following the meteoric rise and fall of its rivals was that of old Jorge Alessandri.

And the driving force behind its evolution from a traditional, state-sheltered industry to a modern, diversified corporation was young Eliodoro Matte Larraín, heir to the family interests, who studied business at Chicago in the early 1970s. "We were different from our elders—totally committed to the notion of free enterprise," the energetic industrialist recounted in 1989.[79]

Having endured the recession by cutting its work force from 5,000 to 3,500 and modernizing its machinery, the firm was reaching $500 million in annual sales by the mid-1980s. Its vast tracts of insignia pine grew quickly, and its researchers developed new uses for paper pulp, such as disposable diapers and wooden pallets for shipping fruit. Matte proudly attributed these achievements to the regime's economic model, and became president of the Center for Public Studies, a prestigious research institute devoted to spreading the free-market gospel. "It is crucial to retain the liberal ideas," he said, "and we must be aggressive in defending them."[80]

After years of quiet deference to military authorities, other big-business leaders set out to build a strong public role in the promotion of economic freedom. Manuel Feliú, elected president of the Confederation of Production in 1986, wrote, "We will gain nothing struggling arduously to raise the gross national product if we don't also succeed in seeing that the principles of free enterprise are shared by the population." It is not enough to be "the engines of development," he added. "It is also necessary to win the battle of ideas."[81]

From a certain perspective, it seemed that Chile's rapid economic development was changing the behavior and outlook of the entire culture. In a best-selling 1987 book called *The Silent Revolution,* Joaquín Lavín portrayed Santiago as an urbane society of shopping malls and consumer marketing, fax machines and cellular phones. Lavín's tour of technical marvels included computerized pricing at supermarkets, direct-dial phone service to twenty-two countries, and video game parlors in every town.

The most important revolution, he maintained, was in attitudes. Chileans were more informed, more resourceful, and less dependent on the state. They obtained health care from ISAPRES and invested their savings in private pension funds. "Everything is changing," Lavín boasted, from what people eat (less meat, more yogurt) to what careers they choose (engineering instead of sociology). "Today, Chile is a leader," fully integrated into the world and "advancing more rapidly than ever before."[82]

To critical observers, however, the swift modernization of

enterprise and life-styles seemed to eclipse a tradition of ethical, or at least discreet, behavior among the affluent. The incomes of the wealthiest 10 percent of Chileans rose 83 percent from 1978 to 1988, and a nouveau riche class of conspicuous consumers emerged even more aggressively than it had in the boom years of the early 1980s.[83] "Today it is more important to be bold than moral, to be rich than hardworking," observed Liliana Mahn. "People have more initiative, but they want everything as soon as possible, and they think you can solve any problem with a computer."[84]

Formed under military rule and insulated in suburban enclaves, Chile's new economic elite had little contact with the working class and no recent experience with democracy. Many members identified more with values of economic choice than with those of political freedom. Over dinner one night in 1989, a young advertising designer described with embarrassed horror the glamorous but authoritarian environment in which she worked:

"The people in my office are the new middle class; they dress fashionably and drive expensive cars, but they don't read, and you can't talk to them about anything of substance," she said. "All that counts with them is the ability to sell and to show off. They spend lavish amounts of money on parties and publicity; the managers speak English and use American nicknames. But underneath they are frighteningly ignorant. They think everyone against the government is a communist, and some of them brag about having friends in the security forces. I don't think they really even know Chile was once a democracy."[85]

As the benevolent state receded and competition sharpened, the traditional boss, who inspected the factory books every Friday and paid stingy wages but remembered his workers' birthdays, was replaced by a striving new breed of money managers who were hostile to unions and hired subcontractors to deal with labor. Many new industries, such as fruit and forestry, thrived on low-paid seasonal labor that enjoyed few benefits and no organized form of protection against exploitation.

At CMPC, the corporate complex featured employee soccer fields and clubhouses, but subcontracted forestry workers toiled in rudimentary logging camps. Eliodoro Matte Larraín acknowledged that "there should be more trickle-down of profits," yet he insisted that Chile's development could not be sacrificed to the demands of a highly protected labor force. "Only growth can bring real social justice," he asserted.

Some young businessmen found success in the new world of

high-stakes capitalism while still clinging to humanistic principles. One was Máximo Pacheco, general manager of a Chilean-Japanese leasing company. As a university student in the Allende era, Pacheco had been a committed socialist at the barricades of change. Now his old classmates would hardly have recognized him, making conference calls to London and Paris from a desk cluttered with copies of *Business Week*.

But Pacheco claimed he had not really changed since those idealistic days. "I have always been a man of action; I wanted to achieve things. When I was in school, everyone was reading Marx and Mao, and we believed the working class was the moving force in society," he reflected. "Today we are living in a different world, where entrepreneurs are the motor of development. That's the frontier I want to be on." Hardly a fan of military rule, Pacheco described Chile as country plagued by schizophrenia. "We may be more modern and efficient, but we are still a stain on the world as long as we are ruled by a dictator," he said.[86]

He was not alone in this assessment. Senior business leaders like Feliú were anxious to change the negative image of businessmen as a greedy, irresponsible group that had profited from dictatorship. They sought to emphasize the role of business as an "engine of progress" and "social harmony" for the nation. Some business groups began holding seminars on unemployment and inviting labor leaders to discussions. "We must never again permit creating enterprises, making money, and getting ahead to be a source of shame and reprehension," Feliú told one group of young executives.[87]

Other businessmen took social responsibility with great seriousness—and not only for altruistic reasons. The Fantuzzi brothers visited Japan to study worker-management relations, and helped support a nonprofit industrial training program for poor teenagers. "Chile needs skilled workers, and if people are cold and hungry, the leftist banner can always be raised again," explained Angel. "It would be a terrible error to go backward, now that we've made so many sacrifices and come so far."

By 1985, moreover, a number of Chile's more thoughtful and open businessmen realized that political change was inevitable, and they wanted to make sure it would occur smoothly, without jeopardizing the free-market model. Some joined a new center-right party, National Renovation, and a handful, including the former economics minister Fernando Léniz, collaborated with opposition leaders on a proposal for political liberalization.

But many captains of industry remained wedded to the regime, by fear as well as by preference. Despite the official philosophy of economic nonintervention, they knew the military state still wielded enormous power to make or break any business venture. Moreover, they deeply mistrusted opposition leaders, whom they suspected of being Marxist patsies. "People thought I was naive or a traitor to my industrial class," recalled Léniz of his attempts to forge political compromise. "They were ironclad with Pinochet, terrified of the communists' coming back, and afraid to criticize the government. To oppose the regime was just bad business."[88]

The average businessman remained indifferent to politics and worried far more about social disorder than about political repression. His instinct was to support the status quo, even if he disdained men in uniform and did not want to be associated with the dictatorial aspects of the regime. When industrial leaders formed "civic committees" in support of Pinochet's continued rule, men like Leonel García joined without hesitation.

"I'm not interested in politics, and we Chileans generally do not prefer military governments, but as a businessman, I owe this one everything I have," García explained in 1987. "Business has finally been freed from the state. No one meddles with us, and we don't ask for special favors. It's not a question of sentiment but of becoming modern. Pinochet has made this country free and orderly, and if no suitable replacement comes along, we will be content with him."

CHAPTER NINE

THE POOR

"When I have a million, when we are rich
I'll buy myself some shoes, I'll buy you a dress
I'll take you to the promenade where the gringos stroll
And I'll buy a whole pack of cigarettes
Water on water, the rain upon the river. . . ."
—*Eduardo Gatti, "The Cobbler"*[1]

ABOVE the Plaza Italia, a rotunda adorned with a majestic military monument, lie the glittering new malls and suburbs of affluent Santiago. Below the plaza, as residents say, lies the other city: a vast grid of crumbling colonial façades that stretches south and west to gritty working-class districts like Pudahuel and Peñalolen, known as poblaciones.

In this marginal world that is home to Santiago's two million poor, men rise at dawn to take three buses to work as machinists, women scrub laundry in dirt yards, and teenagers linger on corners sniffing cans of leather glue. Junk collectors' horse carts clop along the dusty alleys; people crowd around kiosks to read the day's headlines and haunt the flea market displays of doorknobs, tea kettles, socket wrenches, eyeglasses, work boots, and cracked china plates.

The other Santiago includes once elegant sectors like Quinta Normal, where abandoned mansions have been converted to used-furniture stores and rooming houses; modest suburbs like La Florida, where families struggle to meet escalating mortgage payments and send their sons to computer classes; and grimy factory districts like San Miguel, where fuming buses chug so slowly along clogged boulevards that candy peddlers can swing off one and onto the next without missing a step.

Few people in these neighborhoods resemble the blond, slender denizens of Las Condes. Most are mixed race, or mestizo; they often have unexpectedly blue or green eyes, but their faces are round and their hair dark. Their surnames are not Errázuriz or Edwards, but Gómez or Rodríguez. If they were lucky enough to own a television in 1982, the government declared them better off than Chile's 1.8 million "extremely poor," but for the most part they have not seen the fruits of its "silent revolution."[2]

During sixteen years of military rule, their incomes stagnated or fell while those of the wealthy increased; in 1988, the average income in Pudahuel was five times less than the average in Las Condes.[3] For some, once stable factory jobs were replaced by precarious work as grape packers and busboys. More physically removed from centers of commerce, with lower aspirations for the future, they struggled to survive in the old city while a new one beyond their grasp moved swiftly ahead.

CHILE was never as abjectly poor as much of Latin America; since the 1950s, it has been viewed as a "middle-income" country on a par with Taiwan and Costa Rica. By 1960, only 16.4 percent of the population was illiterate.[4] By 1970, the per capita income was $2,236, far higher than that of backward nations like Bolivia and Paraguay, although still below that of more prosperous neighbors such as Argentina and Uruguay.[5]

Poverty persisted under Allende, but his socialist government offered workers and peasants free education and medical care, while fat public payrolls lowered unemployment to a record 3 percent. Forty percent of the work force was unionized, and the poor discovered an exhilarating new sense of worth—a defiant pride that demanded respect from the rich and a share in their economic power.

With the collapse of Allende's economic experiment and the advent of military rule, this dynamic was abruptly halted. Within one year, world recession and government "shock treatment" combined in an apparent reprisal against the poor for their insolent fling with socialism. By 1975, both real wages and per capita social spending had dropped to 63 percent of their 1970 levels.[6] More than 43,000 people were dismissed from public service, and the official unemployment rate reached 18.7 percent.[7] For the next decade, the level of urban joblessness would average 15.7 percent—the highest in all Latin America.[8]

Ramón Pizzaro, a fifty-eight-year-old carpenter from San Miguel, keeps a worn spiral notebook on a shelf in his small, well-scrubbed parlor. Meticulously recorded in his careful script is a list of items he was forced to pawn during the recession of 1976: "September 25: one German screwdriver. November 12: one handmade lathe. December 26: two wedding rings."

Pizarro is a decent, hardworking man. He might have understood if someone had explained that wages had to be cut in order to make the economy strong again, that everyone had to share in the sacrifice. But when the construction industry collapsed—at the peak of police repression in working-class Santiago—he found his livelihood, his dignity, and his physical security stripped away.

"I began taking my tools to pawn. That was how we survived for many months. I had to leave the house before curfew ended at 5:00 A.M. and hide from the soldiers, and my wife always worried until I came home." The grizzled carpenter spoke slowly and painfully. "In the line, we would make fires to keep warm. Some people were embarrassed to be there; they would wear their best clothes and say everything was fine, but it was a lie. I tried to put off pawning my good tools, because they were my capital. But the moment came when I had none left."[9]

To ease the burden of unemployment, the government created the Minimum Employment Program (Programa de Empleo Mínimo, or PEM), which gave idled workers a nominal wage (first $25, then $45 a month) and free medical aid in return for paving roads, tending parks, or preparing school lunches.[10] By 1976, more than 210,000 men and women were enrolled. Although many complained that the work was humiliating, officials feared they would become permanent dependents of the state.

The economy improved after 1978, but unemployment remained high, and when the second crash came, in 1982, it wiped out 62 percent of the construction jobs, along with 44 percent of the employment in mines and 30 percent in factories.[11] By March 1983, more than half a million people were employed by the PEM and a second emergency job program, and 76 percent said they were no longer seeking other work.[12]

Many lower-income Chileans had never recovered from the first recession. Some had borrowed to buy appliances or make home improvements during the boom that followed, so the new crisis was even more devastating. Some families had to choose between buying food and meeting other obligations: by late 1983, more than 100,000 in Santiago alone were no longer paying their electric bills. Reports of malnourishment and infectious diseases rose for the first time in decades.[13]

With one-third of the work force idle, tens of thousands were driven to jobs far below their level of skill: teachers drove taxis; postal workers repaired bicycles. People invented an astonishing array of survival tactics: raising plants to barter for used clothes, cooking empanada meat pies to sell at soccer games, playing the guitar on buses at rush hour. A society of peddlers sprang up, lining the downtown Ahumada Promenade and chanting out their prices as they scanned the block for foot patrolmen. At the sound of a whistle, they snatched up their displays of socks or nail files and vanished into the crowd.[14]

"I'd rather load ten trucks than do this. If there were work, I wouldn't care who the president was," asserted Pedro Urramatos, thirty, who was peddling kitchen knives on the Ahumada one day in November 1985. First he had lost his job as a credit manager, since customers could no longer afford to buy appliances. Then he had lost his house; now he was reduced to hawking trinkets without a license. "The Carabineros declare war on us, but how are we supposed to survive?" he demanded angrily.[15]

A less visible product of mass layoffs was the depression that engulfed many idled workers—and the strains placed on their domestic relations. Some men rose each morning and set out knocking on doors with their toolboxes, but others lapsed into chronic despair: staying home and drinking, fighting with their wives or relatives who had moved in to save money.[16]

"The strongest effect of this period was the disintegration of the family and the daily oppression of problems like overcrowding and debt," observed Father Oscar Jiménez, a priest in Pudahuel from 1974 to 1989. He described Chilean working-class men as "very macho; their custom is to be out working, or going to soccer games with their friends. They are very uncomfortable being at home; they have no role there."

Since it was easy for women to find positions as cooks or maids, thousands of población wives went to work to tide their families over. For some jobless husbands, this double shame was too much to endure. Father Jiménez counseled one laid-off factory worker who was so humiliated at having his wife support him that he refused to eat. "The crisis opened up a new world of opportunities to women, but it seemed to crush many men," the priest said.

"Work was their whole identity, and without it they were nothing."[17]

FOR those who remained employed, the Pinochet era brought bewildering changes in the nature of work and harsh repression of demands for improved wages or benefits. It also brought new opportunities to younger, adaptable workers—but often at a cost to the collective spirit that had made the Chilean labor movement one of the strongest in Latin America.

At first, the junta pledged to respect labor rights, declaring on the day of the coup, "The working sectors have nothing to fear from the new government."[18] Workers who had "mistakenly trusted in traitors" would not be punished. A harmonious productive environment would be created, in which all participants would work together, "without fear, complexes, or rancor," to rebuild the nation.[19]

Almost immediately, however, the armed forces cracked down on all organized labor identified with the left. In November, the regime disbanded the major, leftist-dominated labor federation, the Central Unica de Trabajadores (CUT). In December, it suspended all union elections and ordered vacant posts to be filled by senior company workers, selected by starting date and alphabetical order.[20]

Anti-Marxist labor leaders, eager to collaborate with the authorities, accepted these restrictions and embraced the official concept of a "free," apolitical unionism. In 1974, a number of them appeared at government-sponsored May Day celebrations and traveled to an International Labor Organization conference in Geneva to defend the regime. "To us, the coup seemed like a necessary evil. We were tired of daily confrontations, and we believed the armed forces when they promised to respect labor rights," recalled Hernól Flores, a civil service union leader, in 1989. "How naive we were back then."

Workers initially found a sympathetic ear in Labor Minister Nicanor Díaz, a retired air force general, who created labor mediation panels and asked union officials to comment on proposed legislation. But in 1975, the government further curtailed workers' rights, banning strikes in areas that affected "economic stability" and suspending collective bargaining indefinitely. With unemployment high, workers knew that if they complained, a hundred more were ready to take their place.

Paternalistic labor relations, which had collapsed in three years of strikes and insults, gave way to a tough, impersonal management style. Emboldened by the clampdown on union activity, some employers cheated or humiliated workers in vengeance against their Allende-era defiance. Ramón Pizarro worked for construction bosses who repeatedly fired people after a week without pay or gave them an 11-peso bonus on September 11. "I answered every ad; I defended my family like a cornered cat," the veteran carpenter said. "But when they offer you 40,000 pesos [$133 a month] with no days off, that is beneath a man's dignity."

Among the newly rich, hostility toward workers, such as household servants, was especially pronounced. One woman, after visiting the lavish new home of a friend married to a fruit exporter, was shocked at the couple's treatment of the maids. "They're barely in their thirties, but wealth has already changed them," she said. "They pay the woman a misery, and they said we had to watch her because all the *rotos* steal."

Weakened by unemployment and repressive laws, unions became ineffective and membership declined. In 1972, some 855,000 workers had been organized; by 1983, the number had shrunk to 320,000. Union leaders described their colleagues as passive and fearful of participating. One study concluded that, under Pinochet, unemployment was the most effective form of union repression, with a "wider effect than raids, prison, and exile."[21]

Deeply disillusioned, a group of centrist labor leaders broke with the government in late 1975 and formed a dissident organization known as the Group of Ten. Relations worsened when Díaz was replaced in 1976 by Sergio Fernández, an arch free-marketer who denounced all strikes as "instruments of class struggle" and described Chilean workers as "overprotected" by "utopian" laws.[22]

In response to growing labor criticism, the regime tried to promote a progovernment union movement. Although its leaders were courted by officials, they never gained popular legitimacy; each year on May Day, when they assembled to applaud Pinochet at formal ceremonies, dissidents held a "parallel" rally that was inevitably broken up by riot police.

In mid-1978, the first serious signs of labor unrest were harshly repressed. Workers at the Chuquicamata copper mine boycotted mess halls after failing to win a wage increase, and the protest swelled despite cajoling and threats from officials. In response, the authorities declared a local state of siege and banished seventy-two boycott leaders to mountain villages, denouncing them as communists.[23]

Meanwhile, in response to pleas from frustrated centrist labor leaders, regional and U.S. delegates from the AFL-CIO traveled to Santiago and presented Pinochet with a list of concerns. The government never responded, but five months later, officials suddenly announced that union elections would be held the following week across the country. They also announced a set of new laws that would "free" unions from obligatory dues and affiliation with labor federations.

On October 31, with exactly four days to consider candidates, 510,000 workers chose plant leaders for the first time since the coup. No political activists were permitted to run, and most winners were longtime employees or popular community figures; each had to be approved by the Labor Ministry and swear not to join any political party.

"There was no real way to choose leaders, and people were afraid. I was president of my neighborhood sports club, so I guess that's why they picked me," recalled Humberto Silva, who at twenty-four became head of the Comandari Textile Mill union. In 1981, after months of building up his colleagues' courage, he led a successful strike. "For years, the message was don't get involved, and it was hard to convince people we were a serious force on their behalf," he said.[24]

Despite efforts to create a tame union leadership, most elected officers also turned out to be critics of the regime, and began relying on advice from leftist or Christian Democratic officials, thus enabling persecuted political groups to begin rebuilding their organizations. But the façade of restored union vigor was extremely thin, and the Group of Ten renewed their requests for help from abroad.

In November, the Regional Inter-American Labor Organization voted to ask members to boycott cargo from Chile, along with that from Cuba and Nicaragua. In Santiago, officials denounced the boycott as a plot against Chile by American union leaders and the Carter administration; at a mass rally Pinochet asserted his government had created a "truly free" labor movement and that its enemies were playing their "last cards" in desperation.[25]

Beneath the huffy rhetoric, authorities moved swiftly to prevent the boycott from materializing. José Piñera, the new labor minister, sketched out plans for a massive revision of labor laws. With the American entrepreneur Peter Grace acting as intermediary,

Chilean officials met with George Meany, president of the AFL-CIO, and persuaded him to suspend the boycott.

In January, the regime enacted Piñera's Labor Plan, a masterly combination of permissive and restrictive regulation. Strikes were legalized, but after thirty days an employer could contract new workers, and after sixty days any remaining strikers were considered to have quit. The right to hold unapproved union meetings was restored, but employers could dismiss anyone if it was deemed "necessary." Labor federations were reinstated, but collective bargaining was restricted to the plant level and limited solely to wage demands.[26]

Some union leaders argued that the plan provided an escape valve for worker frustrations, but many dismissed it as a scheme to undermine union strength and were deeply disappointed by the early results. Out of 2,574 contracts negotiated the first year, the average raise was 8 percent—a pittance in view of the 40 percent drop in real wages since 1970.[27]

A spate of amendments to the new law aroused even more alarm. Labor courts were dissolved, which sharply reduced workers' access to legal redress. Employers were allowed to offer new contracts at less than the minimum wages and benefits reached in previous negotiations. Severance benefits were lowered, maximum shifts were extended from eight to twelve hours, and piecework rates were legalized. Many occupational benefits were cut: maids lost maternity leave; stevedores were no longer protected against being ordered to lift more than 176 pounds at once.[28]

Officials defended these measures as producing greater "flexibility" for employers, but others saw them as a retreat from basic labor rights won during decades of struggle. Eduardo Ríos of the port workers called the laws "a monument to the abuse of power, the bullying of entrepreneurs, and the arrogance of fanatical ideologues."[29]

Over time, recession and repression spawned a more radical labor organization, the National Union Coordinator (Coordinadora Nacional Sindical, or CNS), which distanced itself from the Group of Ten after 1978. Its most prominent leader was Manuel Bustos, a Christian Democratic textile worker. Detained and imprisoned in 1981, he grew more outspoken against the dictatorship and more open to the banned Marxist groups that sought formal labor representation.

Despite the government's persistent efforts to drive a wedge of suspicion between its leftist and moderate foes, the labor movement began to sense its potential as a force for change. The one man who seemed able to unite this awakening giant was Tucapel Jiménez, the respected bookkeeper who had headed the white-collar civil service union for two decades.

Squat, shabby, and known for his integrity, Jiménez had initially figured on Pinochet's list of "good" labor leaders. But once he began denouncing repression and public-sector dismissals, he was repeatedly harassed by police agents, and in 1980 he was fired as a troublemaker. But "Don Tuca" continued his crusade undaunted, lambasting the regime and pleading with labor groups to overcome their differences. He brushed off concerns for his safety, saying, "I will only stop defending the rights of workers when I die."[30]

On the morning of February 25, 1982, Jiménez left home for meetings with other labor leaders and vanished en route. When his abandoned car was found with Jiménez slumped at the wheel, shot and stabbed to death, his colleagues knew why—although his murderers were never found or brought to justice. "They killed Tucapel not because he was an extremist but because he was a moderate and had enough credibility to unite the labor movement. He mumbled when he spoke, but people listened to him," said Hernól Flores, a longtime colleague. "The regime couldn't break him, so they singled him out as a dangerous enemy."[31]

THE military government was far from oblivious to the plight of the poor, and Pinochet championed policies aimed at helping the neediest. Widespread poverty provided critics with evidence that the free-market model created injustice, sowed the seeds of unrest, and weakened the stock of "human capital" needed to push the nation ahead. "I am disposed to make the maximum effort so that extreme poverty can be eliminated in Chile," Pinochet vowed on the first anniversary of the coup.[32]

For dedicated officials like Miguel Kast, the war on poverty was both a moral and a technical challenge. Kast believed that, in the past, income redistribution had been unfairly tilted toward middle-class "pressure groups," such as university students. In 1973, he pointed out, the state allocated far more funds to universities, with 144,000 students, than to public elementary and secondary schools, with nearly 2.4 million.,[33] His panacea was to funnel aid directly to needy families, instead of indirectly through tuition, lower mortgage interest rates, or price controls.[34]

Compiling a "Map of Extreme Poverty," Kast's team at ODE-PLAN concluded in 1975 that 21 percent of the population fell into that category.[35] Then it established a plan to decentralize social services and provide individual subsidies through a strict system of controls. Milk was given only to mothers who brought their infants for checkups; caseworkers determined which of three levels of social service discounts each family merited.

"Everywhere we went, we found that the subsidies had gone to the organized sectors and the leftovers to the poor," recalled Patricia Matte, a colleague and admirer of Kast who went on to become secretary for social development and assistance. "We tried to make decisions based purely on technical findings of need, but we came up against many powerful interests. Without the leadership and force of President Pinochet," she said, "there's no way we could have done it."[36]

The ODEPLAN crusade was so successful that by 1982 a second official survey found only 14.2 percent of all Chileans living in "extreme poverty." Sanitation improved so much that by the late 1980s 84 percent of all homes had clean drinking water and 77 percent had sewage systems. Officials were especially proud of programs in preventive health care for needy mothers and children, which led to sharp declines in child malnutrition and infant mortality—from 65.8 deaths per thousand live births in 1973 to 18.1 in 1989, the lowest rate in Latin America.[37]

Yet, while officials heavily publicized these significant achievements, their free-market policies were driving down average living standards and widening the gap between rich and poor. In the period 1978–88, the income share of the wealthiest 20 percent of Chile's households increased from 51.9 percent to 60.4 percent. In the same period, the income of the poorest 40 percent of the families rose only from 11.0 percent to 11.8 percent of the total.[38]

Critics also disputed the government's claim to have sharply reduced extreme poverty, arguing that official statistics placed too much emphasis on the possession of certain durable goods, rather than on more relevant criteria such as wages or calorie consumption, in defining standards of living. At a time of record unemployment, one economist noted that "about 2,000 pesos—the value of a transistor radio—was enough to declassify a family as poor."[39]

In the debate over what constituted poverty and how much was being done about it, statistics could be found to favor both sides. The percentage of state funds spent on social programs nearly doubled between 1973 and 1987, but total social services expenditures fell 13 percent over the same period.[40] Despite the gains in combating extreme poverty, virtually all independent surveys found that general poverty had risen alarmingly. A study by the pro-regime economist Aristedes Torche, based on the ability to meet "basic needs" in food, health, and housing, showed that in 1985 over 45 percent of all Chileans remained poor and that 25 percent of those were "indigent."[41]

Evidence of deteriorated living standards was ample. Between 1977 and 1985, the number of people who walked to work increased from 18 percent to 25 percent. A 1986 survey taken in two poblaciones found that 66 percent and 74 percent of families there consumed less than the minimum calorie requirement for adequate nutrition.[42] In 1988, half the populace still earned less than 45,000 pesos a month ($150), and one-third earned less than the 1970 minimum wage.[43]

On a typical weekday morning in July 1989, janitors hauled out the morning trash from a row of apartment buildings along Vitacura Avenue in Las Condes. By eight-thirty, the scavengers were arriving—a man with a hand-painted horse cart, a father and son on foot—to paw through the barrels. By nine, the neighborhood had filled with a small, ragged army: men with rusty shears and rakes, ringing doorbells in search of odd jobs; peddlers with handcarts singing out the prices of eggs and brooms.

Most of them had traveled great distances by bus or bicycle, hoping to earn a few pesos. The residents tended to ignore them, glancing up with annoyance as they backed their late-model cars out of yards protected by high fences. "There's so much competition now," commented one grimy man, tossing bottles and magazines into his horse cart. "Before, people only sorted glass and metal, but now even paper has become precious. I manage because certain janitors save things for me. Without friends in the jungle, you are lost."

DESPITE the regime's success in preventive and child medicine, the deterioration in general health care was one of its most resounding public policy failures. Chile had long boasted an advanced system of public medicine; its doctors were known to be service oriented, and many—including Allende—were committed socialists. But Pinochet's planners viewed the health system as inefficient and controlled by "pressure groups" of overly paid doctors and their middle-class, state-dependent clients.

Breaking down the National Health Service into twenty-six regional agencies and turning clinics over to municipal governments, the regime encouraged enrollment in the new private health maintenance agencies, ISAPRES, and membership reached 1.4 million by 1988. But the agencies favored healthy, higher-income people, and the left-leaning Chilean Medical Association protested that the new system placed profits over patients. The regime severely curtailed the group's rights and dismissed its complaints as sour grapes, while many doctors found lucrative niches in the burgeoning private health care system.

The government's success in keeping babies alive and healthy came at the deliberate cost of care for the elderly and chronically ill poor. Investment in mother-child care increased 78 percent between 1974 and 1983, while funding for hospital maintenance and equipment fell 91 percent. Overall state spending on health plunged from $283.6 million in 1973 to $134.2 million in 1976, then inched upward for several years only to fall even lower in the mid-1980s.[44]

Conditions in public hospitals deteriorated markedly as public investment fell and wealthier patients switched to ISAPRES. Exposés of horrific conditions appeared in the press and in medical association reports. In community clinics, where budgets were sharply reduced after the transfer to municipal management, long lines of patients formed at dawn in hopes of seeing a doctor by day's end, and sick people entitled to free medicine carried around unfilled prescriptions for months.

The situation became especially critical during the crisis of 1983, when poorer diets and colder houses led to an increase in bronchitis, pneumonia, and hepatitis. At some urban hospitals, patients were asked to supply their own bandages, stocks of antibiotics were often exhausted, and new mothers slept two to a bed.[45] Conditions improved later in the decade, but personal horror stories abounded.

During 1989, a visitor spent several days talking with people crammed onto benches in the outpatient clinic of Barros Luco Hospital in San Miguel. Carmen Zapata, sixty-two, said she had waited all week to see an eye doctor. "My vision gets worse every day, but social security doesn't pay for glasses any more, and where would I get 4,000 pesos?" She and her ailing husband survived on a monthly pension of 7,000, she said, plus the extra she earned by taking in laundry. Suddenly she clutched the visitor's arm, her eyes frightened. "If I go blind, who would take care of him?"[46]

THE proliferation of illegal shantytowns created through *tomas,* or land invasions, during the Frei and Allende years was an especially vexing problem for the new authorities. In 1973, as many as 90,000 Santiago families were living in such camps, which officials saw as breeding grounds for leftist activity and impediments to the development of a modern city.

Moving swiftly to address the issue, the government provided land titles and building subsidies to about 30,000 families. Another 28,000 were forcibly "eradicated," often from inner-city areas to peripheral ones. Some were moved to brick row houses or apartment blocks, others to tiny plots with partly finished kitchen and bath structures.[47] More than 420,000 state-subsidized units were built under Pinochet, who often presided over ribbon-cutting ceremonies himself.[48]

One day in 1984, the general inaugurated a development of 1,200 prefabricated wooden bungalows in San Bernardo, festooned with banners saying, "Thanks to the President." Schoolchildren waved as the motorcade of armored Mercedes arrived and officials took their seats on a wooden stage. A priest blessed the houses, and an official reminded the assembly of new home owners, many relocated from squatters' camps, that "terrorists try to destroy houses" while "the government builds them." Pinochet presented a symbolic door key to a beaming couple, and people cheered as the convoy of Mercedes roared off.

Once settled, however, residents often found they had been "eradicated" to isolated communities, chosen because land was cheap; some critics called it a system of residential apartheid. The housing conditions were a step up, but the areas lacked services and were located hours from work and relatives. La Pintana, a poor suburb whose population leaped from 75,000 to 140,000, was ill equipped to provide bus or garbage-collection service; by 1985, only seven telephones existed in the entire commune.[49]

"I grew up in rented rooms where you had to eat on your bed, so to me this is a palace," said Juan Aravena, a thirty-three-year-old security guard who was relocated to a two-room apartment in La Florida in 1985. "But people here don't know or trust each other, and the only jobs are at the other end of the city. The program solved one problem but created others."

Aravena, a night watchman in an exclusive suburb, commuted almost two hours each way on a series of buses; the ride was too dark for him to read and too jolting for him to sleep. "Where I work, it's like another world," he explained, staring out the bus window. "The houses are like palaces, and it is my job to keep away the people who come to beg or steal. Sometimes I wonder why I'm risking my small life to protect the property of the big people. I don't say it, but I feel it."[50]

The Pinochet government claimed that it did more to house the poor than any previous administration, providing a total of 1.16 million homes, titles, or subsidies by 1987.[51] But public spending for housing, which rose steadily in the 1960s and peaked at $225 million in 1973, fell to an average of $67.8 million for the next decade.[52] Construction increased after 1984, with support from the World Bank, but most subsidies benefited middle-class home buyers, and only under pressure from the bank did officials shift to smaller, more cheaply built units for the poor.[53]

During sixteen years of military rule, Chile accumulated a deficit of nearly half a million housing units.[54] With nowhere to move and less income to spend on rent, hundreds of thousands of families were forced to squeeze in with relatives, a condition called living as *allegados,* or "added on." The 1983 census found 836,800 Chileans sleeping four or more per bedroom.

Chronic overcrowding created severe domestic tensions, especially when married siblings with children moved in with aging parents. "Usually there was only one bathroom; people argued over the use of food and electricity; couples lost their privacy," explained Father Jiménez of Pudahuel. "Kids would fight or hang out on the corners, because there was no room at home."

Beginning in 1980, community groups staged a new wave of *tomas,* in which families camped on vacant land with tents, then built them into makeshift communities. Most were evicted, but in 1983, two huge squatters' camps were erected in La Granja that became symbols of political defiance. In several predawn raids, army troops swept through the camps, detaining all adult men and ransacking homes for guns and propaganda.

"They called us subversives, because we are building something they cannot defeat," said Augustín Guajara, thirty, one of the few leaders left in Camp Raúl Silva Henríquez after a 1984 raid. Sonia Muñoz, a young mother hanging laundry outside her one-room cardboard hut, was not so sure. Her husband had lost his job in the raid, and the family of five slept squeezed onto two cots, surrounded by cooking pots and the stench of paraffin smoke. "When there's nothing left," she confessed, "I take the littlest girls and we go out begging."[55]

THE government's preoccupation with the very poor came at the expense of Chile's lower-middle class, from teachers to railroad clerks, who drifted steadily downward under military rule. Cut off from benefits that had enabled them to achieve respectability, they were thrust into a competitive economy that demanded new skills, paid lower wages, and seemed indifferent to their values of dignity, education, and compassion.

The civil service, which had quadrupled in size since 1920, was purged of over 150,000 white-collar employees.[56] Some found work as cabdrivers or store clerks, but others were reduced to desperate humiliation. A cultured, neatly dressed teacher called on a prominent academic, asking to discuss his latest book; but after a few moments, the visitor confessed in tears that his children had not eaten in a week. A vegetable peddler, chanting out prices from his pushcart, was recognized by an office manager as his former accountant.

They were the losers in Chile's economic revolution, too established to qualify for its welfare programs but not lucky or clever enough to latch on to its free-enterprise fast track. Between 1978 and 1988, the incomes of both the richest and the poorest 10 percent of Chilean households increased by over 80 percent, but among the lower-middle 40 percent of the populace, average incomes rose by less than 14 percent.[57]

Teachers, laid off by the thousands, lost their status as the epitome of Chile's middle-class culture. Enrique Silva, an elementary school teacher and father of five from San Miguel, earned a modest but secure living of 62,000 pesos a month—until one day, after twenty-four years, he was dismissed without warning. With private schools offering only 19,000 to start, he survived by making furniture at home, while his wife, Naomi, knitted and sold sweaters. Although they could no longer afford meat or medicine, the Silvas suffered much more because of an intangible loss.

"When I married Enrique, he was already a teacher, a man who brought books and music home. I don't want him to end up as a furniture maker," Naomi said sadly. "He should be at work, sharing ideas with his colleagues, not hanging around the house. We can survive on odd jobs, but we are left in the air. We live with a permanent worry inside."[58]

Many modest-income families faced the nightmare of the UF (for Unidad de Fomento, or Unit of Promotion), a mechanism by which home mortgages were indexed to inflation. By 1985, half a million families owed 4.2 billion pesos in unpaid mortgage bills.[59] Under pressure from consumer groups, the government urged banks to renegotiate rather than foreclose. But to many the UF remained a hated symbol of official callousness.

Tito Cespedes, a thirty-eight-year-old mining-equipment sales-man, bought his family a small, chalet-style bungalow in La Flori-da in 1983. The cost was 990 UFs, with monthly payments worth 1,000 pesos. "We trusted the system, saved our money, and invested in the future," he recalled over tea in the spotless parlor. But with inflation, the payments gradually quintupled until the family was strangled in debt. By 1988, they had no money for clothing, no telephone, and no savings. "Our situation may not seem so dra-matic," Cespedes said, "but the truth is we are the white-collar poor."

As his own prospects faded, Cespedes keenly felt the differences between himself and those who prospered under military rule. "The managers in my office are so obsessed with getting rich, it seems the classic middle class and its values have vanished," he said. "Today there are two Chiles: one with credit cards and computers, and one that is just trying to survive."[60]

IN its effort to channel aid directly to the poor—and shrink the central bureaucracy as much as possible—the government made local authorities responsible for all social services, beginning in 1981. The process reduced waste and abuse but also placed a lop-sided burden on poor communities, where tax revenues were low-est. In 1986, officials of upper-class Providencia spent 22,000 pesos per resident, while those in improverished Conchalí spent one-tenth that amount.[61]

By personally naming all of Chile's 323 mayors, Pinochet also sought to establish a professional, apolitical style of local govern-ment. These authoritarian bureaucrats acted as the final link in a chain of command from La Moneda; they rarely lived in the dis-trict they served, and their mission was to represent Pinochet, not the local residents. Public management became more decentral-ized, but local political power became tightly controlled at the top.[62]

Some appointed mayors were eager soldiers in the regime's technocratic army, like the widely praised Fernando Alvarez, a soft-spoken architect who served for ten years as mayor of Conchalí. This vast, dilapidated district in northern Santiago housed nearly

400,000 of its poorest residents: in 1988, unemployment was 22 percent and the average income under 26,000 pesos ($86) per month.[63]

Reflecting on his accomplishments in 1989, Alvarez proffered a thick, glossy book detailing the number of roads paved, parks landscaped, and shantytowns eradicated. He spoke proudly of a system that had brought a new spirit of "expertise and public service" to local government, and had virtually eliminated extreme poverty through scientific techniques.

"Conchalí used to be a forgotten corner of Santiago with a terrible image of poverty and delinquency. Nothing was planned; there were thousands of people in squatters' camps," Alvarez recounted. "In the past ten years, there has been tremendous physical and social improvement. We have tried to do our best for the poor, to act impartially, to be creative within scarcity. We hope people will look back and remember that the government of President Pinochet made it possible."[64]

Often, however, bureaucrats were too obsessed with meeting budgets to notice suffering, and people easily fell between the cracks of the newly efficient social programs. One day in 1989, a ragged man appeared at the municipal building in La Cisterna. He was trembling and uncertain; in his arms a small girl coughed incessantly. A bored secretary entered his name in a ledger; twenty minutes later, an official emerged and asked what the problem was.

"I can't take any more," the man began. "I have no job; the house is always full of water. They were supposed to move us, but we were left behind because we didn't have the 5,000 pesos" for a token down payment. He fumbled in his pocket for some papers; the official glanced at the forms and frowned. "I'm sorry, there's nothing I can do. That eradication has been terminated," he said firmly, turning back toward his office. The man's body sagged in defeat, and he began to weep. After a few moments, he picked up the coughing child and shuffled out.

Even in Conchalí, ambitious antipoverty programs could not alleviate the despair and alienation of many families. During one six-month period, a visitor accompanying a social worker on his rounds there entered many homes where alcoholism and violence were rampant and people felt they were struggling alone in a jungle. "The old community spirit has been wiped out," said a stout, gray-haired woman sweeping a pile of garbage out her front door. "Now it's safer to mind your own business and survive the best you can."

THE Pinochet government did attempt to build a network of community support, by creating municipal and regional development boards and by restructuring the four thousand Juntas de Vecinos (Councils of Neighbors) that existed nationwide. The goal was to replace partisan conflict with "intermediate" bodies that would act as vertical conduits between the state and the citizen, but the obsession with control clashed with the desire to encourage civic activism. The regional boards became rubber stamps for the plans of mayors and governors.

The Juntas de Vecinos, whose leaders were designated by local officials, were limited to specific tasks like raising funds for paving. Mistrusted and shunned by many residents, the junta system became largely inactive.[65] In 1987, a movement began to "democratize" junta leadership through elections, but the struggles were vicious and the process slow. Often the initiative came from the left, but junta officers were also expelled for being active Christian Democrats.

Gladys Bustamante, a retired nurse and policeman's wife who headed one junta in Conchalí, expressed effusive gratitude to the regime and pride in her role of providing references to local job applicants. "The municipality knows and trusts us," she explained. Bustamante favored barring "activists" and "communists" who sought to bring back the old junta election system. "If they don't like us, they should ask Mr. Mayor to change us," she said.

But Manuel Hinojosa, a newspaper distributor elected to head another junta in Conchalí, said his greatest pleasure was consulting his neighbors, "not just saying yes." Despite Mayor Alvarez's popularity, he said, most of Conchalí remained Christian Democratic and Socialist. "This regime never learned how to deal with people. It they had, the whole country would be with them," he contended.[66]

It was painful for officials to admit that their imposed good works were not always appreciated and that their intrusive system of "targeting the neediest" was sometimes resented by the recipients. After leaving his post and joining a Catholic charitable institution, Alvarez reflected on the pitfalls of an authoritarian municipal system.

"Objectively we achieved a great deal, and we thought people would see we were planting seeds for the future. But poor people think in immediate terms, and their identification is emotional," Alvarez said. "We had such great mystique about the technical aproach to problems, but you cannot gain people's respect by imposing things. You have to remind them what you've done, or else they forget."

In the shadow of the authoritarian civic structure, a network of dissident community groups competed for the loyalties of the poor and attempted to maintain a spirit of collective grass-roots activism. Often they were formed by banned Marxist groups; in many cases, they were sponsored by local parishes or larger Catholic church programs.

Throughout Santiago, hundreds of groups were formed to teach skills to the jobless or provide shelter for the homeless. Beyond survival strategies, the groups also called attention to social problems and showed the authorities that "popular power" was still a force to be reckoned with. Cultural and sports clubs also served as focal points for community activism, and women's crafts workshops were created to compete with "official" structures like the Mothers' Centers.

The movement was strongest in redoubts of Popular Unity support, such as the tough La Victoria section of San Miguel. Projects from *ollas comunes* (literally, "common cooking pots") to folk-singing fests were organized by Socialist or Communist party activists, and the regime viewed them as fronts for "subversive" organizing. In the early years of military rule, they operated in secrecy, subject to raids and harassment.

Groups which enjoyed support from churches could operate with more impunity. The Vicariate of Solidarity, the Pastoral Workers' Vicariate, and the Academy of Christian Humanism sponsored dozens of projects. The line between religion and politics was often hazy, and many priests sheltered Marxist party activities within Christian Base Communities. Several foreign priests, like Father Pierre Dubois of La Victoria, became so marked as politically "conflictive" that they were expelled from the country in 1986.[67]

"When the Base Communities joined the fight against dictatorship, we worked elbow to elbow with the parties of the left," acknowledged Father Jiménez. His modest chapel, decorated with revolutionary posters, housed countless seminars, workshops, and even meetings of prisoners' families disguised as catechism classes. "We were accused of being Red priests, but we were only accompanying the people. We had to assume a role far beyond anything we had imagined when we took our vows."

After 1980, grass-roots self-help groups multiplied rapidly, numbering more than eleven hundred in Santiago by 1985.[68] The success of the 1983 *tomas* spurred other land invasions and the formation of several competing federations of neighborhood groups. Whenever a protest was called, a handful of poblaciones like La Victoria became battlegrounds of burning barricades and tear gas.

Yet the notoriety of this "alternative culture" exceeded its concrete impact, with many groups never reaching beyond small cores of militants. And the influence of the "liberationist" Catholic church was countered by the rapid growth of the evangelical Protestant movement, which preached aloofness from worldly issues. By the mid-1980s, most poor neighborhoods boasted dozens of storefront temples, and hundreds of thousands of poor Catholics had shifted their religious allegiance.

For Sergio Troncoso, a battle-scarred leftist organizer and janitor from Pudahuel, keeping the Popular Unity spirit alive was a full-time, sixteen-year task. "With so many leaders fallen, we had to convince people the workers' struggle was still alive," he said, rocking a grandchild on his sagging couch. In 1984, he was seized in a mass raid, accused in a supermarket assault, and sent to prison for two years. But once released, he returned to the fray, forming debtors' groups and parallel Juntas de Vecinos. "I was afraid of being tortured again, but this is my destiny," he explained. "It doesn't matter how I live, what my name is. Men pass, but organizations remain."

THE death of Tucapel Jiménez in 1982 was an especially hard blow to the workers' opposition movement, already weakened by recession and ideological splits. That May Day, there were three competing events: General Pinochet's traditional speech in the Diego Portales Building, a low-key commemorative ceremony at Jiménez's union, and a street protest led by Manuel Bustos that was dispersed with riot clubs and tear gas. In December, Bustos was expelled from the country as a political agitator.

Yet the labor movement survived, aided in part by material and moral succor from the Catholic church, which sponsored a workers' vicariate in poor urban districts throughout the Pinochet years and often allowed unions to meet in parish halls and conference centers. Repression also injected a sense of urgency into labor leaders, twelve hundred of whom wrote Pinochet in early 1983 to protest that the working class was being destroyed by economic policies based on "individualism, profit, unchecked competition, and alienating consumerism."[69]

That May, with Chile's economy in its worst crisis since the

1930s, organized labor made its first bold move since the coup, calling for a one-day national strike. The unlikely hero of this initiative was the twenty-nine-year-old Rodolfo Seguel, a long-haired, chain-smoking cashier at the El Teniente copper mine and a militant Christian Democrat. In 1981, he had gained visibility by leading a fifty-nine-day strike at the mine; in February 1983, he was voted president of the 22,000-member miners' union. And barely two months later, he found himself heading the new National Workers' Command (Comando Nacional de Trabajadores, or CNT)— and the May 11 strike.

Whatever the outcome of the strike, Seguel asserted at the time, "we have taken a very important step . . . that of losing fear." Even if he were imprisoned or exiled, he added, others would follow, until the authorities realized that "the crisis cannot be solved with repression, only with change."[70]

Yet, despite their bravado, Seguel and his colleagues were awed by the massive response to their appeal. Not only was the capital paralyzed during the day, but as evening fell, Santiago was filled with an exhilarating cacophony of protest as cars beeped their horns and women clanged kitchen pots out their windows. This first significant challenge to Pinochet unleashed a five-month wave of demonstrations and marked a fundamental turning point in the fortunes of the regime.

"It was a moment of effervescence that broke the dike of dictatorship and transformed my life," Seguel recalled in 1989. The reprisals began immediately: a bomb was placed in his children's school; he was sent to prison three times. When he emerged to freedom after one nerve-wracking detention, a cheering throng awaited him. "At that moment, I asked myself, who am I? And I realized I represented something for the people who were oppressed and humiliated, who had no job and no voice," he said. "I knew then that the dictatorship could not crush us."[71]

But the labor movement's moment of glory was short-lived. At a time of heavy political persecution, unions provided the leadership and organizational strength that parties were not yet able to muster. Once the protests got under way, however, opposition parties and student leaders were able to assume command of the crusade for the regime's liberalization. Labor leaders, on the other hand, found that their members were far too vulnerable to economic reprisal to form a strong, permanent source of antiregime activism.

Thousands of protesters were dismissed from their jobs, forcing family men to choose between taking a stand and protecting what little security they had. Many labor leaders were fired, and the copper workers, seduced by strategic wage concessions, elected new conservative leaders. In size and effectiveness, unions remained weak: in 1970, some 36 percent of the work force had been organized and over seventeen hundred strikes were held; in 1985, when real and minimum wages were far below 1970 levels, only 18 percent of all laborers belonged to unions and fewer than three hundred strikes took place.[72]

"Chilean unionism never found an independent identity. It regained its structure, but no new generation of activists was created," observed Guillermo Campero, the labor analyst, in 1989. "Labor's role in the opposition was largely symbolic; it had no force to confront a Pinochet. And factory workers were not willing to die for that."[73]

REPRESSION and economic reprisal constituted only one factor in the failure of unions to rebound; a far more important reason was the sweeping structural transformation of Chile's economy, which brought dramatic changes in the demand for skills, the conditions and sources of work, the degree of competition for jobs, the relationship between management and labor, and the attitudes of workers.

Between 1973 and 1988, job demand shrank in heavily unionized sectors like mills and manufacturing, and expanded in new areas like data processing and export fruit growing. This shift created entire new categories of workers—one too "modern" to relate to a traditional union and the other too vulnerable and scattered to organize easily.

A parallel phenomenon that worked against the labor movement was the growth of "informal" and self-employed occupations. Temporary survival methods, spawned in a decade of record unemployment, became permanent niches in the underground economy. By 1988, about 30 percent of Santiago workers were occupied in unregulated, untaxed jobs as housemaids, messengers, watchmen, seamstresses, or junk collectors. About 20 percent of the total work force was engaged in personal service and 18.7 percent in commerce and general services.[74]

On average, "informal" workers earned only half the salary of formally employed ones, but they tended to display a more independent, competitive attitude. They rejected both the notion of working for a "boss" and the idea of collaborating with peers for collective gain. Conditioned to surviving by their wits in a hostile environment, the "self-employed" mistrusted institutions of any kind: the welfare state and the military regime, the corporation and the union.

"The informal sector is precarious, but people have adapted and found a modus vivendi, and they don't necessarily long to go back to the factory," observed Campero. "Today there is a new mode of organizing economic life, with fewer rules and less structure. You work in a restaurant for six months, you pack grapes for three months. It is not stable, but it provides opportunities if you're willing to make the switch."

Rafael Cabellero, a fifty-five-year-old father of nine from La Pintana, opened an illegal shoeshine stand on Huérfanos Street when the shoe factory were he worked went bankrupt in 1980. Soon he became a fixture on the block, chatting with steady customers and reading Mark Twain between shines. "I was proud of my craft, but they ruined it with cheap Asian imports. Today you can barely survive in a factory," he observed in 1989. "Here at least I'm providing a service, and I have a certain prestige."

Among organized workers, the creation of a mass consumer culture and the years of propaganda against politics left strong marks. Union members became less committed to a common cause and more personally ambitious. The rise of ISAPRES and private pension funds reinforced this tendency, turning shared social investments into sources of individual profit.

Some of the new job "opportunities" were attractive only to the desperate. One was seasonal labor in fruit orchards and packinghouses, which created 300,000 temporary jobs by 1985. Low-paid and poorly protected, such work required brief periods of arduous effort, then left workers idle for months. Hired by subcontractors and paid by the crate, the *temporeros* earned an average of 700 pesos ($2.50) a day, while packing companies invested huge sums in modern technology.[75]

One project to organize *temporeros* in the grape-picking town of San Felipe, fifty miles north of Santiago, met with resistance from owners and ambivalence from workers, many of them uneducated women. One union delegate proudly described leading a packinghouse work stoppage that forced the manager to provide extra weekend pay. But another delegate, a young mother missing several teeth, had only the vaguest notion of labor rights. "The work is hard, but the boss is okay. If people are rebellious, he just fires them," she said, smiling politely.[76]

UPON taking office in 1985, Finance Minister Büchi adopted policies that kept wages deliberately low, in order to promote exports, savings, and employment, and severely limited social spending in an effort to restore Chile's trade deficit and foreign credit rating. Three years later, the jobless rate had fallen below the double-digit level for the first time since 1975, but 18 percent of the Santiago work force earned less than the monthly minimum wage of 10,000 ($33), and 48 percent earned less than 20,000.[77]

Despite his youthful appearance and bohemian air, critics denounced the minister as a callous technocrat more attuned to the demands of international bankers than to the hardships of the populace. "He will pass into history as the minister of hunger," charged José Sanfuentes, a Communist leader.[78]

In time, the benefits of Büchi's modified free-market scheme began to trickle down to the poblaciones. By 1988, unemployment fell below 9 percent and industrial production climbed almost to pre-crisis levels. At the same time, Chile's economy began to outpace that of most of Latin America, while countries like Peru and Argentina that had dabbled in populist social policies slid toward disaster. Inflation in Chile was 12.7 percent, against a continental average of 760 percent; exports and investment were soaring.[79] After years of criticizing free-market policies as inhumane, opposition economists began to acknowledge they were producing positive results. By the end of the decade, Pinochet's Chile had become a widely touted model of economic reforms for the rest of the continent.

Viewed from Conchalí or La Pintana, however, the new Chile remained a dual society of winners and losers. Despite the government's "investment in human capital," the income gap between rich and poor was wider than at any other time in half a century. The nouveaux riches, roaring through traffic in their expensive sedans, seemed to mock those left behind, trapped in fuming buses.

Statistically, the average Chilean was better off; emotionally, however, the years of economic humiliation remained deeply engraved. Government TV commercials showed pristine hospitals, bustling factories, and carefree families, but in 1988, when opposition spots were finally allowed on the air, millions of Chileans identified with a scene in which a frail, elderly woman purchased tea and a roll for supper. "Two teabags?" asked the grocer. The camera focused on the woman's empty change purse, then on her taut, resigned face. "Just one," she said.

CHAPTER TEN

CHILDREN OF
DICTATORSHIP

"Liberty, as a counterweight to servile docility
which receives everything without scrutiny . . . ,
will without question be the theme of this
university."

—*Andrés Bello,*
founder of the University of Chile, 1843[1]

DURING freshman week at the University of Chile in 1981, General Alejandro Medina, the new rector, astonished students and faculty by parachuting onto the campus grounds. His military stunt, intended in the spirit of fun, was fraught with unintended symbolism. As a soldier placed in command of the nation's most prestigious educational institution, his mission was to ensure order and respect for the authorities, guard against the return of politics to the campus, and assist in the total restructuring of the university system.

To the military authorities, Chile's universities were a symbol of all that had gone wrong with society. In the name of promoting social equality, enrollment had been opened to huge numbers of students, draining state coffers. As the political tide swung leftward during the 1960s, campuses became nerve centers of debate and conflict, until students and faculty were split into bitter camps and academic discipline was abandoned.

For many young Chileans, those were exhilarating times. Student protests erupted in Chicago and Paris; guerrillas battled corrupt establishments in Vietnam and Bolivia; the old order seemed to be trembling. In Santiago, students occupied buildings to force sweeping academic reforms, and universities moved to the center of national politics, with major parties vying for campus leadership. Young people devoured the works of Marx and Marcuse, wept to the ballads of Victor Jara, and dreamed of re-creating the Cuban revolution.

Allende's election made that dream seem possible. On the night of his triumph, he spoke from the balcony of the Federation of Students of the University of Chile (FECH), while thousands of young people danced until dawn in the streets below. "Our hearts were leaping from our mouths. The construction of paradise had begun," recounted Alejandro Rojas, a Communist student leader who was then president of the FECH.

During the Popular Unity years, university campuses such as the University of Chile teachers' college, known as the Pedagógico, became focal points of social and intellectual ferment. New research centers produced ground-breaking studies on poverty; students went to live on Indian reservations; blue-collar workers attended night classes. Enrollment in the cost-free state university system soared from 55,600 in 1967 to 146,450 in 1973. Hundreds of new majors were offered, and faculty slots were filled with political activists, foreign scholars, and high school teachers.[2]

But the search for academic relevance and freedom was undermined by ideological rigidity, as each faction tried to impose its own vision of utopia and student rebels demanded a voice in university policy. At the University of Chile, the conflict became so bitter that whole departments physically split, with Marxist economics taught on one campus and capitalist economics on another.

Edgardo Boeninger, a respected academic and opponent of Allende who headed the University of Chile from 1969 to 1973, worked feverishly to engineer a compromise between enemy factions, but the atmosphere was poisoned beyond repair. "The walls were full of graffiti calling me a Nazi," Boeninger recalled in 1989. "I can laugh now, but at the time it gave one a terribly unpleasant feeling."

In a 1988 essay on his days as a student leader, Alejandro Rojas lamented the climate of confrontation he had helped create, recalling how he once leapt atop a podium where Boeninger was speaking and shouted the rector down. What did such intolerant antics have to do with the "historic task of building a new university?"

he asked in hindsight. "To what point in each Chilean is there a dictator?"[3]

ON September 11, 1973, the revolutionary momentum in higher education stopped cold. Army troops moved onto "conflictive" campuses, rounding up truckloads of students and staff, shutting down classes, and raiding libraries. At the Technical University, a Communist party bastion, armed students barricaded themselves inside buildings and attempted to resist, but were easily overpowered.

One of the junta's first acts was to outlaw the FECH, and its leaders fled underground. "All our illusions were shattered," wrote Rojas, who spent months moving among clandestine safe houses before fleeing into the Finnish embassy and exile. From "riding the glorious wave of history" as part of an "invincible force" for change, he said, "we passed into total uncertainty—a dark night that terrified us like children."[4]

Hoping to prevent a full campus takeover by the military, a group of university rectors met with the junta and pledged to restore order. But conservative academics argued for a full-scale intervention and purge. Otherwise, wrote one, universities would become "refuges of Marxism waiting for the auspicious moment to invade our national life again."[5]

On October 2, the junta decreed that high-ranking military officers would be named to run all Chilean universities, with "broad powers" over them. Admiral Hugo Castro, the new education minister, charged that college classrooms had become centers for "Marxist indoctrination" and "the preaching of hatred." He vowed that true university values would not be destroyed but preserved, by "extirpating" those who had used educational sanctuaries for political ends.[6]

During the next two years, a massive ideological purge was unleashed. New university officials were given sweeping powers to fire faculty and abolish departments. Between 18,000 and 20,000 students and staff members were forced to leave the eight state university branches.[7] Prominent scientists and intellectuals abandoned military-run campuses and joined the ranks of political leaders seeking safe haven abroad.

At the University of Chile, General César Ruiz could dismiss anyone if he deemed it "necessary for higher interests." Conservative faculty and students helped compose blacklists, and special hearings were held to determine whether employees had promoted revolutionary activities. At the University of Concepción, the president canceled all student registrations and appointed twelve rightist students to review re-applications.[8]

The purification process extended deep into academic life. Departments of sociology and Slavic languages were shut down, as were twenty-three research units, including the prestigious Center for the Study of National Reality, at the Catholic University. Student fieldwork was abolished and thousands of social science books were destroyed in bonfires. General Ruiz declared it a "grave infraction" to teach ideological or "sectarian attitudes."

Hernán Larraín, a conservative student leader who became a university administrator under Pinochet, argued later that the purges were unpleasant but necessary. "I'm sure there were injustices done, but in many cases it was justified," he said. "Many universities had created centers that were instruments for political proselytizing, and some professors wouldn't have lasted a year at Harvard or Oxford."[9]

The staff overhaul was less drastic at the Catholic University, because of the more conservative leaning of the faculty and students and the influence of the Catholic church. But the shift in atmosphere was equally dramatic. Instructors were ordered to make no comments on politics or current events, and fear of being denounced or dismissed led to widespread self-censorship.

"The climate became awful. You were not allowed to shut the classroom doors or talk with students in the halls," recalled María Teresa Lladser, a geography instructor who lost her job in 1975. "Sometimes you found unfamiliar people in your class, men with short hair who took notes and then never reappeared. But you didn't complain; you just took orders and taught."

The first purges focused on the left, but by 1975 many Christian Democrats had also been fired or eased out of their positions. After that, dismissals were sporadic or disguised as cost-cutting measures. In 1980, Jorge Millas, a distinguished philosopher and critic of campus repression, was fired from Austral University. In 1981, Malva Fernández, a linguistics instructor whose son had disappeared, was asked to leave the University of Chile after her ties to a human rights group were revealed; upon refusing, she was dismissed "for budgetary reasons."[10]

Faculty members became chronically demoralized by the mediocrity of many superiors and the atmosphere of fear and suspicion.

"There was an absolute breakdown of trust," recalled Pedro Vera, a Christian Democratic faculty leader at the University of Concepción. "You never knew who was going to get a blue [dismissal] folder at the end of the semester."

THE regime made little effort to revamp the ideological content of university teaching, although some courses in military history and national security were introduced. But there was constant pressure on professors to conform to certain "positive" themes. One directive from the Ministry of Education ordered social science instructors to avoid topics leading to "hateful and sterile discussions"; instead, they should promote "national values" and achievements of the armed forces.[11]

By eliminating Marxist texts and "conflictive" disciplines, authorities narrowed students' exposure to ideas. By 1983, only one public university had a sociology program.[12] Most courses were recast in a narrow, technical mold that left little room to raise issues of poverty or power. The president of the Technical University announced that social science teaching would become "more logical" and "without partisan tendencies."[13]

The metamorphosis of Lladser's geography department was illustrative. During the U.P., geography teaching broadened to emphasize the human effects of land and population trends. "We left aside the rivers and mountains and worked on problems of economic and social development," she recalled. "We studied land reform and the effects of industry on towns. Strictly speaking, what we were doing was not geography."

After the coup, this approach ended. "The department heads bent over backwards to adjust to the new regime," Lladser said. "They went back to basic texts, quantitative analysis, and the dry, physical aspects of geography." Similar patterns were repeated in all social disciplines: historians took refuge in colonial times; political scientists turned to diplomatic relations. "Everything shifted back to the narrowest, safest interpretation," she added.[14]

With economics, the regime went further in order to leave an ideological mark, staffing departments with Chicago school disciples. Critics viewed this as an effort to impart the ethics of an ultracapitalistic society: competition and efficiency, reverence for private property, and acceptance of inequality. "All our training was in monetarist theory; the others were never mentioned," recalled Cristián Moscoso, an economist who studied at the University of

Chile from 1978 to 1982. "We tried to hold forums on other theories, but it was not allowed. The Chicago Boys felt they owned the truth."

Education officials denied that they were attempting to impose any political doctrine on students, and insisted that they sought to curb the use of education for ideological propaganda and restore "pluralism" to the classroom. But in a 1976 speech General Pinochet was more blunt in his intentions. "Absolute ideological pluralism" in higher education, he said, was "radically incompatible not only with the current emergency situation of the country but also with the very essence of the regime born on September 11, 1973."[15]

A principal goal of campus intervention, concluded the authors of one study, was to eliminate any intellectual challenge to the regime's legitimacy. "With the expulsion of students and professors, the university community was broken," they wrote. "With the closing of academic units, institutional criticism was dislodged; with the control of student activity, critical expression was killed at the seed."[16]

In their effort to cleanse the universities, officials also sapped their intellectual spirit. Once continental leaders in scholarly innovation, Chilean universities fell behind in many fields, and the reputation of the University of Chile as one of the continent's premier centers of higher learning plummeted. In time, the level of scientific research regained much of its former prestige, but the social sciences and humanities suffered the loss of morale and expertise for years.

Locked out of "official" academe, a number of social scientists created small research centers, many sheltered by the archbishopric of Santiago and financed by foreign institutions such as the Konrad Adenauer Foundation, in West Germany, and the Inter-American and Ford foundations, in the United States. In cramped and drafty houses, these enclaves—notably the Facultad Latinoamericana de Ciencias Sociales (FLACSO) and the Corporación de Investigaciones Económicas para Latinoamérica (CIEPLAN)—kept critical currents of thought alive during the years of military rule.

The centers also allowed dissident intellectuals to meet, reconcile, and analyze the mistakes of the past. "This is where the renewal of the left began. There was a serious reflection on our failures, a rethinking of our entire role," recalled José Joaquín Brunner, a longtime FLACSO scholar who evolved from a student radical into a leading voice for ideological reform in the socialist left.

The regime tolerated these centers in order to avoid antagonizing church and foreign critics, but it banned them from selling books or holding public forums. By the early 1980s, however, the emerging opposition parties and press were relying on them for expertise. Under Edgardo Boeninger, the Centro de Estudios para el Desarrollo (CED) became a meeting ground for intellectual enemies who had not spoken since the coup. "We broke the ice and melted years of hostility," he recalled. "It was critical to get sectors of society to respect each other again."[17]

BEYOND suppressing leftist thought among the young, the Pinochet government sought to create a new, morally pure generation, shielded from the "poison" of ideology and imbued with the virtues of patriotism and hard work. "I am not fighting for me," Pinochet told members of a government youth movement in 1983. "I fight to hand over the country to you, because you are the future of the nation."[18]

The new university rectors aimed to instill the values they had learned as soldiers: patriotism, moral absolutism, obedience, and self-sacrifice. Suspending student governments, officials appointed class leaders of their own choosing. On one campus, all activities were banned that "can be interpreted as an offense to . . . the Honorable Junta." And in Concepción, the military rector vowed that "politics must be put to sleep for a long time."[19]

For conservative students, the new order offered a chance for leadership that had been denied them for years. Under the influence of regime academics like Jaime Guzmán, the *gremialista* movement spread quickly from the Catholic University to other campuses. Many members were named officers of the new "designated" student unions, and later moved into public service as technocratic aides.

"I grew very disillusioned with the left during the U.P., and when I got to the university, I discovered a group of people who still shared my social and economic ideals. They happened to be on the right," explained Andrés Chadwick, who headed the Catholic University student government in 1977. "We had a style, a belief in service, a strong commitment to individual freedom, and our message appealed to people."[20]

Such campus leaders had no qualms about collaborating with the regime; they too believed that Chile's campuses needed a period of enforced calm. "Political agitation is incompatible with the university," argued Eduardo Silva, student president at the University of Chile in 1980. "A new kind of student leader is emerging now, more authentic and healthy, with a true spirit of university service."[21]

Thousands of young conservatives joined the National Secretariat of Youth, a government organization that promoted the regime's values, provided members with camping trips and scholarships, and expected them to rally for patriotic holidays and presidential visits.[22] The secretariat also served as a showcase for young conservative leaders like Cristián Larroulet, who at twenty-three described himself as a firm anti-Marxist and believer in the "principle of authority." Asked if other youth groups should be permitted to form, he replied, "That is a decision the government must make."[23]

Few of the appointed campus leaders were able to achieve wide legitimacy among their peers, except at the Catholic University, where the *gremialistas* had been well established before the coup. But even there, once direct student elections were allowed in 1985, the center-left defeated the right in a majority of schools and departments, and the elite campus was thrust into the center of antiregime politics.

A small movement of thuggish, radical-right youth flourished under military rule, forming "defense committees" or "unity fronts" to intimidate dissident students. Some were linked to groups like Fatherland and Liberty, and all were tolerated by the authorities, even when they provoked violent incidents. In 1985, a gang at the University of Santiago, which was attempting to recruit classmates into an anticommunist command, severely beat up a journalist on campus and then fled to safety in the rector's office.[24]

FOR young people with any rebellious spirit, the early years of military rule were a sobering experience. Guards stood at campus gates, and obedience to campus authorities was regarded virtually as a national-security issue. Students who opposed the coup felt isolated, afraid to voice their opinions and unable to distinguish kindred souls from other classmates who might turn out to be stooges. To disguise their anti-establishment tendencies, they shaved off beards and exchanged ponchos and work boots for neat, non-descript garb.

"The atmosphere was so suffocating that at first it was nearly intolerable," recalled Yerko Ljubetic, a Christian Democratic activist who entered law school at the University of Chile in 1976. "The regime promoted the idea that you go to college to learn a profession, not to worry about others, and at first they were successful," he said. "But gradually we learned to trust each other through simple things like chess and guitar. It was like reweaving a cloth that had unraveled."

For Tatiana Gaviola, a filmmaker who graduated from a progressive high school in 1973, arriving at the University of Chile was a shock. "I went from a whirlwind of debate to a place where no one spoke except in whispers," she recalled. In 1988, Gaviola produced a film called *Angels,* which recaptured the student fervor of the Allende years, but her crew found it hard to re-create a campus era so alien to what they knew. "To us, the university was a place of mistrust and submission," she explained. "We had to gather evidence and reconstruct what it had been like before."[25]

The degree of repression depended on the political background of the student body and the personality of the military rectors. Admiral Jorge Swett, who ran the Catholic University for a decade, was respected by students as reasonable and even-tempered; Colonel Guillermo Clericus, who took over the University of Concepción in 1980, was regarded as an officious martinet.

Swett exuded the aristocratic, formal air of many Chilean naval officers, with a dry wit and a habit of taking high tea. He made high-caliber faculty appointments and firmly steered the university through economic difficulties, tense relations with the Catholic church, and mounting student unrest. Under his stewardship, the university became the most highly regarded in the country. In 1978, his position was ratified by the Vatican, and in 1983, after complex negotiations with the church, he was officially named "canonical rector" by Cardinal Silva.[26]

At the other end of the spectrum, Clericus stomped through campus in a stiff uniform, issuing peremptory orders. At one point, he enacted a series of rules so severe that even appointed rightist student leaders protested. Andrés Chadwick, for example, suggested that Clericus "seems to confuse the university with a Prussian barracks." "This recalls the penal concepts of Hitler's Germany," he added.[27]

The University of Chile, a sprawling institution of seventy thousand students, endured seven military heads in less than ten years. In 1974, General Ruiz declared his mission complete: all employees with "anti-university attitudes" dismissed, all courses examined "for ideological content." The campus mood was described as one of "order, cleanliness, and silence apt for academic meditation."[28]

By 1977, however, thoughtful conservatives began to hint that military control had lasted long enough. Several *Ercilla* articles featured students lamenting the passivity of their peers, and educators decrying the academic "anemia" caused by the loss of many top scholars.[29] In hindsight, even some education officials agreed the armed forces should have retired from campuses sooner. In 1973, "the universities were in chaos and it was crucial to instill order," recalled Admiral Arturo Troncoso, education minister in 1975–76. "But after a prudent time, the power should have been given back."[30]

But other officers, like General Medina, remained convinced that urgent academic reforms required the firm tutelage of military officers. "We had to strike a balance between intellectual freedom and the need for authority, and we were able to do it with impartiality and equanimity," he said. "Under other conditions, it would never have been possible to make the necessary changes."

IN 1981, after seven years of preoccupation with restoring campus order, the regime embarked on an ambitious new plan to revamp and "modernize" the system of higher education. Interior Minister Sergio Fernández vowed that the new policies would ensure that Chile's universities never again became infested with mass politics and "ideologizing experiments."[31]

The new system, based on free-market notions of private competition, aimed to make universities financially self-sufficient and to train professionals and technicians to serve a modern economy. It reversed the course of Chile's educational tradition, in which the state-funded university was dominated by liberal professions and committed to a humanistic culture that incubated poets, politicians, and a refined and cultured middle class.

Officials argued that heavy subsidies for higher education were financially unsustainable and socially regressive, since the taxes of the poor financed the scholarship of the middle classes and the elite. They reduced direct state support and replaced it with student fees, loans, and grants to the campuses that attracted the twenty thousand top-scoring students on college entrance exams. Tuition ranged from 37,500 to 92,700 pesos per year, and the average at eight major universities in 1983 was about 60,000 pesos.[32]

Critics charged that the new system made universities much less accessible to lower-income students and turned education from an intellectual experience into a marketable merchandise. The test-score competition favored private school students, and the new fiscal credit system could not possibly make up for the loss of scholarships and low tuition fees. Eventually, the government had to revise both programs substantially.

Controversy also erupted over the regime's plan to decentralize the state university system and encourage the opening of private colleges and training institutes. The aim was to make academe more competitive and to reduce the power of the University of Chile. Provincial campuses were made autonomous, and controversial departments like journalism were moved to remote Santiago suburbs. Salaries dropped, and faculty morale fell with them.

Some prominent educators were appalled, protesting that the new system had "broken the spine of Chilean culture."[33] But other academics such as Hernán Larraín argued that "the monopoly had to be ended and alternatives created." "Freedom does not mean only what you say in class; it also means being able to choose what and where to study," he contended. "The university should not be for everyone."[34]

The regime's planners envisioned the university as a training ground for an elite corps of professionals to meet the nation's needs, especially in science and technology. They cut back enrollment, from 146,000 in 1973 to 118,000 in 1982, and limited professional degrees to twelve disciplines, nine of them in scientific fields. They offered more grants in science and required higher test scores for entry into those professions. Of 2,200 new places offered in 1982 by the Catholic University of Valparaiso, 820 were in engineering, 400 in biochemistry, 200 in education, 120 in law, 100 in industrial studies, and fewer than 200 in all other humanities and social sciences combined.[35]

To foster academic competition and create a new class of technicians and service workers, the government subsidized new private academic and professional institutes that offered courses such as accounting and computer programming. Each new center was required to apply to the Interior Ministry for permission to open, which was granted only if it was judged not likely to "offend public order and national security."[36]

The trend caught on rapidly; by 1986, Chile boasted twenty-three universities, thirty research centers, twenty-two professional schools, and over one hundred training institutes. Some, like Diego Portales University, built strong reputations in legal or technical fields, but others were academically mediocre and chiefly concerned with turning a profit. After several years, even the regime's enthusiastic supporters recognized the pitfalls of a free-market education system.

"Universities should be reserved for an intellectual elite, and there are plenty of careers that do not need such a degree. The problem was that once the valve was opened, all kinds of people thought they could become educators and get rich on state subsidies," observed Admiral Troncoso. "Education should not be a business, but the government's model made it into one."[37]

On the other hand, critics like José Joaquín Brunner eventually acknowledged that some of the changes had been necessary. "Today you won't find any serious people on the left who defend the old tradition of free state universities," Brunner said in 1989. "The fact is, there must be some payment. The lack of scholarships is leaving many poor but talented kids outside the system. But everyone realizes that, in the past, the state was subsidizing rich students."

THE armed forces did not intervene directly in secondary and elementary schools, but control was just as strict. In 1974, the commander of military institutions announced that he would oversee all issues of security and discipline in schools. Principals were ordered to forward all "proven denunciations" of teachers who made political comments or jokes about regime officials, attended unauthorized meetings, or failed to obey all orders from superiors.[38]

Similar notices were issued by the Ministry of Education from 1973 to 1981, regulating a vast range of behavior. Students and teachers were forbidden to display insignia of political groups or foreign countries. School officials were required to collaborate with all activities by the National Secretariat of Youth. Teachers were not to use unauthorized texts, speak to the press, or participate in class discussions "directly or indirectly linked to national reality."

Elementary school courses emphasizing "patriotic values" were added, and an annual "Fatherland Week" was held that linked the coup to Independence Day festivities of September 19. Military or secret police agents were permitted to suspend parents' meetings at any time.[39] In 1974, one general warned all parent delegates in the suburb of La Reina that failure to attend a certain meeting would be grounds for "immediate arrest."[40]

The degree of official control varied widely. Private and parochial schools maintained considerable autonomy, but state schools were often administered by autocratic regime toadies, and mass layoffs made teachers cautious in their classroom conduct. Over time, the atmosphere loosened, but veteran teachers said the authoritarian regulations sometimes backfired.

"I've taught third- and fourth-graders for years, and now I see in them a great rejection of authority, a hatred for police and people in power," said one teacher from San Miguel. "We have annual homages to the Carabineros, and we say they are there to protect us. But the children in the poblaciones have seen how people in uniform abuse power, and they carry a great burden of resentment with them."

After 1981, in tandem with reforms in higher education, the government began dismantling the central school system. Within five years, virtually the entire system—eight thousand schools and 120,000 teachers—had been transferred to municipal governments, which turned most facilities over to private owners and passed on per student subsidies from the state.

Almost immediately, there were complaints that school operators cut expenses to the bone in order to squeeze the most profit out of state grants. Teachers' unions overwhelmingly opposed the shift to municipal control, complaining of poor wages and appalling conditions. One notorious chain of twenty-eight schools, which paid an average of 30,000 pesos ($100) a month, reportedly received 39 million pesos in monthly subsidies but spent only 9 million, netting over 300 million per year.[41]

Officials dismissed the protests as the carping of a once powerful pressure group, and the new system did make education more accessible and cost-efficient. By the mid-1980s, more than 90 percent of all children were in elementary school, high school attendance had risen to 55 percent, and the illiteracy rate had dropped sharply.[42]

"The changes have been spectacular," said Alfredo Prieto, education minister in the early 1980s. "We introduced the revolutionary idea that families could send their children anywhere they wanted, and now schools even place ads to attract them." While recognizing that the changes had "brutal social costs" for teachers and other employees, he insisted it was necessary to "break the monopoly of the privileged," adding, "Now there are opportunities for all."[43]

ON university campuses, the regime's reforms ignited a protest movement that had been smoldering since 1978. Long before other sectors of society were prepared to challenge authoritarian rule, students began to push against the confines of military-run university life.

The first protests were nervous and tentative; participants were harassed by classmates and the authorities alike. In 1979, when a handful of students rallied at the University of Chile to celebrate the triumph of the Sandinista revolution in Nicaragua, a hostile crowd shouted them down. At the Catholic University that year, 105 students were suspended or expelled for gathering to sing hymns as a form of protest.[44]

Faced with such risks, most students chose safer avenues of expression. By 1980, a number of artistic groups, notably the Agrupación Cultural Universitaria, were organizing folk-song workshops, satirical dramas, and poetry readings. Underground journals with names like Krítica, Chispa (Spark), and La Bicicleta appeared, offering poems, jokes, and political essays.

Often these activities were banned, but students used clever ploys to make their political points. At the Catholic University, students organized a classical music concert and invited campus officials to attend. When the audience was seated, the surprise guest was introduced: Roberto Bravo, a renowned leftist pianist who had just returned from years of exile in Europe. The deans stood up and walked out.[45]

Revolutionary music from the Popular Unity era was taboo, but young artists created a new generation of protest songs called Canto Nuevo (New Song), with more subtle harmonies and introspective lyrics. One ensemble performed Mozart and Bach on Andean instruments like the quena (wooden flute) and charango (armadillo-shell ukulele), which young audiences identified with Allende-era themes but the authorities could hardly censor.[46]

By 1981, dissident student groups were growing larger and bolder, staging hunger strikes and prayer vigils to protest the system of military rectors and government educational policies. The authorities cracked down hard; leaders were expelled, arrested, beaten, and banished to remote villages for ninety days. Little of this conflict appeared in the daily press, but a newsletter published by the Academy of Christian Humanism followed the erupting power struggle in grim detail.

A sampling of items from 1980 follows. November 7: Two students kidnapped from Technical University. November 13: Expelled student beaten by guards at University of Chile. November 14: Students chain themselves inside building. November 21: Bomb found at dean's home. November 25: Hunger strike at University of Chile. November 27: Rightist campus groups paint swastikas. December 4: Four students banished to fishing village. December 22: Nine students begin fast in cathedral. December 24: Fasters take meal of water and salt at midnight. December 28: University of Chile student assassinated.[47]

Pinochet and his aides insisted that a few agitators were responsible, but the unrest gathered momentum. In May 1983, when the copper workers called for a national strike, campuses burst into flame. "A democratic energy exploded that had been submerged for years," wrote one dissident leader. "It was no longer the same old two hundred of us in the courtyards, calling for change. That day there were eight hundred, a thousand, twelve hundred voices that shouted, applauded, and sang."[48]

Over the next five months, a series of student-led demonstrations burst the nation from its cocoon of fear and badly shook the government. Boisterous marchers converged on O'Higgins Avenue, clogging traffic and chanting, "It's going to fall!" as bus drivers honked in rhythm. Riot police battled the tide until long after dark, drenching protesters with clouds of tear gas and jets of water from trucks which students nicknamed guanacos, after the South American llamas notorious for spitting.

On campus, a separate struggle unfolded to "democratize" the student unions—an especially meaningful issue at the University of Chile, where the FECH had produced national leaders for six decades. The campaign encountered multiple obstacles: official hostility, leftist pressure to take power by force or trickery, and demands from Christian Democratic leaders to shun coalitions with Marxist students. But the proponents of a nonviolent, nonpartisan approach finally prevailed, and in October 1984 they staged an open election for FECH leadership, soundly defeating the proregime ticket. That night, the historic FECH banner was brought out of hiding and unfurled for the first time since the coup.

"Not just a student federation was born, but something much more important," wrote Yerko Ljubetic, who was elected FECH president. "A new generation that says unity is possible if we put Chile above personal and party interests."[49] By opening the election to everyone, he recounted later, "we were able to keep our sights on the real issues. We were all sons of dictatorship, but our democratic avocation was stronger."

The FECH was catapulted into leadership of the student movement, which was rapidly moving to the center of a growing national campaign to end military rule. Middle-class students were less vulnerable to economic reprisal than were the labor activists who had sparked the protest movement, and they used this relative immunity to keep pressure on the regime. In 1984, when Pinochet declared a new state of siege, FECH leaders barricaded themselves in buildings and broadcast censored news from loudspeakers. At night, they clustered on O'Higgins Avenue, taunting police and sprinting down side streets as "guanacos" careened by, then regrouping for a new confrontation.

"There was tremendous fear, and many students were skeptical after so many years of antipolitical propaganda. But there was also great excitement in the air," recalled Ljubetic. Although threatened by armed men and detained repeatedly, he had no time to worry about danger. "The country had gone from silence to mobilized effervescence, and we were at the heart of it," he said. "We became an unstoppable engine of change."[50]

Two thousand miles from their own convulsed campus, four student leaders from the University of Antofagasta were playing chess outside a farmhouse on Chiloé Island when a visitor drove up on a warm day in November 1984. They had been detained at dawn, held five days by the secret police, then flown south to serve three-month sentences in a tiny fishing village. Restless and isolated, they were hungry for news from the campus front lines.

"They are trying to neutralize us, but we know the struggle is continuing," asserted Juan Carlos Sánchez, an engineering student. His parents, who had just made a twenty-four-hour bus trip to visit him, beamed with pride. "I'm happy that my son and his friends are fighting for democracy. Because of what happened in 1973, we adults are too fearful to join the struggle," explained Urbano Sánchez, a fifty-three-year-old truck driver.

A strategic setback for the regime came in October 1985, when Ljubetic and ten other students were charged with violating state security laws by calling for a strike. "They persecute us because they fear us," Ljubetic told a huge, cheering campus crowd several days later. "The generation that grew up under dictatorship has transformed itself into the generation that struggles for freedom." From there, hundreds joined a march to the courthouse, where the FECH president turned himself in.

Imprisoned with a number of labor leaders, the students became national heroes. Leading Catholic church officials came to visit them, and the detainees released a poem of protest entitled, "Our hands are clean." As the pressure mounted, aides to Pinochet persuaded him to drop the charges. Freed, the students posed outside the penitentiary gates holding up their palms—and the "clean hands" gesture became an instant symbol of the antiregime struggle.[51]

For a handful of students, the price of activism was much higher. In 1985, an engineering student named Patricio Manzano was seized when police raided a FECH summer project; he died in custody after his heart stopped and police refused to let detained medical students help him. In 1986, the body of Mario Martínez, a Christian Democratic student leader, was found on a rocky beach, apparently strangled. Friends said he had been repeatedly followed and threatened by unknown men.[52]

But by 1985 sustained repression against youthful dissidents had begun to backfire. After armed civilians kidnapped and beat two women students, Qué Pasa demanded swift investigation so as "not to leave the sensation that they have more power and resources than the legal authorities."[53] At Martínez's funeral, former senators and labor leaders joined several thousand students in a candlelit church, and Gabriel Valdés, president of the Christian Democratic party, delivered a eulogy saying Martínez's death had "brought victory closer" to the opponents of dictatorship.

That year, an even more gruesome incident seared the nation's conscience and brought unusually strong condemnation from the Reagan administration. Two teenagers involved in a two-day national protest, confronted in a shantytown by an army patrol, were doused with gasoline, set afire, and abandoned in a roadside ditch. Rodrigo Rojas, a nineteen-year-old exile visiting from Washington, D.C., died of his burns, and Carmen Quintana, eighteen, was left horribly disfigured. After a lengthy investigation, one army lieutenant was given a 300-day sentence for extreme negligence—the first time an army officer had been convicted for an act of repression under military rule.[54]

Student unrest trickled down to Chile's high schools, where many students opposed being shunted over to municipal authority, fearing that the quality of teaching and facilities would fall. In June 1986, students and teachers struck together at several dozen public schools—including the National Institute, which had educated twelve presidents since its founding in 1813. During a week of protests, hundreds of teenagers were arrested and some beaten. The municipal transfer was completed.

At Valentín Letelier High School, striking students barricaded themselves inside the main building and huddled in the frozen cafeteria. Asked about the school atmosphere, they complained that history courses ended with President Alessandri and that teachers who raised political topics were reported by "spies" from the National Secretariat of Youth. "They are trying to crush political thought and turn schools into merchandise," charged Raúl Correa, a senior. "Instead, they are only making us more determined to defend the principles of free education."

The protest movement eventually petered out as political parties emerged to take control of the burgeoning opposition movement. But it did prod the regime to abolish the system of military rectors, and forged bonds with faculty and staff that led to small but significant victories. In 1987, when Pinochet named the widely disliked José Luis Federici rector of the University of Chile, the outpouring of pressure from students and faculty was so overwhelming that he was forced to resign after two months.

Moreover, student elections became closely scrutinized bellwethers of national politics while parties were still legally banned. On campus after campus, opposition forces overpowered proregime factions, with Christian Democratic and Marxist groups forming tactical coalitions even though their national leaders were deeply divided. "The FECH died once before because democratic principles were sacrificed to ideology, and we couldn't let that happen again," explained Ljubetic. "With the regime doing everything it could to neutralize us, our only defense was unity."

IN Pudahuel and San Miguel, a different brand of youth protest erupted with the crisis of 1983. Night after night, after the university students had gone home to their middle-class suburbs, young men in the gritty poblaciones barricaded their streets with burning tires and chunks of cement, hurled rocks and bottles when riot police tried to enter, and punctured their tires with twisted nails called *miguelitos*.

These neighborhood conflagrations were the most visible sign of a festering alienation among shantytown youths. Many came from families with strong leftist roots and burned with rage against the regime. Having few legal channels for self-expression, many turned to the clandestine Communist or Socialist youth brigades, which painted revolutionary murals, leafleted neighborhoods, organized demonstrations, and performed other "tasks" to keep leftist ideals alive among the young and poor.

These were young people with bleak prospects, marginalized from a society that stressed competition and consumption but offered fewer stable job opportunities. Between 1976 and 1979, the unemployment rate averaged 30 percent for fifteen- to nineteen-year-olds and 23 percent for those between twenty and twenty-four; in 1982, 36 percent of all urban youths were jobless. The new, upwardly mobile society of credit cards and designer jeans seemed unattainable to población youths, who turned to video "flippers," marijuana, and jars of Neopren shoe glue for escape.[55]

Authorities drew no distinction between political protesters and "delinquents," and sometimes the line was hazy. Street rallies became excuses to get drunk and shout obscenities. In La Victoria, where youngsters battled police regularly in 1983 and 1984, neighbors warned visitors to watch their purses and beware of young drug addicts. In Conchalí, a drunken fifteen-year-old shot his brother dead; the rifle came from an older boy who was trying to recruit him into a "revolutionary militia."

But for thousands of youths, ideological commitment to a guerrilla struggle became a matter of life and death. Some joined a rejuvenated armed wing of the MIR; others were drawn to the Manuel Rodríguez Patriotic Front, created by the Communist party in 1980. Trained in homemade weaponry and explosives, the "Rodriguistas" and their allies launched a furtive urban war: between 1983 and 1986, such groups were responsible for 3,326 dynamitings (usually of electrical towers), 1,889 acts of sabotage (burning buses or subway cars), 649 armed assaults, and 162 kidnappings or assassination attempts.[56]

One Rodriguista called Gabriel described to the journalist Patricia Politzer how he evolved from a población teenager, seething as he watched troops shove his neighbors to the ground and search them; to a student protester, who found thrills in throwing rocks until he was arrested and tortured; to a member of a Communist Youth "combat unit," where he learned to make explosives and blow up electrical towers.

Upon entering the Front, he was shocked by its rigid, military style. "They were cold and calculating people, and I had thought we would all be friends and brothers," he recalled. The Front demanded hard work and discipline, but rewarded him with challenging "missions"—keeping a kidnapping target under surveillance, planting a car bomb, taking over a radio station, and finally abducting a Carabinero.

An idealist who insisted that Front members were not delinquents and who tried to make people understand why he was stealing their cars, Gabriel was also a steely operative who followed orders without question. "I hate violence and weapons . . . but the government legitimates violence, and you cannot achieve peace by conversing," he explained. "To be in the Front is an honor."[57]

In some poblaciones, these underground warriors were heroes fighting an oppressive establishment, their exploits artistically illustrated on public walls. In Pudahuel, the names of three brothers—Eduardo, Rafael, and Pablo Vergara—became legend. Raised by working-class parents who were active in the Catholic social action movement, the boys were drawn into leftist politics as teenagers after the coup. "We used to pray together before we went to protests," recalled their mother, Luisa Toledo, a woman with iron-gray hair and deeply pained eyes.

In the early 1980s, two of the brothers were expelled from the university and repeatedly detained. Once Pablo came out of prison so badly beaten that he was urinating blood. Soon after that, he told his parents he planned to enter the MIR militia. "We stayed up all night and cried, but he was convinced it was the right thing to do. It was no adolescent whim," Luisa insisted. Rafael, the youngest, soon followed.

In 1985, Eduardo and Rafael were slain in what police called a spectacular shoot-out with the two "political delinquents."[58] Pablo fled to Spain but later slipped back into Chile, sending his parents impassioned but cryptic letters with no return address. "I curse this regime, I curse the complacent rich. . . . I ask God for strength to make the people believe in freedom, in the need for our popular army," he wrote in August 1988. Three months later, he died while allegedly attempting to blow up an electrical tower.

To the Vergara family, who nailed black wooden silhouettes of their sons outside their bungalow in Pudahuel, the boys were neither subversives nor delinquents. To the young people of Villa Francia, where the brothers were memorialized in outdoor murals along with defiant fists and doves of freedom, they were a source of inspiration and courage. "Our sons were struggling to end dictatorship and bring democracy to the poor," said Luisa. "For the marginalized youth of Chile, their lives and deaths are symbols of hope for the future."[59]

DURING the Pinochet years, most students were neither bombing power stations nor chanting in the streets; they were simply trying to get an education and find a niche in adult society. What became of their attitudes and aspirations as they came to maturity under military rule? Did the regime's values of order, patriotism, and competitiveness sink in, or did an older, democratic ethic survive the years of military tutelage?

Unquestionably, repression and propaganda made young people shy away from the political activism that had obsessed earlier generations. In a 1987 survey, only 2.4 percent of all Chileans aged eighteen to twenty-nine said they discussed politics "often," 37 percent said they discussed it "little," and 38 percent "never."[60] Many youths developed a jaundiced view of both socialism and democracy, expressing distaste for politics of any stripe and confusion about various forms of government.

"None of my friends like Pinochet, but maybe democracy would be worse," confided one art student at the Catholic University in 1989. Although her father had been a politician and her mother a voter-registration volunteer for years, this young woman—who had turned three the year of the coup—feared Chile was "not ready for democracy." "Maybe it should only be for a country that has culture and civilization," she mused earnestly.

Although the campus explosions of the mid-1980s seemed massive, only a minority of students became involved in politics. In one poll of students at three universities, two-thirds said student politics were important to the nation, but less than 20 percent had taken an active role in campus elections, and less than 6 percent had been arrested in protests.[61]

Most students described themselves as centrist or center-left but youth activists acknowledged that the level of ideological commitment was far less intense than before 1973. "Our generation is more skeptical, and we don't have gurus," said Cristián Tolosa, thirty, a psychologist and Christian Democratic party organizer. "We get angry, but not too angry; and we don't put all our energy into an idea, because it might fail."

Apathy was most pronounced among affluent students. At Diego Portales University, liberal arts instructors who had come of age in the U.P. found even their brightest pupils disturbingly incurious about social and political issues. Flavio Cortés, a sociology instructor, tried to spark debate about the use and abuse of power, but drew little response from the members of one class, even when he ventured to ask their opinion of torture. Only when he switched to soccer team rivalries did the class perk up.

"I try to get them to reflect on things, but they lead a comfortable and untroubled existence; torture doesn't relate to their lives," Cortés explained. "I have friends and colleagues who were tortured after the coup, and it was difficult enough for them to tell me about it. If I tried to broach the subject in class, these kids simply wouldn't understand," he said in discouragement.

Ricardo Vásquez, a colleague in the psychology department, said many students raised in dictatorship had never learned how to think. "For sixteen years, information has been stuffed into them like sausages, with no room to question," he said. "We are trying to transform them into thinkers again, to show them that reality is not so black-and-white after all. But once you puncture their bubbles, you often find a very vulnerable person within."[62]

Yet surveys showed that although the regime did produce a certain passivity among students across class lines, it achieved only limited success in creating a "new generation" of youth that was purified of so-called political vices—and failed to uproot a stronger, 150-year legacy of democratic culture.

After 1983, opinion polls showed that young people consistently opposed military rule. In one survey, 67 percent of Chileans between the ages of eighteen and twenty-four said they preferred a civilian to a military leader—the highest percentage of any adult age group. When asked whether economic well-being mattered more than democracy, 64 percent of college-age Chileans disagreed—again, a percentage higher than in any other group. Students were also more worried about human rights abuses than older adults were.[63]

And, when asked to rank the importance of certain political values, young people who had grown up under military rule gave answers strikingly similar to those of adults who had known democracy. Freedom ranked the highest among all age groups, with 60 percent mentioning it as important, followed by equality. The major tenets of the regime, such as authority, nationalism, and anticommunism, were chosen by less than 6 percent. And revolution, the idea that had swept Chile into the maelstrom, ranked lowest of all.[64]

By the later 1980s, even conservative student leaders developed a more mellow approach, distancing themselves from the regime and its doctrinaire style. José Antonio Silva, the *gremialista* student body president at the Catholic University in 1988, was frankly critical of state education reforms. "The values were good, but there was too much dogmatism. Instead of rebuilding the universities, they asphyxiated them," he said.[65]

If the government failed to inculcate new political values in Chilean youth, it was far more successful in transforming their professional and economic aspirations. The creation of consumer-oriented culture, permitted by Chile's entry into international markets and promoted by the boom in modern advertising, exposed young people to a wealth of new status symbols, from motorbikes to designer jeans.

At the same time, prolonged economic crisis kept these tantalizing new possibilities beyond the reach of all but a few, and left the rest deeply anxious about the future. In 1987, 28 percent of the college-age adults surveyed in Santiago described their economic situation as "bad," 55 percent as "so-so," and only 18 percent as "good." Asked to predict two years ahead, more than half believed their situation would remain the same or worsen.[66]

Driven both by ambition and by fear of failure, students were easily lured into engineering or business classes, instead of wasting time reading poetry or philosophy. By 1981, the most popular majors at four large universities were civil engineering (16.8 percent), medicine (13 percent), and economics (12.7 percent).[67] Similarly, the most sought-after courses at professional institutes in 1983 were computer studies (22 percent) and business administration (10.7 percent).[68]

Even though university policies placed a strong emphasis on cost-efficiency—regarding education as an "investment in human capital" and setting tuition fees according to the earning potential of each degree—professors from an earlier era were appalled at the narrow pragmatism of students who demanded their money's worth from education, but no more.

"The students see me more as a provider of a service than as a teacher. They are consumers of education," said Cortés, whose university was founded by a group of businessmen with the goal of forming a new technocratic elite. "There is no intellectual relationship between us; they don't like risks and they don't want problems. If they have any rebelliousness at all, it is channeled into consumerism."

The pleasant, businesslike atmosphere of such campuses, where blond-haired future lawyers and engineers planned ski weekends between classes, seemed light-years away from the grim, shabby classrooms in a rundown section of Santiago, where members of the MIR youth gathered for a clandestine workshop one day in 1989. They were somber young men and women who addressed each other in code names; many had parents who had been killed, imprisoned, or forced into exile.

"My dad was in the MIR, and he suffered cruelly for his beliefs. Now I am carrying on the struggle he had to abandon," explained Paulo, a polite but steely-eyed nineteen-year-old. "We are a polit-ical-military party, and we know we can be attacked and killed at any time. We are all prepared to be silent, to endure, to defend ourselves. If you believe in building a truly just society, you are never afraid of death."

Yet even these avenging inheritors of a tragic utopian legacy seemed to be evolving. Their vocabulary was simpler than the obscure leftist jargon of their parents, and they spoke of trying to appeal to 1980s youth without losing their commitment to revo-lutionary change. "We have to be in step with the times," explained Abelardo, also nineteen. "In the past, a MIRista did not dance at parties," he said solemnly. "Now we do."[69]

CHAPTER ELEVEN

THE POLITICIANS

"We are trying to unite all Chileans, and if we got the politicians involved, it would produce polarization all over again. . . . All the work we are doing would be wiped out."

—*Augusto Pinochet, 1975*[1]

"My father used to take me to soccer games with his colleagues from the legislature. He had friends in all the parties. There was one man, a Communist; they would walk and talk together. . . . It seems like a long time ago."

—*Lucía Santa Cruz, 1989*[2]

ON a midwinter morning in August 1985, twenty-one politicians met in the elegant Spanish Circle club and signed a historic manifesto for democracy. It had taken months of delicate negotiations and diplomatic intervention by the new cardinal, Juan Francisco Fresno, to achieve. But now, eleven parties spanning the ideological spectrum, from Socialists who had revered Allende to moderate conservatives who had reviled him, were agreed on a proposal for peaceful political change.

The National Accord for Transition to Full Democracy was a bold alternative to Pinochet's plans for a slow, controlled shift to limited democratic rule. It demanded that all states of emergency be lifted, political parties legalized, and arbitrary exile and internal banishment halted. Looking ahead, it called for free, direct presidential elections, rather than the yes-no plesbiscite with a single candidate nominated by the four military commanders, as spelled out in the 1980 constitution. The Accord also proposed a stronger, elected Congress instead of a partly appointed one, and a more flexible process for amending the 1980 charter.

After twelve years of paralysis and mutual suspicion, the accord brought Chile's political parties together as a responsible and formidable force for change. The Socialists agreed to respect private property, assuaging conservatives' fears and assuring their participation in the agreement. For the first time since the coup, Pinochet appeared isolated and vulnerable, and the possibility of a swift end to dictatorship seemed real.

OF all Chilean institutions, the party system had been most severely damaged by military rule. For many decades, political parties had provided regularly alternating governments, served as intermediaries between citizens and the state, and built public policy through debate and negotiation. But to the generals who seized power over a society in chaos, Chile's parties were incubators of demagoguery and intransigence that had mired the nation in fratricidal conflict.

Chile's political groups were too entrenched to become pliant partners of authoritarianism, as had occurred in Brazil after the 1964 coup. To build a harmonious governing order, the junta members believed, they had to destroy all leftist parties and neutralize the rest. With Congress suspended, political meetings banned, and the media silenced, parties lost their dynamic role in national life and were reduced to a furtive struggle for survival.

Internally, the loss of democracy created a crisis of leadership and authority for all parties. Party elections were banned, so there was no way to test the popularity of particular leaders, and small factions could demand equal recognition. Such power struggles weakened Chile's parties at a time when they could least afford it, leading to fragmentation, drift, and endless arguments on fine ideological points.

The organization best equipped to endure a prolonged period of repression was the Communist party. Founded in 1922, it built a strong working-class base and elected 19 members to Congress by 1941. Growing into the largest Communist party in Latin America, it boasted 250,000 members by the 1970s and became a force for moderation in the U.P. coalition. But the party had also survived a decade of repression after being banned in 1948, developing a tightly organized cell structure and a large central committee that could take repeated blows and still function.[3]

After the coup, these experiences helped the Communists combat infiltration and keep their organization alive despite the constant risk of arrest. Secretary-General Luis Corvalán was captured
and imprisoned, but a new underground leadership was established and the old cell structure reactivated. Using code names to
identify each other, members met in tiny groups, communicating
party instructions and keeping abreast of news through broadcasts
of "Listen, Chile" from Moscow.

Iron adherence to a doctrine of democratic centralism helped
keep the party unified in adversity. "Once matters have been discussed and a decision has been taken, one must obey," explained
the party leader José Sanfuentes, sounding like a well-drilled officer on Pinochet's staff.[4] Patricio Hales, a veteran activist, suggested a different metaphor. "We are very liturgical," he said. "If
you haven't been to mass, you cannot understand the Communist
party."

Above all, survival depended on the commitment of the party
faithful, who addressed each other as *compañero* and nurtured a
subterranean culture with folk music, poetry, and the party newspaper *El Siglo*. Like a religion, communism demanded total commitment to the struggle between good and evil, and in turn it fulfilled
the basic human need to belong.

To a young activist like Eduardo Sabrovsky, who worked
underground for years after the coup, the party provided an all-
consuming identity and purpose, even in terrifying times. "It was
like finding a firm niche in the world. My destiny was totally linked
to that of the party," he explained. "I had a profession and a family, but they were ancillary to my real life."

To Carmen Vivanco, a birdlike widow with penetrating hazel
eyes, party work after the coup was simply another phase in the
struggle she had joined half a century before. As a miner's daughter in the desert nitrate camps of the north, she read smuggled
Marxist pamphlets and dreamed of journeying to a promised land
called Russia. Later, she and her brothers plunged into a whirlwind of labor strikes and campaigns for Marxist candidates. "We
were arrested many times, but it hardened us for what was to come,"
she explained.

Further toughened by the Great Depression and by the tensions
of underground party work after 1948, Vivanco married a fellow

Communist and rose to become a member of the party's powerful disciplinary committee. She campaigned for Allende three times, and his election was the happiest moment of her life. As a provincial governor's wife, she watched in sadness and frustration as the government unraveled, but her faith in the cause of revolution remained unshakable.

After the coup, Vivanco's family returned to clandestine party work, but in August 1976 her husband and son were seized by armed police agents and never seen again. Still undaunted, the petite but determined woman plunged into human rights work, appearing regularly in marches and facing more arrests. "We in the party have a mystique," she explained over tea in her small, spare house, one Sunday in 1985. "There are things one cannot forgive, but history shows us that when the moment is right, the popular explosion will come and our truth will prevail."[5]

Despite such unwavering conviction, party leaders were bewildered by the failure of the Allende experiment and obsessed with determining what had gone wrong. Having supported a slow, peaceful road to revolution, they at first blamed the militaristic posturing of the MIR and the Socialists for having alienated the Christian Democrats.[6] They rejected criticism from the more radical left—and from the Soviet Union—that they should have helped forge a swift revolutionary transformation and a military defense of Allende.[7]

But gradually, haunted by guilt and embittered by persecution, party leaders shifted their interpretation of past events. In 1977, at their first postcoup plenum in Mexico City, central committee members joined the MIR and the more radical Socialists in blasting Allende's government as too "reformist" and passive in the face of attack.[8]

At first, this new perspective did not alter the party's plans. Assuming the dictatorship would ultimately collapse, the Communists urged a broad alliance of "antifascist forces" against military rule. Corvalán, exiled in Moscow, encouraged party leaders to reach out to Christian Democrats and dissident military officers, and to take up the banner of human rights and social injustice.[9] In 1980, the party also authorized its legal experts to collaborate with other groups in drafting an alternative constitution.

But such joint efforts were undermined by mutual mistrust, and the party line hardened in response to the vicious repression unleashed by the DINA. As the secret police penetrated each new layer of security, paranoia and suspicion spread. And as party elders were detained, killed, or forced into exile, they were replaced by younger, tougher militants who sought to push the party toward violent rebellion against military rule.

These young activists had limited experience operating in a democracy, and their frame of reference was one of confrontation and oppression. Some had studied Marxist theory in Leipzig, East Germany, after the coup; others had fought with the Sandinistas in Nicaragua and were inspired by their 1979 revolution. They no longer believed that Pinochet would fall on his own, but they were sure his tightening grip would lead to similar revolutionary conditions in Chile.

The idea of insurrection also appealed to senior party ideologues like Volodia Teitelboim, a former senator living in Moscow, who was impressed by the successful mass uprising against the mighty shah of Iran in 1979.[10] Exile leaders drew other lessons from Nicaragua, where the Communist party had played only a marginal role in the revolution. If a popular revolt developed against Pinochet, Chile's Communists did not want to be left behind by the forces of history. "The old men of the party lived the defeat of Allende with deep personal guilt, and Nicaragua accentuated it," observed an underground leader in 1985. "They felt as if the justification of their entire lives was at stake."[11]

Many party activists opposed the idea of insurrection, including union officials, former legislators, and youth leaders who had been exposed to Eurocommunism while in exile. By 1979, however, most leaders of the younger generation had concluded that Pinochet could be defeated only by a combination of street protest and guerrilla violence. One year later, in Sweden, Corvalán announced a new party line of "Popular Rebellion of the Masses." Faced with fascism, he asserted, the people had no choice but to take up "all forms of struggle, including acute violence."[12]

Once the decision was made, most old-guard militants dutifully acquiesced in the new line, which was soon reinforced by the triumph of Pinochet's plebiscite in 1980. Yet some members objected so strongly to violence that they resigned from the party. "Things returned to Soviet orthodoxy, and the springtime of debate ended quickly," recalled Sabrovsky, one of the dissidents, who blamed the influence of "pre-*perestroika* thinking" on party leaders exiled in the East bloc.[13]

The champions of the insurrectionary line were now in command: tough young professionals like Gladys Marín and José Sanfuentes, described by one critic as "Stalinist" and indifferent to the party's civic traditions.[14] Población youths were recruited into the Manuel Rodríguez Patriotic Front, and their sabotage campaign escalated with the rhythm of street protests, totaling over 1,100 bombings and 350 other attacks in 1984.[15] Exhilarated, the hardliners began to believe they could force Pinochet from power—and foment a workers' revolution at the same time.

"The Front's actions were a form of support to the democratic struggle; they demonstrated our force in the face of dictatorship and sent a double message of encouraging the masses and challenging the dominant classes," explained Jaime Insunza, a party leader, in 1989. Blackouts, he said, "provoked great joy in the popular sectors and great terror in the upper sectors. There were a few grave errors of adventurism, but the Front had a very positive image with the masses."[16]

Such language reflected both the absolute conviction of these militants and their tragic isolation from the dominant mood of the country. Sealed within a rigid structure that placed hierarchical discipline above all other virtues, they could not see that the vast majority of society wanted peaceful change, and they became trapped in a futile military logic that alienated the democratic opposition and fed the paranoia of the regime.

The Communists continued to seek strategic alliances with other opponents of the regime, knowing that a broad political front was needed to make Chile "ungovernable." But their insistence on allowing "all forms of struggle" made groups like the Christian Democrats extremely uncomfortable and led to their exclusion from the multiparty Democratic Alliance (AD), which was formed in August 1983 in the wake of the mass protests.

Scorned and angry, the Communists created their own coalition with the left-leaning socialists, called the Popular Democratic Movement (MDP), which endorsed violent protest.[17] When the National Accord was proposed, they again complained of being excluded but worked feverishly to undermine the pact, which they viewed as a futile, U.S.-concocted plot to return Chile to bourgeois democracy.[18] While the rest of Pinochet's opponents were preparing to negotiate an end to military rule, the Communists were preparing a final offensive to overthrow him.

UNLIKE the Communists, the Socialist party underwent a painful period of self-doubt and schizophrenic divisions after the coup.

Yet, ultimately, this bickering and disorganized party developed a capacity for evolution and renewal that placed its leaders in a far better position to influence Chile's transition back to civilian rule.

Since the party's founding, in 1933, the Socialists had been rent by disputes between members who favored reformist policies and an electoral route to power and those who advocated a violent overthrow of the "bourgeois" state.[19] Drawn leftward by the Cuban revolution, the party declared itself Marxist-Leninist in 1967.

During the U.P. years, firebrand Socialists like Carlos Altamirano, the secretary-general, called for a dictatorship of the proletariat and pushed for violent confrontation as Allende desperately sought compromise. Much of this bravado was hollow, as Altamirano conceded after years in exile. "One thing is what one affirms on the theoretical plane . . . a very different thing is what one does in concrete life," he said in 1989. Where had he imagined that his calls for mass resistance would lead? "The truth is, I didn't think about it," he admitted.[20]

But bravado cost the Socialists dearly. With no underground experience, their leaders were easily tracked down by the DINA. Several thousand members were imprisoned, tortured, and forced into exile. The collapse of the U.P. also left the party stripped of ideological armor against despair. Ricardo Núñez, then a young Socialist academic, found a friend weeping one day. "He said his brother had been killed in the coup, but that at least he had died for a cause. I found myself wondering, what cause?" Núñez recounted. "It had all come crashing down, and there was no cause any more."[21]

The coup provoked a schism in the party that lasted for years, allowing rival factions to emerge in the void left by dead and exiled leaders. One group, the Internal Directorate, called for a merger with the Communists and the creation of a broad, working-class alliance against the regime. Another, the National Coordinator of Regions, called for a "Marxist-Leninist revolutionary vanguard" to rise up against dictatorship.[22]

Further weakened by repression, the rudderless party ultimately splintered into at least fifteen fragments, ranging from moderate reformists to diehard Leninists. They included the Swiss, the Socialist Front, the Twenty-fourth Congress group, the Popular Socialist Union, the Humanist Tendency, the April 19 Consensus, the National Liberation Army, the Spark, the Mandujanos, and groups named for half a dozen individuals.

Abroad, an elaborate party network sprang up. Altamirano first alighted in Havana but was rejected by hardened exiles scheming to launch a military offensive against Pinochet.[23] He finally established headquarters in East Berlin, with Núñez running day-to-day operations while the secretary-general traveled through Europe, cultivating friendships with international Socialist leaders.

Despite their preoccupation with Chile, these men soon discovered that life in the suspicious, heavy-handed systems of the East bloc bore little resemblance to the egalitarian utopia they had envisioned. "I began to realize how emotional our identification with the Cuban revolution had been, and to see the practical difficulties of building a pluralistic socialism," acknowledged Núñez after returning home.

Altamirano grew just as disillusioned with "real" socialism in East Germany, confiding he had been shocked by the lack of freedom and horrified by a system that punished initiative and created a cowed, conformist populace.[24] In 1988, impressed by the changes sweeping the Soviet Union, he condemned Marxism for failing to address deep conflicts in presumably classless societies. "I realized that the division of the world between . . . white and black was not so certain or precise," he said.[25]

The collapse of Allende's experiment provoked great soul-searching throughout the European left, and helped forge a new, more flexible brand of Eurocommunism.[26] This "renewal" also had a profound impact on some Chilean exiles who had long been contemptuous of "bourgeois" democracy. A Rome-based journal called *Chile América* and the Institute for a New Chile, in Rotterdam, became influential sources of their thinking. Setting aside Marx for the writings of Antonio Gramsci, they rejected the notion of "armed struggle" and called for peaceful opposition to Pinochet.[27]

An even larger faction of the Socialist party, however, identified with the more orthodox Marxism of Clodomiro Almeyda, Allende's former foreign minister, also exiled in East Germany. Although a moderating force within the U.P., Almeyda was a doctrinaire ideologue, and his postcoup views evolved with those of the Communists, rejecting Western democracy and supporting close relations with East bloc Communists. Thus, Chile's two dominant Socialists reversed roles: the rabble-rousing Altamirano moved closer to social democracy, while the cautious Almeyda adopted a more militant, confrontational line.

Inside Chile, Almeyda's views prevailed among underground party leaders, and in 1977 the National Coordinator of Regions sent Altamirano a savage letter that disavowed his authority and accused him of collusion with the Christian Democrats.[28] The conflict came to a head in the "Algiers" party plenum of 1978—a code-named meeting held in East Berlin, at which security was heavy and delegates from Chile wore hoods over their heads. Altamirano was barely reelected secretary-general, and a year later he was replaced by Almeyda, who immediately proclaimed the party to be "revolutionary" and Marxist-Leninist.[29]

For Altamirano allies abroad, it was a bitter and uncomfortable moment. "We were harassed by the Germans and by our own people until we had no choice but to leave," recalled Núñez, who briefly moved to Spain. Back home, however, Altamirano supporters called their own congress and reelected him, thus formally splitting the party. Although he had lost much grass-roots support, his ideas were shared by party intellectuals, who published papers opposing violence and promoting a broad push for a return to Chile's traditional democracy.

Despite its weakened position, the "renewed" wing worked hard to build opposition consensus through feverish rounds of meetings and conferences. Altamirano himself, physically and politically spent, retired to a quiet, studious life in Paris. But his faction gradually gained enough support within Chile to elect Carlos Briones, Allende's former interior minister, secretary-general in 1983.

The Socialist renewal also appealed to leftists outside the party, including the Christian Left, whose members joined with Briones in proposing a broad movement called the Socialist Convergence. The effort failed, partly because working-class party "apparatchiks" resented the upper-class "sociologists" in charge.[30] But by 1983, under the emerging influence of an economist named Ricardo Lagos, the Briones Socialists had become an important component of the Democratic Alliance.

The Almeyda Socialists, in contrast, backed the Communist strategy of "popular rebellion" and joined in their Popular Democratic Movement. A group of militants trained in Cuba, Nicaragua, and Libya, known as the *comandantes,* gained influence within the party, which joined in publicly exhorting the "masses" to take up arms against dictatorship.[31]

The continuing Socialist split kept both factions vulnerable to pressure from rival parties and made it difficult to measure the real strength of various leaders. The Almeydistas, overshadowed by the more disciplined Communists, feared losing the support of their followers if they failed to maintain a hard-line posture. The Briones group feared that its moderate followers, tired of violence and radical slogans, would be lured to centrist parties unless it adopted a milder tone.

For years, the Almedya Socialists seemed the stronger faction, because of their vocal support in labor unions and poblaciones, but the moderates came far closer to reading the pulse of the population. Once the political struggle turned from street protests to electoral competition, they easily gained the upper hand. "The Almeydistas were obsessed with blame for the coup, and they insisted on classic Marxist-Leninist definitions," said Núñez. "We believed the past was past; it was time to rebuild the country."

In fact, the Almeydistas had no wish to repeat the bloodbath of 1973, and some were uneasy about allying with the Communists as they persisted in a rigid, revolutionary posture. They felt used by the stronger party and realized they were losing supporters to Briones. This discomfort spread, forcing the *comandantes* to break away and allowing a general shift toward the center. In 1985, when the Briones group helped engineer the National Accord, the Almeydistas cautiously welcomed it, marking a first but significant break from the Communists.

THE Christian Democrats, Chile's sprawling party of moderate reformers, proved far more nettlesome to the regime than did the Marxists. The party, which had polled more than a million votes in the 1973 congressional elections, enjoyed a certain immunity after the coup because of its ties to the Catholic church and European democracies, as well as its role in opposing Allende.[32] With a solid middle-class core and a disciplined organization, the party projected strong democratic values that resisted years of harassment and propaganda.

The party traced its roots to the 1930s, when a group of young Catholics, inspired by the progressive encyclicals of Popes Leo XIII and Pius IX and the writings of French social thinkers like Jacques Maritain, broke away from the Conservative party. Many came to advocate a "third way" between capitalism and communism, rejecting both excess materialism and godless doctrines. Two decades later, the party's fortunes soared when the Chilean Catholic church broke its traditional alliance with the conservative elite and opted for social reform.

The Christian Democrats inhabited a subculture as ingrown as that of the Communists. In formal settings, they addressed each other as "comrade." "Christian Democracy is like a great family," with the strengths and inbreeding of a clan, observed the party leader Enrique Krauss in 1989. "We live exclusively among ourselves. We are a ghetto. Our children marry each other. It is very much like what happens in the military."[33]

After months of battling Allende, senior party leaders, including former President Frei, initially welcomed the coup as the only apparent alternative to a totalitarian takeover. Discreet contact had been made with military officers, and the early influence of Generals Arellano and Bonilla reassured the party that the military would soon turn power over to civilians. Frei told his son he had been assured that elections would be held within six to twelve months of the coup.[34]

In a letter to *El Mercurio* on Christmas Day, 1973, the acting party president, Osvaldo Olguín, expressed confidence in the junta and said he welcomed the political "recess" after the trauma of the Allende years. "For a time we want to rest, to reorder our ranks," he wrote. "In future years, we will return renewed and whole, to serve Chile better."[35]

But some Christian Democrats strongly opposed the coup, and twelve members led by Bernardo Leighton quickly published a statement condemning it as immoral and avoidable. "The declaration marked us all deeply," recalled one signer, Ignacio Balbontín. "For the military we became dangerous, and for many of our friends we became traitors."[36]

The split cut across party culture and loyalties and led to a reluctant estrangement between Leighton and Frei, two lifelong friends. In an anguished exchange of letters in 1975, the former president protested Leighton's association with leftist exiles in Rome, but Leighton insisted it was crucial for Chilean parties to reunite, arguing, "The struggle is not between us, but against the dictatorship."[37]

For years afterward, Frei's acceptance of the coup remained a topic of bitter disagreement within the party.[38] In hindsight, some Christian Democrats who had supported the coup vehemently denied it. European democracies condemned the party as responsible for the events of 1973, and a U.S. congressional investigation raised charges of CIA support for the Christian Democrats during the 1960s.[39]

But Frei and his cohorts soon grew alarmed at the intense persecution of the left and the junta's indifference to their views. Shortly after the coup, the former president refused to shake hands with Pinochet at a special public mass.[40] Relations deteriorated further as the party continued its activities in defiance of the political "recess." "The military said we betrayed them. They never understood it was an issue not of opportunism but of moral opposition," explained the party leader Edgardo Boeninger.

By mid-1974, Christian Democrats were being removed from academic and civil service posts. Party meetings were spied upon, party media were suspended, and two former legislators, Claudio Huepe and Renán Fuentealba, were sent into exile. In a series of acrimonious letters to Bonilla, the party president, Patricio Aylwin, objected strongly to the junta's authoritarian policies. But with Bonilla's death and Arellano's retirement, the key military contacts were lost. Demoralized and exhausted, Aylwin abandoned his post.

In 1975, Frei definitively broke with the regime, publishing a monograph called *The Mandate of History,* which criticized its economic policies and human rights abuses.[41] The work was banned, but friends printed a thousand copies on mimeo machines hidden inside a truck. The day the book came out, the government staged an elaborate military parade to counter the blow from Chile's most respected political figure.

The rift between the Christian Democrats and military authorities caused Cardinal Silva and other Catholic officials to lose hope of influencing the regime, and the escalating repression against party leaders led to a permanent split between church and state. Suddenly, party activists were being harassed by right-wing thugs; Bernardo Leighton and his wife were nearly assassinated in Rome; and Jaime Castillo, Frei's former justice minister, was seized and forced into exile.

In 1977, officials denounced an alleged plot by Andrés Zaldívar, Aylwin's successor, to overthrow the regime. Police searching his wife's luggage at the airport found documents criticizing the government and outlining a plan for an alternative, democratic one. On March 11, officials presented the documents as evidence of "subversion" and accused the authors of abetting foreign "calumny" against them.[42] That day, the junta decreed all parties dissolved.

From then on, the progovernment press dutifully identified the Christian Democrats as an "ex-party," and its attempts to reassert a public role were quashed. In 1978, when some militants tried to organize support for a "no" vote in the referendum on Pinochet's rule, they were seized and banished to small villages. Yet party

leaders continued to behave as if they were respected professionals, maintaining a solid party structure and creating institutes to
keep research and debate alive, with help from Catholic and international foundations.

In 1979, the Christian Democrats launched an ambitious underground campaign to draft an alternative constitution, bringing
together lawyers, academics, and labor activists from center and
left parties in secret work sessions across the country. "It was the
rebirth of organized democracy, but it was totally clandestine.
Someone always kept watch, and there was the feeling that at any
moment, the knock on the door would come and it would be over,"
recounted Balbontín.

As the 1980 plebiscite approached, government officials accused
the group of being in league with the Communists and denied them
all access to television. The sole public act permitted the opposition, a rally in the Caupolicán Theater featuring Eduardo Frei,
backfired badly. Official newscasts focused not on his message but
on revolutionary catcalls from the audience—a disconcerting
reminder of the past to many voters.

Pinochet's triumph at the polls was a sharp blow to Christian
Democratic leaders, and those who had taken visible opposing roles
suffered harsh reprisal. Zaldívar, arriving home on a flight from
Europe, was confined to the plane and forced into immediate exile.
The expulsion shocked some conservatives and prompted a stinging editorial in *Qué Pasa,* which called it "an error of vast dimensions."[43] The regime then offered Zaldívar a chance to come home,
provided he swear allegiance to the new constitution. Upon refusing, he was banned from Chile for three years.

Unnerved by the loss of their chief officer, party leaders slowed
their pace and lost contact with grass-roots militants. The demor-
alization was deepened by the economic boom, which had lulled
many party members into accepting prolonged military rule. "There
was a great sense of defeat," recalled Eugenio Ortega, Frei's son-
in-law. "Everyone went back into their caves. People were afraid
to go to meetings, and it became exhausting just to keep hope
alive."[44]

The party felt isolated, and the election of Ronald Reagan as
president that November undermined its claim to close ties with
Washington. The new administration opened cordial relations with
the regime, and Ambassador Theberge pointedly turned his back
on its democratic opponents. The administration also restored trade

credits, reestablished annual joint navy exercises, and returned to approving multilateral loans to Chile, which totaled more than $1.7 billion in Reagan's first term.[45]

The new conservative policymakers in power viewed Pinochet as an important anticommunist ally who was far more likely to respond to "quiet diplomacy" than to punitive sanctions. The defiant general, however, was not easily swayed. When Reagan's personal envoy, Jeane Kirkpatrick, paid him a cordial call in 1981, she refused to meet with Jaime Castillo, the distinguished Christian Democrat who headed the Chilean human rights commission. Less than a week later, Pinochet ordered Castillo arrested and expelled from the country for the second time.

ALTHOUGH the Christian Democrats were largely spared the trauma of physical abuse, their party was deeply damaged by dictatorship. Leadership positions were frozen, so younger activists could not ascend. Local leaders were cut off from Santiago, and they resented the growing dominance of urban professionals and academic institutes in policy decisions. And the perennial split between left- and right-leaning sectors, which intensified under military rule, could not be resolved, because of the ban on party elections.

The progressive faction (known as the *chascones*, or longhairs) welcomed a coalition with Marxist groups and supported a strategy of public protest. The conservatives (known as the *guatones*, or potbellies) were strong anticommunists and party chauvinists who favored negotiations with the right and the armed forces. This rivalry never erupted into open warfare, but only because party officials, determined to avoid a painful split, made sure both groups were represented in important committees and posts.

The greatest blow to the Christian Democrats, though, was dealt by nature. Eduardo Frei, who had just turned seventy-one, entered a clinic for routine surgery in January 1982. While still hospitalized, he suddenly died, leaving the party in emotional shock and Chile deprived of the only man who could challenge Pinochet's pretensions to power.

The funeral arrangements were tense. Against the family's wishes, Pinochet insisted on attending the cathedral mass with his entire cabinet, which was forced to endure a pointed homily from Cardinal Silva praising Frei's dedication to justice. For two days, while mourners filed past the coffin, Zaldívar and three other exiled party leaders fought for permission to pay their last respects. But when their planes landed, they were detained and placed on departing flights. At the mass, four empty chairs draped with red copihue lilies bore the exiles' names.[46]

With the Christian Democrats' unrivaled leader gone, heavy competition for the party presidency soon erupted. To cut short the unseemly factional infighting, officials agreed on a compromise: Gabriel Valdés, a left-leaning party elder who had been Frei's foreign minister. Many members doubted that Valdés could fill Frei's shoes, but he proved to be a man of strong principles and personality, who injected new hope and determination into the party.

First, Valdés set about rebuilding the organization, which had dwindled to 25,000 hard-core loyalists. Tapes were sent to 1,500 local groups, containing stirring music and messages from Valdés exhorting all "comrades" to join the crusade for democratic restoration.[47] Then he began reaching out to the Socialists, a delicate task that required overcoming deep fear and resentment among many colleagues. Members in urban areas responded positively, but those in small towns remained fearful and reluctant to work with the left.

Despite the success of the 1983 protests and the formation of the Democratic Alliance, the opposition was rent by discord; coalitions continually broke down amid personal and ideological quarrels. But Valdés and his colleagues persevered, arranging meetings with Socialist politicians. Labor and student leaders forged their own links with Marxist cohorts, and gradually the years of mistrust began to recede.

The Christian Democrats were thrust into leadership of the opposition, and the regime tacitly acknowledged its new national stature by permitting leaders like Zaldívar to return.[48] In the face of persistent protests, the junta also sought a more conciliatory strategy toward the opposition. Sergio Onofre Jarpa, the interior minister appointed in late 1983, invited the Democratic Alliance to negotiate an early transition to democracy, thus defusing the crisis engendered by the protests.

But within a year the talks collapsed as it became clear that Pinochet had no intention of backing his minister's promises, much less of agreeing to the alliance's unrealistic demands that he resign. A new spate of demonstrations erupted, and the regime responded by declaring a new state of siege. For three months, tanks patrolled the streets and troops raided "conflictive" poblaciones, rounding up and questioning more than 32,000 people in three months.[49]

It was in this tense climate that Cardinal Fresno launched his quiet campaign to forge a unified democratic opposition, much to the chagrin of the authorities. At first, they had celebrated the Vatican's decision to replace the retiring Cardinal Silva with Fresno, a clergyman of conservative reputation; First Lady Lucía Hiriart was even heard to remark, "Our prayers have been answered."[50] But although politically cautious, Fresno soon became a defender of the church's mission to the oppressed, and a promoter of national reconciliation.

With help from three prominent civilians—Sergio Molina, Fernando Léniz, and a Christian Democratic businessman named José Zabala—Fresno arranged a series of private meetings with a variety of politicians; views were exchanged through intermediaries. Socialists and conservatives balked repeatedly at each other's demands, but by August 1985 the National Accord was a fait accompli.[51]

Three months later, at the peak of his prominence, Gabriel Valdés addressed half a million citizens in O'Higgins Park, demanding that Pinochet bow to the accord. "The people are on their feet, saying enough dictatorship, enough decay, enough repression," he cried from a huge platform overlooking a sea of Communist, Socialist, and Christian Democratic banners. "You, Mr. Captain General, Augusto Pinochet Ugarte, are the obstacle to democracy in Chile!"[52]

TO Chile's traditional rightist parties, the Liberals and the Conservatives, democracy had always been a matter of deep patrician pride. For half a century, while their peers in Argentina or Peru were bankrolling military putsches, Chilean rightists vied against moderates and Marxists in regular elections. But the organized right weakened in the 1950s, with the populist success of the strongman president Ibáñez, and was dealt a fatal blow by the rise of the Christian Democrats. In 1965, Chile's two major conservative groups merged as the National party in order to stave off further decline.[53]

Having thrown their weight behind Frei in 1964, the rightists were so angered when he championed land reform and other programs to promote the poor that they decided to back their own candidate in 1970—thus propelling Allende into La Moneda. For three years, National party legislators battled the U.P., moving in 1973 to an openly subversive strategy, and finally joining the Christian Democrats in drafting the resolution that condemned Allende's government as being unconstitutional and seeking to "deny all possibility of democratic life."[54]

Once the military was in power, this eloquent concern for democracy vanished. Relieved to have the government in firm hands, the right made no protest when the junta disbanded Congress.[55] A few National party legislators were indignant at their enforced withdrawal from political life, but the party president, Jarpa, supported a full recess—and a majority of members dutifully agreed. As one dissenter put it years later, the party "simply erased itself."[56]

Like other Chileans, many conservatives assumed that the junta would withdraw from power after a brief interregnum. But most were content to return to private life and had little objection to repression against the left. "The right followed the politics of the ostrich," commented one moderate conservative in 1989. "The regime brought order and progress, and that was what really mattered."

As the regime became entrenched, some conservative politicians did try to rein in its authoritarian ambitions. But most were so terrified of the left that they supported the 1980 constitution without question—and some even expressed doubts about the wisdom of universal suffrage, which had been championed by rightist leaders in the nineteenth century.[57] Comfortable in the cocoon of authoritarian rule, the political right lost all ambition, and seemed to have "no conscience about its public responsibilities," lamented Pedro Ibáñez, a senior National party figure, in 1985.[58]

After a full decade, a handful of conservatives finally distanced themselves from the regime, expressing their frustration with its "antagonism" against the "system of liberty which distinguished us."[59] Forming a group called the Republican Right, they joined the Democratic Alliance in 1983, lending legitimacy to the opposition but provoking resentment from their peers. "They consider us traitors, and they cannot forgive us," explained Javier Díaz, a leader of the group.[60]

While most of the conservative establishment retired from public life, two rightist groups—the *gremialistas* and the *nacionalistas*—competed fiercely to become the party of the regime. The *nacionalistas*, who bore no relation to the National party, were hard-line authoritarians closely allied with the secret police. They had emerged in the early 1900s and gained visibility with the rise of fascism in Europe, but never made serious inroads into Chilean politics. With Allende's election, however, nationalism found new expression in Fatherland and Liberty, the fascist-style paramilitary movement.

The group dissolved itself after the coup, but its leader, Pablo Rodríguez, a lawyer with a Hitlerian mustache, and several other nationalists became occasional advisers to Pinochet. Inspired by Franco's Spain, they disdained liberal democracy for a corporatist-style regime, and some hoped to consolidate a permanent military state.[61] Yet they never achieved real influence under Pinochet, and their dreams of creating progovernment civic campaigns were repeatedly foiled by the junta's mistrust of politicians and popular movements.

In their crude, single-minded patriotism, the nationalists despised the Chicago Boys as elitists with foreign economic schemes, and they felt vindicated by the economic collapse of 1983. On the tenth anniversary of the coup, they launched a fascistic movement called Avanzada Nacional (National Advance), with a stark credo: either one was with the armed forces, or one was with the "anti-fatherland," the "bankrupt" parties, the technocrats, and the rich.[62]

"For us, the fatherland is an historic mission," explained José Ramón Molina, a leader of Avanzada, in 1989. "We assume the legitimacy of the government which rescued Chile from Marxist tyranny, and we identify with the spirit of the armed forces." The crew-cut philosophy instructor, who had once been active in leftist student politics but had gone on to study Nietzsche in Franco's Spain, described Pinochet as "the greatest statesman of the twentieth century."[63]

Avanzada was strongly promoted by the secret police, and one of its chief officers was Major Alvaro Julio Corbalán, the infamous CNI agent.[64] But Pinochet continued to shun the nationalists in favor of the Chicago Boys, with their professional style and modern vision of the world. After a vain attempt to soften their image by aligning with other conservatives, the nationalists receded into the shadows, while Avanzada dwindled to the hard-line faithful like Molina.

In contrast to the nationalists' frantic quest for public legitimacy, the *gremialistas* preferred to toil quietly in the bureaucracy, developing their apolitical, capitalist utopia. Not until 1979 did they begin to publicize their views, through a new journal, *Realidad*, and a research center, the Institute for a Free Society. Their mission was not only to battle Marxism and Christian Democracy but also to make sure the nationalists were unable to undermine the 1980 constitution and the emergence of a libertarian society. Fortunately, as one *gremialista* put it, "the fascists got here too late."[65]

With the rapid opening of the political system after 1983, the *gremialistas* took another step that seemed even more out of character. They founded a political party, the Independent Democratic Union (Unión Democrática Independiente, or UDI), under the leadership of Jaime Guzmán. Embraced by former officials and staffed by young technocrats, UDI build a grass-roots base through municipal patronage, becoming known as the "party of the mayors."

Yet UDI leaders insisted their movement was independent, dedicated to building a free society and willing to criticize the regime.[66] "We are neither right nor left, because in Chile both are statist. What we are for is freedom, profound personal freedom," explained Gerardo Jofre, and amiable UDI member and former regime economist. "We are trying to build a democracy that doesn't restrict liberty."[67]

After a decade of dormancy, the conservative establishment was awakened by the crisis of 1983. Economic collapse shook conservatives' confidence in the regime, protests made them fear a Marxist comeback if the transition was not speeded up, and the resurgence of the Christian Democrats stirred their competitive juices. When Interior Minister Jarpa resigned after his talks with the opposition failed, the old National party leader plunged back into the fray, forming a new center-right party called National Union (Unión Nacional).[68]

Jarpa and his cohorts soon clashed with the brash young technocrats of UDI. Concluding that the regime's stubbornness was only fueling the Marxist left, they pushed for speedier party legalization and congressional elections. Andrés Allamand, a young official of National Union, warned that if the "intransigence of the opposition" was met by the "obstinacy of the government, we will only be dousing fire with gasoline."[69] With Jarpa's blessing, Allamand took the bold step of endorsing the National Accord.

DEMOCRATIC opposition leaders also found a new, unexpected ally in the Reagan administration, which was fast abandoning its strategy of "quiet diplomacy" toward Pinochet. Washington's disillusionment had begun in late 1984, shortly after Reagan's reelection, when Minister Jarpa's talks with the opposition collapsed and Pinochet imposed a state of siege. Influential American conservatives, including the academic Mark Falcoff, began to argue that Pinochet's repressive rule could create "another Nicaragua" by exacerbating leftist unrest.[70]

Yet the administration continued to send mixed signals to Pinochet. In early 1985, the State Department called Chile's human rights performance "the greatest disappointment" in the Western Hemisphere, but when A. Langhorne ("Tony") Motley, the assistant secretary of state for inter-American affairs, visited Santiago that month, he announced that Chile's future was "in good hands."[71] That year, in an unusual gesture of protest, the administration abstained on four multilateral loans to Chile—yet between Reagan's reelection and mid-1987 the White House backed eighteen other loans, worth a record $2.1 billion.[72]

By mid-1985, however, a more consistent, critical policy was being fashioned by officials such as Elliott Abrams, Motley's replacement, who believed that Pinochet's harsh grip on power had become a dangerous obstacle to peaceful political change. Moreover, the administration was committed to thwarting the leftist Sandinista regime in Managua, and increased pressure on Pinochet helped counter charges that it held to a double standard.[73]

To establish a new American image in Santiago, Theberge was replaced by Harry G. Barnes, Jr., a distinguished career diplomat who had just completed a tour as ambassador to India. Upon presenting his credentials to Pinochet, Barnes calmly observed that "the ills of democracy can best be cured by more democracy."[74] The new ambassador immediately established ties with democratic and human rights leaders, while remaining cool to Marxist parties, and endorsed the National Accord. In response, Pinochet banned him from La Moneda, ordered the press to crop him from ceremonial photos, and ranted against "the interference of certain ambassadors" in Chile's "internal affairs."[75]

In early 1986, the fall of the Duvalier and the Marcos dictatorships in Haiti and the Philippines further strengthened the hand of U.S. officials who believed it wiser to support democratic reform movements than unpopular autocrats in the Third World.[76] In March, President Reagan vowed to "oppose tyranny in whatever form, whether of the left or the right," and for the first time since the Carter years, the United States sponsored a UN resolution condemning Chile for human rights abuses.[77]

That July, several weeks after the burning death of Rodrigo Rojas, Abrams told a congressional committee he was "skeptical that Pinochet wants any kind of transition," and asserted that the administration would begin regarding human rights as an important criterion for multilateral votes. Asked about an upcoming $250 million World Bank loan, Abrams said, "I would recommend we vote no."[78] This threat provoked a wave of official indignation in Santiago, although in fact, the United States abstained and the loan was easily approved.

THE signing of the National Accord left the regime badly shaken and its opponents emboldened. A consensus began to build that Pinochet could not last until the plebiscite he had planned for 1989, at the end of his eight-year term, or that the military commanders would at least choose someone else as president for the next eight years. But despite these high hopes, the Accord failed to dislodge the general or modify his transition plans, while the fragile opposition alliance crumbled under pressure from symbiotic adversaries on both extremes: the Communist party and the hard-line Pinochetistas.

Pinochet flatly rejected the proposal, warning that as long as leftist terrorism stalked the land, a firm military hand was needed. Although his junta colleagues and numerous aides hinted that some liberalizations were desirable, Pinochet refused to meet with Accord leaders or permit any of his aides to negotiate with them. On Christmas Eve, when Cardinal Fresno called on the president and asked him to reconsider, Pinochet brushed him off, saying, "No, no, it is better if we turn the page." The meeting came to an abrupt end.[79]

At the same time, the general worked hard to undermine conservative support for the accord, hammering away at the threat of Marxist chaos, the treachery of the Christian Democrats, and the disloyalty of allies who turned against him. Business leaders were reluctant to alienate the regime and vulnerable to reprisal: one executive who endorsed the Accord was threatened with a cutoff of crucial state credits. Others, comfortable with authoritarianism, had simply lost all commitment to Chile's democratic traditions.

In the absence of a common enemy like Allende, old feuds and rivalries flared up among conservative politicians. Pacts were made and broken, and the movement of the "enlightened right" sputtered into factionalism. "The right always had a haughty, antidemocratic quality, and the regime destroyed what coherence we had. Now we have descended into anarchy," lamented one former National party senator.[80]

A far more critical factor in the failure of the accord, however, was the disagreement between parties that believed popular protest was needed to force the regime to make political concessions, and those that opposed violence and street actions, fearing they would alienate the middle class and undercut chances of a negotiated end to military rule.

The Socialists and left-leaning Christian Democrats argued that protests had made the Accord possible and that the regime would never negotiate unless the pressure was sustained. Although leery of including the Communists in a formal agreement, they were willing to work with them to mobilize demonstrations, and they feared losing working-class support to their leftist rivals if they appeared to be too soft on the dictator.

The conservatives and right-leaning Christian Democrats contended that more demonstrations would make it difficult for the armed forces to negotiate and that the visible role of the far left in the protest movement exposed democratic leaders to the regime's charges that they were Marxist dupes. Such accusations were especially effective in undercutting conservatives' support for the Accord, because they were afraid of losing middle-class support to the far right. As the politicians wrangled, Pinochet watched with glee.

Soon after the National Accord was signed, these internal contradictions emerged sharply over the issue of student elections at several universities, where Christian Democrats formed joint slates with their Communist allies. Party leaders decided not to disavow their actions—thus seriously compromising their new understanding with the right, while reinforcing Pinochet's intransigence. "We can't accept the Christian Democrats' alliance with the Communists," Allamand said at the time. "Pinochet will never sit down at the table as long as the left persists in the tragic illusion that it can force him out."[81]

Hoping to keep the Accord alive, the Christian Democrats formally distanced themselves from the Communists while seeking other channels to pursue joint tactics. In early 1986, the Assembly of Civility, a grass-roots amalgam of labor and civic groups, was formed to sponsor new demonstrations without official party approvals. But this initiative also fizzled, as the Christian Democrats grew alarmed over the Communists' refusal to disavow the use of force. "Only the totally peaceful path," Valdés rebuked them, would lead back to democracy.[82]

But the Communists, following their own internal logic, had a very different scenario in mind. They envisioned 1986 as the "decisive year" in which an accelerating pattern of protests and sabotage would make the country "ungovernable" and demoralize the military. The regime would collapse, clearing the way for a new form of popular democracy—not the bourgeois variety outlined in the Accord. "The armed forces have been shaken by our actions; they have no ideals or cohesion," asserted an underground party leader in November 1985. "When they see that the people are united against them, they weaken and become afraid."

By midyear, a series of events made it clear that the Communists' commitment to violence was far more than rhetorical. For months, the Patriotic Front had been secretly stockpiling weapons through Sergio Buschmann's "fishing" operation in the village of Vallenar. When security forces pounced, they uncovered arsenals containing more than three thousand automatic rifles, 275 rocket launchers, two million rounds of ammunition, and tons of explosives. It was enough to supply several combat battalions—and to vindicate Pinochet's direst warnings of a terrorist threat.[83]

With its long-term plans unraveling, the Front decided to push ahead with its most audacious plot of all: the assassination of Pinochet. Code-named Operation Twentieth Century, the mission was planned with meticulous care. Its two dozen direct participants were motivated by revolutionary idealism and personal vengeance: several were sons of executed or disappeared Communist party militants; all were prepared to die in the name of "annihilating the tyrant."

In July, the team rented a safe house in a strategic spot near Route G-25, the highway leading to Pinochet's Melocotón mansion, and prepared a plan to ambush his regular weekend convoy into the city. Using a series of disguises, the commando leaders "Ernesto" and "Tamara" posed as an affluent couple to rent vehicles, while the hidden assault team practiced military drills, studied Pinochet's travel routines, and sang the Patriot Front hymn to keep their morale high.

At dusk on Sunday, September 7, a lookout's telephone call signaled the high-speed approach of Pinochet's heavily guarded caravan. Within minutes, the commando team was launched, and at 6:37 P.M., a distraught voice crackled over military radio: "They're attacking the convoy!" In the barrage of high-power fire, a LOW rocket hit the Mercedes in which Pinochet rode with his grandson Rodrigo, but it failed to explode. As the general sped to safety, five of his bodyguards lay dying. The attackers, fleeing in vans and disguised as security agents, melted into the city. Only when Pinochet appeared on television that night, defiantly brandishing a bandaged hand, did the revolutionaries realize they had missed their target.[84]

The failed attack transformed the Communists' "decisive year" into a debacle. Pinochet's mystique was reinforced by his miraculous escape, and a devastating witch-hunt was launched against the left. Hundreds of political activists were seized and interrogated, while investigators tracked down nine of the twenty-five commandos from Operation Twentieth Century, and all were sent to prison under military death sentences. In 1988, "Comandante Tamara" and her lover were reportedly discovered operating a guerrilla camp in central Chile. Several days later, their bodies were found floating in a nearby river.

Although angered by the repressive excess that followed the assassination attempt, most politically active Chileans were equally horrified by the crime itself. The Communists' effort to trigger a revolutionary situation had backfired. The Christian Democrats recoiled from all further collaboration with the Communists, and even the Almeyda Socialists distanced themselves from their long-time allies.

"They never warned us they were preparing an assassination attempt. We felt angry and betrayed," recalled Osvaldo Puccio, a leader of the Almeyda faction. "The Communists were sure that if Pinochet died, an explosion of popular jubilation would erupt, but I think the generals would have just moved in and taken over," Puccio added. "I was at the theater that night, and a woman announced Pinochet had been killed. Nobody celebrated; everyone was terrified of the consequences."[85]

In their revulsion against the Communists' violent schemes, the two Socialist factions were finally drawn together, and the Almeydistas began to work with the democratic opposition. In a long "open letter" to the left, Núñez, named the new secretary-general of the Briones group, condemned political terrorism and called for "the construction of one great Socialist party" to press for a return to democracy.[86]

Although ostracized and demoralized, Communist party leaders failed to see that their actions had strengthened Pinochet and undermined the opposition. "If the attempt had succeeded, we would have been called heroes," asserted Jaime Insunza in 1989. "A perfect revolutionary situation had evolved; the government was isolated and the people wanted it to leave. But the divisions in the opposition were too great, and the moment passed," he added. "The bourgeois option prevailed, and the masses gave up in disillusionment."[87]

The attack on Pinochet's motorcade dealt a critical blow to the already crumbling National Accord. Conservatives rallied around Pinochet, arguing it was best to accept the regime's transition timetable and pressing National Union leaders to back off from their opposition partners. The economy began to improve, diminishing the sense of urgency for change. The Reagan administration, shocked by the scope and audacity of the Communists' military plans, substantially toned down its support. Finally, the Accord collapsed.

The opposition, further weakened by the spate of harsh political repression that followed the attack, splintered into quarrelsome factions. The general, having again proven his uncanny ability to survive, quickly seized the initiative, and authorities began to publicize elaborate legal preparations for a presidential plebiscite. Only months before, most Chileans had believed Pinochet would be forced to modify his itinerary and perhaps even step down. Now, once again, he seemed invincible.

CHAPTER TWELVE

REBIRTH OF A NATION

"Don't forget that in the history of the world, there was a plebiscite, in which Christ and Barabbas were being judged, and the people chose Barabbas."
—*Augusto Pinochet, October 25, 1988*[1]

THE twin rows of soldiers stood motionless at attention, facing each other across a narrow red carpet that stretched from O'Higgins Avenue to the Ministry of Defense. One by one, at three-minute intervals, the commanders of Chile's navy, air force, and Carabineros emerged from their sedans, strode between the rows, saluted, and entered the building. Then, after a slightly longer pause, General Pinochet made his entrance. The wooden portals swung shut, and the secret deliberation began.

Five hours later, the Interior Ministry announced that the four commanders had "unanimously" chosen Pinochet as the sole candidate for the presidential plebiscite. The news was greeted with quiet dismay among democratic leaders, and with rock-throwing defiance by youths who battled riot squads far into the night.

But in the cavernous hall of the Diego Portales Building, where Pinochet's candidacy was anointed that evening, the atmosphere was one of serene majesty. Military and civilian officials arrived in formal dress, passing hallway exhibits of confiscated Soviet weapons. Onstage, Pinochet sat upright in an ornate red velvet chair, slightly apart from the other three commanders. After two nominating speeches, he arose from his throne and strode to the podium.

Resplendent in white dress tunic and presidential sash, the silver-maned general praised the "glorious" military act that had liberated the nation from Soviet "tyranny" in 1973. But he warned that Chile was not yet free of the "destructive and dissolute presence of Marxism" and that the task of building a "protected" democracy and a prosperous economy was reaching a critical stage. "With God's help," Pinochet vowed to guide it to fruition.[2]

IT was August 30, 1988, and seventy-three-year-old Augusto Pinochet was in fine fighting form. Generals Matthei and Stange had both opposed his candidacy, and even Admiral Merino had hinted that he preferred a civilian to preside over the transition to democracy.[3] Regime insiders and conservative leaders, from Jaime Guzmán to Andrés Allamand, had sought a less divisive electoral formula. The conference of Catholic bishops had pleaded for a consensus candidate, warning that Pinochet's formula could dangerously polarize the nation.[4]

But Pinochet had survived far more formidable obstacles during his fifteen-year reign: the rivalry of General Leigh, the scandals surrounding the DINA, the protests of 1983, even a terrorist attempt on his life. He was convinced that his firm hand must steer the nation into a new era, and he was loath to abandon La Moneda for the vulnerable and humiliating existence of a retired dictator.

The general believed that the "yes-no" plebiscite, enshrined in the 1980 constitution, would guarantee him eight more years in power. It had been presented to him as another perfunctory "consultation" on military rule, and it had been designed so that even if the No vote won and the official candidate lost, Pinochet would remain in power another seventeen months while presidential elections were prepared and held. In either case, he could remain as army commander for eight additional years.

During 1987, the president fended off all opponents by a shrewd combination of political co-optation, dazzling public relations, and suspenseful silence. Conservative politicians were asked to lunch at La Moneda and invited to join the Yes campaign. National Union and UDI joined to form a new party, Renovación National (National Renewal), hoping to persuade the commanders to select a civilian candidate. But Pinochet astutely named Sergio Fernández, one of UDI's founders, to become his "campaign" interior minister in July—and the rightist alliance quickly collapsed.

While barring its opponents from television, the regime began a preelectoral advertising campaign that showed smiling workers, clean hospitals, and bustling schools—then flashed to Pinochet in a cheering crowd and faded to a lingering shot of the "Christ of the Andes" monument, high in Chile's snowcapped mountains.

Despite his tense relations with the Catholic church, Pinochet also managed to turn a visit by Pope John Paul II in April to his advantage. The pontiff referred to Chile as a "dictatorship" and made several embarrassing gestures, including an embrace for the badly burned Carmen Quintana and a symbolic mass of bread and tea in one of Santiago's poorest poblaciones. But Pinochet orchestrated several symbols of his own, tricking the pope into blessing the chapel inside La Moneda while he and the first lady knelt devoutly nearby. The resulting photographs were splashed across proregime tabloids within hours.[5]

As conservatives floated rumors of alternative candidates and the opposition struggled to unite against the Yes vote, Pinochet confounded them all by refusing to divulge whether he planned to run and when the plebiscite would be held. Once the date was announced—October 5, 1988—he plunged into campaigning with confidence and vigor. Abandoning his uniform and dictatorial scowl, he became a smiling, grandfatherly candidate in business suits— bussing babies, waving at crowds, and donning miners' helmets and Indian blankets as he traveled the country promoting the government's good works and the importance of "projecting" them into the future.

During the year before the plebiscite, the government stepped up its production of homes for the poor, aided by over $200 million in loans from international financial institutions. Critics had opposed the loans on grounds that they would be used to bolster Pinochet's candidacy, and, indeed, presidential campaign stops were often coordinated with ribbon-cutting ceremonies for low-income developments.[6]

Behind this beneficent image was a massive, efficient campaign, backed by the purse of an authoritarian state and conducted like a military operation. Army officers acting as regional and provincial governors were responsible for campaign progress in their areas—and eager to make the best possible impression with their superiors. Secret marching orders also went out to the nation's mayors from the Interior Ministry, instructing them to use all available resources to "consolidate" and "project" the regime. "The responsibility falls on the mayors for the best [election] result in each of the towns they lead," it said.[7]

The collaboration of UDI was crucial. By 1988, many new mayors were party members with political ambitions—and a heavy Yes turnout was their ticket to the future. In blue-collar La Cisterna, the handsome young mayor, Gonzalo Stefani, embarked on a whirl of goodwill community appearances, while some of his staff members became UDI activists and spent increasing amounts of time on the campaign, also hoping for a political reward after the Yes victory.

"We have been the sustainers of the government's ideology and principles, and we want to see it continue," Stefani explained. Asked if he had used his office to promote the Yes campaign, Stefani replied, "We never used municipal money, but we changed our style. Before, streets were paved and clinics opened, but no one talked about it. Now we make an effort to inform people about the good works being done." Would he bar the opposition from municipal facilities? The mayor shrugged. "Why give them the advantage when they want to overturn everything we've done?" he said. "This is a battle between freedom and Marxism."[8]

Avanzada Nacional was equally eager to support the campaign, and attempted to mobilize a "Great Civic Front" for the Yes, while General Contreras and several associates publicly promoted Pinochet's candidacy. Among other rightist groups, however, the general's nomination created bitter divisions. Renovación Nacional, which had strongly opposed Pinochet's nomination once UDI left its ranks, now had no choice but to back him—or forfeit all aspirations to national leadership.

Businessmen were at first concerned that the general's insistence on running could jeopardize the entire free-market model. But eventually the skeptics were persuaded that Pinochet was a safer investment than the possible alternative—a left-leaning government bent on avenging fifteen years of humiliation and dismantling the Chicago Boys' policies. By mid-1988, prominent business leaders were at work raising funds for the Yes campaign.

An especially formidable weapon in the campaign arsenal was the first lady's volunteer army. "Women . . . cannot remain at rest; we must be prepared to carry the offensive," Lucía Hiriart exhorted a meeting of a thousand CEMA volunteers in 1987.[9] Supplied with posters and pamphlets, the women infused their members with enthusiasm for the Yes and strongly urged them to attend rallies for the president.

At one campaign event in Conchalí during August 1988, the new municipal recreation area was jammed with CEMA ladies bused in from all over Santiago, who lofted posters of the beaming candidate as the air was flooded with amplified lyrics to the song "Free, We are Free!" "The president saved Chile from the communist dogs, and I hope I live to thank him for all he has given us. Now we are in a free fatherland, and my vote is 'yes,' " said sixty-year-old Hilda Valenzuela, nearly weeping with eagerness to catch a glimpse of Pinochet.[10]

Despite the ban on campaign graffiti until one month before the plebiscite, the regime sent out nocturnal brigades—often reported to be police or municipal workers—to paint slogans for the Yes. In Concepción, identical blue letters appeared on every curb and telephone pole, saying "Pinochet Yes." But when slogans for the No appeared on public walls, they were systematically painted over, and the perpetrators, if spotted, were arrested.

PINOCHET'S opponents, having denounced the official transition rules as illegitimate, were reluctant to accept the plebiscite as a fait accompli and divided over how to respond. In early 1987, still hoping to press a democratic-election formula on the regime, a group of opposition leaders launched a crusade for an open presidential race with multiple candidates rather than the up-down choice of a single nominee.

For months, the free-election drive occupied much of the opposition's time and energy. Along the way, it drew support from some of Pinochet's top aides, who believed he would fare better in an open race against a hodgepodge of opposition candidates. But Pinochet was unrelenting, and in the face of sustained official resistance, the free-election crusade petered out.

Meanwhile, the regime's electoral preparations drew the nation's attention to the upcoming plebiscite. In February 1987, voter registration opened amid heavy publicity, and Pinochet registered with great fanfare at the traditional voting booth of Chile's presidents, becoming "Citizen Number One," as *Cosas* magazine noted admiringly.[11] One month later, the government permitted all non-Marxist parties to become legal, as long as they collected signatures from about 35,000 registered voters.

The new parties law presented Pinochet's opponents with an agonizing dilemma. Should they join in the process and try to defeat the dictator by his own rules, at the cost of dividing the left and legitimizing a military-controlled, potentially fraudulent election? Or should they boycott the plebiscite, at the risk of being isolated from a process that was rapidly becoming the only political game in Chile?

The issue provoked intense debate among the opposition parties, and none wanted to take the first step toward registering. The Humanist party, a youthful new movement emphasizing environmental causes, broke the ice and began a signature drive. In mid-year, the Christian Democrats followed suit, bringing back Patricio Aylwin, a figure of serene style and traditional values, to replace Gabriel Valdés as president and lead the party into elections.

For the moderate Socialists, led by Ricardo Núñez, the decision was painful because the rest of the left was excluded from the process. Trying to ease partisan rivalries, Núñez and his colleague Ricardo Lagos proposed creating a new, broad-based movement called the Party for Democracy. Although meeting with little support, they registered their party anyway—a masterful move which gave the left a neutral vehicle to participate in the election.

An eloquent advocate for registration, Núñez called it "an act of rebellion, not of submission." On the day he signed up to vote, Núñez declared his motive was to recover his "rights as a citizen." "It was Pinochet who burned the electoral registers in 1973," he recalled, "and today all Chileans must recover this right, in order to tell the government they will not accept its continuity."[12]

The Almeyda Socialists, legally banned and long allied with the Communists, endured a wrenching period of soul-searching. In March of 1987, the sixty-five-year-old Almeyda sneaked into Chile and turned himself in to the courts, challenging charges that he was an apologist for violence and totalitarianism. Although banished to a small village and later sentenced to 541 days in prison, the veteran politician brought new stature to his party. Even *El Mercurio* sent a team to interview and photograph him, drifting contemplatively in a rowboat.[13]

Mistrustful of the regime's institutional framework, the party at first joined the Communists in denouncing the plebiscite as a "trap." But Almeyda, recoiling from the assassination attempt against Pinochet, pushed the party to back off from its revolutionary allies and aim at defeating the general through the polls. By 1988, both Socialist groups were actively committed to the No campaign—and working together for the first time in ten years.

The Communist party, now totally isolated, was thrown into turmoil. Moderate members argued it was time to abandon the path of armed insurrection, but leaders of the Manuel Rodríguez Patriotic Front refused to be reined in, and one splinter group continued to stage bombings and assaults. "We believe we are a necessity. The people need to defend themselves," explained one hooded commander, adding that the combatants were "products of the violence of this regime."[14]

The doctrinal discipline that had long fortified the party now deafened its leaders to the urgent need for change. When activists like Patricio Hales called for participation in the electoral process, they were ostracized as traitors.[15] "Too many boys were being sent out to die," Hales recalled bitterly, but the issue was not open for discussion. "The earth may revolve around the sun, but if the Vatican says no, Galileo remains excommunicated," he added.[16]

Eventually, the party softened its position, but only after facing near-mutiny from the rank and file. One Sunday in August 1987, Christian Democratic and Socialist leaders were discussing the No campaign at a community meeting in Renca, a working-class suburb of Santiago. A high-level Communist official interrupted them, arguing vehemently that the system was a fraud.

Finally, a white-haired man rose from his bench. "I have been a militant of the party for sixty years, but you are making a grave mistake," he said quietly. "An election is a form of struggle too, and we feel we must do everything possible to defeat the dictatorship. If you continue with this line much longer, you are going to have a revolt on your hands." The room burst into applause, and the party official sat down, speechless.

HAVING agreed to play by Pinochet's rules, his opponents now had to convince the voters that the process was credible. Apathy and skepticism were high, and the task of registering seven million voters was daunting. Rumors circulated that hidden cameras would be able to detect how a person marked his ballot. In public opinion surveys, a majority of those polled said they planned to vote against Pinochet—yet a majority also said they believed he would win.[17]

Conditions were hardly conducive to public confidence in a fair, open vote. Under the permanent "states of exception," the regime could detain anyone for three weeks, censor the press, and ban public meetings. From January to June 1988, the Vicaría reported 1,780 political arrests. In July, Americas Watch charged that "an extraordinary degree of intimidation" pervaded the preplebiscite atmosphere and that no fair vote could be held unless the states of exception were lifted.[18]

During the campaign, offices being used by No supporters were firebombed, rallies for the No were forcibly dissolved, and opposition volunteers were harassed or beaten. Voters in poor communities reported more subtle forms of pressure, ranging from offers of new bicycles if they supported the Yes to veiled threats of canceled housing subsidies if the No triumphed.[19]

At one rally for the Yes in San Miguel, a working-class crowd watched silently while a succession of politicians fulminated against the opposition from an outdoor stage, and youths with UDI banners cheered lustily. Men with crew cuts roamed the crowd, murmuring into walkie-talkies. One elderly onlooker, asked if he planned to vote Yes, nodded curtly and turned away. But after two security agents moved out of earshot, the old man apologized. "I'm for the No. Everyone in this neighborhood is for the No," he explained. "But it is not safe to say so."

To overcome such fears, opposition groups staged mock ballots and volunteers from the nonpartisan Civic Crusade knocked on doors with brochures explaining the plebiscite. Many opposition leaders believed that Pinochet was incapable of accepting defeat and would do anything necessary to remain in power. But they hoped that with a maximum number of voters registered, the victory for the No would be resounding—and that if the regime attempted to deny it, the resulting outcry would force Pinochet from power.

The legal design of the plebiscite also made it less vulnerable to tampering than the 1980 referendum had been. One reason was the courage of the Constitutional Tribunal, a panel of conservative regime-appointed jurists which—to the dismay of hard-liners like Justice Minister Hugo Rosende—took its mandate of legal vigilance with extreme seriousness.

First, the panel insisted on setting up an independent electoral commission because the spirit of the constitution required it, even if the law did not. Then, as election laws were drafted, the members reviewed them in order to safeguard the process. Voter registration procedures were scrupulous, each registered party was permitted a poll watcher at each voting table, and each ballot was to be opened and counted in full public view. When the tribunal was done, the plebiscite was virtually fraud proof.

"Rosende wanted the plebiscite to be like 1980, and he thought he could manipulate us. But we argued that to be constitutional, it had to be transparent," recalled Eugenio Valenzuela, the most determined tribunal member. "Few people knew it at the time, but we changed the course of Chilean politics. We made the process something people could believe in."[20]

A second source of insurance was the opposition's design for a fast, reliable parallel vote count. This required having at all 22,131 voting tables poll watchers who could relay information to Santiago, where it was to be tabulated in computers operated by the Command for the No and the Committee for Free Elections. The recruitment and training of poll watchers was agonizingly slow, but a sophisticated computer system was set up in several secret locations and ready well before voting day.

Pressure from Washington also affected the regime's decision to permit a "real" election. The administration had latched on to the plebiscite as the only way to ease the regime from power without jeopardizing its economic policies. During 1987, the United States abstained on several multilateral loan votes to signal its close scrutiny of the process, and the State Department called for an end to television censorship and emergency powers.

American officials also provided funds for activities to promote a fair election. The Reagan administration channeled $1.2 million to the work of the Civic Crusade, and Congress appropriated $1 million to the National Endowment for Democracy to finance opinion polls, media consultants, and the parallel vote count.[21] Officials denounced these measures as "foreign intervention," and Pinochet blasted Ambassador Barnes as an agent for the opposition who had been "imposed on this small country" to destroy his government.[22]

Ironically, the most important guarantee of a clean vote was Pinochet's conviction that he could win. Regime officials, shaken by the spectacle of the Philippine dictator Ferdinand Marcos's disgrace in the fraudulent 1986 elections, feared their victory would also be discounted—and that their best defense was to make fraud impossible. Weeks before the plebiscite, Pinochet also lifted the states of exception and announced that all remaining exiles were free to come home. "If I were the dictator they say I am," the smiling candidate insisted, "I would not have conducted the political process we are about to culminate."[23]

The general's self-confidence stemmed from two sources. His aides constantly reassured him that "decent" Chileans appreciated his long sacrifice, and the enthusiasm of the crowds at orchestrated rallies seemed to prove it. Pinochet was also contemptuous of his opponents, whom he viewed as a motley crew of demagogues unable to compete with his solid record. Most polls showed him likely to lose, but the president dismissed them as deliberately slanted, clinging instead to more optimistic official data and the high number of voters who described themselves as "undecided."[24]

In fact, many polls reflected a deep division among voters. For the affluent, the Pinochet years had been a time of public order and private freedom that many wished to see continue; for the poor, they had brought certain welfare benefits that would be painful to give up. By 1988, Chile was in its third year of healthy growth and urban unemployment had dropped to 10 percent. Among voters leaning to the Yes, especially women, security and stability appeared repeatedly as issues of concern.

For many other Chileans, military rule had been an experience of humiliation and deprivation. Families had been sundered and dignity violated; a proud democratic tradition had been replaced by the furtive, arbitrary atmosphere of authoritarianism. To see dictatorship end, a substantial portion of society—including the majority who opposed any form of Marxist rule—was willing to risk the uncertain alternative represented by the No.

Privately, the regime was deeply worried about these voters, and attempted to revive their latent anticommunist fears. On the stump, Pinochet portrayed the Yes as a vote for security and order, the No as a vote for communism and chaos, and himself as the hero of a Manichaean struggle. "What is truly at stake," he thundered in his final campaign speech, "is the freedom of Chile."[25]

The boldest attacks, however, were unleashed in the nightly television campaign that began six weeks before the plebiscite. Ads for the Yes alternated scenes of a bright, prosperous Chile with grim footage of food lines and violence under Allende. In one horrific "re-creation," a mother and child fled from a mob brandishing clubs and red banners. "If we return to the past, the first innocent victim could be in your family," the announcer warned as the camera froze on smashing glass and the woman's silent scream.

AGAINST this onslaught, opposition leaders struggled to unify their disparate forces and reassure voters of their ability to deliver peaceful, democratic change. A loose coalition of fourteen parties, formed in early 1988, was initially frustrated by partisan mistrust, but the campaign for the No gained coherence and credibility as respected figures like Aylwin and Lagos visited towns and poblaciones.

Lagos, always articulate and direct, glavanized the campaign during a television interview in April. Turning to the camera, he pointed his finger at an imaginary Pinochet. "You promise the country eight more years of torture, assassination and human rights violations," he charged. "To me, it seems inadmissible that a Chilean would be so ambitious for power as to pretend to hold it for twenty-five years." When the interviewers tried to cut him off, he politely persisted, saying, "I speak for 15 years of silence."[26]

Aylwin, the moderate Christian Democratic president, emerged as a key figure in the campaign. To refute the regime's portrait of the No coalition as an unstable, leaderless hodgepodge, the party pushed for a single platform and symbolic "candidate" to embody the No. The opposition could not agree on an individual, but chose Aylwin as "spokesman" for the No, a choice that placed an avuncular, reassuring figure in a highly visible role.

The campaign remained plagued by quarrels and confusion until August 1988, when the Command for the No, representing sixteen parties, was officially opened. The indefatigable Genaro Arriagada was named to direct the operation, with little money but one priceless resource: a network of former local activists who had been in hibernation for fifteen years. Unlike the regime's military governors and imported mayors, these men knew their turf—and were thrilled to be back at work.

In Maipú, Edgardo Cavíz, the onetime Popular Unity organizer, emerged from his fifteen-year debate with the television set and started knocking on neighbors' doors. In Mulchén, former Mayor Alfredo Kunkar, long haunted by his role in the death of a Communist alderman, was happy to refurbish his warehouse for a No rally.

Thousands of other volunteers were drawn to the campaign through the freewheeling, nonpartisan spirit of the Party for Democracy. One was Ronald Ramm, a reclusive architect who became the party's coordinator in Los Angeles. "I've never been involved in politics, but I know what is right, and the time has come to unite against a dictator," Ramm explained. "If you vote Yes, you are approving all the murders they have committed since 1973. I care too much about my country to let that happen."[27]

Voter registration began slowly, but by the cutoff date of August 30, a record 92 percent of the voting-age population—7,435,913 Chileans—had signed up. Three opposition parties—the Christian Democrats, the Humanists, the Radicals, and the Party for Democracy—managed to collect 35,000 signatures, register to participate, and train 120,000 poll watchers. On the regime side, only Renovación Nacional and Avanzada Nacional achieved the same success.[28]

The real spirit of the No emerged in the nightly, competing television spots. Officials assumed that the opposition parties would squabble over airtime and that no one would watch the late-night ads. Instead, the creative, upbeat No segments captured the nation's imagination. Each night, a kaleidoscope of Chileans—from bus drivers to ballerinas—kept time to the theme song "Joy Is Coming." The message was an optimistic, simple appeal for dignity and democracy, and Patricio Bañados, a prominent newscaster who had quit state TV to protest censorship, urged, "Without hatred, without fear, vote No."

Wary of frightening voters away, campaign aides chose subtle images to convey the abuses of military rule: the elderly woman purchasing her tea bag, a soccer star revealing that his mother had been beaten by the police. After years of propaganda that ignored their own troubles, viewers were riveted. Some ads were so powerful that the regime clumsily attempted to refute them, and one tape of Judge Rene García denouncing torture was yanked from the air. But the damage was done: the government had lost control of the truth, and the opposition had run away with it.

AS October 5 approached, tension rose throughout the country. Officials stepped up near-hysterical warnings that a No victory would bring revolution and anarchy. Small-town opposition leaders received anonymous threats and sent their children to stay with relatives. "We were all terrified that if the Yes won, we would have to go into hiding the next day," recalled Ronald Ramm.

At the final rally for the No, half a million Chileans crammed onto a twenty-block stretch of highway through Santiago, swaying to the "Waltz of the No" and listening to emotional speeches from newly returned exiles, including the family of Allende. The next day, backers of the Yes formed a massive, honking caravan through the upper-class suburbs, but there was a vengeful undertone to their exuberance. "If the No wins, we will rise up against the Russian *rotos*, just like we did on September 11," warned a fashionable matron carrying a Pinochet poster.

By night, disturbing incidents were afoot: power blackouts and pamphlets calling for mass insurrection; a break-in at one of the opposition's secret computer sites; the mysterious theft of a number of Carabinero buses. The Communist party, which had belatedly urged its members to vote No, denied any link to the incidents, but returning leftist exiles like Volodia Teitelboim alarmed voters by exhorting the masses to rise up and defend the opposition triumph against expected official fraud.

One week before the plebiscite, police officials privately contacted leaders of the No campaign and the Civic Crusade, and warned them of possible plots to sabotage the election. Rumors circulated of a plan by right-wing commandos to stage false police raids on election night, provoking riots and a coup. These reports reached Ambassador Barnes, and on Sunday , October 2, the State Department called in Chile's ambassador to express its grave concern. On Monday, the department announced it had information that the regime might seek to "cancel the plebiscite or overturn the results."[29]

At the Command for the No, worried leaders met with General Jorge Zincke, commander of the election-day "security zone" in Santiago, and exchanged private telephone numbers. Through Radio Cooperativa, the command appealed to supporters to vote early and return home, ignore "official" results, and wait for the No campaign to broadcast its own figures. Someone wanted things to go wrong, and only mass public restraint could prevent it.

OCTOBER 5 dawned hot and clear. By eight o'clock, when schoolyard polls opened, hundreds of thousands of voters were already in line. All morning, they moved closer to the tables, perspiring and silent, many dressed in their Sunday best. The old customs were observed: men voted separately from women, and military officers monitored each facility with impeccable politeness. People grumbled about the heat, but no one wished to spoil the solemn ritual. "For Chile, it's today or never," said Eduardo Acuña, a forty-seven-year-old carpenter waiting to vote in La Bandera.

At the National Institute, the traditional polling place of presidents, Pinochet's caravan of silver Mercedes pulled up just before 11:00 A.M. Bodyguards leapt out, clearing a path through the crowd as the beaming president strode up the steps in a brown business suit. Photographers surged around as he signed the registry and stepped into the booth, but the lines of voters watched in silence until the entourage had swept out of the building and back to the bulletproof limousines.

By late afternoon, the first tables were closing. With trembling precision, officials chosen from among the 350 voters at each table counted each of the folded ballots, signed and opened them, and began calling out the results. Small crowds gathered in each classroom, and excitement built as the piles of paper grew. Invariably, if the final count favored the No, a spontaneous cheer went up.

By 9:00 P.M., the opposition's parallel count showed the No ahead with half a million votes counted, but an hour later the government had released results from only 677 tables, favoring the Yes. In La Moneda, as the bad news continued to pour in, Pinochet's men grew desperate. A call went out to the Carabineros, asking them to lift the downtown security cordon so that Yes supporters could celebrate—a clear invitation to clashes with supporters of the No. In an act of prudent defiance, Carabinero officials refused.

Fearful that public patience would wear thin, Arriagada began broadcasting his own results. By 11:00 P.M., the No command claimed a 58 percent to 40 percent lead, with 40 percent of the votes counted. But state television announced the Yes ahead, with 3.4 percent of the vote counted—then abruptly switched to cartoons and a rerun of the American comedy series "Moonlighting."

Now even more alarmed, Arriagada spoke with worried friends at Renovación Nacional headquarters and persuaded them that his results were correct. Renovación leaders repeatedly called the Interior Ministry, threatening to acknowledge a No victory. But by midnight no new results had been announced, so Sergio Onofre Jarpa joined Patricio Aylwin on Catholic University television, and the two men—adversaries from three decades of democratic politics—calmly agreed that the No appeared to be winning.

Thirty minutes later, reporters spied General Matthei entering La Moneda. "I am certain the No has won, but we are calm," he told them. But inside the palace, the three commanders found a stunned and enraged president, raving that he had been betrayed by his advisers and outflanked by his enemies. At one point, Pinochet blustered about demanding emergency powers or resigning, but his colleagues gently reminded him they had all sworn to uphold the constitution. Finally the exhausted general sank back, muttering, "All right, do whatever you want."[30]

At 2:40 A.M., the under secretary of the interior appeared on television and tersely announced that with 71 percent of the vote counted, the No was leading by 53 percent to 44 percent. At the Command for the No, pandemonium erupted and volunteers surged into the empty streets, singing and hugging embarrassed Carabineros.

Five hundred miles south, Alfredo Kunkar and two friends were driving ballot results to Los Angeles, nervous and depressed because the Yes had won heavily in Mulchén. When the news from Santiago came over the radio, Kunkar jammed on the brakes and the men jumped out onto the deserted highway, dancing for joy under the starlit sky.

TWENTY-FOUR hours later, with official results tabulated at 54.7 percent to 43 percent in favor of the No, Pinochet appeared on television. Gone was the affable civilian candidate; in his place was a haggard dictator in a military tunic. "I recognize and accept the verdict expressed by a majority of citizens," he said stiffly, but warned there would be no change in the regime's "constitutional order." The armed forces "will firmly maintain their commitment to the principles that inspired the glorious effort of September 11, 1973," Pinochet declared. "My honor as a soldier is now, as then, at the service of this end."[31]

Despite the gallant rhetoric, Pinochet was a humiliated man, rejected by voters in ten of the twelve national regions. The general who had crushed or outwitted every adversary for fifteen years had now been defeated by ordinary Chileans, betrayed in the final battle by the instincts and ambitions that had sustained him for so long. How could it have happened?

First, he misread the will of the people. Flattered by sycophants and lulled by official publicity, he failed to realize how desperately most Chileans wanted change. He overestimated their fears of a communist threat, and underestimated their democratic vocation. Enthralled by the success of the free-market model, officials also failed to see that it had left many people behind—people who identified more with the elderly woman buying one tea bag than with glittering ads for "Chile, a Winning Country."[32]

Having assumed that the poor would vote for him out of gratitude, Pinochet could only conclude they had failed to do so because of manipulation by his enemies. Revealing both a contempt for the masses and a deep persecution complex, Pinochet reminded a group of CEMA-Chile volunteers that another mob had once chosen to save the thief Barabbas from the cross, instead of Jesus Christ.[33]

Second, the general had insisted on clinging to the letter of his constitution, against all demands and advice, portraying it as the armed forces' prime legacy to the nation. Now that he had been defeated by his own rules, Chile's military establishment was not prepared to sacrifice honor and unity to salvage his ambitions—especially not at the cost of substantial bloodshed.

Ultimately, Pinochet was betrayed by his own ambition, which overcame his judgment and allowed him to believe he was indispensable. And none of his minions, trapped in the hierarchical logic of authoritarianism, dared let the truth filter through. "The media campaign was awful, but there was no feedback. Even those of us who raised the funds were never allowed to express ourselves," said Eugenio Hieremans, a prominent insurance executive.[34]

In La Cisterna, Sofía Burgos, a mill forelady and CEMA leader, wept over the thank-you note she received from La Moneda for her volunteer work for the Yes campaign. "All the women worked so hard; we marched to the plaza even when the Marxists threw rocks at us," she recounted. "But the midlevel managers tricked the president. They made people go to rallies, but they pocketed the money and they didn't really want our help," Burgos added angrily. "Finally, people here became disillusioned and gave up."[35]

Inside La Moneda recriminations abounded, but wiser conservatives latched on to the widening mood of consensus. At the Center for Public Studies, Director Arturo Fontaine Talavera addressed a roomful of gloomy but attentive rightist leaders. "We cannot keep fighting phantoms that are no longer in people's minds," he said, describing the plebiscite as a "great secular communion" and quoting Aristotle: "For the state to endure, it needs more than commerce and security," he said. "It needs civic fraternity."[36]

DESPITE their euphoria, opposition leaders knew that the general was far from totally defeated. Under the law, he would remain in power for seventeen months, until presidential and congressional elections were held and a new government installed. All laws shaping the transition would be crafted by the military commanders, who could retain their posts for another eight years. Officially, nothing would change until March 11, 1990.

Yet Pinochet's opponents had won a strong mandate for change, and they were determined to reform his constitution before the virtually unamendable charter was set in stone. The most troubling provisions outlawed all Marxist and "antifamily" parties, permitted current authorities to name nine of twenty-six new senators, and created the National Security Council, dominated by military officials, with vaguely worded veto powers over presidential and congressional decisions.

Moderate aides in the government were willing to consider some changes, but the constitution was a crucial instrument of power to Pinochet, and a sacrosanct guarantee of future privilege to the armed forces. General Zincke, newly promoted to the post of army vice-commander, warned that the military would tolerate an opposition president only if he adhered to the charter. "Otherwise," he said, "we have the example of 1973."[37]

Army officials were also infuriated by demands that Pinochet step down as commander. In June 1989, when Patricio Aylwin called on Pinochet to resign in the interests of national reconciliation and military professionalism, army officials accused him of waging an "open attack" on the basic laws of society—laws they would not hesitate to uphold, if necessary, by "the use of legitimate force."[38]

To buy time and goodwill, Pinochet named a new interior minister, Carlos Cáceres, to take a more conciliatory approach to the opposition. But Renovación Nacional leaders, eager to assert their political independence and ease transition tensions, called his bluff by sitting down to discuss constitutional reforms with leaders of the opposition, now called the Concertación para la Democracia (Concertation for Democracy).

In April, the two groups proposed a package of amendments, neatly undermining regime hard-liners who had argued that the demand for reform was a conspiracy by radical leftists to dismantle the policies of the Pinochet era. Now leaders representing 70 percent of the political elite had endorsed sweeping changes to make the charter more democratic—a mandate that pragmatic officials could not ignore.

Cáceres delicately broached the subject of certain reforms with Pinochet, but the general rejected all but a few cosmetic changes. In a stunning move, Cáceres announced his resignation, and three other ministers threatened to accompany him. Since the other junta members and army officials privately supported them, the cornered dictator had no choice but to relent.[39]

For the next month, Cáceres seesawed between tense negotiations with the Concertación and the president. The talks repeatedly collapsed, but Jarpa and Aylwin persuaded their colleagues that a smooth transition to democracy was more important than clinging to a particular clause. "Huge efforts at compromise were made on all sides," recounted Miguel Luis Amunátegui, a lawyer from Renovación. "We all gave up legitimate differences in search of a peaceful transition."[40]

The final proposal of fifty-four reforms replaced the ban on groups espousing Marxism with a prohibition against promoting violence. It increased the number of elected senators to thirty-eight, expanded the National Security Council's civilian membership and downgraded its authority.[41] Finally, it eliminated the requirement that all future constitutional amendments be approved by two consecutive sessions of Congress. On June 1, Pinochet approved the proposal; on July 30, voters overwhelmingly endorsed it at the polls.

WITH this lofty achievement behind them, Chile's opposition parties turned to the December elections. It had been difficult enough to defeat a dictator in the name of democracy; now seventeen parties had to agree on a presidential nominee, hammer out a national policy, select and promote candidates for 158 seats in parliament, and begin planning how to govern the nation.

Proregime forces assumed that once the competition for the presidency and Congress began, the Concertación would crumble amid partisan squabbles. But to give themselves an extra edge, officials drafted a convoluted electoral law that gave rightist candidates the advantage. Congressional districts were redrawn to allot more deputies to rural areas, where the Yes had been strongest, and fewer to densely populated urban areas, where the No had prevailed.[42]

The electoral laws also skewed the requirements for earning a congressional seat so that the winning (presumably opposition) ticket could carry 65 percent of the vote and still earn only one of two district seats, while the second-place (proregime) ticket needed only 33 percent of the vote to earn the other seat.[43]

In choosing a presidential candidate, the Concertación confounded its enemies' predictions of a catfight, when leftist parties agreed to accept a Christian Democrat. Within that party, the nomination process touched off a bitter rivalry among Valdés, Aylwin, and Eduardo Frei, the former president's son, threatening to undermine the opposition. But by midyear, the nomination was firm for Aylwin, a man of seventy-one who described himself as a "typical middle-class Chilean"—a leader whose conciliatory style had won wide respect and whose only noticeable flaws were a preference for baggy sweaters and a somewhat beatific facial expression.

Selecting congressional candidates was a more complex and agonizing process. The political pie had to be divided, with no formal way to prove which groups deserved the larger pieces. Dozens of would-be candidates, whose political careers had been truncated by the coup, had to sacrifice their ambitions to satisfy a delicate partisan balance. But by employing tact and toughness through weeks of negotiations, Concertación members, under the skillful leadership of Edgardo Boeninger, finally agreed on candidates for each seat.

The Communist party presented an extra problem, insisting on creating a "parallel" slate of candidates at the risk of undermining the Concertación's united electoral front. But here, too, a compromise was found: The Concertación would run a single "master" ticket, while the Communists would compete separately in a number of races and support Concertación hopefuls everywhere else. It was a small step for democracy, and a decisive boost for the opposition.

WHILE the Concertación gained cohesion and confidence in adversity, the right seemed unable to recover from the debacle of the plebiscite and refocus its energies on the campaign. Relations between Renovación and UDI degenerated into public mudslinging, and proregime forces splintered into a dozen factions, with multiple tickets competing for legislative seats. Years of complacent abdication to authoritarian rule had cost the right its edge, its leadership, and its sense of purpose.

To many conservatives, the obvious choice for president was Jarpa, a wily political veteran skilled at oratory and horse-trading, and the most attractive party to carry the conservative banner was Renovación. But to purists in the regime, Jarpa and his team embodied the most contemptible qualities of "politicking," and businessmen who had flourished under the free-market model did not trust Jarpa's statist proclivities.

The preference of regime insiders and the business elite was Hernán Büchi, the brilliant young finance minister. Under his hand, the economy had recovered steadily, and now Chile stood poised for prosperity while neighbors like Peru and Argentina sank into a mire of debt and poverty. Inflation had leveled at under 20 percent, key export earnings had nearly doubled in four years, and urban unemployment was at its lowest point since the coup.

Moreover, the thirty-nine-year-old minister, a dedicated runner and yogurt addict with a Prince Valiant haircut, projected a modern, youthful image that was far removed from the darker side of dictatorship. "Büchi represents splendidly the desire for a whitewashed future, without memory of bloody acts, with clean hands full of dollars," wrote Marco Antonio de la Parra in *Caras* magazine.[44]

There was one problem, however: the intensely private minister had no desire to be president—and after a month of wooden campaign appearances, he suddenly withdrew from the race in May. "I am an engineer. My medium is silence. . . . I have no vocation as a candidate," Büchi confessed to the nation. "I have forced myself to the limit, but I have not been able to overcome this vital contradiction."[45]

But the rightist establishment pressed the tormented candidate to change his mind, and in July a repackaged Büchi bounded back into the race. This time, he had the grudging endorsement of Renovación and the financial backing of proregime business groups.[46] Meanwhile, a minor rival emerged in Francisco Javier Errázuriz, a self-made millionaire who appealed to poor voters by railing against the Chicago Boys and who lured hard-line nationalists with his anticommunist ardor.[47]

For all intents and purposes, however, the race became a rematch between the Yes and the No. Büchi symbolized a sixteen-year effort to change the political and economic habits of the nation and to "project" that change into the future. Aylwin represented the essence of Chile's democratic past and a belief that this tradition, tempered by two decades of trauma, was still the strongest bulwark against extremes.

As the campaign unfolded, a curious role reversal emerged. Büchi, who had slashed social spending to satisfy foreign lenders and reduce inflation, promised to provide "a million new jobs," one hundred thousand new houses each year, and health insurance for everyone.[48] Aylwin, whose politics the regime had denounced as venal and demagogic, made few promises and warned that democracy would not cure Chile's social and economic problems overnight.

Moreover, although Aylwin counted on strong Socialist support, his economic platform incorporated many of the regime's innovations. Opposition economists like Alejandro Foxley, who had criticized Pinochet's economic policies for years, gave speeches that pleasantly surprised the Chicago Boys. Despite the painful social cost, Pinochet's policies had stabilized, expanded, and modernized the economy—and the opposition had no wish to undermine these achievements.

Opinion polls consistently showed that Aylwin would defeat his opponents by a margin similar to that of the plebiscite vote. By November, there was little doubt that his message—Chile's need to recover dignity, compassion, and freedom—would prevail and that the lavish effort to "market" Büchi as the symbol of a modern, upwardly mobile society could not shake his image as a soulless protégé of dictatorship.

In his final appearance before a jubilant multitude in O'Higgins Park, Aylwin, serene and confident, pledged to heal the wounds of war and rebuild a society at peace with itself. Chile had learned from history, he asserted; a new tolerance would replace the divisive utopian pretensions of the past. "Never again will our differences convert us into enemies."[49]

On December 14, voters delivered a resounding victory to the Concertación, electing Aylwin with 55.2 percent of the vote while Büchi and Errázuriz divided the remainder with 29.4 percent and 15.4 percent, respectively. This time, there was no threat of violence or foul play, and by 10 P.M. both losing candidates had graciously conceded. Just after midnight, Aylwin appeared on a hotel balcony to proclaim, "Chile has recovered its freedom!" while fireworks exploded and confetti showered on an ecstatic crowd jamming O'Higgins Avenue.

In the legislative races, the regime's skewed electoral formula and designation of nine senators gave conservative forces a small but critical majority.[50] But the Concertación gained 72 of 120 seats in the Chamber of Deputies and 22 of 38 contested Senate seats. Across the nation, voters selected Christian Democrats, "renewed" Socialists, and moderate conservatives, while rejecting candidates from the fascist right and revolutionary left. After sixteen years of polarization, Chileans had chosen to put the war behind them and return to a civilized, consensual brand of politics.

TO General Pinochet, the battle was still not over. In public, he acted the statesman who had nobly conceded defeat and was now exclusively concerned with delivering a healthy nation to his successors. In numerous ceremonies, he bestowed "Mission Accomplished" awards on aides and supporters. Yet he could not mask his deep suspicion of the opposition, telling one women's group he must remain army commander to safeguard the nation against "those who appear today like docile sheep" but "carry hatred and infamy in their hearts."[51]

Behind closed doors, meanwhile, the president scrambled to prevent as much power as possible from escaping into his successors' hands, and to protect military loyalists from future humiliation. He upgraded laws that banned civilian interference with military budgets, promotions, or education; guaranteed the armed forces a percentage of all sales of state copper; and even had the titles to his fleet of Mercedes and Lo Curro mansion transferred to the army.

Although unrepentant over the use of violence to eradicate the Marxist threat, Chile's security forces dreaded facing trials similar to those held in Argentina after the "dirty war" of the 1970s. Pinochet also knew that once Aylwin took office, the Letelier assassination could return to haunt General Contreras and possibly himself.

At military ceremonies, Pinochet assured his troops he would shield them from "unjust" prosecution, partly by remaining army commander as long as the law allowed. "The day they touch any one of my men, the state of law is ended," he warned in October 1989.[52] To make sure the loyalty was returned, he reshuffled the high army command, promoting confidants and hard-liners like the former CNI chief General Hugo Salas.[53]

Preparing the intelligence services for a future under civilian rule was a more delicate matter, made especially distasteful by the eruption of vicious internal sniping that accompanied the shadow warriors' denouement. Major Alvaro Julio Corbalán of the CNI accused the Carabinero intelligence squad of plotting to murder him; Contreras sued three CNI officers who testified against his son, calling one "a danger to society."

During the last months of military rule, several secret police veterans were assassinated—possibly by insiders fearful that they knew too much. When Roberto Fuentes Morrison, the retired air force antisubversive squad commander, was gunned down in June 1989, the Manuel Rodríguez Patriotic Front claimed credit. But no manhunt was launched, no officials attended the funeral, and the eulogy by his brother alluded bitterly to the "disloyalty" of his colleagues."[54]

During the campaign, both Aylwin and Büchi called for the CNI's dismantling, but authorities were reluctant to dismiss several thousand men with lethal skills and powerful secrets.[55] Instead, Pinochet decided to fold the agency into army intelligence—a step which both shielded it from civilian prying and secured military control over a useful but volatile resource.[56] Once Aylwin was elected, however, the incoming president pledged repeatedly to seek "the truth" about regime abuses after 1978, making it unlikely that the crimes of the CNI would be completely erased.

Pinochet was equally anxious to "project" his future power over another subservient institution—the Supreme Court. His method in this case was an appeal to greed: he offered all justices over seventy-five a generous bonus to retire early. Despite a national outcry over such a crude attempt at manipulating the courts, only four of ten eligible members declined the offer, including the eighty-three-year-old Rafael Retamal. Thus, during his last eighteen months in office, Pinochet was able to name nine jurists to life terms on the sixteen-member high court.[57]

From the Central Bank to the National Television Council, Pinochet moved to place loyalists in long-term positions before his term ended. Having brutally purged his predecessor's bureaucracy, he now drafted a law protecting all civil servants from dismissal. To keep state-owned enterprises out of its successors' hands, the government also attempted to privatize some of its prized assets—television stations, newspapers, even the national airline.

But despite the cunning of these moves, there was also something pathetic about Pinochet's frantic efforts to lash down all loose objects on his sinking ship. The old warrior seemed unable to acknowledge that the country had voted for peace and that the forces of history were passing him by.

AS the inauguration of March 1990 approached, signs of emerging consensus and reconciliation abounded. The labor leader Manuel Bustos, banished to a tiny village for most of 1989, now appeared in *El Mercurio* shaking hands with business leaders as they negotiated a social pact. General Matthei, who had dismissed the Concertación as a "clown's patchwork," called on Aylwin with congratulations and support. Transition-team economists called for "fiscal prudence," while conservative legislators-elect acknowledged the need to be "socially responsible."

Chile was still a society of ghettos, in which the breaches between *rotos* and *momios,* soldiers and civilians, were as wide as ever. And more than 40 percent of the population, after all, had chosen to continue Pinochet's rule. But the peaceful outcome of both elections—and the triumph of civic maturity over threats, uncertainty, and alarmist propaganda—suggested that two decades of fear and alienation had implanted lessons different from those that Chile's military tutors wished to impart.

In some respects, Chilean society had evolved enormously since 1973; it was more worldly, more skeptical of the state, and more aggressive in pursuing its ambitions. In other aspects, though, the old democratic culture had strongly reasserted itself. There was a new appreciation for the values of moderation and compromise that had once been bitterly discarded—and a firm rejection of the utopian visions that had inspired and scarred a generation.

The forces of extremism hovered close, their symbiotic struggle far from exhausted. In September 1989, Jécar Neghme, a spokesman for the MIR, was executed by an anonymous hit-and-run team. Six months later, two gunmen strolled into General Leigh's office and shot him in the face; the retired junta member barely survived. But only a few years before, the establishment would have winked at Neghme's murder, and the underground left would have fought to take "credit" for the assault on Leigh. This time, the condemnation of both crimes was universal.

After two decades of trauma, Chileans were tired of violence, and tired of hating each other. Augusto Pinochet could rave about the "rats" and "germs" coming to power; Volodia Teitelboim might dream of the "masses" rising up in revolution. But the people had rejected this dire, conspiratorial logic, and each major political group had made enormous concessions to ensure that the political transition would take place.

As his days of real power drew to an end, General Pinochet still schemed to control the symbolic trappings of his exit. Although Aylwin planned to hold the inauguration on March 14, Pinochet insisted it take place on the eleventh in memory of the coup. When several democratic heads of state refused in advance to greet Pinochet, he canceled their invitations. And although custom called for the outgoing president to depart on foot after turning over his sash, the general demanded a full, Prussian-style cavalry escort away from the new Congress in Valparaiso.

Nevertheless, proof of Pinochet's humiliation pervaded the inauguration. The general, his archaic blue uniform clanking with medals and sword, sat stiffly on the dais next to Gabriel Valdés, the newly elected Senate president, and surveyed the sea of incoming officials he had once excoriated, imprisoned, or exiled. Outside, after the ceremony ended and Pinochet stepped into his open limousine between rows of matching white horses, the last of South America's modern-day dictators was pelted with tomatoes and eggs.

The next evening, in his inaugural address before an audience of seventy thousand at the National Stadium, President Aylwin struck a very different tone, vowing to rebuild a climate of respect and trust among all Chileans, "whether civilians or military men." Interrupted by boos, he insisted, "Yes, compatriots, between civilians and military men!" With that, the stadium burst into cheers.[58]

The night was rich in symbols: a free-flowing outdoor ballet with figures from every ethnic and social group, a medley of songs once banned from the airwaves, a list of disappearance victims illuminating the scoreboard. Later, the accounting would come; a middle ground between vengeance and impunity would have to be found. But at least there were private satisfactions: as Cecilia Castro's name flashed by on the screen, her parents turned to proudly watch their grandchild, Valentina, dance in the inaugural ballet.

Later still, in the vast courtyard of La Moneda, four thousand guests sipped champagne under the flowering orange trees. Most had never set foot inside the palace before; several had been dragged out of the building on September 11, 1973. Orlando Letelier's widow was there and several relatives of the disappeared, priests and politicians and poets. At one point, someone called for silence, and the national anthem was struck up. This time Claudio Huepe, the new congressman from Arauco, sang with gusto.

NOTES

Unless otherwise indicated, all interviews took place in Santiago, Chile.

CHAPTER ONE: THE WAR

1 Patricia Verdugo, *Los zarpazos del puma* (Santiago: CESOC, 1989), 27–28.
2 Allende's last broadcast is reproduced in Patricio Quiroga, ed., *Salvador Allende obras escogidas (1970–1973)* (Barcelona, Spain: Editorial Crítica, 1989), 397–98.
3 That day, recalled the retired air force general Nicanor Díaz Estrada, one of the coup plotters, Pinochet acted as if he "owned the show." See Sergio Marras, *Confesiones* (Santiago: Ornitorrinco, 1988), 111.
4 Many details of this account come from Ignacio González Camus, *El día que murió Allende* (Santiago: CESOC, 1988), 242–44. González reconstructed Pinochet's radio dispatches from tapes and interviews with former military aides.
5 Augusto Pinochet, *El día decisivo* (Santiago: Andrés Bello, 1980), 145, and González, *El día que murió Allende*, 295.
6 In his reconstruction of the coup, Gonzáles Camus makes a persuasive case that Allende expected to die and took his own life as the troops approached. James Whelan, in *Allende: Death of a Marxist Dream* (Washington, D.C.: Council for Inter-American Security, 1981), gives extensive treatment to statements by Dr. Guijón, whose testimony is crucial to the suicide thesis. See also Nathaniel Davis, *The Last Two Years of Salvador Allende* (Ithaca: Cornell Univ. Press, 1985). When Allende's body was exhumed for reburial in Santiago, Chile, on Sept. 4, 1990, witnesses, including family members, confirmed Dr. Guijón's account.
7 González, *El día que murió Allende*, 92.
8 One La Legua leader, Carlos Echeverría, later described a fierce battle in which "the entire population seemed to be on the firing line" against marauding troops, and the neighborhood ran with "rivulets of blood." His gripping, if exaggerated, account was published in Samuel Chavkin, *The Murder of Chile* (New York: Everest House, 1982), 170–73.
9 Pinochet, *El día decisivo*, 134.
10 *Ercilla*, Sept. 26, 1973, 29–35.
11 Pinochet voices these fears in his account of the coup. See *El día decisivo*, 128, 141.
12 *Ercilla*, Sept. 26, 1973, 30, and Verdugo, *Los zarpazos del puma*, 52–53.
13 Interview with Colonel Gastón Elgueta, Aug. 1, 1989, Concepción. Another local

government source said the army feared that it would take months to subdue the area and considered bombing the bridge separating Lota from the city of Concepción.

14 *Ercilla,* Sept. 26, 1973, 31.

15 Interview, July 11, 1989, Puente Alto.

16 *El Mercurio,* Sept. 26, 1973, 22.

17 *Ercilla,* Sept. 26, 1973, 16–17.

18 Decree Law 5, Sept. 12, 1973, said, "The state of siege decreed for internal disturbance, in the circumstances in which the country is living, should be understood as a state or time of war, for the purpose of applying the penalties of this time established by the Code of Military Justice and other penal laws." *100 primeros decretos leyes dictados por la junta de gobierno de la República de Chile* (Santiago: Editorial Jurídica, 1973), 16.

19 Ascanio Cavallo, Manuel Salazar, and Oscar Sepúlveda, *La historia oculta del régimen militar* (Santiago: La Epoca, 1988), 26–30.

20 Interview, April 19, 1989.

21 The estimates are from Organización de los Estados Americanos, Comisión Interamericana de Derechos Humanos, *Informe sobre la situación de los derechos humanos en Chile* (Washington, D.C.: OEA, 1985), 55. These include up to 250 people executed without trial, up to 35 executed after being condemned by war councils, 30 to 50 killed "trying to escape," and others shot in confrontations or military custody. It is possible that as many as 2,000 people died after the coup, including cases of personal score settling and rural killings where victims' relatives have been too fearful to come forward.

22 For a discussion of the origins and evolution of Chilean democracy, see Arturo Valenzuela, "Chile: Origins, Consolidation, and Breakdown of a Democratic Regime," in Larry Diamond, Juan J. Linz, and Seymour Martin Lipset, eds., *Democracy in Developing Countries; vol. 4, Latin America* (Boulder, Colo.: Lynne Rienner, 1989), 159–206.

23 Interview, May 2, 1989.

24 The income figures are from James W. Wilkie, ed., *Statistical Abstract of Latin America,* vol. 20 (Los Angeles: UCLA Latin American Center Publications, 1980), 12.

25 U.S. Senate, *Covert Action in Chile, 1963–73,* Staff Report of the Select Committee to Study Governmental Operations with Respect to Intelligence Activities (Washington, D.C.: GPO, Dec. 18, 1975), 14–17. The comparison with the expenditures in the U.S. election comes from Arturo Valenzuela, *The Breakdown of Democratic Regimes: Chile* (Baltimore: Johns Hopkins Univ. Press, 1978), 118.

26 Quoted by Seymour Hersh, in *New York Times,* Sept. 11, 1974, 14.

27 U.S. Senate, *Covert Action,* 19–26. The attempted kidnapping and unintentional assassination of General René Schneider, commander of the Chilean army, a central event in this bungled plotting, will be discussed in chapter 2. An additional tragedy of this episode was the disgrace of the U.S. ambassador, Edward M. Korry, who was deliberately kept in the dark about the CIA operations and spent years trying to prove his lack of complicity.

28 For studies of the Allende years, see Paul Sigmund, *The Overthrow of Allende and the Politics of Chile* (Pittsburgh: Univ. of Pittsburgh Press, 1977), Manuel Antonio Garretón and Tomás Moulián, *Análisis coyuntural y proceso político: Las fases del conflicto en Chile* (San José, Costa Rica: Editorial Universitaria Centroamericana, 1978), and Valenzuela, *Breakdown.*

29 Interview, Aug. 17, 1987.

30 Interview, Aug. 7, 1989, Concepción.

31 Interview, Aug. 6, 1989, Chillán.
32 Studies of the Chilean economy under the UP include Stefan de Vylder, *Allende's Chile: The Political Economy of the Rise and Fall of the Unidad Popular* (Cambridge: Cambridge Univ. Press, 1976), and Sergio Bitar, *Transición, socialismo y democracia: La experiencia chilena* (Mexico: Siglo XXI, 1979). See also the economic essays published in Pablo Baraona Urzúa et al., *Visión crítica de Chile* (Santiago: Edición Portada, 1972).
33 Interview, May 2, 1989.
34 Valenzuela, *Breakdown*, 57.
35 U.S. Senate, *Covert Action*, 1–8, 26–31.
36 Interview, June 18, 1989.
37 García interview, Aug. 21, 1988. Santa Cruz interview, Aug. 17, 1989.
38 Interview, Nov. 21, 1985.
39 Letter from Radomiro Tómic, in Carlos Prats, *Memorias: Testimonio de un soldado* (Santiago: Pehuén, 1985), 497.
40 Interview, July 20, 1989.
41 Interview, June 20, 1989.
42 Interview, June 30, 1989. Although a senator, Bulnes was a key figure in the backroom negotiations leading to the resolution.
43 The speech, which was viewed by the military as a literal call to armed insurrection, is reproduced verbatim in Patricia Politzer, *Altamirano* (Buenos aires: Grupo Editorial Zeta, 1989), 189–94.
44 U.S. House of Representatives, Subcommittee on Inter-American Affairs of the Committee on Foreign Affairs, *United States and Chile during the Allende Years, 1970–1973* (Washington, D.C.: GPO, 1975), 94–115. Kubisch's testimony was given on Sept. 20, 1973.
45 Interview, Aug. 3, 1986.
46 Eugenia Weinstein et al., *Trauma, duelo y reparación* (Santiago: FASIC / Editorial Interamericana, 1987), 112.
47 Joan Turner, *Victor Jara, un canto no truncado* (Concepción: Editorial LAR, 1988).
48 *Qué Pasa*, Feb. 19, 1976, 30–31.
49 *Análisis*, Aug. 28, 1984, 25.
50 Chavkin, *Murder of Chile*, 187.
51 Interview, April 19, 1989.
52 *Qué Pasa*, Oct. 4, 1973, 8–9.
53 Politzer, *Altamirano*, 145–47.
54 *Análisis*, Aug. 28, 1984, 24–32.
55 Chavkin, *Murder of Chile*, 105. The best account of life on Dawson Island comes form Sergio Bitar, Allende's minister of mines, in his book *Isla Diez* (Santiago: Pehuén, 1987).
56 Interview, Aug. 6, 1989, Talcahuano.
57 OEA, *Informe*, 53.
58 Interview, May 2, 1989.
59 Interview, Aug. 21, 1988.
60 Interview, Aug. 4, 1989. For details of the incident and ensuing court case, see Arzobispado de Santiago, Vicaría de la Solidaridad, *Donde están*, vol. 7 (Santiago: Vicaría de la Solidaridad, 1979), 1555–56, 1560–74.
61 Interview, April 19, 1989.
62 *Qué Pasa*, Aug. 10, 1989, 11.
63 Interview, Aug. 10, 1989.
64 One colonel from Calama recalled receiving "an infinite number of anonymous denunciations." See Verdugo, *Los zarpazos del puma*, 69.

65 According to U.S. Senate, *Covert Action,* 40, two CIA collaborators aided in preparing the White Book.

66 Verdugo, *Los zarpazos del puma,* 27–29.

67 Numerous accounts of Arellano's tour have been pieced together by Chilean journalists. The most detailed, and critical, is found in Verdugo's book *Los zarpazos del puma,* which includes interviews with a number of local military officials. See also the testimony of Joaquín Humberto Lagos in *Apsi,* Dec. 15–28, 1986, 18–21.

68 Verdugo, *Los zarpazos del puma,* 133.

69 Pinochet, *El día decisivo,* 162–67.

70 Ibid.

CHAPTER TWO: THE SOLDIERS

1 Gonzalo Bulnes, *Guerra del Pacífico,* vol. 3 (Santiago: Editorial del Pacífico, 1974), 328. Bulnes describes a war force composed predominantly of patriotic civilians who, like those of Napoleon's army, "each carried in his knapsack a marshal's baton."

2 The characterization of the Prussian army as the first professional military force is found in Samuel P. Huntington, *The Soldier and the State* (New York: Vintage Books, 1964), 31. For descriptions of the Chilean army, see Frederick M. Nunn, *The Military in Chilean History* (Albuquerque: Univ. of New Mexico Press, 1976), 67–70.

3 See Frederick M. Nunn, "Emil Körner and the Prussianization of the Chilean Army: Origins, Process, and Consequences, 1885–1920," *Hispanic American Historical Review* 2 (May 1970): 300–322. See Also Florencio Infante Díaz, *Escuela militar del libertador Bernardo O'Higgins* (Santiago: Dirección de Bibliotecas, Archivos y Museos, 1985), 64–67.

4 *Ercilla,* Aug. 18, 1965, 4.

5 José M. Barceló Lira, "La evolución del ejército chileno," *Revista del Ejército, Marina y Aviación,* no. 5 (1935), 207, cited in Arturo A. Valenzuela, "The Chilean Political System and the Armed Forces, 1830–1925" (M.A. thesis, Department of Public Law and Government, Columbia Univ., 1967), 46.

6 The friction between the professional, middle-class officer corps and a promotion system that favored the sons of the upper classes was an important factor in the civil-military crisis of the 1920s. See Valenzuela, "Chilean Political System."

7 Interview, July 11, 1989.

8 Sergio Marras, *Confesiones* (Santiago: Ornitorrinco, 1988), 39–40.

9 *Cosas,* Dec. 22, 1983, 31. Since the War of the Pacific, in 1879, the Chilean armed forces have engaged no external foe, although there have been periodic moments of military tension with neighboring Peru and Argentina.

10 Interview, July 11, 1989, Puente Alto.

11 Ibid.

12 Biographical information on Pinochet comes from Augusto Pinochet, *El día decisivo* (Santiago: Andrés Bello, 1980), 17–45, *Diccionario biográfico de Chile* (Santiago: Empresa Periodística, 1959–61), 1028, Raquel Correa and Elizabeth Subercaseaux, *Ego sum Pinochet* (Santiago: Zig-Zag, 1989), 15–39, and other sources.

13 See Pinochet, *El día decisivo,* 18, 34.

14 *El Mercurio,* Aug. 24, 1988, 8.

15 Augusto Pinochet, *Política, politiquería y demagogia* (Santiago: Editorial Renacimiento, 1983), 115.

16 Pinochet, *El día decisivo*, 18–19.

17 Correa and Subercaseaux, *Ego sum Pinochet*, 38–39.

18 Pinochet, *El día decisivo*, 20.

19 Interview with Mónica Madariaga, March 12, 1990.

20 Pinochet, *El día decisivo*, 20–21.

21 Ibid., 25.

22 Ibid., 23–29.

23 Nunn, *Military in Chilean History*, 249–52.

24 Interview, Aug. 18, 1989.

25 *Qué Pasa*, Sept. 10–16, 1981, 9.

26 Marras, *Confesiones*, 42.

27 Interviews were conducted with several active-duty army officers with the ranks of colonel and general who insisted on strict anonymity.

28 Marras, *Confesiones*, 65–66.

29 James W. Wilkie, ed., *Statistical Abstract of Latin America*, vol. 20 (Los Angeles: UCLA Latin American Center Publications, 1980), 146, and Lawrence L. Ewing and Robert C. Sellers, eds., *Armed Forces of the World* (Washington, D.C.: Sellers & Associates, 1966).

30 Data on military expenditures as a percentage of GNP are from Wilkie, ed., *Statistical Abstract of Latin America*, 146.

31 Florencia Varas, *Conversaciones con Viaux* (Santiago: Eire, 1972), 55. In every conversation with the authors, military officers inevitably described the severe feeling of frustration and humiliation felt by high-ranking officers in the 1960s.

32 Carlos Prats González, *Memorias: Testimonio de un soldado* (Santiago: Pehuén, 1985), 103, 127. It is interesting to note that Pinochet, for all his antipolitical bravado, does not mention any of these incidents in his books or interviews, nor do other officers remember his position on political issues. Pinochet preferred to be cautious—to go along rather than take a stand.

33 See Nathaniel Davis, *The Last Two Years of Salvador Allende* (Ithaca: Cornell Univ. Press, 1985), 8–10, 16, U.S. Senate, *Covert Action in Chile, 1963–73*, Staff Report of the Select Committee to Study Governmental Operations with Respect to Intelligence Activities (Washington, D.C.: GPO, Dec. 18, 1975), 10–11, 23, and Nunn, *Military in Chilean History*, 267. The CIA maintained that, because it was not directly supporting Viaux's group at the time of the kidnapping, it did not share responsibility for what happened.

34 Pinochet, *El día decisivo*, 47.

35 Correa and Subercaseaux, *Ego sum Pinochet*, 56–57.

36 Pinochet, *El día decisivo*, 63.

37 U.S. Senate, *Covert Action in Chile*, 28, 38.

38 From U.S. Senate hearings on the nomination of Henry Kissinger as secretary of state, Sept. 17, 1973, as cited from the official transcript in James Petras and Morris Morley, *The United States and Chile: Imperialism and the Overthrow of the Allende Government* (New York: Monthly Review Press, 1975), 131–32.

39 From David A. Phillips, head of the CIA's Western Hemisphere division at the time of the coup, cited in Davis, *Last Two Years of Salvador Allende*, 349. In secret testimony before Congress, William Colby, then CIA director, also denied direct agency involvement.

40 Books that set out these allegations of direct U.S. involvement in the coup include Robinson Rojas, *The Murder of Allende* (New York: Harper & Row, 1976), and Thomas Hauser, *The Execution of Charles Horman: An American Sacrifice* (New York: Harcourt Brace, Jovanovich, 1978), which was the basis for the Costa-Gavras film. Davis's account is from his *Last Two Years of Salvador Allende*.

41 U.S. Senate, *Covert Action,* 28.

42 Prats, *Memorias,* 487–89.

43 There are several versions of this incident. Pinochet wrote in *El día decisivo,* 115, that Allende asked him for the resignations of four generals and that he refused for reasons of "honor." Prats wrote in *Memorias,* 495, that Pinochet told him he had tried to get numerous top generals to resign and that they had refused, so he had decided to postpone the request. A third version suggested Pinochet did not want his action to appear political, and preferred to have the generals removed later through the annual army promotion and retirement process. See Genaro Arriagada, *La política militar de Pinochet* (Santiago: Salesianos, 1985), 65–67.

44 Marras, *Confesiones,* 105–8, contains an account of the meeting of generals and Díaz's comments about the plotters' suspicions of Pinochet.

45 Sergio Arellano Iturriaga, *Más allá del abismo: Un testimonio y una perspectiva* (Santiago: Editorial Proyección, 1985), 47.

46 Ignacio González Camus, *El día que murió Allende* (Santiago: CESOC, 1988), 92–93, and Florencia Varas, *Gustavo Leigh: El general disidente* (Santiago: Editorial Aconcagua, 1979), 129–30, contain slightly different versions of this meeting and the note from Merino. Mónica Madariaga, Pinochet's relative and close aide for many years, was convinced that Pinochet moved to support the coup out of fear for his own safety. Interview, Dec. 4, 1985.

47 Pinochet, *El día decisivo,* 107.

48 Pinochet's version of the coup plotting is found in Correa and Subercaseaux, *Ego sum Pinochet,* 87–92, and in Pinochet, *El día decisivo,* 60–75.

49 Pinochet, *El día decisivo,* 112.

50 Correa and Subercaseaux, *Ego sum Pinochet,* 91.

51 See Arriagada, *La política militar,* 65. A number of officers described Pinochet's contingency plans as applicable to any emergency situation, and as having been completed by July. If the information they contained had relevance for an offensive against the government, Arriagada wrote, it was used only after Pinochet pledged to support the coup on Sept. 9.

52 Pinochet, *El día decisivo,* 77, 84.

53 See Patricia Verdugo, *Los zarpazos del puma* (Santiago: CESOC, 1989), 16–23, and General Nicanor Díaz Estrada's account in Marras, *Confesiones,* 104.

54 See Samuel Chavkin, *The Murder of Chile* (New York: Everest House, 1982), 148–50. According to Edelstam, the officer who told him he had ordered Lavandero's execution was "a Colonel Espinoza." This was probably Colonel Pedro Espinoza, who became a high-ranking official in the Chilean secret police and was indicted in the United States for the 1976 assassination of Orlando Letelier. Also see Verdugo, *Los zarpazos del puma,* 22–23, and Ascanio Cavallo, Manuel Salazar, and Oscar Sepúlveda, *La historia oculta del régimen militar* (Santiago: La Epoca, 1988), 26.

55 Interview, Jan. 6, 1990, Potomac, Md.

56 Ibid.

57 The text of Pinochet, *El día decisivo,* 245–52, describes various reasons for the coup but never mentions Plan Z. Curiously, a postcoup press account describing the plan was reprinted as an appendix to Pinochet's book, again without being mentioned in the text.

58 Verdugo, *Los zarpazos del puma,* 22.

59 *Apsi,* July 18, 1990, 11.

60 Verdugo, *Los zarpazos del puma,* 43.

61 Interview with Jaime Guzmán, Dec. 3, 1985.

62 Interviews, July 20 and 25 and Aug. 17, 1989. Chapter 4 details the role of several

army officers in the killings, including Colonel Espinoza, who later became top-level agents of the Chilean secret police and may already have been acting in that capacity.

63 Ibid. See also Cavallo et al., *La historia oculta*, 79.

64 See Taylor Branch and Eugene M. Propper, *Labyrinth* (New York: Viking Press, 1982), 66–69, and John Dinges and Saul Landau, *Assassination on Embassy Row* (New York: Pantheon Books, 1980), 139–42. Both accounts, although differing in some details, describe the involvement of Chilean secret police agents and Argentine intelligence services in the assassination.

65 Interview, July 19, 1989.

66 Correa and Subercaseaux, *Ego sum Pinochet*, 80–87.

67 Arriagada, *La política militar*, 104, 181.

68 *Qué Pasa*, Oct. 24, 1985, 19. See also Arriagada, *La política militar*.

69 Cavallo et al., *La historia oculta*, 212–13.

70 By 1984, all but two proven loyalists in the corps of generals were at least ten military academy classes behind Pinochet. See Arriagada, *La política militar*, 194–96.

71 *Cosas*, Sept. 6, 1984, 10–14.

72 Interview, July 28, 1989.

73 Interview, Dec. 15, 1989.

74 *The Almanac of World Military Power* (Presidio, Calif., 1980), 97, *El Mercurio*, April 2, 1989, D5, and *Cauce*, Aug. 18–24, 1986, 18–21. If expenses for police and intelligence services are added, by 1979 the Chilean state was spending a full 32.9 percent of its budget on the security sector. See Carlos Portales and Augusto Varas, "The Role of Military Expenditure in the Development Process: Chile, 1952–1973 and 1973–1980: Two Contrasting Cases," *Iberoamericana* 12 (1983): 21–50. An excellent article which documents the surge in military spending on salaries and equipment purchase is Jorge Marshall, "El gasto público en Chile, 1969–1979," *Colección Estudios Cieplan*, no. 5 (July 1981):53–84.

75 Carlos Huneeus and Jorge Olave, "La partecipazione dei militari nei nuovi autoritatismi il Cile in una prospettiva comparata," *Rivista Italiana di Scienza Politica* 17, no. 1 (April 1987): 69, and Charles L. Taylor and David H. Jackson, *World Handbook of Political and Social Indicators* (New Haven: Yale Univ. Press, 1983), 37–38.

76 For a detailed description of these activities, see chapter 4.

77 This legislation, pressed annually by Senator Edward M. Kennedy, Democrat of Massachusetts, was finalized in the International Security Assistance and Arms Export Control Act of 1977. The law was weakened in 1981 to allow a restoration of aid upon certification by the president that Chile had showed "significant progress" in human rights, but no such finding was ever made, and the law remained in effect through the entire period of military rule.

78 *El Mercurio*, Oct. 22, 1985. The incident occurred at a ceremony in Santiago for the Inter-American Defense Board, of which Schweitzer was then president.

79 Interview, June 5, 1989.

80 *Qué Pasa*, Aug. 10, 1989, 11.

81 Interview, Aug. 18, 1989.

82 *Cosas*, Dec. 22, 1986, 31.

83 *Ercilla*, Aug. 27, 1975, 13.

chapter three: The Dictator

1 *Newsweek,* March 19, 1984, 18.
2 Ascanio Cavallo, Manuel Salazar, and Oscar Sepúlveda, *La historia oculta del régimen militar* (Santiago: La Epoca, 1988), 23, and *Ercilla,* July 3, 1974, 8–9.
3 *Ercilla,* March 21, 1984, 9.
4 *Hoy,* Nov. 30, 1983, 13–14.
5 Interview, June 12, 1985.
6 Cavallo et al., *La historia oculta,* 22–24.
7 Florencia Varas, *Gustavo Leigh: El general disidente* (Santiago: Editorial Aconcagua, 1979), 33, 54.
8 Cavallo et al., *La historia oculta,* 140–41.
9 Ibid., 145–46.
10 Varas, *El general disidente,* 21.
11 The most complete account of these events can be found in Cavallo et al., *La Historia Oculta,* 179–82. Leigh also describes them in Varas, *El general disidente,* 17–22, and in numerous interviews. The authors are grateful to Jorge Olave for further clarification.
12 Press conference of Aug. 2, 1978, cited in Cavallo et al., *La historia oculta,* 183.
13 *Ercilla,* Aug. 2, 1978, 9.
14 Ibid., Aug. 20, 1975, 9.
15 *Hoy,* June 26, 1979, 7.
16 *La Segunda,* Aug. 8, 1984, 3.
17 Augusto Pinochet *Política, politiquería y demagogia* (Santiago: Editorial Renacimiento, 1983), 70.
18 *Cosas,* Sept. 22, 1981, 180.
19 General Nicanor Díaz Estrada quoted in Sergio Marras, *Confesiones* (Santiago: Ornitorrinco, 1988), 100.
20 The literature on Portales is voluminous. See Francisco Antonio Encina, *Portales,* 2 vols. (Santiago: Editorial Nascimiento, 1964), and Jay Kinsbruner, *Diego Portales: Interpretative Essays on the Man and Times* (The Hague: Martinus Nijhoff, 1967).
21 Bordaberry's plan was rejected by the Uruguayan armed forces, however. The authors are indebted to Jaime Guzmán for this insight and for making available the mimeographed transcripts of Bordaberry's speeches before the Uruguayan military council, which Pinochet had read.
22 Speech at Chacarillas, July 9, 1977, in Augusto Pinochet, *Patria y democracia* (Santiago: Andrés Bello, 1983), 86.
23 From a speech of June 9, 1977, cited ibid., 15.
24 See Cavallo et al., *La historia oculta,* p 250–252.
25 *Apsi,* special ed., Oct. 21, 1980, 12. This issue contains one of the most complete accounts of the events surrounding the adoption of the 1980 constitution.
26 Interview with José Luis Cea, July 27, 1989.
27 Interview with Francisco Bulnes, June 30, 1989.
28 *Apsi,* special ed., Oct. 21, 1980, 51.
29 Cited in Pinochet, *Patria y democracia,* 232.
30 *Qué Pasa,* Sept. 10, 1981, 10, and Raquel Correa and Elizabeth Subercaseaux, *Ego sum Pinochet* (Santiago: Zig-Zag, 1989), 10–12. The one exception to Pinochet's healthful life-style was his smoking, especially during tense meetings.
31 Interview with Jaime Guzmán, Aug. 22, 1987.
32 *Qué Pasa,* Sept. 10, 11–13.
33 *Análisis,* Sept. 17, 1990, 31–34.

34 See *Cauce*, May 15, 1984, 4–13, and special report, 10. Also see *Análisis*, Oct. 30, 1989, 30–34, and Nov. 6, 1989, 30–34.

35 Interview, June 25, 1990.

36 *Qué Pasa*, Nov. 19, 1987, 35.

37 Ibid., Sept. 12, 1988, 10–11.

38 *Ercilla*, Aug. 20, 1975, 9.

39 *Qué Pasa*, July 2, 1987, 38.

40 Ibid., Nov. 19, 1987, 38.

41 Ibid., April 24, 1986, 13–20.

42 *Cosas*, Sept. 29, 1988, 19.

43 *Newsweek*, March 19, 1984, 18–19.

44 Speech to women's group in Concepción, June 1, 1983, quoted in Pinochet, *Patria y democracia*, 248.

45 *Qúe Pasa*, April 24, 1986, 17.

46 *Hoy*, Sept. 15, 1982, 7–9.

47 Speech, April 6, 1979, cited in Pinochet, *Patria y democracia*, 197.

48 Cavallo et al., *La historia oculta*, 254.

49 Interview, Aug. 22, 1987.

50 *Qué Pasa*, April 24, 1986, 13–20.

51 Ibid., 14.

52 Ibid., July 10, 1975, 11.

53 Correa and Subercaseaux, *Ego sum Pinochet*, 47.

54 *Facts on File*, Nov. 20, 1976.

55 This comment was made in 1986 to A. Langhorne Motley, the assistant secretary of state for inter-American affairs. See *New York Times*, May 15, 1986, 1.

56 *New York Times*, Jan. 15, 1986, 6, and Reuters cable, Jan. 16, 1986.

57 *Washington Post*, July 12, 1986, 14, and *Boston Globe*, Aug. 17, 1986, 22.

58 Correa and Subercaseaux, *Ego sum Pinochet*, 113–23.

59 *Newsweek*, March 19, 1984, 18.

60 *Qué Pasa*, July 2, 1987, 35–41.

61 Ibid.

62 Junta message, Sept. 18, 1973, cited in Pinochet, *Patria y democracia*, 83.

63 Interview, June 9, 1989.

64 Interview, Aug. 24, 1989.

65 Interview, March 16, 1990.

66 *Qué Pasa*, July 2, 1987, 35–41.

67 Interview with Cristián Larroulet, June 2, 1989.

68 This incident is described in detail in Cavallo et al., *La historia oculta*, 215–22.

69 Marras, *Confesiones*, 25–26.

70 Cavallo et al., *La historia oculta*, 123.

71 *Qué Pasa*, March 22, 1974, 9. An especially strong example of Merino's vitriolic anti-communist rhetoric was a speech reported in *El Mercurio*, Aug. 31, 1988, C4.

72 *Qué Pasa*, Sept. 14, 1978, 38.

73 *El Mercurio*, July 30, 1989, D1–2.

74 *Cosas*, June 30, 1983, 12.

75 *Qué Pasa*, March 19, 1987, 13.

76 Ibid., Aug. 29, 1985, 34.

77 See Genaro Arriagada, *La política militar de Pinochet* (Santiago: Salesianos, 1985), for this insight.

78 Interview, March 9, 1990.

79 Off-the-record interview, Aug. 16, 1989.

80 *Cosas*, July 10, 1986, 10.

81 Interviews, April 19 and June 28, 1989.
82 Ibid.
83 *El Mercurio*, Aug. 24, 1988, 11.
84 Interview, Jan. 6, 1990.
85 *Qué Pasa*, Nov. 19, 1987, 35–40.
86 Marras, *Confesiones*, 26.
87 Interview with Jaime Guzmán, July 22, 1987.
88 Cavallo et al., *La historia oculta*, 376–77.

CHAPTER FOUR: ARMY OF THE SHADOWS

1 Interview, June 22, 1989.
2 The contents of the secret articles were rumored for years, and finally revealed in 1985. See Roberto Garretón, "Las leyes secretas de Chile," *Revista Chilena de Derechos Humanos*, 1st trimester 1985, 35–37.
3 See John Dinges and Saul Landau, *Assassination on Embassy Row* (New York: Pantheon Books, 1980), 126, 155–56.
4 *Apsi*, Aug. 14, 1989, 18–21. Also Ascanio Cavallo, Manuel Salazar, and Oscar Sepúlveda, *La historia oculta del régimen militar* (Santiago: La Epoca, 1988), 32–33.
5 Frenz, whose human rights activities and outspoken opposition to the Pinochet government led to a deep split among German Lutherans in Chile, was expelled from the country in June 1975.
6 Interviews, April 10 and 30, 1989.
7 Cavallo et al., *La historia oculta*, 73–75, and Brian H. Smith, *The Church and Politics in Chile: Challenges to Modern Catholicism* (Princeton: Princeton Univ. Press, 1982), 292–93. For an overview of the ambivalent church-state relations under Pinochet, see ibid., 283–355.
8 Interview, June 23, 1989.
9 Interviews, Aug. 15 and 20, 1989.
10 Organización de los Estados Americanos, Comisión Interamericana de Derechos Humanos, *Informe sobre la situación de derechos humanos en Chile* (Washington, D.C.: OEA, 1985), 78–79.
11 One of many accounts of this incident is in Cavallo et al., *La historia oculta*, 87–90.
12 David Becker et al., *La experiencia teurapéutica con víctimas de represión política en Chile y el desafío de reparación social* (Santiago: Instituto Latinoamericano de Salud Mental y Derechos Humanos, 1989), 9.
13 Interview, July 19, 1989. Bacciarini became so ill from torture that she was transferred to a psychiatric hospital, but in 1974 a war council headed by Contreras sentenced her to two years in prison for subversive activities before the coup. With help from a lawyer, she was able to serve the rest of her sentence in a convent. A gripping book-length memoir called *Tejas Verdes* was written by the prisoner Hernán Valdés and published in Spain (Barcelona: Laia, 1978).
14 Interview, Aug. 21, 1989.
15 Patricio Orellana, *Violación de los derechos humanos e información* (Santiago: FASIC, 1989).
16 *Análisis*, Oct. 1, 1985, 14.
17 Eugenia Weinstein et al., *Trauma, duelo y reparación* (Santiago: FASIC Editorial Interamericana, 1987), 123.
18 *Cauce*, July 23, 1985, 2–16.
19 Interviews, Aug. 15 and 20, 1989.

20 Weinstein et al., *Trauma, duelo y reparación*, 41.

21 *Cauce*, July 23, 1985, insert pp. 1–16.

22 From an interview with the *Washington Post*, Feb. 6, 1987, A1. Much of this detail comes form Fernández's court statements in the United States after he fled Chile in 1987.

23 *Cosas*, March 16, 1989, 28.

24 The 1975 hearings held by the Select Senate Committee to Study Governmental Operations with Respect to Intelligence Activities, under the chairmanship of Senator Frank Church, detailed the role of the CIA in assassination plots against four foreign leaders in the 1960s, as well as the conspiracy against General Schneider, the sabotage of the 1964 election in Chile, and the three-year effort to undermine the Allende government. The committee issued an interim report on Nov. 20, 1975, and numerous volumes of hearings material, including the *Covert Action in Chile* report, dated Dec. 4–5, 1975.

25 *Apsi*, Aug. 14, 1989, 18–21.

26 Cavallo et al., *La historia oculta*, 108.

27 Interview, April 15, 1989.

28 Interview, Aug. 15, 1988.

29 Ibid.

30 Sergio Marras, *Confesiones* (Santiago: Ornitorrinco, 1988), 54.

31 Quoted by his son, Sergio Arellano Iturriaga, in *Más allá del abismo* (Santiago: Editorial Proyección, 1985), 64.

32 Interview, Aug. 20, 1987.

33 *Análisis*, April 30, 1990, 31–34.

34 Cavallo et al., *La historia oculta*, 104.

35 Interview, Aug. 20, 1987.

36 Townley's mission to Mexico is described in detail in Taylor Branch and Eugene M. Propper, *Labyrinth* (New York: Viking Press, 1982), 235–49.

37 The DINA link to the Prats murder is described in Branch and Propper, *Labyrinth*, 66–69, and Dinges and Landau, *Assassination*, 139–43. The Leighton attack is described in Branch and Propper, *Labyrinth*, 307–11, and in Dinges and Landau, *Assassination*, 157–64.

38 Interview, July 10, 1989.

39 Details of the bombing are drawn from Dinges and Landau, *Assassination*, 207–14, and Branch and Propper, *Labyrinth*, 17–31.

40 The woman agent's identity remained a mystery until April 1990, when a former nightclub dancer named Mónica Lagos confessed to Santiago's *La Epoca* newspaper that she was Liliana Walker. The paper, and a subsequent court investigation, essentially confirmed her story.

41 See Dinges and Landau, *Assassination*, 101–15, 373–76.

42 See Branch and Propper, *Labyrinth*, 494–503.

43 *Washington Post*, Jan. 23, 1979, A5.

44 Ibid., Feb. 26, 1979, A12.

45 Letter of April 29, 1979, cited in *Chile: La memoria prohibida* (Santiago: Pehuén, 1989), 3:172.

46 *El Mercurio*, April 29, 1990, D6.

47 *Apsi*, July 4, 1990, 6–10.

48 Letter of June 29, 1979, cited in *Chile: La memoria prohibida*, 3:128. See also Dinges and Landau, *Assassination*, 394–96.

49 Dinges and Landau, *Assassination*, 242–43, 309–18, 372–73, 383–87, 392–96. The visit by Townley and Fernández to Washington had multiple CIA connections, but most seem to have been fabricated by the DINA. The two men initially obtained

U.S. visas on Paraguayan passports after letting U.S. diplomats believe they had CIA approval. George Landau, the U.S. ambassador, grew suspicious and notified the CIA, which told him no mission had been approved, so Landau canceled the visas. Traveling to Washington on false Chilean passports, the agents called the CIA in search of General Walters. This raises questions about why the agency did not keep closer tabs on their visit, failed to provide relevant evidence to U.S. investigators, and insisted that the DINA could not have been involved in the crime. Although Ambassador Landau had photographed their Paraguayan passports, it took months for investigators to identify the two DINA men, who had used several false names.

50 See Branch and Propper, *Labyrinth*, 51, 168, 355, 493, 584, and Dinges and Landau, *Assassination*, 242–44.

51 This is Section 701 of the International Financial Institutions Act of 1977.

52 *New York Times*, Nov. 30, 1979, 1.

53 Ibid., Sept. 13, 1980, 2.

54 See the accounts in *Hoy*, Feb. 9–15 and 16–22, 1987, and in *Washington Post*, Feb. 5, 1987, A12. In 1989, Pinochet dismissed Fernández's testimony by asking, "How much did they [the United States] pay him?" and by reiterating Contreras's assertions that the CIA had committed the crime. See Raquel Correa and Elizabeth Subercaseaux, *Ego sum Pinochet* (Santiago: Zig-Zag, 1989), 129–31.

55 *Washington Post*, Feb. 6, 1987, A1. Fernández was sentenced to up to seven years in prison, but was released in Sept. 1987, in view of his ongoing collaboration with U.S. investigators.

56 Mena's father, an army intelligence officer whose name was Reinaldo, gave his son a "code" name that mirrored his own—hence, Odlanier.

57 See the interview with Mena, *Qué Pasa*, April 5, 1979, 12, and *Hoy*, Aug. 5, 1980, 14–16.

58 Letter from Townley to Gustavo Etchepare, April 29, 1979, cited in *Chile: La memoria prohibida*, 3:78.

59 See Dinges and Landau, *Assassination*, 308–9, and *Qué Pasa*, Aug. 10, 1978, editorial, "Donde están los documentos de la DINA?"

60 *Qué Pasa*, Aug. 7, 1980, 5.

61 *El Mercurio*, May 11, 1980, cited in *Hoy*, June 24, 1981, 15.

62 Contreras interview cited in *Qué Pasa*, July 24, 1980, 13. Puga's column is quoted in *Hoy*, July 23, 1980, 12.

63 Cavallo et al., *La historia oculta*, 231.

64 Ibid., 265–72. The forest camp was allegedly part of a plan to overthrow Pinochet, orchestrated with assistance from guerrilla groups in neighboring countries. No evidence of this collaboration has been made public.

65 *Cauce*, March 10, 1986, 37.

66 Interview, Nov. 23, 1985.

67 *Las Ultimas Noticias*, Jan. 13, 1982, cited in *Chile: La memoria prohibida*, 3:417–18.

68 *La Tercera*, June 26, 1981, cited in *Chile: La memoria prohibida*, 3:415. The details of this case, including extensive public statements by individuals charged, are reported exhaustively on pp. 381–435 of this 1,500-page chronicle of human rights abuses under Pinochet.

69 *La Tercera*, June 26, 1981, cited in *Chile: La memoria prohibida*, 3:418.

70 See *Cauce*, Aug. 6, 1985, 34–38, for a history of the crime and the complex relationship between Chilean intelligence agencies.

71 *Hoy*, Nov. 30–Dec. 6, 1983, 6.

72 Several books and numerous articles have been written about the Jiménez assassi-

nation, notably Aldo Signorelli and Wilson Tapia, *Quien mató a Tucapel* (Santiago: Ariete, 1986), and Rodolfo Sésnic, *Tucapel: La muerte de un dirigente* (Santiago: Bruguera, 1986.) For a summary account, see Cavallo et al., *La historia oculta*, 283–85.

73 *Cauce*, May 5, 1986, 24–27.

74 Amnesty International, *Chile: Evidence of Torture* (London: Amnesty International, 1983), 5.

75 Ibid., 35.

76 *Cauce*, Aug. 13, 1985, 38–39.

77 For a detailed description of these events, see Patricia Verdugo and Carmen Hertz, *Operación siglo XX* (Santiago: Ornitorrinco, 1990), and Cavallo et al., *La historia oculta*, 389–95. See also *Hoy*, Aug 18, 1986, 6–9, and *Qué Pasa*, Sept. 4, 1986. For the government's version, see Pedro Vara Lonfat, *Chile: Objetivo del terrorismo* (Santiago: Instituto Geográfico Militar, 1988), 56–60.

78 *Cauce*, March 16, 1987, 34.

79 See *Apsi*, Aug. 3, 1987, 29–44. The article reproduces an exhaustive report by the Chilean Human Rights Commission on the five CNI raids of June 15–19, 1987, in which official descriptions of "armed confrontations" were contradicted by numerous witnesses.

80 Report of the Chilean Human Rights Commission, reproduced ibid., (quotation, p. 42).

81 *Qué Pasa*, July 31, 1980, 9.

82 *Cosas*, Jan. 19, 1989, 52.

83 Ibid., Dec. 22, 1988, 76.

84 *Las Ultimas Noticias*, Nov. 24, 1990, 15, *La Epoca*, Nov. 20, 1990, 23, *El Mercurio*, Nov 18, 1990, D3, and *Hoy*, Nov. 19, 1990, 9–12.

85 See *Análisis*, Dec. 3, 1990, 4–7, *Hoy*, Nov. 19, 1990, 4–7, and *Apsi*, Nov. 15, 1990, 6–9.

86 *Cosas*, March 16, 1989, 27–33.

CHAPTER FIVE: THE LAW

1 *Qué Pasa*, July 2, 1987, 38.

2 See below, n. 58.

3 Off-the-record interview, Dec. 21, 1989.

4 See Andrés Echeverría and Luis Frei B., *La lucha por la juridicidad en Chile* (Santiago: Editorial del Pacífico, 1974), 3:160.

5 Ibid., 176.

6 Ibid., 1:209–10.

7 *El Mercurio*, Sept. 13, 1973, 1.

8 *Hoy*, April 26, 1978, 14–16.

9 *El Mercurio*, March 29, 1974, C1, C12.

10 Interview, Dec. 19, 1989.

11 Interview, Aug. 5, 1989, Los Angeles.

12 Interview, Jan. 6, 1990, Bethesda, Md.

13 Montealegre's research for these trials led to his authorship of a ground-breaking legal text, *La seguridad del estado y los derechos humanos* (Santiago: Academia de Humanismo Cristiano, 1979).

14 Interview, July 17, 1989.

15 Vicaría de la Solidaridad, *Noveno año de labor* (Santiago: Arzobispado de Santiago, 1984), 66.

16 Pinochet's full letter and Silva's response are reproduced in Vicaría de la Solidari-

dad, *El Comité de Cooperación por la paz en Chile: Cronología de dos años de labor* (Santiago: Vicaría de la Solidaridad, 1975).

17 Interview, June 12, 1989.

18 For a compelling summary of the Vicaría's accomplishments, see Americas Watch, *The Vicaría de la Solidaridad in Chile* (New York: Americas Watch Committee, 1987).

19 See Eugenio Velasco, *Expulsión* (Santiago: Sociedad Editora Copygraph, 1986), 77–78, and interview, Aug. 25, 1988.

20 Interview, Aug. 20, 1988.

21 Velasco, *Expulsión*, 263.

22 *El Mercurio*, Aug. 25, 1976, 1, 12, also cited in Velasco, *Expulsión*, 172.

23 *Apsi*, Jan. 12, 1987, 13.

24 Velasco, *Expulsión*, 144–45.

25 Organización de los Estados Americanos, Comisión Interamericana de Derechos Humanos, *Informe sobre la situación de los derechos humanos en Chile* (Washington, D.C.: OEA, 1985), 179.

26 Off-the-record interview, Aug. 2, 1989, Concepción.

27 The court case and family statements are detailed in Arzobispado de Santiago, *Donde están,* vol. 7 (Santiago: Vicaría de la Solaridad, 1979), 1661.

28 *Ercilla,* Feb. 26, 1975, 13.

29 Vicaría de la Solidaridad, "Presentación al presidente de la Corte Suprema" (Santiago: Vicaría de la Solidaridad, March 1976, mimeo).

30 OEA, *Informe,* 181.

31 Vicaría de la Solidaridad, "Presentación al presidente."

32 Interview, Aug. 17, 1987.

33 *Qué Pasa,* March 4, 1976, 9, and *Hoy,* May 24, 1978, 12.

34 *Hoy,* May 9, 1979, 20–21.

35 OEA, *Informe,* 85, 210.

36 *Qué Pasa,* March 4, 1976, 7.

37 Off-the-record interview, July 19, 1989.

38 Off-the-record interview, Aug. 2, 1989, Concepción.

39 Off-the-record interview, Dec. 21, 1989.

40 This principle was quoted verbatim by several of the judges interviewed by the authors. It is Article 1, Paragraph 1, of the Chilean Civil Code.

41 Interview, June 15, 1989.

42 Echeverría and Frei, *La lucha,* 3:176.

43 Interview, Dec. 4, 1985.

44 Interview, Dec. 21, 1989.

45 *El Mercurio,* June 16, 1978, 1, 33.

46 OEA, *Informe,* 47.

47 Interview, Dec. 4, 1985.

48 OEA, *Informe,* 166.

49 For a complete listing see *Ordenamiento constitucional* (Santiago: Editorial Jurídica, 1980), 65–107.

50 OEA, *Informe,* 167.

51 Interview, July 27, 1989.

52 Roberto Garretón, "Las leyes secretas en Chile," *Revista Chilena de Derechos Humanos,* 1st trimester, 1985.

53 República de Chile, *Diario Oficial,* no. 30.042, April 19, 1978.

54 Sergio Marras, *Confesiones* (Santiago: Ornitorrinco, 1988), 136.

55 *La Epoca,* Aug. 8, 1989, 18.

56 Interview, June 15, 1989.

57 *Hoy,* April 27, 1983, 19–20.
58 Eugenio Hojman, *Memorial de la dictadura* (Santiago: Emisión, 1989), 104. The actual phrase he used was "me tienen curco," a colloquialism that suggests an intolerable burden on the shoulders—a monkey on the back.
59 José Cánovas Robles, *Memorias de un magistrado* (Santiago: Emisión, 1987), 107.
60 Velasco, *Expulsión,* 167.
61 Off-the-record interview, March 15, 1990.
62 Off-the-record interview, July 19, 1989.
63 See Americas Watch, "Chile News in Brief," Sept. 18–Nov. 14, 1986, 3–4.
64 The victims were Santiago Nattino, an artist; José Manuel Parada, a human rights activist; and Manuel Guerrero, a teacher. All were unarmed and kidnapped in broad daylight in the presence of numerous witnesses. See *Qué Pasa,* Feb. 6, 1986, 16. For a detailed chronology of the case, see *Cauce,* March 31, 44–45.
65 Cánovas, *Memorias,* 87.
66 Ibid., 99.
67 Interview, April 7, 1989.
68 Interview, July 13, 1989.
69 See OEA, *Informe,* 63, 109, 166, and *Hoy,* Aug. 29, 1979, 11–13.
70 Interview, July 27, 1989.
71 *Cauce,* June 27, 1988, 9.
72 *Qué Pasa,* May 3, 1984, 40–43.
73 Cánovas, *Memorias,* 55–58.
74 *Cauce,* June 27, 1988, 5–6.
75 Interview, July 17, 1989.
76 For the full text of the 1980 constitution, see Luz Bulnes Aldunate, *Constitución política de la república de Chile: Concordancias, anotaciones y fuentes* (Santiago: Editorial Jurídica, 1981), 309–96. Transitory articles are listed ibid., 133–50.
77 Ibid., 310.
78 OEA, *Informe,* 38.
79 Bulnes, *Constitución,* 145–46.
80 OEA, *Informe,* 43.
81 The most complete account of the events surrounding the adoption of the 1980 constitution is found in *Apsi*'s special ed., "Informe sobre el plebiscito de Pinochet," Oct. 21–Nov. 3, 1980.
82 Interviews, May 29 and July 27, 1989.

CHAPTER SIX: THE CULTURE OF FEAR

1 Nadezhda Mandelstam, *Hope against Hope: A Memoir* (New York: Atheneum, 1970), a portrait of life under Stalin.
2 *Cosas,* March 29, 1988, 93.
3 *El Mercurio,* Oct. 3, 1973, 21.
4 Interview, Aug. 16, 1987.
5 Interview, May 12, 1989.
6 Interview, April 11, 1989.
7 Interview, June 5, 1989.
8 Interview, Aug. 25, 1989.
9 Interview, April 19, 1989.
10 Interview, Dec. 21, 1989.
11 Interview, May 19, 1989.
12 Interview, May 2, 1989.
13 Interview, May 8, 1989.

14 Interview, July 15, 1989.

15 Interview, June 4, 1989.

16 Interview, June 18, 1989.

17 Off-the-record interview, May 10, 1989.

18 Figures from United Nations and World University Service records, cited in Liliana Muñoz, "Grief and Loss in Exile" (Ph.D. diss., 1984). Univ. of Sussex, England. Thousands more fled unofficially and never registered abroad as exiles; after the economic recession of 1982, the flow was augmented by economic refugees. By some estimates, as many as 200,000 people left the country between 1973 and 1986.

19 The United States, in contrast, accepted relatively few, and the refusal of U.S. embassy officials to help leftists seeking asylum during the horrific days after the coup deepened the bitterness and suspicion of many Chileans toward the U.S. government.

20 Interview, July 10, 1989. The political impact of exile on Chile's Socialist and Communist parties will be discussed in chapter 11.

21 Muñoz, "Grief and Loss."

22 Interview, May 4, 1989.

23 Interview, May 16, 1989.

24 The incident is related by Mónica Madariaga in Sergio Marras, *Confesiones* (Santiago: Ornitorrinco, 1988), 84–85.

25 Interview, April 24, 1989.

26 Interview, Aug. 6, 1989.

27 *El Mercurio,* Sept. 29, 1973, 31.

28 *New York Times,* Feb. 19, 1976.

29 Interview, Dec. 18, 1989. The article published in Brazil was entitled "Terroristas chilenos no interior da Argentina," and it appeared on the front page of the June 25, 1975, edition of the *O Dia* newspaper in Curitiba.

30 See Organización de los Estados Americanos, Comisión Interamericana de Derechos Humanos, *Informe sobre la situación de los derechos humanos en Chile* (Washington, D.C.: OEA, 1985), 82.

31 *Cauce,* March 27–April 9, 1984, 23–28. CIA support for *El Mercurio* before the coup has been well documented. According to the 1975 report by the U.S. Senate Select Committee to Study Governmental Operations with Respect to Intelligence Activities [the Church committee], *Covert Action in Chile, 1963–1973* (Washington, D.C.: GPO, Dec. 18, 1975), 29, at least $1.5 million was channeled to *El Mercurio* in 1971 and 1972.

32 Interview, July 20, 1989.

33 *El Mercurio* began an ambitious modernization plan in 1981, incurring such heavy debts that in 1985 Edwards was forced to guarantee his personal estate in order to reach an agreement with the paper's creditors. See Arturo Navarro, "El sistema de prensa bajo el régimen militar," in ILET / CERC, *La prensa: Del autoritarismo a la libertad* (Santiago: ILET / CERC, 1989), 131.

34 Interview, July 20, 1989.

35 For an especially poetic diatribe against the Allende era, see an editorial entitled "Today, Two Years Ago," *Qué Pasa,* Sept. 11, 1975, 9.

36 Interview, Dec. 18, 1989. The editorial ran on Aug. 14, 1975, 9.

37 Interview, June 14, 1989.

38 Francisco Reyes Matta, Carlos Ruiz, and Guillermo Sunkel, eds., *Investigación sobre la prensa en Chile (1974–1984)* (Santiago: CERC / ILET, 1986), 232–33.

39 Chilean census data, quoted in Joaquín Lavín, *Chile: La revolución silenciosa* (Santiago: Zig-Zag, 1987), 31. According to Lavín, this is more than six times higher than the 1970 figure.

40 See José Joaquín Brunner, *La cultura del autoritarismo en Chile* (Santiago: FLACSO, 1981), 91–95.

41 *Qué Pasa*, Feb. 14, 1980, 24–27.

42 "La tiranía de la desinformación," *Hoy*, May 25, 1983, 39–40.

43 Ascanio Cavallo, Manuel Salazar, and Oscar Sepúlveda, *La historia oculta del régimen militar* (Santiago: La Epoca, 1988), 135–36.

44 *Ercilla*, April 6, 1977, 13–14.

45 See the remarks by Interior Minister Sergio Fernández, cited in *Qué Pasa*, June 28 1979, 6.

46 Interview, May 26, 1989.

47 Interview, May 3, 1989.

48 Interview, March 19, 1990, Cambridge, Mass.

49 Bórquez's harangue was prompted by the press-driven release of the prime official suspect in a chain of bizarre murders in Viña del Mar. Later, the crimes were linked to two members of the secret police.

50 Cavallo et al., *La historia oculta*, 131–38.

51 *Qué Pasa*, Nov. 8, 1984, 32–36.

52 *Hoy*, April 7, 1982, 31, and May 21, 1980, 21.

53 Ibid., April 7, 1982, 31.

54 *Qué Pasa*, March 6, 1975, 18–19.

55 See Brunner, *La cultura autoritaria*, 47.

56 The role of the National Secretariat of Youth under military rule is explored in chapter 10, in connection with the regime's efforts to mold a new breed of Chilean youth. The political organization of the Councils of Neighbors is discussed in chapter 9, in conjunction with municipalities, antipoverty programs, and alternative community organizations.

57 *Cosas*, Sept. 24, 1981, cited in Augusto Pinochet Ugarte, *Patria y democracia* (Santiago: Andrés Bello, 1983), 188.

58 *Qué Pasa*, Nov. 16, 1973, 16–18.

59 Gloria Cruz, Ana María de la Jara, and Paulina Sabal, "Mujeres: Ciudadanas o pedestales de la patria?" (Santiago: Cordillera, Programa de Desarrollo Comunal, June 1988, mimeo), 1.

60 Susana Levy and Norbert Lechner, "CEMA-Chile y secretaría nacional de la Mujer," in M. Angélica Meza, ed., *La otra mitad de Chile* (Santiago: CESOC, n.d.), 85.

61 Cavallo et al., *La historia oculta*, 213–14.

62 Interview, Aug. 21, 1988.

63 See Levy and Lechner, "CEMA-Chile," 81–99.

64 From *La Nación*, March 20, 1984, cited in Cruz, de la Jara, and Sabal, "Mujeres: Ciudadanas," 1.

65 Interview, May 19, 1989.

66 FLACSO, *Encuesta sobre la realidad político-social de Chile* (Santiago: FLACSO, 1986), 13.

67 Interview, May 14, 1989.

68 This issue will be discussed in chapter 9.

69 Off-the-record interview, Aug. 4, 1989.

70 Interview, Aug. 4, 1989, Santa Bárbara.

CHAPTER SEVEN: THE TECHNOCRATS

1 "Ha oído hablar de los Chicago Boys?" *El Mercurio*, June 4, 1989, D11–13.

2 Arturo Fontaine Aldunate, *Los economistas y el presidente Pinochet* (Santiago: Zig-Zag, 1988), 20.

3 This account is based on numerous interviews, including several with Saénz, who asserted that to his knowledge all funds had come from corporate donors in Europe, Latin America, and the United States. It is likely that some aid was provided by the CIA. According to the 1975 report by the U.S. Senate Select Committee to Study Governmental Operations with Respect to Intelligence Activities, the CIA helped finance "an opposition research organization" during the U.P. See *Covert Action in Chile, 1963–73* (Washington, D.C.: GPO, Dec. 18, 1975), 30.

4 Interview by Nina Serafino, Nov. 12, 1979.

5 Interview, Nov. 16, 1985.

6 Fontaine, *Los economistas*, 16–17.

7 A. Bardón, C. Carrasco, and A. Vial, *Una década de cambios económicos* (Santiago: Andrés Bello, 1985), 35–37, and Banco Central de Chile, Departamento de Estudios, *Informe económico de Chile* (Santiago, 1983), 46.

8 Daniel Wisecarver, "Regulación y derregulación en Chile: septiembre 1973 a septiembre 1983," *Estudios Públicos*, no. 22 (Autumn 1986): 120.

9 Fontaine, *Los economistas*, 42.

10 Ibid., 24. For a deeper examination of how Chicago school economics came to Chile, see Juan Gabriel Valdés, *La escuela de Chicago: Operación Chile* (Buenos Aires: Grupo Zeta, 1989).

11 "Los Chicago Boys: Como llegaron al gobierno," *Qué Pasa,* Oct. 8, 1981, 22–29.

12 Interview, May 29, 1990.

13 The break between the Christian Democrats and the Pinochet government will be discussed in chapter 11. Christian Democrats who left the government out of loyalty to the party included Jorge Massad and Juan Villarzú.

14 Interviews, Aug. 5, 1988, and June 1, 1990. The authors gained further insight into this period from interviews with Cristián Larroulet, Aug. 5, 1986, and June 9, 1989.

15 Details of this pivotal meeting were drawn largely from Fontaine, *Los economistas,* 53–57. Complementary information came from interviews with current and former officials, including José Piñera, Hugo Araneda Dörr, Arturo Fontaine A., Cristián Larroulet, and Fernando Léniz.

16 Joseph Ramos, *Neoconservative Economics in the Southern Cone of Latin America, 1973–1983* (Baltimore: Johns Hopkins Univ. Press, 1984), 102.

17 Between Jan. 1973 and Jan. 1974, the world oil price increased 349 percent. See Bardón et al., *Una década,* 43. The price of copper, which averaged 93 cents a pound in 1974, dropped sharply at the end of the year and averaged only 56 cents in 1975. See Banco Central de Chile, Dirección de Estudios, *Indicadores económicos y sociales, 1960–1982* (Santiago: Banco Central, 1983), 139. See also Ramos, *Neoconservative,* 108.

18 "El consejo del profesor," *Ercilla,* April 2, 1975, 19–22. Friedman's full remarks were published in Fundación de Estudios Económicos, Banco Hipotecario de Chile, *Milton Friedman en Chile: Bases para un desarrollo económico* (Santiago: Editorial Universitaria, 1975).

19 Although it was largely unnoticed at the time, Decree Law 966 also gave Pinochet sweeping powers of "executive prerogative" to name all top government officials, an authority previously shared by all four junta members.

20 Fontaine, *Los economistas,* 62. Actually, this maxim is derived from Harberger's well-known phrase "The cat's tail must be cut off in one blow," a prescription for quick, harsh economic readjustment policies.

21 Interview, Dec. 4, 1985.

22 Interview by Nina Serafino, Nov. 12, 1979.

23 There was one more, little-known reason why military officials quickly embraced the Chicago Boys' prescriptions: their fear that economic weakness would leave

the Chicago Boys' prescriptions: their fear that economic weakness would leave Chile vulnerable to attack by neighboring Peru or Argentina, with which it had had territorial disputes for many years.

24 The Nixon administration, which had sought to "make the economy scream" under Allende, was eager to make it purr under Pinochet. U.S. economic aid to Chile was immediately revived, and between 1974 and 1976 the amount totaled $183.6 million—as compared with $19.8 million in U.S. aid during the entire Allende government. See Heraldo Muñoz and Carlos Portales, *Una amistad esquiva* (Santiago: Pehuén, 1987), 90–95. Other experts have calculated the total aid amount at an even higher level. After 1976, however, congressional prohibitions reduced U.S. aid to a trickle.

25 See W. Frick Curry, Center for International Policy, "Aid Memo" (Washington, D.C., May 30, 1986). This report contains a detailed list of all multilateral loans to Chile, as well as the U.S. voting record for each loan under the Ford, Carter, and Reagan administrations.

26 *Washington Post*, Aug. 3, 1979, 16, and Associated Press cable, Washington, Nov. 30, 1979.

27 The first figure is adjusted for inflation. See Bardón et al., *Una década*, 56.

28 Pilar Vergara, "Changes in the Economic Functions of the Chilean State," in J. Samuel Valenzuela and Arturo Valenzuela, eds., *Military Rule in Chile* (Baltimore: Johns Hopkins Univ. Press, 1986), 91.

29 See *Ercilla*, May 7, 1975, 11–15. As part of the policy change, the escudo, which had averaged 990 to the dollar in 1974, was replaced by the peso, which averaged 5 to the dollar in 1975. See Banco Central, *Indicadores*, 135.

30 For a detailed description of these economic measures from the government point of view, see Bardón et al., *Una década*, esp. 38–54.

31 "Sectors that can't be efficient with 10 percent protection don't deserve the right to use productive national resources," de Castro remarked at the time. See *Ercilla*, March 22, 1978, 31.

32 Ramos, *Neoconservative*, 18.

33 See Bardón et al., *Una década*, 50–53, and Vergara, "Changes in the Economic Functions," 84–89. The human effects of this recession, as well as those of the even graver economic crisis of 1982, will be discussed in chapter 9.

34 *Ercilla*, May 7, 1975, 15.

35 See the description in Fontaine, *Los economistas*, 26.

36 Interview, March 9, 1990. The incident is described in Ascanio Cavallo, Manuel Salazar, and Oscar Sepúlveda, *La historia oculta del régimen militar* (Santiago: La Epoca, 1988), 65–66.

37 A major developer of these statist theories was Raúl Prebisch, an Argentine economist and first head of the UN Economic Commission for Latin America, whose 1950 manifesto became the bible of Latin American economic thought. As long as poor countries relied exclusively on exporting raw materials for income, he argued, they would always lag behind the countries whose more sophisticated products they needed.

38 Vergara, "Changes in the Economic Functions," 78.

39 Interview by Nina Serafino, Nov. 12, 1979. For a more complete exposition of de Castro's views on this issue, see his "La realidad socio-económica chilena y su proyección en la década 80," *Realidad*, no. 23 (April 1981): 37–40.

40 The phenomenon is not a new one. The economist Albert O. Hirschman, in his remarkable book *Journeys toward Progress* (New York: Norton, 1963), 240–41, described how leaders in Chile, Colombia, and Brazil had often been seized with a "rage to want to conclude," or a "headlong rush toward the pseudo-insight," cast-

ing off past policies with contempt in their search for "the next Comprehensive, Fundamental, Integral Solution."

41 *Cosas*, Feb. 17, 1977, Cited in Vergara, "Changes in the Economic Functions," 97.

42 *Ercilla*, March 23, 1977, cited in Pilar Vergara, *Auge y caída del neoliberalismo en Chile* (Santiago: FLACSO, 1983), 96.

43 See Claudio Garate, "Ha oído hablar de los Chicago Boys?" *El Mercurio*, June 2, 1989, D11.

44 While encouraging the development of Kelly's team at ODEPLAN, Pinochet typically kept a separate team of economic planners, dominated by army officers, operating under Colonel Julio Canessa, known to be skeptical of the Chicago Boys. This strategy had the double effect of keeping the army involved in sensitive areas and of giving Pinochet the latitude to choose between groups with opposing policy views.

45 See Joaquín Lavín's revealing biography, *Miguel Kast: Pasión de vivir* (Santiago: Zig-Zag, 1988).

46 Interview, June 9, 1989. Kast himself, Lavín notes dutifully, made a substantial amount of money on investments in timber, aided by generous state subsidies.

47 Lavín, *Kast*, 92.

48 *Hoy*, May 28, 1980, 26.

49 See Vergara, *Auge y caída*, 98–99.

50 Interview in *El Mercurio*, June 17, 1979, sec. D., cited in Vergara, *Auge y Caida*, 163.

51 *Qué Pasa*, May 31, 1979, 31.

52 Ramos, *Neoconservative*, 20, 52.

53 Ibid., 55.

54 *Ercilla*, March 22, 1978, 30.

55 *El Mercurio*, Sept. 17, 1989, D7.

56 Fontaine, *Los economistas*, 49, refers to the high losses incurred by state firms under Allende.

57 Ramos, *Neoconservative*, 52.

58 Cavallo et al., *La historia oculta*, 210–11.

59 See Fontaine, *Los economistas*, 125–28.

60 Bardón et al., *Una década*, 55, states this clearly. Also see *Qué Pasa*, Dec. 4, 1980, 8–11.

61 For a detailed analysis of this issue, see Cristián Larroulet, "El estado empresario en Chile," *Estudios Públicos*, no. 14 (Fall 1984). The statistics are from p. 148.

62 Interview, Aug. 22, 1987. Guzmán was a key figure in the evolution of Pinochet's thinking from corporativist to liberal lines. He told the authors that his discovery of von Hayek had significantly altered his own views since 1974, when he wrote the regime's declaration of principles, with its corporativist tone.

63 This account is drawn from Fontaine, *Los economistas*, 128–32, and interview with José Piñera, Aug. 21, 1987.

64 The most eloquent argument for this holistic approach to the liberalizing of society is found in a pivotal article by Jaime Guzmán, "El camino político de Chile," *Realidad*, no. 7 (Dec. 1979), also reprinted in *El Mercurio*, Dec. 26, 1979.

65 Interview, Nov. 29, 1985. Piñera clashed with de Castro in general cabinet meetings, reflecting his disdain for the more narrow, technical vision of the monetarists.

66 *El Mercurio*, Sept. 12, 1979, 1.

67 The threatened U.S. boycott, and the labor legislation that resulted, will be dealt with in chapter 9.

68 *Hoy*, March 5, 1980, 23–25.

69 One study estimated that the adjusted sale price of the twenty-five largest firms and banks sold over fours years ranged from 63 percent to 77 percent of their net worth. See Vergara, "Changes in the Economic Functions," 90.

70 See Alejandro Foxley, "The Neoconservative Economic Experiment in Chile," in Valenzuela and Valenzuela, eds., *Military Rule in Chile*, 33. Also see the chart in Fernando Dahse, *El mapa de la extrema riqueza* (Santiago: Editorial Aconcagua, 1979), 180–81, comparing value and sales prices of numerous transactions, based on figures from CORFO and the Superintendency of Anonymous Societies.

71 "Quién protege a Cruzat y Edwards?" *Análisis*, Feb. 14, 1984, 22–25; also see Dahse, *El mapa*, 27.

72 See Dahse, *El mapa*, 140–47, 159, and Foxley, "Neoconservative," 45. These groups will be described in more detail in chapter 8.

73 Ramos, *Neoconservative*, 66.

74 *Ercilla*, March 22, 1978, 31.

75 Serafino interview, Nov. 12, 1979.

76 *Qué Pasa*, May 31, 1979, 30–33.

77 Ramos, *Neoconservative*, 69, 104, 108.

78 *Ercilla*, Dec. 27, 1979, 6–11.

79 Amid a rash of complimentary articles, Peter Dworkin's "Chile's Brave New World of Reaganomics," *Fortune*, Nov. 2, 1981, 136–44, was especially laudatory. Also see World Bank, *World Development Report 1981* (Washington, D.C.: World Bank, 1981).

80 Kirkpatrick's essay on this topic, "Dictatorships and Double Standards," first appeared in the Nov. 1979 issue of *Commentary*.

81 *Washington Post*, Aug. 13, 1981, 25.

82 Theberge addressed the House Subcommittee on Inter-American Affairs on Sept. 17, 1974. See the official transcript of the hearings, held between July 1, 1971, and Sept. 18, 1974, *United States and Chile during the Allende Years, 1970–1973* (Washington, D.C.: GPO, 1975), 309–19, 634–38.

83 From Theberge's remarks at his swearing-in ceremony, cited in *New York Times*, March 5, 1982, 4.

84 UPI cable, Miami, Oct. 14, 1982.

85 The statistics are from Banco Central, *Indicadores*. Opposition economists such as Patricio Meller argued that official growth figures were misleading and exaggerated. He suggested that the average growth rate for the period was 6.5 percent a year. See his "Una revisión del milagro económico chileno, 1976–1981," *Colección Estudios Cieplan*, no. 15 (Dec. 1984):5–109.

86 Banco Central, *Indicadores*, 1960–1988, 185.

87 Interview, July 24, 1989.

88 *El Mercurio*, Aug. 28, 1980, 1, 12.

89 *Realidad*, no. 23 (April 1981):43.

90 Ramos, *Neoconservative*, 48.

91 The debt figures are from World Bank, *World Debt Tables: 1989–90*, vol. 2 (Washington, D.C.: World Bank, 1989).

92 Sebastián Edwards and Alejandra Cox Edwards, *Monetarism and Liberalization: The Chilean Experiment* (Cambridge, Mass.: Ballinger, 1987), 196.

93 The data are from Banco Central, reported in Manuel Delano and Hugo Traslaviña, *La herencia de los Chicago Boys* (Santiago: Ornitorrinco, 1989), 198–99. The export data are from Ramos, *Neoconservative*, 88.

94 Vergara, *Auge y caída*, 191.

95 *El Mercurio*, March 30, 1982, A3. This was one of several unusually critical edi-

torials that led *El Mercurio*'s owner, Augustín Edwards, to fire the editor Arturo Fontaine Aldunate.

96 Fontaine, *Los economistas,* 160–61.

97 Kast had recently been named head of the Central Bank. See Lavín, *Kast,* 86.

98 Cavallo et al., *La historia oculta,* 299.

99 The higher rates, set by Federal Reserve Board Chairman Paul Volcker in an effort to bring down double-digit inflation in the United States, had a direct effect on all dollar-based lending worldwide. Chilean industry was especially vulnerable because 60 percent of its foreign debt had been contracted at variable rates. See Felipe Larraín, "The Economic Challenges of Democratic Development," in Paul Drake and Iván Jaksic, eds., *The Struggle for Democracy in Chile, 1982–1990* (Lincoln: Univ. of Nebraska Press, 1991), 5.

100 *Realidad,* no. 30 (Nov. 1981):7.

101 Interview, July 24, 1989. See also "El día en que Chile enloqueció," *Qué Pasa,* Jan. 5, 1984, 34–49.

102 Ramos, *Neoconservative,* 23.

103 Ibid., 66.

104 See Vergara, *Auge y caída,* 236, and Foxley, "Neoconservative," 47–48.

105 *Qué Pasa,* Nov. 1, 1984, 12.

CHAPTER EIGHT: THE RICH

1 See Constantine Menges, "Public Policy and Organized Business in Chile: A Preliminary Analysis," *Journal of International Affairs* 2 (1966):343–65. See also David Cusack, "The Politics of Chilean Private Enterprise under Christian Democracy" (Ph.D. diss., Univ. of Denver, 1970).

2 Interview, Aug. 25, 1987.

3 Maurice Zeitlin and Richard E. Ratcliff, "The Concentration of National and Foreign Capital in Chile," in Arturo Valenzuela and J. Samuel Valenzuela, eds. *Chile: Politics and Society* (New Brunswick, N.J.: Transaction Books, 1976), 301–5.

4 For a detailed breakdown of the pattern of business expropriations, see Cristián Larroulet, "El estado empresario en Chile," in *Estudios Públicos,* no. 14 (Fall 1984): 131, 148. Also see Patricio Rozas, "Elementos de un diagnóstico sobre la situación del empresariado nacional durante el régimen militar (1973–1983)," *CED: Materiales de Discusión,* no. 56 (Nov. 1984):53–54.

5 Interview, Nov. 16, 1985.

6 Guillermo Campero, *Los gremios empresariales en el periodo 1970–83* (Santiago: ILET, 1984), 93–95.

7 Ibid., 102.

8 *Ercilla,* Nov. 20, 1974, 26–27.

9 Arturo Fontaine Aldunate, *Los economistas y el presidente Pinochet* (Santiago: Zig-Zag, 1988), 47–48.

10 Campero, *Los gremios,* 109–10.

11 *Ercilla,* April 23, 1975, 11.

12 *Qué Pasa,* Nov. 4, 1982, 8–9.

13 Campero, *Los gremios,* 120, 123, and passim.

14 *Ercilla,* June 30, 1976, 9. For detailed statistical information, see Banco Central de Chile, Dirección de Política Financiera, *Indicadores económicos y sociales, 1960–82* (Santiago: Banco Central, 1983).

15 For a detailed examination of the fortunes of the textile industry, see Patricio Frías et al., "Industria textil y del vestuario en Chile," *Colección Estudios Sectoriales PET,* no. 4 (1987):59–60.

16 *Qué Pasa*, Dec. 8, 1977, 30.
17 Banco Central de Chile, Dirección de Estudios, *Indicadores económicos y sociales, 1960–1988* (Santiago: Banco Central, 1989), 251.
18 Interview, May 8, 1989.
19 *Ercilla*, July 7, 1976, 12–13.
20 *Qué Pasa*, July 1, 1976, 6–9.
21 Letter ibid. from Jorge Yarur Amador, Nov. 18, 1982, 6.
22 In 1976, Chile's economy grew 3.5 percent, but for each of the next three years its growth exceeded 8 percent. See Banco Central, *Indicadores* (1989), 26.
23 Banco Central, *Indicadores* (1989), 370.
24 Manuel Delano and Hugo Traslaviña, *La herencia de los Chicago Boys* (Santiago: Ornitorrinco, 1989), 61, and *Qué Pasa*, March 6, 1980, 23.
25 *Qué Pasa*, Feb. 7, 1980, 42–43.
26 *Hoy*, Aug. 17, 1977, 20.
27 "Secretos del consumismo," *Hoy*, April 2, 1980, 23–27.
28 Interview, May 9, 1989.
29 *Qué Pasa*, June 26, 1980, 38–40.
30 *Economía y Sociedad*, Sept. 1983, 8.
31 For a detailed breakdown of Vial's holdings through the BHC group, see Fernando Dahse, *Mapa de la extrema riqueza* (Santiago: Editorial Aconcagua, 1979), 41–46.
32 *Hoy*, Aug. 26, 1981, 22–24.
33 Interview, July 21, 1983.
34 "El millonario invisible," *Hoy*, Sept. 16, 1981, 19–21, and "Los diez hombres más ricos de Chile," *Qué Pasa*, Sept. 3, 1981, 16.
35 See Dahse, *El mapa*. The list of Cruzat's holdings appears on pp. 29–35.
36 *Qué Pasa*, March 24, 1983, 10–15.
37 *El Mercurio*, April 10, 1980, cited in Campero, *Los gremios*, 218–19.
38 Campero, *Los gremios*, 151.
39 Ibid., 155–56.
40 *Qué Pasa*, Oct. 9, 1980, 19–20.
41 *Hoy*, March 4, 1981, 21–22.
42 Quote from José Pablo Arellano cited in *Hoy*, Sept. 17, 1980, 32–33.
43 See "Lo que hay detras de CRAV," *Hoy*, July 8, 1981, 24–27, and "CRAV," *Análisis*, Special supplement, July 1981, 1–9.
44 Banco Central, *Indicadores* (1989), 26; Delano and Traslaviña, *La herencia*, 99–102. The bankruptcy figures are from the National Syndicature of Bankruptcies.
45 *El Mercurio*, Oct. 24, 1982, cited in Guillermo Campero, "Los empresarios chilenos en el régimen militar y el post-plebiscito" (Paper prepared for presentation at the Conference on Transformation and Transition in Chile, Univ. of California, San Diego, 13–14 March, 1989), 25.
46 See Delano and Traslaviña, *La herencia*, 99–100, and Campero, *Los gremios*, 267–70.
47 *Hoy*, March 16, 1983, 16–17.
48 Interview, May 11, 1989.
49 *Hoy*, June 21, 1982, 17.
50 The stockholders' meeting is briefly mentioned in Delano and Traslaviña, *La herencia*, 102.
51 See Alejandro Foxley, "The Neoconservative Economic Experiment in Chile," in J. Samuel Valenzuela and Arturo Valenzuela, eds., *Military rule in Chile* (Baltimore: Johns Hopkins Univ. Press, 1986), 45–47.
52 Numerous political and personal factors figured in this contrasting treatment. See

"Quién protege a Cruzat y Edwards?" *Análisis,* Feb. 14, 1984, 22–26; and Delano and Traslaviña, *La herencia,* 114.

53 See "El caso de los pirañas que se devoraron," *Cauce,* Dec. 17, 1987, 38–41; "Avalancha desde la torre," *Qué Pasa,* Feb. 2, 1984, 8; and Ascanio Cavallo, Manuel Salazar, and Oscar Sepúlveda, *La historia oculta del régimen militar* (Santiago: La Epoca, 1989), 292–95, 299–301.

54 Interviews, July 21, 1983, and May 18, 1989.

55 "La cesantía en los ejecutivos," *Qué Pasa,* April 15, 1982, 8–11.

56 Interview, Jan. 6, 1990, Washington, D.C.

57 *Hoy,* Feb. 9, 1983, 20–23.

58 *Qué Pasa,* Nov. 4, 1982, 8–10.

59 *Economía y Sociedad,* Feb. 1985, 5.

60 *Análisis,* Aug. 28, 1984, 12.

61 *Hoy,* May 30, 1984, 37–39.

62 Fontaine, *Los economistas,* 179–83.

63 Interview, June 9, 1989.

64 Interview, Richard Newfarmer, Feb. 12, 1989, Washington, D.C.

65 For a detailed description of these mechanisms, see Juan Andrés Fontaine, "Los mecanismos de conversión de deuda en Chile," *Estudios Públicos,* no. 30 (Fall 1988):137–57.

66 W. Frick Curry, "Aid Memo" (Washington, D.C.: Center for International Policy, June 30, 1987), material compiled from World Bank reports.

67 Interview, Aug. 16, 1988.

68 Joaquín Lavín, *Chile: La revolución silenciosa* (Santiago: Zig-Zag, 1987), 115.

69 Interviews, Aug. 24 and 25, 1989.

70 *Journal of Commerce,* July 22, 1987, 4.

71 Lavín, *La revolución silenciosa,* 44–60.

72 Chile's economic recovery was clearly aided by an increase in copper prices, however, from 62.3 cents a pound in 1986 to $1.32 in 1989. Büchi also established the Copper Stabilization Fund, which set aside any copper profits beyond those expected for the year, thus protecting the peso from overappreciating and providing a cushion in case prices fell.

73 Some critics saw "popular capitalism" as chiefly a public relations scheme, rather than as a serious attempt to disperse private ownership. See Patricio Rozas and Gustavo Marín, *1988: El mapa de la extrema riqueza 10 años después* (Santiago: CESOC / PRIES-Cono Sur, 1989), 66. For a detailed look at one case, see Harald Beyer, "La privatización de la distribución de energía Eléctrica: El caso de Chilectra Metropolitana," *Estudios Públicos,* no. 32 (Spring 1988):156–57.

74 The most exhaustive study of recent foreign investment in Chile is found in Rozas and Marín, *1988: El mapa.* See pp. 70–75 for a list of foreign investors in privatized Chilean enterprises.

75 Ibid., 284.

76 In two years, the state lost about $600 million by selling off firms at an average 40 percent of their nominal value. See Mario Marcel, "La privatización de empresas públicas en Chile, 1985–88," *Notas Técnicas CIEPLAN,* no. 125 (Jan. 1989).

77 *Hoy,* Oct. 27, 1986, 32–34.

78 *Estrategia,* Aug. 14, 1989, 18–19.

79 Interview, Dec. 19, 1989.

80 Ibid. See also *El Mercurio,* Sept. 17, 1989, D1–2.

81 Manuel Feliú, *La empresa de la libertad* (Santiago: Zig-Zag, 1988), cited in Campero, "Los Empresarios," 42.

82 Lavín, *La revolución silenciosa,* 11, 155.

83 The data are from Delano and Traslaviña, *La herencia*, 167.

84 Interview, May 19, 1989.

85 Interview, Aug. 25, 1989.

86 Interviews, May 10 and 30, 1989.

87 *El Mercurio*, Aug. 20, 1986, cited in Campero, "Los Empresarios," 48.

88 The authors interviewed Léniz five times between 1985 and 1990. These remarks come from an interview on June 1, 1989. Some businessmen who signed the National Accord were penalized by the government, including one mine owner whose government loan was suddenly denied.

CHAPTER NINE: THE POOR

1 Recording of "El Botero" by Eduardo Gatti on his *Escencialmente así no más*, cassette album released by RCA / Ariola, Chile, 1986.

2 In his 1988 book *Los silencios de la revolución* (Santiago: Puerta Abierta), the sociologist Eugenio Tironi offered a systematic rebuttal to Joaquín Lavín's *Chile: La revolución silenciosa*, arguing that Chile's rapid modernization came at a high cost to the majority of its poor and moderate-income citizens.

3 Mariana Schkolnik and Berta Teitelboim, "Encuesta del empleo en el gran Santiago" (Santiago: PET, Nov. 1988), 78.

4 Banco Central de Chile, Dirección de Estudios, *Indicadores Económicos y Sociales, 1960–1988* (Santiago: Banco Central, 1989).

5 From data reported in Inter-American Development Bank, *Economic and Social Progress in Latin America* (Washington, D.C: IDB, 1989), 463.

6 See José Pablo Arellano, "La situación social en Chile," *Notas Técnicas CIEPLAN*, no. 94 (June 1988): 8, 19.

7 "El 'Boom' de la pobreza," *Qué Pasa*, Aug. 5, 1976, 31.

8 See Banco Central, *Indicadores*, 254–56, for Chilean statistics. For comparative figures, 1980–88, see United Nations, Economic Commission for Latin America, *Economic Survey of Latin America and the Caribbean, 1988* (Santiago: ECLA, 1989), 62. For prior years, see the *Economic Survey, 1981*, 27.

9 Interview, May 16, 1989.

10 *Qué Pasa*, July 8, 1976, 30–31.

11 Banco Central, *Indicadores*, 277.

12 Ibid., 303–5. See also *Qué Pasa*, March 17, 1983, 12–14.

13 See Jorge Jiménez de la Jara, "La salud pública en Chile, 1985," *Vida Médica*, 36, no. 1 (March 1985): 40–41.

14 For a survey of street peddlers during this period, see PREALC, *Sobrevivir en la calle: El vendedor ambulante en Santiago* (Santiago: PREALC, 1988).

15 Interview, Nov. 15 1985, originally cited in Pamela Constable, "A Growing Defiance," *Boston Globe Magazine*, March 9, 1986, 50.

16 An exceptionally revealing series of interviews with thirteen unemployed men and women was published by the Chilean playwright David Benavente. See *A medio morir cantando* (Santiago: PREALC, 1985).

17 Interview, April 8, 1989.

18 Bando no. 9 of the military junta, Sept. 11, 1973, published in *El Mercurio*, Sept. 26, 1973, 22.

19 Bando no. 31 of the military junta, Sept. 14, 1973, ibid., 23.

20 Decree Law 198, in *101-200 decreto-leyes dictados por la junta de gobierno de la República de Chile* (Santiago: Editorial Jurídica, 1974), 298–304.

21 See Jaime Ruiz-Tagle, *Sindicalismo y estado en el régimen militar chileno* (Santiago: PET, 1986), 8 (statistics are from pp. 15–17).

22 See Rodrigo Alamos, "La modernización laboral," *Estudios Públicos*, no. 26 (Fall 1987): 149–92.

23 Ascanio Cavallo, Manuel Salazar, and Oscar Sepúlveda, *La historia oculta del régimen militar* (Santiago: La Epoca, 1989), 186–87.

24 Interview, June 20, 1989.

25 *El Mercurio*, Dec. 7, 1978, C1.

26 See Manuel Barrera and J. Samuel Valenzuela, "The Development of Labor Movement Opposition," in J. Samuel Valenzuela and Arturo Valenzuela, eds., *Military Rule in Chile* (Baltimore: Johns Hopkins Univ. Press, 1986), 250–51, 264.

27 See ibid., 253–60, and *Hoy*, Feb. 13, 1980, 24–28.

28 *Hoy*, Dec. 31, 1980, 27.

29 *Hoy*, Aug. 26, 1981, 27–30, and Barrera and Valenzuela, "Development," 258.

30 *Hoy*, Nov. 26, 1980, 19.

31 Interview, May 4, 1989.

32 Presidential message to the nation, Sept. 11, 1974, cited in Augusto Pinochet; *Patria y democracia* (Santiago: Andrés Bello, 1983), 134.

33 Miguel Kast Rist, *Distribución del ingreso y desarrollo económico* (Santiago: ODEPLAN, 1976), 8–11.

34 Ibid., 31.

35 *Qué Pasa*, April 8, 1976, 31–32.

36 Interview, June 26, 1989.

37 See *El Mercurio*, April 16, 1989, B1, and Secretariat for Social Development and Assistance, "Evolution of Extreme Poverty in Chile" (Santiago, Aug. 1988). For comparative data on infant mortality, see CEPAL, *Statistical Yearbook for Latin America and the Caribbean* (Santiago: CEPAL, 1989), 15. For an overview of regime social policies, see Tarsicio Castaneda, "Innovative Social Policies for Reducing Poverty: Chile in the 1980s" (Manuscript, Washington, D.C., 1989). For a study of infant mortality, see Dagmar Raczynski and C. Oyarzo, "Porqué cae la tasa de mortalidad infantil en Chile?" *Colección Estudios Cieplan*, no. 6 (Dec. 1981):45–84.

38 See Manuel Delano and Hugo Traslaviña, *La herencia de los Chicago Boys* (Santiago: Ornitorrinco, 1989), 170. Other works that deal with income distribution include Eugenio Ortega and Eugenio Tironi, *Pobreza en Chile* (Santiago: CED, 1988), 44, and Ricardo Ffrench-Davis and Dagmar Raczynski, "The Impact of Global Recession and National Policies on Living Standards: Chile, 1973–87," *Notas Técnicas CIEPLAN*, no. 97 (March 1987): 34. The Secretaría de Desarrollo y Asistencia Social, in "La lucha contra la pobreza: Politicas y resultados en Chile" (Santiago: Secretaría de Desarrollo y Asistencia Social, 1989), 14–15, argues that income distribution became slightly more egalitarian. Ffrench-Davis and Raczynski, in "Impact," 34, argue that that conclusion was based on faulty assumptions.

39 Arellano, "La situación social," 28.

40 See Secretaría de Desarrollo y Asistencia Social, "La lucha," 6. Also Banco Central, *Indicadores* (1989), 406. The decline of social spending as a percentage of total government programs is reported in Mabel Cabezas, "Revisión metodológica y estadística del gasto social en Chile: 1970–86," *Notas Técnicas CIEPLAN*, no. 114 (May 1988). The 13 percent decline figure is found on p. 2.

41 See Aristedes Torche Lazo, "Distribuir el ingreso para satisfacer las necesidades básicas," in Felipe Larraín, ed., *Desarrollo económico en democracia* (Santiago: Universidad Católica, 1987), 175–78.

42 See Mariana Schkolnik, *Sobrevivir en las poblaciones José Maria Caro y lo Hermida* (Santiago: PET, 1988).

43 See Delano and Traslaviña, *La herencia*, 167, and Ffrench-Davis and Raczynski, "Impact," 33.

44 Banco Central, *Indicadores*, 406. According to Delano and Traslaviña, *La herencia*, 148, public spending on health, in dollars per capita, dropped steadily, from $28.80 in 1973 to $10.90 in 1988.

45 See "Hospitales en estado de coma," *Qué Pasa*, Aug. 1, 1985, 11–13, also Jiménez, "La salud pública," 42–43.

46 Interview, Aug. 31, 1989.

47 See Dagmar Raczynski, "Costos y lecciones de la erradicación de los pobladores," *Revista Cieplan*, no. 12 (April 1988): 23–28.

48 See Castaneda, "Innovative Social Policies," 112. A detailed description of all government housing programs is found on pp. 112–47.

49 See Raczynski, "Costos y lecciones," 25. See also Tironi, *Los silencios*, 23–28, and *La Epoca*, May 17, 1989, 14.

50 Interview, May 21, 1989.

51 Secretaría de Desarrollo y Asistencia Social, "La lucha," 11–12.

52 Banco Central, *Indicadores* (1989), 406. The number of houses built per 1,000 inhabitants, which averaged 3.5 in the 1960s and 4.3 in the Popular Unity years, fell to 2.8 from 1974 to 1981, and again to 2.5 in 1982. See Ffrench-Davis and Raczynski, "Impact," 51.

53 Even sympathetic studies showed that some programs intended for the needy were often economically unworkable, so the units went to higher-income families instead. See Castaneda, "Innovative Social Policies," 112–42. For the role of the World Bank, we have relied on conversations with World Bank economists conducted in Washington, D.C., between 1987 and 1990. For a general discussion of housing policy, see José Pablo Arellano, "Políticas de vivienda popular: Lecciones de la experiencia chilena," *Colección Estudios Cieplan*, no. 9 (Dec. 1982): 41–73.

54 Delano and Traslaviña, *La herencia*, 153.

55 From the authors' visit to Camp Raúl Silva Henríquez on Nov. 15, 1984.

56 *Hoy*, April 16, 1980, 24–25. The statistics are from *Qué Pasa*, May 20, 1981, 7–8.

57 Delano and Traslaviña, *La herencia*, 167–68.

58 Interview, April 29, 1989.

59 *Cauce*, Sept. 10, 1985, 38–39.

60 Interviews, Aug. 15 and 26, 1989.

61 Eduardo Morales, Hernán Pozo, and Sergio Rojas, *Municipio, desarrollo local y sectores populares* (Santiago: FLACSO, 1988), 61. Some revenues were redistributed through the Common Municipal Fund, but the balance remained heavily tilted toward wealthier communes.

62 For a detailed study of the role of municipal government under Pinochet, see Alfredo Rehren, "The Impact of Authoritarian Policies at the Local Level: The Case of Chile, 1974–1984" (Manuscript, Instituto de Ciencias Políticas, Universidad de Chile, 1989).

63 Mariana Schkolnik and Berta Teitelboim, *Pobreza y desempleo en poblaciones: La otra cara del modelo neoliberal* (Santiago: PET, 1988), 78, 83.

64 Interview, June 27, 1989.

65 See Cordillera, Programa para el desarrollo comunal, "Las juntas de vecinos," *Cuadernos de Trabajo*, no. 15, 1988. Also *Cauce*, Aug. 17, 1987, 26–29.

66 Interviews, July 4 and 9, 1989, Conchalí.

67 Dubois, a Frenchman, was one of numerous European priests working in Chile during military rule. See "Los curas extranjeros . . . conflictivos," *Qué Pasa*, Oct.

24, 1985, 52–56. He and two colleagues were arrested and expelled during a state of siege in Oct. 1986.
68 For a study of 495 groups in the greater Santiago area, see Luis Razeto et al., *Las organizaciones económicas populares* (Santiago: PET, 1986).
69 The open letter to General Pinochet was published as a special supplement to *Análisis* in Feb. 1983.
70 *Hoy*, May 4, 1983, 9.
71 Interview, May 23, 1989.
72 Oscar MacClure, *Negociación colectiva, sindicalización y huelga: Chile, 1932–1985* (Santiago: CEDAL, 1987), cited in Tironi, *Los silencios*, 72.
73 Interview, June 13, 1989.
74 Schkolnik and Teitelboim, "Encuesta del empleo," 26.
75 See "Las uvas de la ira," *Cauce*, Feb. 9, 1987, 24–26.
76 Interviews, July 5, 1989, San Felipe.
77 Schkolnik and Teitelboim, "Encuesta del empleo," 24–33, 60.
78 *La Epoca*, April 4, 1989, 10.
79 ECLA, *Economic Survey*, 41, 53.

CHAPTER TEN: CHILDREN OF DICTATORSHIP

1 *Hoy*, Jan. 14, 1981, 12.
2 José Joaquín Brunner, *Informe sobre la educación superior en Chile* (Santiago: FLACSO, 1986), 32.
3 Rojas's candid essay on his experiences as a leftist student leader and then as a political exile is found in Ricardo Brodsky, ed., *Conversaciones con la FECH* (Santiago: CESOC, 1988), 105–64.
4 Brodsky, ed., *Conversaciones*, 150–51.
5 Essay by Juan Antonio Widow in *Tizona*, Sept.–Oct. 1973, cited in L. Silver and J. P. Mery, "Universidades chilenas e intervención militar" (Manuscript, Santiago; FLACSO, 1975), 26–27.
6 *El Mercurio*, Oct. 3, 1973, 1.
7 The estimates are cited by Brunner, *Informe*, 42. The estimated number of those forced to leave campuses is somewhat higher in Silver and Mery, "Universidades."
8 Silver and Mery, "Universidades," 20–38. This unpublished study is the only known effort to systematically document the postcoup university purges. In their introduction, the authors note that their research, conducted in 1975, was hindered by the "fear and insecurity" prevailing on campuses at the time.
9 Interview, April 12, 1989.
10 *Hoy*, July 2, 1980, 11–13.
11 Silver and Mery, "Universidades," 105.
12 Academia de Humanismo Cristiano, *Boletín Realidad Universitaria*, no. 24 (Jan.–Feb. 1983), 15.
13 Silver and Mery, "Universidades," 32–39.
14 Interview, May 8, 1989.
15 Cited in Brunner, *Informe*, 45.
16 Silver and Mery, "Universidades," 45–46.
17 Interview, Aug 18, 1989. Beginning in 1984, the authors held numerous conversations with Boeninger and periodically attended seminars at CED.
18 The speech, delivered in Puerto Montt on Feb. 18, 1983, is excerpted in Augusto Pinochet, *Patria y democracia* (Santiago: Andrés Bello, 1983), 205.
19 Silver and Mery, "Universidades," 57–62.
20 Interview, May 17, 1989.

21 *Hoy*, May 14, 1980, 19–20.

22 See Programa Interdisciplinario de Investigaciones en Educación (PIIE), *Las trans-formaciones educacionales bajo el régimen militar,* vol. 2 (Santiago: PIIE, 1984), 421.

23 *Hoy*, Aug. 10, 1977, 22–24.

24 *Cauce*, Oct. 29, 1985, 45–46.

25 Interview, April 18, 1989.

26 See the profile in *Ercilla,* July 13, 1977, 36–39.

27 *Boletín Realidad Universitaria,* no. 2 (Jan.–Feb. 1981):9.

28 *Qué Pasa,* June 28, 1974, 12–14.

29 *Ercilla,* Dec. 21, 1977, 37–41, and Sept. 27, 1978, 28–32.

30 Interview, May 3, 1989.

31 Brunner, *Informe,* 59–62.

32 *Boletín Realidad Universitaria,* no. 24 (Jan.–Feb. 1983): 2–3, 14–15, for a complete list of tuition fees at Chilean universities.

33 Ibid., no. 2 (Jan.–Feb. 1981):13.

34 A detailed and comprehensive essay arguing in favor of the new university legislation can be found in Jaime Guzmán and Hernán Larraín, "Debate sobre nueva legislación universitaria," *Realidad,* no. 22 (March 1981):19–32.

35 *Cauce,* Nov. 18, 1983, 28–29, and *Boletín Realidad Universitaria,* no. 22 (Nov. 1982):32–33.

36 Brunner, *Informe,* 86.

37 Interview, May 3, 1989.

38 Circular issued Aug. 12, 1974, by the Army Command of Military Institutes, cited in PIIE, *Las transformaciones educacionales,* 481–84.

39 See Ibid., 481–96, for a detailed list of these and other circulars.

40 Silver and Mery, "Universidades," 107.

41 *Cauce,* July 23, 1985, 15–17.

42 The figures are from Banco Central de Chile and UNESCO, cited in Tarsicio Castaneda, "Innovative Social Policies for Reducing Poverty: Chile in the 1980s" (Manuscript, Washington, D.C., 1989), 28. Public school reforms are described in depth on pp. 11–37.

43 Interview, April 11, 1989.

44 *Hoy*, May 16, 1979, 8–9.

45 Interview with Enrique París, April 4, 1989.

46 The term "Canto Nuevo" was used to distinguish the new style from protest music of the precoup era, known as Nueva Canción. See Nancy Morris, *Canto porqué es necesario cantar: The New Song Movement in Chile, 1973–1983,* Research Paper Series no. 16 (Albuquerque: Univ. of New Mexico, 1984). Also see Fernando Paulsen, "El nuevo canto," *Análisis,* Jan.–Feb. 1982, 4–9.

47 *Boletín Realidad Universitaria,* nos. 1 and 2 (Nov. and Dec. 1980). All items are paraphrased.

48 Esteban Valenzuela, *Fragmentos de una generación* (Santiago: Emisión, 1988), 26–27.

49 Brodsky, ed., *Conversaciones,* 208.

50 Interviews, April 20 and 26, 1989.

51 See *Qué Pasa,* Oct. 10, 1985, 8–9, and *Análisis,* Oct. 4, 1985, 7–8.

52 *Cauce,* Aug. 10, 1986, 43.

53 *Qué Pasa* editorial, July 18, 1985, 7.

54 *El Mercurio,* Aug. 25, 1989, C1, 12. The incident is described in Pamela Constable, "Teen-ager's Burning in Chile Arousing Outrage," *Boston Globe,* July 13, 1986, 22.

55 See Raúl Urzúa, "Juventudes populares, involución social y sobrevivencia," *Documento de Trabajo*, no. 24 (Santiago: Centro de Estudios del Desarrollo, 1985), 34, 38.

56 Milan Marinovic, "Hipótesis del terrorismo," *Cuadernos de Ciencia Política* (University of Chile), cited in *Qué Pasa*, Sept. 24, 1987, 17.

57 Patricia Politzer, *La ira de Pedro y los otros* (Santiago: Planeta, 1988), 33–59.

58 Details and conflicting accounts of their deaths are outlined in Comité de Defensa de los Derechos del Pueblo, *Hermanos Vergara Toledo* (Santiago: CODEPU, 1986).

59 Interviews, May 6 and 14, 1989.

60 FLACSO and CED, *Opinión pública y cultura política* (Santiago: FLACSO, Aug. 1987), 156.

61 Poll by the Centro de Estudios de la Realidad Contemporanea (CERC), published in Academia de Humanismo Cristiano, *Realidad Universitaria*, Sept. 1987.

62 Interviews, May 16 and June 8, 1989.

63 Brockbank and Associates, "National Public Opinion Survey," May–June 1988, Santiago. Also given in Centro de Estudios Públicos, "Encuesta nacional de opinión pública," May–June 1988 (Santiago: CEP, June 1988).

64 FLACSO and CED, *Opinión pública*, 189–219.

65 Interview, April 3, 1989.

66 Centro de Estudios Públicos, "Encuesta nacional," 55, 60.

67 *Boletín Realidad Universitaria*, no. 22 (Nov. 1982):18–19.

68 Ibid., no. 24 (Jan.–Feb. 1983):39.

69 Interviews, Aug. 26, 1989.

CHAPTER ELEVEN: THE POLITICIANS

1 From *Ercilla*, Aug. 26, 1975, cited in Luis Alejandro Salinas, *Sursum corda* (Santiago: Todos, 1984), 35.

2 Interview, June 5, 1989.

3 *Qué Pasa*, June 12, 1986, 12. This general account draws from a number of readings, including Carmelo Furci, *The Chilean Communist Party and the Road to Socialism* (London: Zed, 1984), and from interviews with party activists, including Patricio Hales, Jaime Insunza, and several anonymous individuals.

4 *Qué Pasa*, June 12, 1986, 12.

5 Interview, Aug. 3, 1986.

6 See the declaration of the party's central committee in June 1974, published in Buenos Aires and reprinted in *El Mercurio*, June 22, 1974, 35.

7 Boris Ponomariov, the highest Soviet Foreign Ministry official dealing with Latin America, made this argument in "La situación mundial y el proceso revolucionario," *Revista Internacional*, no. 6 (1974), cited in José Miguel Insulza, "Eurocomunismo y socialismo en Chile," *Foro Internacional* 21: no. 3 (Jan.–Mar. 1981): 289–303. Also see the writings of Kiva Maidanik, a Soviet scholar whose criticisms after the coup provoked an angry protest from Chilean party leaders to Soviet officials. Although the Soviets initially were cautious about antagonizing the junta, they soon began to mount a strong campaign against Chile's new leaders.

8 See *Qué Pasa*, Dec. 22, 1977, 33–35, and *Apsi*, May 18, 1987, 8.

9 See *El Mercurio*, June 25, 1977, 10, for the contents of the party plan published on the previous day by Granma in Cuba. See *El Mercurio*, Aug. 31, 1977, 8, and *Qué Pasa*, March 1, 1984, 37, for Corvalán's message to the plenum.

10 See the interview with Teitelboim in *Cauce*, Dec. 10, 1985, 12–13.

11 Interview, Nov. 20, 1985. Although some party activists were public by this time, important party leaders were still working clandestinely. In this case, the interview

was arranged through intermediaries and conducted in a house with all curtains drawn, reached via numerous changes of transportation. The name of the party leader, a nondescript middle-aged man, was not given.

12 *Qué Pasa,* July 28, 1983, 1. For an overview of the speech, see ibid., March 1, 1984, 37–39. Also see Furci, *Chilean Communist Party,* 165.

13 Interview, July 31, 1989. Also see *El Mercurio,* Dec. 19, 1982, 3C, and *Apsi,* May 18, 1987, 8.

14 *Apsi,* May 18, 1987, 8.

15 *La Segunda,* July 28, 1981, 2, and *Qué Pasa,* July 28, 1983, 16, and Sept. 24, 1987, 17.

16 Interviews, Aug. 29 and 31, 1989.

17 In Jan. 1985, Chile's Constitutional Tribunal declared the Popular Democratic Movement unconstitutional, ruling that it defied the legal ban on groups that propagated Marxist doctrine. See *Solicitud de inconstitucionalidad del MDP* (Santiago: Editorial Opinión, 1984) for a full transcript of the complaint filed by thirty prominent conservative citizens, including Sergio Fernández and Jaime Guzmán, which led to the banning of the MDP.

18 These views were reflected in the authors' interview with an underground Communist leader, which took place on Nov. 20, 1985, just as the Accord was being negotiated.

19 See Benny Pollack and Hernán Rosenkranz, *Revolutionary Social Democracy* (London: Frances Pinter, 1986), Paul Drake, *Socialism and Populism in Chile* (Urbana: Univ. of Illinois Press, 1978).

20 Patricia Politzer, *Altamirano* (Buenos Aires: Grupo. Editorial Zeta, 1989), 105, 122. This is a book-length interview conducted in Paris, where Altamirano lived in exile for many years.

21 Interviews, April 13 and July 10, 1989.

22 The "Inside Leadership" position was spelled out in the "March Document" of 1974, which became the permanent reference for all party debate. For a detailed description of these developments, see Ricardo A. Yocelevsky, "El partido Socialista de Chile bajo la dictadura militar," *Foro Internacional* 27, no. 1 (July–Sept. 1986):102–131.

23 Politzer, *Altamirano,* 149. Their ambitious plan, which never materialized, even called for landing on Chile-owned Easter Island, 2,000 miles out in the Pacific.

24 Ibid., 150–51. In 1979, he confessed some of these doubts in an interview with *Hoy,* but the regime, uninterested in such subtleties, temporarily shut down the magazine as punishment for airing the views of a hated Marxist. See *Hoy,* June 20, 1979, 22–25.

25 Politzer, *Altamirano,* 150–53, 164–66.

26 The reflections of Enrico Berlinguer, secretary-general of the Italian Communist party, were crucial to this change. His 1977 writings are cited in José Miguel Insulza, "Eurocommunismo y socialismo en Chile," *Foro Internacional* 21, no. 3 (Jan.–March 1981):294.

27 See José Antonio Viera Gallo, "Chile: Una crisis en perspectiva," *Chile América,* nos. 10–11 (1975), and the response by Jorge Arrate in Rotterdam, "Una perspectiva gramsciana de la crisis chilena," ibid., no. 25, both cited in Insulza, "Eurocommunismo," 289–303.

28 *El Mercurio,* Aug. 9, 1977, 6. For a full text of the public party document criticizing Altamirano, see ibid., Aug. 11, 1977, 21.

29 *El Mercurio,* May 3, 1979, 12, and May 4, 1979, 36. Almeyda is cited in *Hoy,* June 13, 1979, 21.

30 See Yocelevsky, "El partido Socialista," 126.

31 *Qué Pasa,* March 1, 1984, 39.

32 Arturo Valenzuela, *The Breakdown of Democratic Regimes: Chile* (Baltimore: Johns Hopkins Univ. Press, 1978), 85.

33 *Apsi,* July 10, 1989, 25.

34 Lester A. Sobel, ed., *Chile and Allende* (New York: Facts on File, 1974), 145.

35 *El Mercurio,* Dec. 25, 1973, 49.

36 Interview, June 20, 1989.

37 Letters from Frei to Leighton, May 22, 1975, and from Leighton to Frei, June 26, 1975, both in possession of the authors.

38 In interviews conducted with one of the authors in Feb. 1974, Frei argued that the coup had become inevitable. He strongly denied that he had sought a "soft" coup which would make possible his reelection to the presidency after a short interval, saying his own contacts in the military had persuaded him that any takeover would be bloody. And yet, at no point did Frei use his influence to try to stop a coup. Interviews conducted with Sergio Arellano Iturriaga, the son of General Sergio Arellano, confirmed that several key Christian Democratic leaders were in active contact with the architects of the coup and that Frei was informed of these conversations. The Arellano interviews were conducted on July 20, July 25, and Aug. 17, 1989.

39 U.S. Senate, *Covert Action in Chile, 1963–73,* Staff Report of the Select Committee to Study Governmental Operations with Respect to Intelligence Activities (Washington, D.C.: GPO, Dec. 18, 1975), 14–22.

40 Frei expressed this view in an interview with one of the authors in Santiago in Feb. 1974.

41 *Ercilla,* May 28, 1975, 8–12.

42 *La Tercera,* special supplement, March 12, 1977.

43 *Qué Pasa,* Oct. 23, 1980, 5. The expulsion is described in *Hoy,* Oct. 22, 1980, 7–9.

44 Interview, Aug. 16, 1989.

45 See the testimony by W. Frick Curry, Center for International Policy, before the Subcommittee on International Development Institutions and Finance of the Banking Committee of the U.S. House of Representatives, Washington, D.C., July 21, 1987.

46 "La muerte de Frei," *Hoy,* Jan. 27, 1982, 6–10.

47 *Qué Pasa,* June 24, 1982, 11.

48 *Qué Pasa,* March 22, 1984, 35–40.

49 Washington Office on Latin America, "WOLA Update" (Washington, D.C.: March / April 1985), 5. The great majority of detainees were released after a few days.

50 Eugenio Hojman, *Memorial de la dictadura* (Santiago: Emisión, 1989), 183, and Ascanio Cavallo, Manuel Salazar, and Oscar Sepúlveda, *La historia oculta del régimen militar* (Santiago: La Epoca, 1989), 309.

51 Cavallo et al., *La historia oculta,* 353–60, gives a detailed account of this negotiating process.

52 *Boston Globe,* Nov. 22, 1985, 3.

53 "Que se hizo la derecha," *Qué Pasa,* July 4, 1985, 31.

54 *El Mercurio,* Aug. 23, 1973, 1.

55 *La Segunda,* Sept. 25, 1973, 11.

56 See *Qué Pasa,* Nov. 2, 1978, 18.

57 *Qué Pasa,* Nov. 2, 1978, 20.

58 *Qué Pasa,* July 4, 1985, 30.

59 *Hoy,* Sept. 14, 1983, 21.

60 Interview, Nov. 20, 1985.

61 See interviews with Rodríguez in *Hoy*, April 9, 1980, 15, and *Qué Pasa*, Dec. 3, 1981, 25. Also see Alvaro Puga in "Los secretos del nacionalismo," *Qué Pasa*, April 7, 1983, 12–14.

62 From the Basic Statutes of Avanzada Nacional, cited in *Cauce*, July 28, 1986, 29.

63 Interview, July 24, 1989.

64 See *Cauce*, July 28, 1986, 29, for details of links between the CNI and Avanzada.

65 *Hoy*, Sept. 30, 1981, 18–19.

66 *Qué Pasa*, Oct. 6, 1983, 35. A detailed account of the history of the *gremialistas* is found on pp. 14–18.

67 Interview, April 10, 1989.

68 Jarpa's role as interior minister and his views are discussed in *Qué Pasa*, Dec. 1, 1983, 8–11.

69 *Qué Pasa*, March 22, 1984, 16–17.

70 See Falcoff's article "Pinochet: The Next Somoza," in *Policy Review* 34 (Fall 1985) 18–24.

71 *Washington Post*, Feb. 23, 1985, 12.

72 See W. Frick Curry, Center for International Policy, Washington, D.C., "Aid Memos," May 30, 1986, and June 30, 1987, for detailed breakdowns of these loans and the U.S. voting record. Some U.S. officials, notably Ambassador Theberge, argued that the opposition to loans deprived Washington of what little "leverage" it had over the regime, since military aid had long been banned. Two of the approved loans, each worth $250 million, were crucial instruments that enabled Chile to refinance its foreign debt.

73 See the articles by Susan Kaufman Purcell and Mark Falcoff in Mark Falcoff, Arturo Valenzuela, and Susan Kaufman Purcell, *Chile: Prospects for Democracy* (New York: Council on Foreign Relations, 1988).

74 *New York Times*, Jan. 27, 1986, 6.

75 *El Mercurio*, Dec. 3, 1985, 1. Also see the profile of Barnes in *Boston Globe*, July 16, 1986, 3.

76 See Mark Falcoff, "The Coming Crisis in Chile," *Policy Review* (Oct. 1985):18–24, and Pamela Constable and Arturo Valenzuela, "Is Chile Next?" *Foreign Policy* 63 (Summer 1986):58–75.

77 *New York Times*, March 13, 1986, 1.

78 *El Mercurio*, Aug. 2, 1986, 1. The Reagan administration had abstained on votes on multilateral loans to Chile once before, in Feb. and March 1985, shortly after Pinochet extended a state of siege imposed the previous Nov.

79 This incident is recounted in Cavallo et al., *La historia oculta*, 379.

80 See "Que se hizo la derecha," *Qué Pasa*, July 4, 1985, 35–36. The comment is from an off-the-record interview with the authors.

81 Interview, Oct. 23, 1985.

82 *Hoy*, Jan. 27, 1986, 8.

83 For a detailed description of these operations, see Cavallo et al., *La historia oculta*, 389–96. See also *Hoy*, Aug. 18, 1986, 6–9, and *Qué Pasa*, Sept. 4, 1986.

84 Patricia Verdugo and Carmen Hertz, *Operación siglo XX* (Santiago: Ornitorrinco, 1990), and Cavallo et al., *La historia oculta*, 389–95. For the official version, see Pedro Vara Lonfat, *Chile: Objetivo del terrorismo* (Santiago: Instituto Geográfico Militar, 1988), 56–60.

85 Interview, June 20, 1989.

86 "Carta abierta a los dirigentes y militantes de la izquierda chilena," *Apsi*, Dec. 29, 1986, eight-page insert.

87 Interviews, Aug. 29 and 31, 1989.

CHAPTER TWELVE: REBIRTH OF A NATION

1 *La Epoca,* Oct. 26, 1988, 12.
2 *El Mercurio,* Aug. 31, 1988, C4.
3 *La Epoca,* June 11, 1987, 8.
4 Ibid., Aug. 12, 1988, 11.
5 *La Segunda,* April 2, 1987, 1. For an extensive description of the pope's visit, see Ascanio Cavallo, Manuel Salazar, and Oscar Sepúlveda, *La historia oculta del régimen militar* (Santiago: La Epoca, 1989), 407–22.
6 In public opinion polls during the campaign, Chileans gave the regime exceptionally high marks for housing. Answering a survey conducted in May–June 1988, 83 percent of the respondents said the regime's performance in providing housing had been "good" or "very good." See Centro de Estudios Públicos, "Encuesta nacional de opinión pública" (Santiago: CEP, June 1988).
7 Associated Press report, printed in *Miami Herald,* Aug. 27, 1987.
8 Interview, May 11, 1989.
9 Gloria Cruz, Ana María de la Jara, and Paulina Sabal, "Las mujeres: Ciudadanas o pedestal de la patria?" Cordillera, *Cuadernos de Trabajo,* no. 15, 1988, 2.
10 *Boston Globe,* Aug. 28, 1988, 20.
11 *Cosas,* Sept. 29, 1988, 19.
12 *La Epoca,* May 16, 1987, 8.
13 See *El Mercurio,* March 25, 1987, A1. Almeyda's trial is described in *Las Ultimas Noticias,* Oct. 1, 1987, 13.
14 *Apsi,* April 27, 1987, 15–16.
15 María Maluenda, a former party legislator who had lost two family members to military violence, was also shunned for supporting voter registration. See *Apsi,* May 18, 1987, 10.
16 Interviews, Aug. 15 and 20, 1989.
17 In one poll, conducted by Gémines in Aug. 1987, only 22.8 percent of the respondents said they would vote for Pinochet (30 percent would vote against, and 47 percent either did not reply or did not plan to vote). But a full 59 percent said they believed he would win.
18 Americas Watch, "Chile: Human Rights and the Plebiscite" (New York, July 1988), 1–10.
19 See ibid., 118–30. See also Americas Watch, *Chile News in Brief,* bulletins 1–4, Santiago, Aug.–Sept. 1988, and *Boston Globe,* Aug. 15, 1988, 3.
20 Interview, Dec. 12, 1989.
21 *New York Times,* Nov. 18, 1988, B6.
22 *La Epoca,* Nov. 28, 1988, 9.
23 *Cosas,* Sept. 29, 1988, 19–23.
24 One series of polls, conducted by the Centro de Estudios de la Realidad Contemporanea between April 1987 and July 1988, showed Pinochet losing by between 10 and 19 percent. See CERC, "Informe Encuesta Nacional" (Santiago, July 1988), 10. But other polls showed up to 35 percent of the voters "undecided" or not responding.
25 *La Tercera,* Oct. 2, 1988, 7.
26 *New York Times,* June 30, 1988, A4.
27 Interview, Aug. 19, 1988, Los Angeles, Chile.
28 In addition, three parties collected enough signatures to run candidates in local regions: the National, Radical Democracy, and Social Democracy parties.
29 For accounts of the plotting and events on the night of the plebiscite, see "Chile Factions United to Safeguard Voting," *Boston Globe,* Oct. 13, 1988, 1, Cavallo et

al., *La historia oculta,* 439–56, "La historia de un golpe frustrado," *Apsi,* Oct. 24, 1988, 4–7, and "El día mas largo," *Qué Pasa,* Oct. 7, 1988, 6–8.

30 These details are described in Cavallo et al., *La historia oculta,* 455.

31 *El Mercurio,* Oct. 7, 1988, A8.

32 Indeed, postplebiscite polls showed that the No media campaign far outclassed the Yes ads in terms of credibility and appeal. See Brockbank Associates, "Estudio nacional de opinion publica de Chile" (Santiago: CEP, Sept. 1988), 3.

33 *La Epoca,* Oct. 26, 1988, 12.

34 Interview, May 4, 1989.

35 Interview, May 13, 1989.

36 *Boston Globe,* Oct. 16, 1988, A27, and Oct. 24, 1988, 3.

37 *La Epoca,* May 19, 1989, 11.

38 Ibid., April 11, 1989, 9, *El Mercurio,* June 23, 1989, C3, and *La Epoca,* June 24, 1989, 9.

39 *Qué Pasa,* May 4, 1989, 9–13.

40 Interview, May 24, 1989.

41 The constitutional language regarding the National Security Council is open to interpretation. It gives the members the right to "represent" to civilian authorities their objections to policy decisions. Some experts argued that this was only an advisory function. Others argued that it would provide legal justification for a coup, should the authorities refuse to heed the council's warning. According to this view, the lack of such authority had prevented the Chilean military from acting sooner in deposing Allende. The "legislative history" of the constitution is found in Sergio Carrasco Delgado, *Génesis y vigencia de los textos constitucionales chilenos* (Santiago: Editorial Jurídica, 1980). The most valuable source for the Constitution of 1980 is Luz Bulnes Aldunate, *Constitución política de la república de Chile* (Santiago: Editorial Jurídica, 1981).

42 Thus the twenty smallest districts, with 1.5 million people, would elect forty deputies; the seven largest, with a similar population, could choose only fourteen. A vote in the conservative District 52 would be worth three times a vote in the opposition District 18. See *La Epoca,* April 6, 1989, 10.

43 For a more detailed explanation, see Pamela Constable and Arturo Valenzuela, "Chile's Return to Democracy," *Foreign Affairs* 68 (Winter 1989–90):176–77.

44 *Caras,* July 12, 1989, 91.

45 *La Epoca,* May 15, 1989, 8.

46 One of Büchi's key financial backers was Julio Ponce Lerou, Pinochet's son-in-law. See the interview with him in *La Epoca,* July 25, 1989, 9.

47 See *La Epoca,* Aug. 27, 1989, 14, for a strong endorsement of Errázuriz by Avanzada Nacional.

48 See the typical campaign speech in *El Mercurio,* Oct. 13, 1989.

49 *La Epoca,* Dec. 11, 1989, 12.

50 In the senate race for Conchalí, the Socialist candidate, Ricardo Lagos, received nearly twice as many votes as the UDI candidate, Jaime Guzmán. But because of the way results were totaled, by ticket rather than by individual, the seat earned by one of the regime's most outspoken opponents was awarded instead to one of its foremost ideologues.

51 *La Epoca,* Oct. 18, 1989, 13.

52 Ibid., Oct. 11, 1989, 13.

53 "Las puas del bunker," *Apsi,* Oct. 16, 1989, 8–11.

54 *Análisis,* June 19, 1989, 23–24.

55 Ibid., 23–26.

56 Some military officers were appalled at this camouflage maneuver and reluctant to

welcome into the professional army men they viewed as untrustworthy "delinquents." See "La CNI se camufla," *Apsi,* Oct. 23, 1989, 16–19.

57 *El Mercurio,* Sept. 24, 1989, D1.

58 *La Epoca,* March 13, 1990, 8.

INDEX

Page numbers in italics denote illustrations.